Trust and Supply Chains

This research volume aims at outlining the substantial role of information asymmetry in agri-food chains and how building trust and mitigating this problem could enhance the performance of these chains. The supply chain covers a systemic sequence of linked companies with material and information exchange. Sharing information about capabilities, inventories, and needs is vital to streamline channels, reduce uncertainty, and enhance performance, but economic agents may be reluctant due to opportunism. Information asymmetry can cause problems in quality assurance and distort the supply chain's functioning. Building trust is crucial, and solutions include guarantees, standards, licensing, and hybrid governance. *Trust and Supply Chains: Information Asymmetry in the Agri-Food Sector* is based on real-world examples and case studies from the agri-food industry (cheese, apples, pasta and bakery, beef, organic products, and more), providing practical solutions to building trust and sharing information. It offers academics, practitioners, and advanced students a comprehensive overview of the various aspects of information asymmetry and trust in agri-food supply chains.

Michał Pietrzak is a highly accomplished economist and strategic management researcher and practitioner. He currently holds the position of Full Professor at the Institute of Economics and Finance, Warsaw University of Life Sciences. Additionally, he serves as Vice Chairman of the committee responsible for the university's strategy. Professor Pietrzak's research interests are centered around economics, with a particular focus on new institutional economics and hybrid organizations such as cooperatives, chains, and networks.

Joanna Domagała (PhD) is Associate Professor in the Department of Logistics at the Institute of Economics and Finance at Warsaw University of Life Sciences (WULS), Poland. Her primary research interests include enterprise efficiency, internationalization, and globalization of the food industry sectors, logistics systems in agribusiness, management and planning of logistics in enterprises, and supply chain management.

Aleksandra Chlebicka holds a PhD in Economics. Currently, she is employed in the Institute of Economics and Finance of Warsaw University of Life Sciences (WULS), Poland. Her main research interests lie in the areas of business cooperation and interorganizational linkages, with a specific focus on the role of trust and social capital.

ROUTLEDGE STUDIES IN TRUST RESEARCH
Series editors: Joanna Paliszkiewicz and Kuanchin Chen

Available Titles in this Series:

Artificial Intelligence, Management, and Trust
Edited by Mariusz Sołtysik, Magda Gawłowska, Bartłomiej Śnieżyński and Artur Gunia

Privacy, Trust and Social Media
Edited by Joanna Paliszkiewicz, Kuanchin Chen and Jerzy Gołuchowski

Communication, Leadership and Trust in Organizations
Edited by Joanna Paliszkiewicz and Jose L. Guerrero Cusumano

Trust and Organisational Resilience
Iwona Otola, Marlena Grabowska and Zoran Krupka

Trust and Artificial Intelligence
Development and Application of AI Technology
Edited by Joanna Paliszkiewicz and Jerzy Gołuchowski

Trust in Social and Business Relations
Theory and Practice
Edited by Joanna Paliszkiewicz, Kuanchin Chen and Marta Mendel

Trust and Brand Management
The Role of Brand Heritage
Hanna Górska-Warsewicz

Trust and Supply Chains
Information Asymmetry in the Agri-Food Sector
Edited by Michał Pietrzak, Joanna Domagała and Aleksandra Chlebicka

Trust and Supply Chains

Information Asymmetry in the Agri-Food Sector

Edited by Michał Pietrzak, Joanna Domagała and Aleksandra Chlebicka

Routledge
Taylor & Francis Group
NEW YORK AND LONDON

First published 2025

by Routledge
605 Third Avenue, New York, NY 10158

and by Routledge
4 Park Square, Milton Park, Abingdon, Oxon, OX14 4RN

Routledge is an imprint of the Taylor & Francis Group, an informa business

ISBN: 978-1-032-62329-0 (hbk)
ISBN: 978-1-032-63371-8 (pbk)
ISBN: 978-1-032-63372-5 (ebk)

DOI: 10.4324/9781032633725

Typeset in Times New Roman
by Newgen Publishing UK

Contents

Figures

Tables

Foreword by Wim Heijman

As food supply chains grow more complicated, the importance of information for both consumers and intermediaries becomes increasingly evident. For consumers, trust in the information provided on product labels is paramount. If consumers do not believe the information, they are unlikely to purchase the product. They need assurance that the product is safe to consume and that it possesses all the qualities claimed.

However, consumer communication is only one aspect of the issue. The other critical aspect is ensuring the integrity of the seller's information. This requires rigorous verification that the provided information is accurate. Trust and control are therefore inseparable. Contrary to the often-attributed quote from Lenin, "trust is good, control is better", in the context of the food supply chain, control and trust must work hand in hand. Effective control systems should foster trust, and both elements are equally crucial. The fundamental question is how to assure the integrity of the entire supply chain.

Once trust is lost, it is exceedingly difficult to regain it quickly: "It arrives on foot, but leaves on horseback". Trust is built through long-term, robust control systems and by providing clear, convincing information to consumers and intermediaries throughout the supply chain.

This book, *Trust and Supply Chains: Information Asymmetry in the Agri-Food Sector*, addresses the critical issue of bridging the information gap between buyers and sellers – a challenge that is not new but has become increasingly significant as the distance between producers and consumers has expanded dramatically over the years. Trust between buyers and sellers is no longer a given within a small, familiar group; it now requires systematic efforts.

This book is essential for understanding the problems related to control, trust, and communication within supply chains, and it explores potential (technological) solutions to these issues.

Prof. Dr. Wim Heijman
Czech University of Life Sciences Prague

Foreword by Helga Pavlić Skender

Contemporary supply chains are characterized by dynamism and complexity, and above all by a large number of participants that are interlinked through material, financial, and, especially, information flows. In such a complex environment, having the right information at the right time is crucial for the effective management of business processes. It is for this very reason that this book is of particular importance, as it addresses an extremely important dimension, information asymmetry in supply chains, with a special focus on agri-food chains. The exchange and verification of information between stakeholders enables the efficiency and effectiveness of supply chains.

*Trust and Supply Chains: Information Asymmetry in the Agri-Food Secto*r, by the editors Michał Pietrzak, Joanna Domagała, and Aleksandra Chlebicka, is a high-quality and original work containing the research results of scientists and experts not only from Poland but also from Italy, France, Germany, the Czech Republic, Croatia, South Africa, and the United States. The multidisciplinary team made it possible to bring together theoretical and practical knowledge from the fields of logistics, organization and management, supply chain management, agribusiness, agricultural economics, and information and communication sciences.

To emphasize the importance of information asymmetry and trust in agri-food supply chains from a theoretical and practical perspective, the book is divided into two parts. The first part of the book is theoretical and focuses on the theoretical characteristics and the role of information, information asymmetry, and trust in supply chains. This part includes six chapters that present the knowledge about logistics, supply chains, information, knowledge, organizational learning, information asymmetry, trust, and information technology in supply chains. The second part of the book is the result of empirical research. Seven chapters present the research findings, that is, examples and case studies from the agri-food supply chains. These studies show the impact of information asymmetry on the efficiency and effectiveness of the agri-food supply chain.

The research results represent a contribution to the body of knowledge from the world of agri-food supply chain management. Therefore, the research results can be of particular importance for a wide range of users, scholars, and students, not only from the fields of economics, management, and supply chain management but also from other higher education institutions, and also for all professionals and managers involved in international business, agribusiness, agricultural economics, and food quality management and beyond.

Helga Pavlić Skender, PhD
Faculty of Economics and Business, University of Rijeka

Preface

Michał Pietrzak, Joanna Domagała, and Aleksandra Chlebicka

The supply chain concept has evolved from focusing on logistics within a single company to encompassing a sequence of linked companies. These companies are viewed as links in the whole system, which involves the exchange of materials and information from sourcing raw materials to delivering final products to end users. Informational integration is crucial to the supply chain, not just mutual alignments in the physical flow of goods. Sharing information about capabilities, inventories, product conditions and locations, international shipments, and buyer needs can streamline information channels and reduce uncertainty. This, in turn, leads to cost reduction and enhanced resilience of the entire supply chain.

Despite advancements in digital connectivity and data standards, information sharing is not always willingly done. Information asymmetry, where information is imperfect and varies among different agents, emerges as a significant challenge. Limited cognition, bounded rationality, and opportunism further exacerbate this challenge. Information asymmetry is particularly challenging in agri-food chains where quality issues arise, and differences in quality can be difficult to verify in advance. Downstream buyers at successive stages of the chain can experience difficulties distinguishing good products from poor ones, leading to problems in quality assurance throughout the supply chain.

The responsibility for the quality of final products is strongly dispersed across many actors in the chain, while the problem of information asymmetry plagues interrelations between them. The structure of incentives can be shaped so that a better-informed party can economize on costs by lowering product quality without punishment, leading to misbehavior in conducting different activities within the chain and distorting the functioning of the entire agri-food chain. Building trust within the supply chain is key to addressing the reluctance to share information. Several solutions can help build trust, such as guarantees, brand names, private or public standards, licensing and certification, and hybrid forms of governance (such as long-term contracts, franchising, cooperatives, etc.).

The book has a twofold purpose. First, it outlines the significant role of information asymmetry and trust and their impact on the performance of agri-food supply chains. It provides a detailed analysis of the theoretical aspects of information asymmetry, incorporating behavioral assumptions such as bounded rationality and opportunism, as well as the social capital context, offering insight into the role of trust in the agri-food supply chains. Second, it suggests a variety of remedies to mitigate informational asymmetry and approaches to building trust or creating its substitutes, which are crucial in complex agribusiness networks plagued by opaque information and quality concerns.

The main body of the book is divided into two parts. The first part is theoretical and examines the concept of information asymmetry, its impact on the supply chain, and the role of trust, trust-enhancing solutions, and information technologies. The second part presents real-world examples and case studies from the agri-food chains, providing practical insights into how information asymmetry can affect the performance, quality, and safety of the agri-food supply chain. This empirical part also explores various practical solutions, such as certificates and labels, brand names, private and public standards, and hybrid forms of governance, for overcoming the challenges of information asymmetry in the agri-food chain. These actionable strategies are useful for industry professionals and policymakers looking to improve their performance.

The first part, entitled "Theoretical Background of the Role of Information and Trust in Chains", consists of six chapters. **Chapter 1** serves two main purposes. First, it provides an overview of the evolution of logistics and how it has transformed into the concept of the supply chain. It examines different approaches to the supply chain phenomenon. Second, it emphasizes the crucial role of information sharing in achieving integration within the supply chain. In **Chapter 2**, the role of information in managing complex systems, particularly supply chains, is discussed. The relationship between information, knowledge, and organizational learning is described. The chapter also distinguishes between the precise technical definition of information and the broad social view on information. It highlights the importance of adopting a socio-technical approach that connects the meaning behind the data with the organizational practices. **Chapter 3** aims to explore the challenge of information asymmetry and discuss the critical role of information sharing in enhancing agri-food chain performance in the world of functional and geographical division of labor. It develops the model of the supply chain as a learning system. Additionally, it establishes a general framework that addresses the main issues tackled in the book. Namely, the issues of information asymmetry and trust are structured by three vertices of a triangle: coordination of physical flow, mechanisms for securing quality, and governance structures. These components form the basis for further theoretical and empirical exploration in the book.

The purpose of **Chapter 4** is to provide a comprehensive overview of the fundamental aspects of trust within inter-organizational relationships, in order to establish a solid knowledge base for the empirical parts of the book. The review explores and offers an understanding of the nature of trust rooted in the game-theoretical approach. To address the issue of information asymmetry, partners in the chain must establish a way of cooperation that reduces the risk of opportunism and ensures value creation. Credible strategic moves, repeated interactions, and reputations constitute three significant elements that could foster cooperation within inter-organizational relationships and alleviate uncertainties within these relationships. **Chapter 5** is dedicated first to discussing how trust and formal contracts can complement each other to reduce information asymmetry issues in supply chains. Second, it explores hybrid modes of governance based on both formal and informal coordination mechanisms that can enhance trust within supply chain relationships.

Chapter 6, the last one in the first part of the book, is devoted to discussing the role of information technology in mitigating the problem of information asymmetry and distrust. First, it identifies the most commonly used technologies in supply chain management. Second, it highlights technologies that monitor the flow of products as pivotal in mitigating information asymmetry. Specifically, traceability, blockchain, and tokenization are discussed, along with their benefits and limitations.

The second part of the book, titled "Empirical Illustrations of Information Asymmetry and Trust in Agri-Food Chains", comprises seven chapters. **Chapter 7** explores the topic of food labeling. Apart from ensuring transparency of ingredients, origin, and quality of products, certified labels improve the credibility of products and increase trust within the supply chain, thereby reducing information asymmetry. This is particularly crucial for food products distinguished by their high added value, regional features, or traditional recipes, such as specialty cheeses, which are investigated in this chapter. This chapter highlights the mixed success of geographical indications as branding labels. **Chapter 8** delves into the topic of geographical indications as compared with club varieties (brand names used by club members within the entire chain). Both approaches to branding aim to reduce information asymmetry, increase transparency, and ensure that food products meet consumer expectations. The chapter compares these two solutions as mechanisms orchestrating incentives for investment in the quality of fresh apples across the whole supply chain, highlighting their limitations and benefits.

In **Chapter 9**, the importance of different governance structures in improving trust and reducing information asymmetry is analyzed. Three cases of supply chains for premium grain products are empirically studied, with different forms of integration and contractual arrangements (including formalized control systems and certifications) used in each chain to ensure quality. **Chapter 10** focuses on the possibilities of improving information flow and transparency throughout the beef supply chain. It analyzes the beef meat quality labeling scheme, which aims to differentiate meat based on quality aspects. Despite the low coverage of this scheme, the system based on third-party certification proves to assure interested consumers of the accuracy of information provided by suppliers.

Chapter 11 addresses issues related to organic products, where information plays a crucial role in providing traceability for food safety and quality. It outlines how producers and retailers of organic food perceive the most important factors of information exchange and how this exchange affects trust in organic food supply chains. This empirical study highlights the differences in attitudes between retailers and producers of organic food regarding the exchange of information. **Chapter 12** outlines the problem of asymmetric information and the lack of trust in the renewable energy supply chain, namely in the biogas sector. It focuses mainly on the interface between the procurement stage (biomass supply) and the energy generation stage. For producers of green energy from biomass, it is crucial to ensure the supply of substrate with appropriate quality parameters, as poor-quality substrate can destabilize biotechnological processes. The analysis, based on interviews with the managers of energy facilities, shows that regular suppliers and occasional written contracts help maintain trust and ensure quality.

Chapter 13 focuses on tokenization, a solution for achieving higher levels of transparency and traceability by using decentralized blockchain technology. The purpose of the chapter is to determine the opportunities and challenges related to the use of blockchain technology and non-fungible token (NFT) technology in the market of premium beehive products, with a particular focus on enhancing food safety and quality assurance measures. The results show that NFT technology can play a positive role in positioning valuable beehive products on the market. However, financial constraints are a barrier to the broader adoption of this technology.

The book draws on insights from a range of disciplines, including supply chain management, value chains, knowledge management, organizational learning, system thinking, new institutional economics, game theory, agribusiness, agricultural economics, and food quality management, providing a holistic and interdisciplinary perspective on the undertaken topics. All these topics are explored by an international team of experts representing different countries and academic backgrounds. This book will be useful for both academics and industry professionals. It provides a comprehensive analysis of supply chain management and policymaking, as well as practical solutions for these areas. The target audience includes academics, researchers, and students in fields such as supply chain management, logistics, agribusiness, agricultural economics, and food science. The book will also appeal to industry professionals involved in the agri-food supply chain, including marketing and sales managers, procurement managers, logistics managers, quality assurance managers, supply chain analysts, and sustainability officers. Additionally, policymakers and regulators in the agri-food industry will find the book valuable in understanding the impact of information asymmetry on the supply chain and identifying policies and regulations to improve information disclosure, promote information sharing, and build trust among supply chain actors. Finally, the book will be useful for courses related to supply chain management, logistics, agribusiness, agricultural economics, and food science.

This book is the result of collaborative efforts within our community. We extend our heartfelt gratitude to everyone whose help, support, and inspiration contributed to its creation. While it is impossible to name each individual, we wish to acknowledge a few. Special thanks go to the esteemed scholars who reviewed our work: Wilem Heijman and Helga Pavlić Skender. We are also deeply appreciative of the outstanding researchers who provided critical yet inspirational comments, remarks, and suggestions: Piotr Gołasa, Anna Kłoczko-Gajewska, Paweł Kraciński, Radim Lenort, Andrzej Parzonko, Celina Sołek-Borowska, Dariusz Strzębicki, Elżbieta Szymańska, Ludwik Wicki, Marcin Wysokiński, and Rafał Zbyrowski. Our gratitude extends to Joanna Paliszkiewicz, the editor of the "Routledge Studies in Trust Research" book series, for inspiring us to begin work on this book. Finally, we wish to thank the supportive editors from Routledge, Taylor & Francis Group – Brianna Ascher and Jessica Rech – for their invaluable assistance during the preparation of this book.

About the Editors

Michał Pietrzak is Full Professor at the Institute of Economics and Finance, Warsaw University of Life Sciences (WULS), Poland, where he also serves as Vice Chairman of the committee responsible for the university's strategy. He is a highly accomplished economist and strategic management researcher and practitioner. Professor Pietrzak's research interests are centered around economics, with a particular focus on new institutional economics and hybrid organizations such as cooperatives, chains, and networks. He is also highly knowledgeable in the areas of strategic management, organizational learning, and logistics. In addition to his academic work, Professor Pietrzak has extensive experience as a consultant, providing strategic analyses and strategy development services, as well as implementing Balanced Scorecard methodologies for various industries and sectors, including agribusiness, automotive, energy, professional services, municipal services, public agencies, and universities. Professor Pietrzak was also the head of the MBA program and postgraduate studies for several years.

Joanna Domagała (PhD) is Associate Professor in the Department of Logistics at the Institute of Economics and Finance at Warsaw University of Life Sciences (WULS), Poland. Her primary research interests include enterprise efficiency, internationalization, and globalization of the food industry sectors, logistics systems in agribusiness, management and planning of logistics in enterprises, and supply chain management. With over 150 scientific publications to her credit, Prof. Domagała is an established scholar in her field. She has also actively presented her research at various international conferences and has completed foreign internships at the University of Georgia (United States) and Shanghai Ocean University (China). In addition, she has served as a reviewer and guest co-editor for several international journals. Prof. Domagała is a member of various academic associations, including the Polish Logistics Society, the European Association of Agricultural Economists, and the Association of Agricultural Economists and Agribusiness. She also serves as the head of the Department of Logistics and head of Postgraduate Studies in Logistics at WULS.

Aleksandra Chlebicka is currently employed in the Institute of Economics and Finance of Warsaw University of Life Sciences (WULS), Poland. She holds a PhD in Economics. Her main research interests lie in the areas of business cooperation and inter-organizational linkages, with a specific focus on the role of trust and social capital. Aleksandra has authored 60 scientific publications and has worked as an expert for the OECD in the field of agricultural markets and trade. She was also a member of a focus group for knowledge transfer and innovation of EIP-AGRI, European Commission. Aleksandra has authored numerous reports and studies on the establishment and performance of agricultural producers' organizations, commissioned by the Ministry of Agriculture and Rural Development in Poland and the European Commission. For several years, she served as the head of the Department of Analysis of Agricultural Policy, a part of the Foundation of Assistance Programmes in Agriculture – a think tank established by the World Bank in Poland.

Contributors

Filippo Arfini (PhD) is Full Professor in Agricultural Economics at the Department of Economic and Management Science of the University of Parma, Italy. His research activity focuses on the economics of food quality schemes, the assessment of CAP, and rural development policies in developed countries. He has participated in several research projects in the framework of the European Research Project (from FP4 up to H2020), as well as several Research Tenders from DG-Agri and the EU Parliament. The results of his research activity are published in several Italian and international scientific journals.

Valentin Bellassen is a senior researcher in environmental economics and evaluation of public policies at National Research Institute for Agriculture, Food and Environment – INRAE (France), since 2014. He holds a PhD in Environmental Sciences (2010), and his current research covers the multi-criteria evaluation of food value chains and the evaluation of policies impacting food systems and diets.

Agnieszka Biernat-Jarka (PhD) works at Warsaw University of Life Sciences in Economics and Finance Institute (Poland). She graduated from Postgraduate Studies of European Integration and a course organized by the Cornell University (United States) and the Mellon Foundation on "Experimental economics" and "Marketing economics". Her area of interest includes EU policy, project management, European funds, and project for enterprises. She twice completed an internship at the University of Groningen in the Netherlands. She is a participant and speaker at conferences and national and international seminars. She has published articles in national and international scientific journals.

Grzegorz Dobiesz (MEng) is an employee of one of the largest technology companies in the world. He is a graduate of the Faculty of Mechanical Engineering at Gdansk University of Technology and the Faculty of Management at Warsaw University of Technology (Poland). He is an enthusiast about new technologies such as Blockchain and AI, and their adaptation in the industry. He is one of the authors of the project to use blockchain technology in production traceability and cattle monitoring in Poland.

Wojciech Florkowski is Professor in the Department of Agricultural and Applied Economics, University of Georgia, USA. He has experience in research, project management, and training. His areas of specialization and expertise include agricultural economics and international business, with an emphasis on marketing and consumer studies, technology transfer and assessment, environmental policy analysis, and research policy. He is the author of over 200 publications. He has been a reviewer and a guest co-editor for a number of international journals. He has actively participated in presenting research results at various international conferences. He has successfully supervised many PhD students, leading them to completion of their degrees. He co-founded the Association of Agricultural Economists and Agribusiness in 1993 in Poland. He was elected as the Vice President of the Association for the 1993–1995 term. The Association holds its annual meetings and publishes proceedings.

Dušanka Gajdić (univ.spec.oec.), since 2010, is Senior Lecturer at the Križevci University of Applied Sciences (KUAS, Croatia) in the fields of management and organization, trade, quality management, and accounting. She currently serves as the head of the Undergraduate Professional Study of Agriculture. She obtained the academic title of university specialist in business economics, majoring in Quality Management in 2010, by defending her specialist post-graduate thesis entitled "Food Safety Management Systems in the Croatian Food Industry". She is a PhD student in the Faculty of Economics, University of Rijeka. She defended her doctoral thesis entitled "The Impact of Collaboration and Trust on Performance in the Organic Food Supply Chain". She is an authorized internal auditor of the quality management system according to the ISO 9001 standard, as well as an active participant of national and international conferences in the fields of quality management, trade, agribusiness, and food safety. Her areas of research interest are agri-food supply chains, relationship management in food supply chain, sustainability of agri-food chains, food quality and food safety, food waste, and food losses. She continuously engages in empirical research and publishes works in the aforementioned areas. As a researcher, she has participated in several international projects, including cross-border cooperation projects INTERREG VA Hungary-Croatia.

Monika Gębska obtained her PhD in Animal Sciences from Warsaw University of Life Sciences (WULS, Poland). Her main research interests are farm management, sustainable production, including animal welfare issues, data economy in the food system, and digitalization of agriculture operations. For the last ten years, she has done research on social and economic aspects of animal welfare and sustainable production. In this area, she has worked on several international projects.

Roman Grzesiak holds Master of Capital Investments and Enterprises Financial Strategies. He is a member of the Board of IDFS Ltd., AGREGO Project Coordinator, and co-creator of AGRO BLOCK CHAIN FOR BEEF (Poland). He is also a specialist in the field of innovative IT solutions for agriculture, both meat and plant industries. On a daily basis, he coordinates the work and activities of the project, managing the work of the IT team, and designing and testing the functionality of the system. He has 20 years of experience in consulting in the agricultural industry. He is a speaker and participant in numerous conferences, trainings, and discussions.

Wiktor Ignaciuk (MSc) is an advisor to the board of Bio-Power (Poland) and the Polish agricultural biogas market expert (author of numerous articles published in the trade press). Besides developing a business career, since 2021, he has entered into long-term scientific cooperation with researchers from the Department of Economics and Organization of Enterprises, Institute of Economics and Finance (WULS). The partnership has resulted in his contribution to scientific papers published in 2021 and 2023, in which the state of the European and Polish biogas industries was a central topic of analysis. Moreover, throughout 2021, he has been a participant in the research project carried out at the Ecotechnology Laboratory of the Poznan University of Life Sciences ("Research on the preparation process of methane fermentation of chicken manure": 10/2021/U). He has also participated in meetings of an intra-governmental working group (set up by the Ministry of Energy and Climate) focusing on the issue of local gas network development.

Sławomir Jarka (PhD) works in the Management Institute of Warsaw University of Life Sciences (WULS, Poland). He graduated from postgraduate managerial studies at the Warsaw School of Economics and a course organized by the Cornell University (United States) and the Mellon Foundation on "Experimental economics". He is a participant and speaker at conferences and national and international seminars, including Mansholt Graduate School and Wageningen University. His area of interest includes management problems in agricultural enterprises, the use of IoT, and blockchain technology in the process of building food safety and increasing their efficiency. He twice completed an internship at the University of Groningen in the Netherlands. He has published numerous articles in national and international scientific journals. His hobbies include beekeeping. He is a co-founder and President of the Beekeeping and Sustainable Development Academy Foundation.

Pavel Kotyza is Assistant Professor at Czech University of Life Sciences in Prague since 2014, from which he received his PhD in 2016 with a dissertation on cooperation between farmers in Visegrad countries. His areas of interest include agricultural cooperation, rural development, food security, self-sufficiency and competitiveness, sustainability, and development studies. He teaches topics related to rural development, sustainable growth, and agricultural development. He is involved in international projects and actively participates in the rural development working group of the EuroLeague for Life Sciences (ELLS). At the same time, he is involved in international value chain analysis studies (VCA4D – Georgia, Niger) for the European Commission.

Christiaan Maasdorp is Lecturer in the Department of Information Science at Stellenbosch University in South Africa and Study Director of the Postgraduate Programs in Information and Knowledge Management. He lectures and supervises postgraduate research on knowledge management and organization theory. His research focuses on knowledge and technology in organizations.

Edward Majewski (PhD) is Full Professor at the Institute of Economics and Finance of Warsaw University of Life Sciences, Poland. The main fields of his scientific interests are sustainable agriculture, farming systems, impacts of CAP reforms on Polish agriculture as well as food supply chains sustainability. Majewski plays a leading role in disseminating sustainability concepts, specifically the implementation of Integrated Farming System (IFS), in Poland. His research activities include studies on farm-level impacts of agricultural policy measures, farmer strategies, adoption of agro-environmental measures and more sustainable farming practices, and sustainability indicators for short and long food supply chains. Prof. Majewski has been extensively co-operating with a number of partners from the EU and CEE countries, as well as being the coordinator of EU-funded research and educational projects.

Agata Malak-Rawlikowska (PhD) works as Associate Professor in the Institute of Economics and Finance of Warsaw University of Life Sciences, Poland. Her main scientific interests are focused on agricultural production and food chains, and concern vertical integration in the food supply chain (including bargaining power, information asymmetry, and contractual relations), sustainability of short and long food supply chains, agricultural and farm economics and management, and agricultural policy and its impact on production. She has experience in 21 international projects both as a core-team member and coordinator.

Katharina Meyer has been a researcher at the Research Institute of Organic Agriculture (FiBL), Germany, since 2018. Her tasks include project management and coordination, networking of actors, data collection and analysis, and expert interviews. On behalf of FiBL, she is responsible for the

"Wasserschutzbrot" (Water Protection Bread), acting as the core contact for the value chain members involved in this initiative and the public relations work. She holds a Master of Science in "Global Change: Ecosystem Science & Policy", a joint degree of University College Dublin (Ireland) and Justus-Liebid-Universität Gießen (Germany), and did her Bachelor in Environmental Management.

Konrad Michalski (PhD) works in the Department of Logistics at the Warsaw University of Life Sciences (WULS, Poland). He is a graduate of the University of Szczecin, where he has defended the PhD thesis in economics on logistics. He also completed his postgraduate studies in HR and social psychology. His main scientific interests include logistics, changes in processes of adjustment of organizational structures, and processes within an organization to requirements of innovative technologies. He has many years of experience in the business.

Maurizio Notarfonso works as an EU funding manager at Federalimentare, the Italian National Association of Agrofood Industries. He has more than 16 years of experience in the management of European multilateral projects on the environment, technology transfer, and entrepreneurship topics. He is an experienced manager specialized in dissemination and communication actions to food industry networks. He is also managing the application of SPES to the EU call for proposals.

Adam Patkowski is a master of finance and monetary policy, CEO of IDFS Sp. z o.o., co-founder of AGREGO and AGRO BLOCK CHAIN FOR BEEF. He is an expert in the agro industry (20 years of experience), in building integration among producers, market organization, and shortening the supply chains. He is involved in the process of integration of Polish agriculture, cooperation with all entities from the agricultural environment (state institutions, consulting companies, banks, suppliers of production means and machinery equipment, and recipients of agricultural products), as well as farmers and agricultural producer groups. He creates and manages agricultural producers' groups. He is a speaker and participant in numerous conferences, trainings, and discussions. He has participated in the work on the Polish Beef 2022 Strategy.

Monika Roman (PhD) is Assistant Professor in the Department of Logistics, Institute of Economics and Finance, Warsaw University of Life Sciences (WULS, Poland). Her research interests include several topics: spatial economies, agricultural economics, quantitative methods, transport, logistics systems in agribusiness, and optimization of logistics processes in enterprises. She is the author or co-author of more than 70 scientific publications. She has participated in foreign internships at the University College Cork (Ireland), the National University of Life and Environmental Sciences of Ukraine, and the Czech University of Life Sciences Prague. She has been a reviewer and a guest co-editor for several international journals. She is a member of the Polish Logistics Society, Polish Society of Production Management, and Association of Agricultural Economists and Agribusiness.

Tania Runge works as a senior scientist at the Thünen Institute, Germany. She is an agronomist and holds a PhD in environmental planning. She has a long-lasting experience with topics at the interface between agriculture and environmental protection, including the design and development of practical solutions. While working in Brussels for Copa-Cogeca (European Farmers and Agricultural Cooperatives), she was responsible for biodiversity, water, sustainability, and research and innovation. In 2017, she returned to research and has been involved in EU projects, including CONSOLE. She is currently the project manager of a program, with 28 national climate projects.

Piotr Sulewski (PhD) is Associate Professor in the Department of Economics and Organisation of Enterprises, Institute of Economics and Finance, Warsaw University of Life Sciences (WULS, Poland). The main fields of his scientific interest are farm efficiency, risk production in agriculture, fertilizer market, agricultural biogas production, and the potential reduction of GHG from the agricultural sector. He is the author of a number of articles and books in his field of study. He is a lecturer on courses in agricultural economics, farm management, strategic management, risk management in agriculture, risk management in logistics, and organization and management of production processes. He is a member of the European Association of Agricultural Economists and Association of Agricultural Economists and Agribusiness. He is the referee of several scientific journals and coordinator or partner in a number of research projects in the fields of sustainable development, risk management in agriculture, renewable energy sources, and potential of agricultural biorefineries.

Stefano Targetti (PhD) is Junior Assistant Professor in the Department of Agricultural and Food Sciences, University of Bologna (Italy), since 2021. He has worked in several research institutions, including INRAe, the University Aix-Marseille, and the University of Natural Resources and Life Sciences, Vienna (Austria). His research activity concerns agri-environment policies, climate change adaptation in agricultural systems, and ecosystem services. He is the author or co-author of more than 20 SCOPUS-indexed papers, with c.a. 500 citations (H-index= 11, March 2023 SCOPUS), and co-author of over 60 publications, including conference contributions, book chapters, and monographs.

Davide Viaggi is Full Professor in Agricultural Economics and Rural Appraisal, University of Bologna (Italy). He has been working since almost 30 years in the field, with research interests focused on bioeconomy, agricultural policy evaluation, economics of water use in agriculture, environmental evaluation, economics of agri-environmental schemes, and farm management. He was the coordinator of the FP7 projects CAP-IRE and CLAIM and of the H2020 projects PROVIDE and CONSOLE, all of which related to the role of the CAP in rural areas and the provision of environmental and climate public goods. He is now coordinating the BBI project BIOBEC. He also participated in several other EU projects in these fields, including many closely connected to the measurement of CAP impact on the environment (e.g., LIFT, SPARD, BIOBIO) and the bioeconomy (Transition2Bio, Coopid, BIOGOV.NET). Davide was editor-in-chief of the journal *Bio-Based and Applied Economics* and published in 2018 the book *The Bioeconomy. Delivering Sustainable Green Growth*, CABI, UK. He is part of the steering group of the international master "Bioeconomy in the Circular economy – BIOCIRCE" and of the Coordination Group of the European Bioeconomy University.

Adam Wąs (PhD) is Associate Professor in the Department of Economics and Organisation of Enterprises, Institute of Economics and Finance, Warsaw University of Life Sciences (WULS), Poland. The main fields of his scientific interest are building economic models for farms; assessing the impact of agricultural policy on farm organization and structure of the farm sector; estimating external effects of agricultural production; mitigating GHG emissions in agriculture; and analyzing risk management in agricultural production. He is the author of a number of articles and books in his field of study. He is a lecturer on courses in agricultural economics, farm management, quality management in agriculture, and business planning. He is the coordinator or partner in a number of research projects in the field of structural changes in the farming sector, potential effects of agricultural biorefineries, risk management in agriculture, and renewable energy sources. He is the referee of several scientific journals. He is a member of the European Association of Agricultural Economists and International Farm Management Association.

Zdeňka Žáková Kroupová (PhD) is Associate Professor in the Department of Economics, Faculty of Economics and Management, Czech University of Life Sciences Prague (CULS). Her research focuses on the competitiveness of agriculture (especially milk) and food production, with particular emphasis on technical efficiency and productivity. Furthermore, her research interests also include the environmental dimension of agricultural production – the provision of public goods and externalities. She has participated in various international and national research projects, for example, the BRIGHTSPACE project – a research project funded under EU's Horizon Europe; the VALUMICS project (funded under EU's H2020); and the COMPETE project (supported by the European Commission's

Seventh Framework Programme). She is the author or co-author of more than 90 scientific publications. She is a member of the Czech Academy of Agricultural Sciences, the European Association of Agricultural Economists, the International Association of Agricultural Economists, and the Society for Agricultural Economics.

Matteo Zavalloni (PhD) is Senior Assistant Professor in Agricultural Economics and Rural Appraisal at the University of Urbino Carlo Bo (Italy). His research interests are at the interface between environmental and agricultural economics. He has mostly worked on theoretical analysis related to agri-environmental policies and to cooperation on natural resource management. Increasingly, he is working on the economics of land use zoning, including its impact and its political economy determinants.

PART I

Theoretical Background of the Role of Information and Trust in Chains

1 From Logistics to Supply Chain Management

Joanna Domagała
Warsaw University of Life Sciences – SGGW, Poland

1.1 Introduction

In any economy, there is a spatial dispersion of the places of origin of raw materials for production, the places of production of final products, and the places of their consumption and utilization. It is necessary to take into account not only the spatial but also the temporal aspect of economic activity in that the volume and structure of production are most often not aligned over time with the volume and structure of product consumption and utilization.

Regardless of the type of products produced, and especially in the case of agricultural production, spatial and temporal gaps occur. The increasing specialization of production and, consequently, its wider dispersion in space as well further exacerbate it. Moreover, physical flows of raw materials and agri-food products are characterized by certain specificities. This specificity is mainly due to the transfer of living organisms, organic raw materials, or their products. Therefore, the main challenge is to ensure the quality of fresh products, which are easily subjected to decomposition, spoilage, or other forms of deterioration during the flow. The utility of space and time is therefore extremely relevant in this context. The spatial and temporal gaps make it necessary to carry out activities to ensure the delivery of raw materials to the places of processing into final products, which in turn reach the places of consumption and utilization. Therefore, measures must be taken to meet a specific customer need and to ensure the physical availability of specific products. The sphere of economic activity that is primarily concerned with the material and informational processes of the flow of material products within a company and between business entities is known as logistics.

Logistics provides utility of place by moving goods from places where there is surplus production to locations where there is demand for them. Logistics thus extends the physical boundaries of the market and adds new economic value to goods – the utility of place. Logistics creates utility of place mainly through transportation, for example, shipping crops by train or truck from farmland to

DOI: 10.4324/9781032633725-2

markets or directly to processors. Goods and services not only need to be available wherever consumers need them but also when they are needed. Logistics therefore also creates time utility by maintaining proper inventory levels and proper placement of goods in the supply chain. In some cases, transportation can also contribute to the creation of time utility by moving goods more quickly to places where there is demand for them (Coyle et al., 2010).

The basic logistics paradigm is the belief that the integrated action of enterprises in organizing the flow of products provides greater benefits for companies than independently implemented processes. Enterprises are often viewed as organizational units that conduct business independently of other entities. These units compete for customers and resources needed for operations in order to gain a competitive advantage or just survive in the market. The philosophy of solitary struggle can be self-destructive for even the best enterprises. No single company can win with a supply chain in which, through the deepened cooperation of its links, synergistic effects are achieved, leading to growth potential that could not be achieved by suppliers, manufacturers, and distributors working together on a transactional basis. The concept of an integrated supply chain represents a new challenge for modern companies. The benefits that can be achieved by the entire supply chain and its individual participants are obvious, but achieving a high level of integration of links and creating trust-based partnerships between them is an extremely challenging task (Fechner, 2007).

It should be emphasized that in the supply chain, it is information that initiates and accompanies the flows of material goods. It holds a key place connecting all the basic components of the logistics system. In Chapter 2, the historical development of ideas about information in organizations is described, and the related concepts of data, knowledge, and learning are considered. Chapter 2 distinguishes between the technical definition of information in information theory and the social view of information in management. Moreover, it is argued that information becomes useful in organizations only when knowledge is applied as a basis for evaluating and interpreting information.

There are many reasons for the lack of information and informational mismatch between supply chain partners. They give rise to a number of consequences that negatively impact service levels and overall supply chain costs. Chapter 5 discusses solutions for overcoming information asymmetry and enhancing trust in supply chains, and Chapter 6 attempts to identify the most commonly used information technologies for mitigating information asymmetry in the supply chain.

The aims of this chapter are twofold. First, it attempts to explain the supply chain phenomenon, describing the evolution of logistics toward supply chain and exploring different approaches. Second, it proposes insights into the role of information sharing in chain integration.

1.2 Literature review

1.2.1 Definition and evolution of logistics

Recent years have seen the spread of the term logistics in business practice, as well as in economic literature. The most well-known and widely distributed definition of logistics developed in the United States by the Council of Logistics Management is: "logistics is the process of planning, implementing and controlling procedures for the efficient and effective transportation and storage of goods including services and related information from the point of origin to the point of consumption for the purpose of conforming to customer requirements and includes inbound, outbound, internal and external movements". A similar definition is given by Bozarth and Handfield (2007), assuming that logistics is the part of the supply chain process that deals with the planning, initiation, and control of the efficient and effective flow of goods, services, and related information from the point of origin to the point of consumption in order to satisfy consumer demands. In turn, Sołtysik (1994) defines logistics as the field of knowledge of logistical processes in the economy and the art of effectively managing these processes.

From the presented definitions of logistics, it can also be concluded that three main tasks are assigned to logistics:

- Coordination of the flow of material goods from their place of origin to the final recipient (consumer),
- Minimizing the cost of this flow (taking care of process efficiency),[1]
- Subordinating logistics activities to the requirements of customer service, including ensuring the availability of products to the customer.

This last task of logistics places special emphasis on the spatial and temporal dimensions of logistics. It is worth additionally recalling at this point the other demands placed on logistics: right product, right quantity, right value, right place, right time, right customer, right price.

Systematizing the definitions of logistics, it can be assumed that three main approaches stand out in the literature. First, logistics is treated as the physical flow of material goods within and between enterprises and the flow of information streams reflecting material processes and used in controlling these processes. Second, logistics is treated as a certain concept, a philosophy of managing goods flow processes based on a systemic and integrated view of these processes. Third, logistics is treated as a field of economic and management knowledge, studying the regularities and phenomena of the flow of goods and information in the economy, as well as in individual links. Logistics is to effectively deliver products to customers while taking care of the efficiency dimension of processes. Only the existence of physical goods flow and information processes makes it possible to develop logistics as a certain management concept and even as a discipline of economic knowledge, studying the flow of goods and information in the economy. In this book, the authors considered all approaches to logistics because they are complementary and should be analyzed together.

The origins of logistics are difficult to define. The practical activity of interest to logistics – the movement of goods – has existed since trade began. The issue, therefore, is not when logistics was created but when it began to be distinguished as a separate type of activity. The contemporary meaning of the *logistics* term comes from the military sphere. Since ancient times, logistics has functioned alongside tactics and strategy as one of the foundations of the art of war, conditioning the conduct of all military operations. Researchers locate this moment in different periods and places – in ancient Egypt, ancient Greece, or ancient Rome. The most common source for the theoretical basis of military logistics is the work of Swiss General A. H. de Jomini *Outline of the Art of War* published in 1837. The *logistics* term was used by him to describe the activity of transporting, housing, and supplying military troops (Beier & Rutkowski, 1993). An extremely important stage in the development of logistics as the pillar of the art of war was the Second World War, during which logistics provided transport and supply processes on the fronts of Europe, Africa, and Asia. In turn, specialists consider the greatest logistical success in the military sphere to be Operation Desert Storm in the Persian Gulf in 1991 (Fertsch, 2008).

As mentioned above, logistics in civilian applications developed in parallel with the development of trade. However, logistics as a separate theoretical concept has been adopted in the economy in the early 1960s in the United States. In the early 1970s, logistics concepts became widespread in Western European countries and Japan. Since then, there has been a steady and very dynamic development of logistics in the world.

Logistics has gone through a long evolution. Initially, individual processes such as transportation, storage, inventory, and distribution were considered autonomously. Logistics issues were solved in a fragmented way. Tasks related to the organization of the purchase of materials were formulated and solved separately, warehousing separately, and the organization of distribution separately. The implementation of individual tasks was broken down among enterprise functions at the operational level. Subsequently, the analysis of logistics processes involving going beyond the internal structures of the enterprise led to an emphasis on the dependencies between the entities involved in product and information flows and the introduction of the *chain* term – in which each link has a certain independence, but this is limited by obligations to the upstream link – the supplier – and the downstream link – the customer. Thus, certain relationships of dependence are established between entities, and logistics processes are considered in a comprehensive, integral way within the supply chain treated as a certain *whole*.

In the literature, the development of logistics is presented in chronological terms, distinguishing a different number of stages. The classification presented below distinguishes 4 phases in the development of logistics (Coyle et al., 2010; Ross, 2003).

The zero phase is called the era of logistics decentralization, which was characterized by non-integrated logistics activities. Often companies fragmented logistics into stand-alone activities and placed control under different company departments. The result was a disjointed, relatively uncoordinated, and costly management of logistics activities. The first stage occurred in the period extending from the early twentieth century to the mid-1950s (Ballou, 2004).

The first stage is associated with the explosive growth of large-format stores that took place in the late 1940s and early 1950s in the United States. Supermarkets focused mainly on physical distribution. Physical distribution was the activity of transporting products, warehousing, packaging, inventory management and after-sales service. At the time, logistics referred to the handling of retail trade carried out by large stores and required the coordination of tasks and processes within distributions.

It was realized that even the most efficient distribution would not ensure the availability of products in retail stores if there were delays in production or supply of materials. The second phase of logistics development known as the integration phase began. By the mid-1970s, companies began to merge logistics functions formally under a single manager. It was this manager's responsibility to make decisions that would benefit the whole logistics system and not just local departmental optimization. Logistics began to deal with the movement of goods throughout the enterprise – from procurement to distribution. The goal was to structure logistics so that total costs, and not just the cost of one logistics activity, are minimized. This required processing large amounts of information and was therefore supported by information technology (IT) solutions (Kisperska-Moroń & Krzyżaniak, 2009).

Meeting customer needs for basic products and increasing customer wealth have caused customers to look for more complex products and begin to pay attention to additional product-related services. Technological advances have made it possible to meet these demands. However, the increase in product complexity led to an increase in the complexity of logistics systems, which in turn led to the development of logistics system design methods, and the third phase of logistics development was called the logistics engineering phase or the logistics systems phase.

The next phase in the development of logistics was associated with a change in the behavior of enterprises. Enterprises began to cooperate with each other both in the spheres of procurement, production, and distribution. Logistics integration began to take place not only at the enterprise level, but also across enterprises, that is, within logistics chains. In logistics, there was a shift from a functional orientation to a flow approach. Hence, the fourth phase of logistics development is the phase of supply chains. Since the second half of the 1990s, there has been a development in the management of global supply chains. During this period, the development of IT, the Internet, and modern integrated management systems contributed to the emergence of logistics supply chains. Some researchers point out that this is the era of Supply Chain Digitization.

1.2.2 The essence of supply chains

According to Coyle et al. (1992), traditionally, responsibility for various logistic functions and tasks was dispersed among various departments of enterprises. The individual entities existed as independent, functional units that performed separate tasks and made decisions independently, without agreement with other group participants. Due to the lack of process coordination, companies had to duplicate their activities at each stage of the goods movement process (transportation, storage, etc.) (Schary & Skjott-Larsen, 2002). The concept of supply chain, which appeared in management, initially focused on the integration of logistics operations within enterprises in order to reduce costs (Camps, 2004, p. 18). Gradually, these responsibilities began to be integrated within materials management and physical distribution, and consequently, all of these issues were integrated within the logistics supply chain.[2]

The supply chain began to be thought of in a broader context, that is, beyond the boundaries of a single company (Camps, 2004, p. 18; Sweeney, 2011, pp. 38–41) and covering a series of sequentially related enterprises (Lazzarini et al., 2001, p. 7; van der Vorst, 2004, pp. 105–106). Integration and mutual alignment are at the heart of the supply chain idea (Christopher, 2011; Storey et al., 2006). According to Fawcett and Magnan (2002), four levels of integration can be identified: internal (cross-functional), backward (with direct suppliers), forward (with direct buyers), and complete backward and forward (from supplying suppliers to direct suppliers to customers purchasing from direct customers). Initially, the concept of supply chain concerned the first level, but nowadays it is usually interpreted in terms of the fourth level of integration. In this broader sense, the term supply chain was first used in the early 1980s by consultants R. K. Oliver and M. Weber (1982).

However, the concept of supply chains has lived to see a wide variety of definitions, often with little consistency. Some authors treat a supply chain as a sequence of activities performed sequentially by different companies (process approach). An example is the definition by the European Committee for Standardization (1997), according to which "a supply chain is the sequence of processes which create value added to a product during its flow and processing from raw materials through all intermediate forms to the form consistent with the requirements of the end-client". The APICS (Association for Operations Management) organization definition of supply chain also fits into the functional approach. The APICS organization defined the supply chain as: the processes that occur from the acquisition of the initial supply materials to the consumption of the final product, linking across the supplier and customer, and the functions inside and outside the enterprise that enable the value chain to produce products and deliver services to customers (Cox et al., 1995).

The second, entities-oriented approach defines supply chains as a set of cooperating organizations interconnected vertically by some modes of governance. According to Witkowski (2003), a supply chain is a collaboration of suppliers, manufacturing, trading, service companies, and their customers in different areas, between which flow streams of products, information, and financial resources. Some authors also add knowledge flows to the triad of streams listed above. Mentzer et al. (2001, p. 4) define a supply chain as "a set of three or more entities (organizations or individuals) directly involved in the upstream and downstream flows of products, services, finances, and/or information from a source to a customer". Sterman (2000) assumes that chains consist of cascades of companies, each receiving orders and adjusting production to meet changes in demand and each maintaining and controlling inventories of material and finished product. The distinguishing feature of the various links in the supply chain is the temporal and spatial succession concerning the manufacture and movement of a product from the location of the raw materials necessary for its manufacture to the location of the demand for the product (Poluha, 2007). These views of the supply chain treat supply chain management as the operation of a vertical structure of interconnected companies involved in exchange processes.

Within the entities-oriented approach, it can be noticed that some researchers treat the supply chain as a network of interrelated and interdependent organizations that, working in cooperation with each other, control and improve material and information flows from suppliers to end users (Christopher, 2000). A network view of the supply chain is presented by Harland (1996), who defines supply chain management as "the management of a network of interrelated enterprises involved in the ultimate delivery of packages of products and services required by the end customer". The network nature of supply chains is related to the increase in the number and heterogeneity of actors in the various phases of the flow of goods, information, and finance, which in turn causes logistics linkages to become less sequential and linear and increasingly complex and multiple. The network view of the supply chain treats supply chain management as a complex network of organizations involved in exchange processes.

Thus, given the diversity of approaches to defining a supply chain, in this book the supply chain will be understood as a set of organizations interconnected vertically by some modes of governance that coordinate the flow of products, information, and financial resources, with the goal of adding value to the product as it flows up to a form that meets the requirements of the final customer. Food supply chains include all entities involved in the production of food and its delivery to consumers. The distinguishing feature of the various links in the agri-food supply chain is the temporal and spatial succession concerning the manufacture and movement of a product from the location of the raw materials necessary for its manufacture to the location of the demand for the product. In addition, chain membership is variable, and individual organizations that are participants in the chain pursue their own goals. They may also compete with each other for a position in the chain, a share of profits, or even access to participation.

Bechtel and Jayaram (1997), based on a review of definitions of supply chains, identified four basic schools of supply chain analysis. The first school is the functional supply chain awareness school, which emphasizes the role of product flow and the fact that multiple actors, including suppliers and manufacturers, are involved in the processes of adding value to a product. The second school of logistics emphasizes the role of linkages between different functional areas in the supply chain at the interface of which there is an opportunity to improve management and thus achieve a significant competitive advantage over other supply chains. Another school – the information one – emphasizes that in addition to the flow of products through the chain, the flow of information is also important, being an essential element of its final results. The furthest in its assumptions goes the last integrative school, which divides the supply chain into horizontal blocks, which include individual business processes that are the subject of optimization efforts.

The issues described in this book outline the significant role of information asymmetry and trust and their impact on the functioning of agri-food supply chains; therefore, they fit into the interests of information schools. The book provides a detailed analysis of the theoretical aspects of information asymmetry, incorporating behavioral assumptions such as bounded rationality and opportunism, as well as the social capital context, offering insight into the role of trust in the agri-food supply chains. Second, it suggests a variety of remedies to mitigate informational asymmetry and approaches to building trust or creating substitutes, which are crucial in complex agribusiness networks plagued by opaque information and quality concerns. The second part presents case studies from the agri-food chains, providing practical insights into how information asymmetry can affect the performance, quality, and safety of the agri-food supply chain.

It should be noted that supply chain analysis is part of a systems approach. The essence of the concept of the system is that the whole is greater than the sum of its parts (von Bertalanffy, 1972).

It can be said that the system is a product of the interaction of elements that make up a given system. When depicting the chain as a system, we will use the hierarchical structure of systems (i.e., systems within systems), which are built from subsystems, which, in turn, are divided into subsystems, etc. (Simon, 1962).The supply chain is an open and relatively isolated system, because on the one hand it has defined boundaries and is separated from its environment, and on the other hand it interacts with its environment through the exchange of matter and information. The supply chain influences the environment through its outputs and is susceptible to external influence through inputs. Thus, the supply chain is constantly adapting to its environment, but the environment influences the behavior and shape of the supply chain much more than the reverse.

The systems approach in supply chains involves a holistic view of phenomena rather than an analytical consideration of individual components separately. This holistic viewpoint stems from the fact that the properties of the system as a whole are not identical to the properties that characterize its component parts. The elements that make up the structure of thc system are therefore subject to laws that are relevant to the whole.

In a supply chain treated as a system, it is necessary to avoid suboptimization, which occurs when individual links in the chain are evaluated according to separate, individual criteria. In addition, it is also a matter of examining the interaction of individual links in the chain when implementing product and information flows. According to the description of the economic system proposed by Kornai, the processes taking place in it can be divided into two categories: The real sphere and the control sphere. The real sphere includes the material processes taking place in the economic system, such as production and delivery (including products and services), sale, and consumption. The control sphere includes the thought processes occurring in the economic system, such as perception, transmission, and the processing of information, preparation, and decision-making, which govern the material processes in the real sphere (Kornai, 1971; Pietrzak, 2023).

Chapter 3, according to the system theory, describes the company in three systems: causal, response, and normative, pointing out the essence of the sharing of information in the system and how information feedback enables the learning process, which could take the form of single-loop or double-loop learning.

As a result of applying the principle of thinking of the whole, the so-called synergy effect appears, which consists in achieving additional benefits from combined actions compared to the sum of the results of actions taken separately. Most often, the synergy effect is achieved as a result of joint process planning and scheduling of resource use in the supply chain. In the context of the supply chain, the synergistic effect of systemic analysis and rationalization of logistics costs and comprehensive customer service is characteristic. In addition, in a systems approach to the supply chain, it is important to treat logistics costs from a holistic perspective. This view of costs avoids a situation where a reduction in costs in one link of the supply chain will affect such a significant increase in costs in another area that it will ultimately increase total logistics costs.

A review of the literature also reveals a heated discussion of how the terms *logistics* and *supply chain* relate to each other. Larson and Halldorsson (2004), attempted to systematize this issue. The result of their work was the identification of four groups of views.

- Traditionalists are willing to view the supply chain as a part of logistics, along the lines of external or inter-organizational logistics. In this view, logistics is a concept far beyond the supply chain.
- Re-labelings – They use the two terms interchangeably. This group renames logistics: what was logistics is now supply chain management.
- Unionists represent the opposite view to the traditionalists. In their view, the supply chain term includes the logistics term. They limit logistics to one of many business processes.
- Intersectionists believe that logistics covers the operational decisions and the supply chain concept covers strategic aspects stretching both within the company and across the supply chain. The supply chain is not the union of logistics, marketing, operations management, purchasing, and other functional areas. Rather, it includes strategic, integrative elements from all of these disciplines.

The authors do not determine which approach is the right one. Instead, they point out the consequences of opting for one of them. The traditionalist and re-labeling positions result in a narrow approach to the supply chain, while the unionist and intersectionist approaches imply a broad definition of the supply chain.

1.2.3 Supply chain integration and the importance of information exchange

The management of complex, multi-level organizational structures such as supply chains requires the participating entities to meet a number of postulates crucial to the success of the process. These postulates can be presented as follows (Mentzer, 2001):

- integration of processes/activities carried out by different links in the chain;
- orientation toward full cooperation of chain links in the implementation and management of processes in the chain;
- striving by all members of the supply chain toward the common interest of providing the best possible service to the chain's ultimate customers;
- the building of long-term relationships by supply chain participants based on partnership principles;
- sharing the risks and benefits of the chain's activities;
- sharing of information by chain participants.

The last of the abovementioned postulates is of particular importance, as it conditions the realization of the others. Many authors on the subject of supply chain management emphasize that effective exchange of information increases the efficiency of these structures (Hult et al., 2004; Lee & Whang, 2000; Zhou & Benton, 2007). Following Kembro and Selviaridis (2015), it can be stated that information exchange in the supply chain takes place at three levels: operational, tactical, and strategic. Information in the supply chain relates to the product and its flow. The first group (product data) includes information related to the development of a new product, its design, preparation and planning of its production, management of the material structure of the product, its variants, configurations, and production flow, as well as related to its documentation, commercialization, and servicing. Moreover, in agri-food supply chains, the key product data is information about product quality. Many agri-food product traits belong to the categories of experience and credence attributes. In contrast to search attributes (those that can be easily identified before purchase, such as color, size, or weight), experience attributes are difficult to evaluate before purchase, such as the taste of the food. Credence attributes are those that are difficult to evaluate even after purchase, such as the chemical residues in foods, fair trade, the welfare of livestock animals, and environmental impact, among others. The buyer could experience difficulties distinguishing a quality product from a poor one, which creates problems in quality assurance through the supply chain. These issues will be deeply discussed in Chapter 3.

The second group of information (flow data) is the result of controlling the flow of products in the supply chain in order to track the movement and source of products (track & trace) at all stages of processing and flow. Such flow data are important for food safety and are most relevant to improving the traceability of food in supply chains (Szymczak, 2012). There are several different types of food tracing systems, each with its own benefits and drawbacks. Some common methods of food tracing include barcode scanning, radio-frequency identification (RFID) tags, and blockchain technology (cf. deeper discussion about this issue in Chapters 6 and 13).

Zhou and Benton (2007) highlight three key aspects of the information exchange process in the supply chain: information quality (understood as, among other things, availability, accuracy, timeliness, internal consistency, completeness, usefulness, or comprehensibility), technology supporting information exchange (primarily software), and information content (dependent on its source – the chain link) (Lee et al., 2002).

Integration emphasizes the coordination of separate activities of entities aimed at achieving common interests in the flow of materials and products. These interests include serving the ultimate customer and ensuring the efficiency of the operations comprising the chain (Cooper & Ellram, 1993). The goal of supply chain integration, therefore, is to achieve efficient flows of products and services, information, and capital to maximize stakeholder value. The importance of cooperation between partners to achieve strategic goals therefore becomes crucial. This implies the need to build trust, share information, and share risks.

The relationships of various individual organizations that make up the supply chain must be examined. Most supply chains are comprised of a large number of companies, for example, suppliers, producers, retailers, or wholesalers. All these enterprises are independent commercial entities, each with their own business objectives and profit goals. As a result, the control of many supply chains is traditionally fragmented between these companies, and relationships are often adversarial. The individual goals of individual entities in the supply chain may be consistent with the interests of the whole supply chain (which will encourage cooperation), but they may also be contradictory (which will result in competition). In some cases, one company (often a major manufacturer) may have gained control of other entities either upstream (e.g., suppliers) in a process of vertical integration in order to gain control of a greater part of the supply chain and thereby permit more systematic management of the system. This is the case with some Japanese car manufacturers who have control of component suppliers and dealerships and also a large retail chains working with small food manufacturers and agricultural producers (Taylor, 1997). Governance structures and organizational learning (cf. deeper discussion about this issue in Chapters 2 and 3) are intended to make companies aware that there is a set of common interests within the supply chain and to encourage them to implement them. It is also important to assess which organizations are most powerful, as in reality it is likely that only the most powerful members of the chain will be able to force through initiatives that require significant changes of operational practice across the chain.

Referring to the previously mentioned evolution of logistics management, as well as developing relationships between supply chain partners, the following levels of supply chain integration can be distinguished (Poirier, 2004):

- Level I – functional integration. This level of internal integration is focused on cooperation between functional departments of the enterprise. It is oriented toward intuitive decision-making, usually in the area of cost reduction related to logistics activities. Improvements and focus are in the internal areas of the enterprise, not in the relationships with other supply chain partners. There is a lack of synchronization of supply and demand.
- Level II – internal excellence. Focusing on improvements within the enterprise, but paying particular attention to information flow and greater coordination of supply and demand synchronization information flows. Implementing integrated enterprise management systems. Focusing on internal excellence.
- Level III – cooperation with partners. Systematically establish partnerships with business partners. Establishing partnerships to improve efficiency and customer service, which requires acquiring and processing information and sharing it with business partners. At this level of chain maturity, real-time access to information by all partners is important.

- Level IV – value chain collaboration. Cooperation between managers of all links in the supply chain to reduce costs, allocate resources more efficiently, improve customer service, and meet customer needs and market position. It is important here to maintain the solidarity influence of all links in the supply chain and develop common information systems. The coordination of flows between the individual links dispersed in the global market intensifies the demand for and use of modern ICT.
- Level V – networking. Within the supply network, information is shared and joint decisions are made on the better functioning of the entire network through improvements, coordination, and synchronization of material, information, and cash flows. A prerequisite for cooperation in a network is its formalization, which should ensure: on-time delivery, high quality, price, terms of delivery and returns, consequences for failure to meet deadlines, quantity and location of inventory storage, etc. Networking is aimed at strengthening ties between network members to better and jointly focus attention on buyer needs.

In business practice, levels of supply chain integration vary widely and, unfortunately, are still far from being perfect. Each level of progression requires time and patience to accomplish. The necessary understanding and requisite behavioral change (business transformation) is not easy and requires sustained executive endorsement. An empirical study conducted by Fawcett and Magnan (2002) among purchasing, manufacturing, and logistics managers in the United States found that almost half of companies limit themselves to integrating processes only within their organization, a third focus on integration with first-tier suppliers, 11% of companies focus only on integration with key customers, and 8% of the companies surveyed systematically integrate their processes with first-tier suppliers and customers.

The key to internal and external integration is cooperation between partners based on trust and information sharing. While already managing the flow of information in a single organization is not an easy task, its implementation at the inter-organizational level is a particularly difficult challenge. When discussing information management in the supply chain, special emphasis should be placed on the issues of obtaining and sharing information. The role of efficient information flow in the supply chain is widely emphasized in the literature (Fawcett et al., 2007; Handfield & Nichols 1999; Simchi-Levi et al., 2000). It is referred to as infopartnership, in which entities commit to ensuring the proper and uninterrupted flow of information between each other (the above-mentioned level 3 and 4 supply chain integration). It is an essential element of popular strategic supply chain management solutions based on collaborative planning to synchronize the flow of resources and their efficient use, which have been formalized in the form of the CPFR (Collaborative Planning, Forecasting, and Replenishment) concept (cf. deeper discussion about this issue in Chapter 3). On its basis, such solutions as VMI (Vendor Managed Inventory), ECR (Efficient Consumer Response), JIT (Just in Time), or QR (Quick Response) have been developed. Information management in modern supply chains should be organized in such a way that the 3 Vs (visibility, velocity, versatility) principle is realized in the supply chain. Transparency focuses on resources, especially inventories (inventory visibility), and means their visibility in the supply chain, the ability to see them from any link, and therefore the ability to monitor their level throughout the supply chain. Velocity refers to the ability to meet needs (fulfillment velocity) or fulfill a contract in a short period of time. Versatility, on the other hand, is the ability to work with suppliers and customers in the face of different delivery conditions (coordination versatility).

Full integration of activities in supply chains should therefore cover three areas: information, operational, and relational integration. Information integration refers to the flow of information, while it is realized through communication channels and technologies that support the flow of information between companies in the supply chain. Operational integration involves joint undertaking of activities, coordination of decision-making processes, and standardization of processes. Relational integration refers to the strategic adaptation of ties between companies characterized by trust, commitment, and long-term orientation. Achieving full integration of supply chain links, across all areas, is a difficult, long-term, and multi-stage task. It requires the commitment of all participants, especially the supply chain leader, and the support of the top management of these companies. A key aspect is also the willingness to share information and the mutual trust of chain partners in each other.

1.3 Summary and conclusions

Logistics encompasses the flow of products as well as the management of information in order to offer the right product and level of service to the customer at a reasonable cost. The flow of physical goods can be analyzed from different perspectives. First, we can distinguish the flow of products and information within various departments of the company. Second, there is a flow of products from points of origin to points of final consumption (external supplies from suppliers and a flow of supplies to final customers).

Looking through the perspective of the flow of goods from the sources of their acquisition to the final recipients, we are talking about a flow in which we can distinguish many links forming a supply chain. Supply chains are a set of organizations interconnected vertically by some modes of governance that coordinate the flow of products, information, and financial resources, often consisting of farms producing agricultural raw materials and companies processing and distributing products to final customers (from field to fork). The flow of products thus crosses both functional boundaries (production, inventory storage, and transportation) and organizational boundaries (manufacturers, carriers, distributors, and customers). It also often crosses geographic boundaries, as it involves global supply and global markets. Proper management of products, information, and financial flows within supply chains treated as a certain system forming a whole can be a source of competitive advantage. However, this requires a focus on cooperation and coordination among supply chain partners.

Building a partnership arrangement is a costly undertaking – you need good communication, regular coordination of activities, and the ability to share risks. The key issue is to find solutions that reconcile the often conflicting interests of supply chain partners. This requires increased trust and cooperation. The issue of trust and cooperation naturally weaves into the theme of cooperation and the belief that the place of value creation is a chain of enterprises, not a single company.

A supply chain cannot function without information flowing between its links, as no transaction resulting in the movement of any resources would then take place. Conversely, it is not possible to market and deliver any good through a supply chain without the exchange of data and information between its links. The consequences of information asymmetry in the supply chain can be manifold, including the following:

- Lost sales – caused by a lack of up-to-date information about demand and the resulting lack of inventory,
- High inventory costs or lack of inventory – both situations are caused by misdiagnosed demand and lack of inventory information from customers,
- Quality problems – where differences in quality exist, which are difficult to verify in advance, creating an incentive to deliver low-quality products. This is often the case in agri-food chains, where many product traits belong to the categories of experience (such as the taste of the food) and credence attributes (such as the chemical residues in foods, the welfare of livestock animals, and environmental impact),
- Underestimated customer service levels – as a consequence of incorrect forecasting and the inability of the supply chain to react quickly to changes in demand.

Holding information also raises problems due to: different information and data formats of trading partners, different information media, different IT systems or lack thereof, high costs of implementing IT systems, and electronic data interchange (EDI). The choice of the method of information exchange and its principles and supporting IT tools is a strategic decision for supply chains, affecting the quality, security, and efficiency of carrying out tasks in logistics processes, and consequently also the competitiveness of supply chains. Despite the huge progress in digital connectivity, information technologies, and data standardization, economic agents are still reluctant to share information. People are limited in cognition and rationality (bounded rationality) and susceptible to opportunism, and information asymmetry aggravates the problem in supply chains. Therefore, the aim of integrated chain governance takes effort to implement. The following chapters of the book provide an in-depth description of information, knowledge, and organizational learning in supply chains, the issue of informational asymmetry in supply chain governance, trust in inter-organizational relations, solutions for overcoming information asymmetry, and then many of these theoretical issues are demonstrated with case studies of specific agri-food chains.

Notes

1 Thanks to the integration of supply chain links, it is also possible to achieve benefits other than cost reduction. Gradually, as the concept of supply chain management developed, the focus on costs was replaced by the idea of customer value (Camps, 2004, p. 18). An illustration of this trend is the definition of supply chain proposed by Lazzarini et al. (2001, p. 7) – "a set of sequential, vertically organized transactions representing subsequent stages of value creation". In this approach, the concept of the supply chain breaks away from the operational orientation towards a strategic orientation (Sweeney et al., 2018) – focused on building a broadly understood competitive advantage, constructed on the scale of the entire chain. Then the concept of the supply chain comes close to the idea of a value system (Porter, 1998 [1985] p. 35), but it is much more conceptually developed.

2 Supply chains are not recent manifestations; they have been in existence for many centuries. Supply chains through about 1750 are best characterized as trading supply chains – set of trading partners that engaged in moving goods from one location to another, usually without transforming the goods at intermediate locations.

References

Ballou R. H. (2004). *Business logistics/supply chain management*. Pearson/Prentice Hall.

Bechtel, Ch., & Jayaram, J. (1997). Supply chain management: A strategic perspective. *International Journal of Logistics Management*, *8*(1), 15–34.

Beier, F.J., & Rutkowski, K. (1993). *Logistyka* (Logistics). Oficyna Wydawnicza SGH.

Bozarth, C., & Handfield, R. B. (2007). *Wprowadzenie do zarządzania operacjami i łańcuchem dostaw* [Introduction to operations and supply chain management]. Wydawnictwo Helion.

Camps, T. (2004). Chains and networks: Theory and practice. In T. Camps, P. Diederen, G. J. Hofstede, & B. Vos (Eds.), *The emerging world of chains and networks: Bridging theory and practice* (pp. 13–32). Reed Business Information.

Christopher, M. (2000). *Logistyka i zarządzanie łańcuchem dostaw* [Logistics and supply chain management]. PCDL.

Christopher, M. (2011). *Logistics and supply chain management: Creating value-adding networks*. Prentice Hall.

Cooper, M., & Ellram, L. (1993). Characteristic of supply chain management and its implications for purchasing and logistic strategy. *International Journal of Logistics Management*, *4*(2), 13–24.

Cox, J. F., Blackstone, J. H., & Spencer, M. S. (1995). *APICS dictionary*. American Production and Inventory Control Society.

Coyle, J. J., Bardi, E. J., & Langley, C. J., Jr. (1992). *The management of business logistic*. West Publishing Company.

Coyle, J. J., Bardi, E. J., & Langley, C. J., Jr. (2010). *Zarządzanie logistyczne* [Logistics management]. PWE.

European Committee for Standarisation. (1997). *Logistics – Structure, basic terms and definitions in logistics*.

Fawcett, S. E., Ellram, L. M., & Ogden, J. A. (2007). *Supply chain management. From vision to implementation*. Pearson Education.

Fawcett, S. E., & Magnan, G. M. (2002). The rhetoric and reality of supply chain integration. *International Journal of Physical Distribution & Logistics Management*, *32*(5), 339–361. DOI:10.1108/09600030210436222

Fechner, I. (2007). *Zarządzanie łańcuchem dostaw* [Supply chain management]. Wyższa Szkoła Logistyki.

Fertsch, M. (2008). *Podstawy logistyki* [Basics of logistics]. Biblioteka Logistyka.

Handfield, R. B., & Nichols, E. L. (1999). *Introduction to supply chain management*. Prentice Hall.

Harland, C. M. (1996). Supply chain management: Relationships chain and networks. *British Journal of Management*, *7*, 63–80.

Hult, G. T. M., Ketchen, D. J., & Slater, S. F. (2004). Information processing, knowledge development, and strategic supply chain performance. *Academy of Management Journal*, *47*(2), 241–253.

Kembro, J., & Selviaridis, K. (2015). Exploring information sharing in the extended supply chain: An interdependence perspective. *Supply Chain Management: An International Journal*, *20*(4), 455–470.

Kisperska-Moroń, D., & Krzyżaniak, S. (2009). *Logistyka* [Logistics]. Biblioteka Logistyka.

Kornai, J. (1971). *Anti-equilibrium: On economic systems theory and the tasks of research*. North-Holland.

Larson, P. D., & Halldórsson, Á. (2004). Logistics versus supply chain management: An international survey. *International Journal of Logistics*, *7*(1), 17–31. DOI:10.1080/1367556031000161924O

Lazzarini, S. G., Chaddd, F. R., & Cook, M. L. (2001). Integrating supply chain and network analyses: The study of netchains. *Journal of Chain and Network Science*, *1*, 7–22.

Lee, H. L., & Whang, S. (2000). Information sharing in a supply chain. *International Journal of Manufacturing Technology & Management*, *1*(1), 79–93.

Lee, Y. W., Strong, D. M., Kahn, B. K., & Wang, R. Y. (2002). AIMQ: A methodology for information quality assessment. *Information & Management*, *40*(2), 133–146.

Mentzer, T. (2001). What is supply chain management? In J. T. Mentzer (Ed.), *Supply chain management*. Sage Publications.

Mentzer, J. T., DeWitt, W., Keebler, J. S., Min, S., Nix, N. W., Smith, C. D., & Zacharia, Z. G. (2001). Defining supply chain management. *Journal of Business Logistics, 22*(2), 1–25.

Oliver, R. K., & Webber, M. D. (1982). Supply chain management: Logistics catches up with strategy. In M. Christopher (Ed.), *Logistics: The strategic issues* (pp. 63–75). Chapman and Hall. ISBN 978-0412415500.

Pietrzak, M. (2023). Should we rethink supply-chain management? Insights from global-value-chain approach. In J. Domagała, A. Górecka, & M. Roman (Eds.), *Sustainable logistics. How to address and overcome the major issues and challenges* (pp.101–138). Routledge, Taylor & Francis Group.

Poirier, Ch. C. (2004). *Using models to improve the supply chain*. CRC Press, Taylor & Francis Group.

Poluha, R. G. (2007). *Application of SCOR model in supply chain management*. Cambria Press.

Porter, M. E. (1998 [1985]). *Competitive advantage: Creating and sustaining superior performance* (with a new Introduction). The Free Press.

Ross, D. F. (2003). *Introduction to e-supply chain management: Engaging technology to build market-winning business partnerships*. St. Lucie Press.

Schary, P. B., & Skjott-Larsen, T. (2002). *Zarządzanie globalnym łańcuchem podaży* [Global supply chain management]. PWN.

Simchi-Levi, D., Kaminsky, Ph., & Simchi-Levi, E. (2000). *Designing & managing the supply chain. Concepts, strategies, and case studies*. Irwin/McGraw-Hill.

Simon, H. A. (1962). The architecture of complexity. *Proceeding of the American Philosophical Society, 106*(6), 467–482.

Sołtysik, M. (1994). Istota i cechy zarządzania logistycznego [The essence and features of logistics management]. *Gospodarka Materiałowa & Logistyka, 7–8*, 145–146.

Sterman, J. D. (2000). *Business dynamics. Systems thinking and modeling for a complex world*. Irwin/McGraw-Hill.

Storey, J., Emberson, C., Godsell, J., & Harrison, A. (2006). Supply chain management: Theory, practice and future challenge. *International Journal of Operations & Production Management, 26*(7), 754–774. https://doi.org/10.1108/01443570610672220

Sweeney, E. (2011). Towards a unified definition of supply chain management. *International Journal of Applied Logistics, 2*(3), 30–48. https://doi.org/10.4018/jal.2011070103

Sweeney, E., Grant, D. B., & Mangan, J. (2018). Strategic adoption of logistics and supply chain management. *International Journal of Operations & Production Management, 38*(3), 852–873. https://doi.org/10.1108/IJOPM-05-2016-0258

Szymczak, M. (2012). Współczesne tendencje rozwojowe łańcuchów dostaw produktów żywnościowych [Contemporary development trends in food supply chains]. *Logistyka, 5*, 7–10.

Taylor, D. H. (1997). *Global cases in logistics and supply chain management*. Cengage Learning (EMEA).

van der Vorst, J. G. A. J. (2004). Supply chain management: Theory and practices. In T. Camps, P. Diederen, G. J. Hofstede, & B. Vos (Eds.), *The emerging world of chains and networks: Bridging theory and practice* (pp. 105–128). Reed Business Information.

von Bertalanffy, L. (1972). The history and status of general systems theory. *The Academy of Management Journal*, *15*(4), 407–426. https://doi.org/10.2307/255139

Witkowski, J. (2003). *Zarządzanie łańcuchem dostaw. Koncepcje, procedury, doświadczenia* [Supply chain management. Concepts, procedures, experiences]. PWE.

Zhou, H., & Benton, W. C., Jr. (2007). Supply chain practice and information sharing. *Journal of Operations Management*, *25*(6), 1348–1365.

2 Information, Knowledge, and Organizational Learning in Supply Chains

Christiaan Maasdorp
Stellenbosch University, South Africa

2.1 Introduction

Improvements in information technology have led to the incorporation of data gathering, processing, and sharing systems into all aspects of management, primarily as management information systems to improve decision-making, coordination, and control in organizations. Today, the importance of information in management increases with developments in data analytics, big data, and machine learning. The management of modern organizations depends heavily on information for decision-making, process optimization, and strategic planning. Although information systems improved organizations' ability to collect, process, and manipulate information, they also massively increased the amount of information to be processed. Information is not just an internal resource for organizations; it is also a primary conduit for interacting with their external environment, which largely consists of other organizations. In supply chains, diverse organizations pursue their own goals that partially overlap with the goals of their upstream and downstream partners. Information is the medium through which mutual adjustment is made possible in this dynamic configuration. In fact, supply chains would be impossible without the exchange of financial and other information between firms, as this is the basis on which they coordinate their actions and manage the interface with each other. Therefore, it is hardly surprising that the quality and efficiency of information sharing between supply chain actors is coming under increased scrutiny (Chen, 2003). One phenomenon of particular interest is the situation where some participants possess better or more information than others. The management research devoted to this phenomenon is called information asymmetry. This phenomenon is fluid over time because interacting parties may start out with information in common, and asymmetries can emerge over time for a variety of reasons.

Research on information asymmetry proceeds from game theory foundations to analyses of organizational behavior regarding planning, control, coordination, contracting, and pricing. The common view of information as data given form treats information as unproblematic. This has also been the case with much of

DOI: 10.4324/9781032633725-3

the treatment of information in economics in general and specifically in research on information asymmetry. In the context of management information systems, the nature and role of information in organizations need deeper reflection. Luckily, the related fields of information theory, cybernetics, systems thinking, information management, and knowledge management grappled with the conceptual issues around information and how it relates to other concepts like data, knowledge, and learning. Ultimately, the challenge of connecting relevant information with business outcomes remains at every level of decision-making and in all domains of supply chain management.

This chapter aims to set the necessary background for the case studies on information asymmetry in supply chains in the agri-food sector that follow in the empirical part of this book. There are many perspectives on the role of information in management and organization; given the vastness and complexity of these concepts, a complete view is not possible within one chapter. Instead, this chapter offers an interpretation of the historical development of the mainstream understanding of information in organizations, along with the related concepts of data, knowledge, and learning. This interpretation is just one perspective among many plausible ones and seeks to introduce the relation between these concepts, thereby laying the groundwork for discussions in the later chapters.

The next sections trace the thinking regarding information in the disciplines of economics, mathematics, and management. We start by discussing how three areas of economics—game theory, information economics, and institutional economics—conceive of information. Then we turn to information theory and the influence it had on subsequent reflection about the relation between data, information, and knowledge. Lastly, we consider knowledge management and organizational learning as disciplines focused on the role of management to bundle the knowledge and skills of workers to make it productive. Whereas economics and information theory tend to conflate information with data and its processing, the emphasis in knowledge management and organizational learning shifts to information being imbued with meaning because of its combination with knowledge in the pursuit of practices.

2.2 Information Asymmetry in Supply Chains

Information asymmetry refers to a condition where information is not equally distributed between parties in a transactional relationship and where the asymmetry matters, namely that the party without information held by the other party could have made better decisions with that missing information (Ren et al., 2010, p. 82; Shen et al., 2019, p. 4898). This situation is worsened if the missing information is counterintuitive rather than confirmatory information because guesses made under uncertainty would be incorrect. In supply chains, managing this asymmetry is important to facilitate coordination between supply chain partners, fairness in contracting, and ensure overall efficiency of the entire chain.

It seems obvious that sharing information to improve feedback processes and learning is the way to counteract information asymmetry, but the information relationship is a dynamic one where parties that start out with equal information diverge over time into an asymmetric relationship.

Information asymmetry is studied not only in supply chains but in broader management research. Bergh et al. (2019) provide a recent overview of information asymmetry in management research, describing the foundational work on this phenomenon, and categorizing research in the subfields of entrepreneurship, human resource management, international business, organizational behavior, organization theory, and strategic management. A famous example of classic information asymmetry research is presented by Akerlof (1970), who demonstrated how market failure can result when transacting agents have asymmetric information about product quality. He modeled the second-hand car market, where the seller has perfect information about the quality of the vehicle offered, but the purchaser only has information about the likelihood that the vehicle is of poor quality. In this situation, buyers will offer the same price for both good and bad cars, because they base their offer on their expectation of likely quality. As a result, sellers with higher-than-average quality cars will be driven out of the market, and the proportion of lower quality vehicles will increase, which in turn will adjust the expectations about the likelihood of bad quality cars being offered, leading to market failure caused by the information asymmetry between buyers and sellers.

Bergh et al. (2019) also reveal that the asymmetry may be the result of a wide array of information attributes and identify five types of asymmetries based on different notions of information studied in the field of management research. The first is privileged (or private) information, which might be proprietary and, therefore, legally restricted, or simply because the information requires specialized expertise (Bergh et al., 2019, p. 128). The second is different information because of the natural condition where some people know things that others do not (Bergh et al., 2019, p. 129; Stiglitz, 2000, p. 469). The third is hidden information that makes opportunism during contracting possible (Bergh et al., 2019, p. 129). The fourth is imperfect information that is incomplete from the perspective of buyers (Bergh et al., 2019, p. 130), as evidenced by Akerlof's model of the used-car market. Lastly, the impact of information can manifest as an asymmetry (Bergh et al., 2019, p. 130), because the extent to which information becomes embedded differs among participants according to their learning capabilities so that they end up with a different amount or quality of information over time (Williamson, 1985).

In their review of research on information asymmetry in supply chain coordination, Vosooghidizaji et al. (2020) found that most papers focused on the asymmetry of cost and demand information, and other types of information asymmetry were less studied. By far, the most widely used coordination mechanisms are various types of contracts based on wholesale price, quantity discount, or profit sharing. This shows that the body of research on information asymmetries in supply chains overall perceives information to be financial and stock information and oversimplifies the nature of asymmetry in a way that may not be the case in real-world supply chains.

2.3 Views on Information in Economics

The work on information asymmetry is based on theories about information developed by economists. This section describes the contributions of the subdisciplines of economics. Without delving deeply into the specifics, there are three general perspectives on the role of information in the field of economics corresponding with the sub-disciplines of game theory, economics of information and communication, and institutional economics. These three perspectives emphasize different aspects of information, but, as we will argue in this section, information is relatively under-theorized in economics.

Game theory is a subdiscipline of economics focused on decision-making under various game conditions, each with their own information requirements and rules for acquiring further information. Classic strategy boardgames like chess are perfect information games (Mycielski, 1992), meaning that there is no hidden information, and players always have the same information about the game state available. In contrast, many classic card games, such as poker, are imperfect information games because gameplay depends on some information being hidden from opponents. The famous prisoner's dilemma (Kuhn, 2019) is a situation in which two parties may benefit from cooperation or suffer from not doing so, but coordination is very difficult because the parties have no way of obtaining new information about the other's action.

In game theory, information is the raw material used as input for decision-making, and the lack of accurate information, because of ambiguity or uncertainty, is considered an increased risk. Accordingly, information asymmetry is typically studied as a condition for decisions in game theory. However, game theory largely sees information as an unproblematic concept. Information is assumed to be a kind of disembodied content that can be communicated as a message. This seems quite simple, as it is close to our common notion of information, but it neglects the interpretation and application of information required to make it productive in an organization.

Hayek (1945) was one of the first economists interested in the coordinating role of information and knowledge (used interchangeably) in society. This interest marks the second community of economists, those interested in the economics of information and communication. Although they are interested in information as an analytical lens for studying coordination, the transition from industrial to informational modes of development raised the profile of their work considerably. Hayek's (1945, p. 519) basic insight was that knowledge is dispersed among people, with each possessing incomplete or partial information about the situation. In such an environment, an integrated overview and central control is in principle impossible. The price mechanism communicates information about the state of supply and demand that permits coordination without central control. This idea was investigated further by Hurwicz (1969), who essentially argued that modern economies are too complex to be centrally steered and that information flows provided by the market mechanism achieve a decentralized coordination of economic agents who act as rational information processors on locally available information through a process of mutual adjustment. In their wake followed writers like Akerlof (1970), Arrow (1984), and Williamson (1985) interested in the role of information in the economy. However, more than half a century after Hayek, the field has not achieved a general theory of information. Even insiders like Arrow (1996) and Stiglitz (2000) note that the field is faced with a lack of consensus regarding the various kinds of information that characterize the informational economy. Lamberton (1998) explicitly doubts whether such a general theory of information is feasible or even desirable for further development of the field. The problem, it seems, is that information sometimes appears like stock (as data) and other times like a flow (as messages).

Like game theorists, researchers who study the coordinating role of information in the economy typically imagine the economic actor as an information processor with the goal of using information in the service of improved decision-making. However, it is obvious that rationality is not achievable in the real world because information is rarely fully available in time for a decision to be made, and even with complete and timely information, decision-makers also need a fully integrated set of assumptions without trade-offs to act completely rationally. Simon's (1978) solution to this problem is his notion of the satisficing (as opposed to optimizing) behavior of boundedly rational agents who make decisions that are good enough given their informational constraints. With this shift, it becomes clear that the individual economic agent is a poor basis for modeling information processing because a lot of preprocessing of information is done before an individual faces a moment of decision. Organizations are primarily information processing structures in the Simonian view. Through organization, the cognitive load is reduced for individual members whose decision-making is scaffolded by reusable scripts or standard operating procedures in the form of organizational routines developed for handling typical recurring situations.

At this point, we can consider the contribution of institutional economists to the role of knowledge in preference to information. In particular, they do not use the terms knowledge and information interchangeably. Nightingale (2003, pp. 149–150) explains that Nelson and Winter (1982) tried to synthesize the information processing paradigm (based on the work of Simon) with the tacit knowledge tradition based on the work of Polanyi. By tacit knowledge, Polanyi meant know-how that the owner can use skillfully but not necessarily communicate explicitly, meaning that "we can know more than we can tell" (Polanyi, 1967, p. 4). While Simon's standard operating procedures are organizational routines that help to simplify the information processing, Nelson and Winter (1982, Chapter 4) see these organizational routines as a form of organizational knowledge; more precisely, routines are collectively held tacit knowledge. It is tacit since, for the most part, individual participants of a routine cannot specify it in its entirety, nor the contributions of other participants, because they have decidedly partial knowledge of the unwritten rules governing the collective action forming the routine. In fact, participants are often inaccurate in their application of these rules, which in turn leads to variation in the routines from one situation to the next. In their view, these variations become the basis for the evolution of firm capabilities as some routine variations are selected in a process analogous to natural selection. What is significant here is that the variation is the result of participants acting differently on the same information. Institutional economists consider information as colored by background knowledge to an extent that classical economists and game theorists do not. In fact, routines as a form of collective skillful behavior are taken for granted by those involved to the extent that it becomes automatic. This stands in stark contrast with the neoclassical view of the economic agent deliberating to maximize choice (Nelson & Winter, 1982, p. 94).

This shift in view leads to the development of a sub-field with an interest in process innovation, specifically focused on the meta-routines capable of producing variations leading to new routines. Normally routines are relatively stable over time and evolve slowly, especially if the situations facing the organization remain familiar. There are, however, dynamic routines too that involve experimentation and the development of new knowledge in the form of processes (Teece et al., 1997, p. 510). Teece and Pisano (1994, p. 1) define these as dynamic capabilities, where the first term points to the changing nature of the environment and the second to the conglomerate of organizational knowledge, skills, and resources available for navigating that environment. Importantly, it is a major departure from the information processing paradigm that assumes a natural flow of already existing information without accounting for new knowledge creation.

At this point, knowledge is no longer considered a kind of stock built up through information flows but approaches a sociological conception as a capacity for action. This development proved to be fertile ground for the ideas of Nonaka (1994) about knowledge creation in opposition to the information processing view of organization. Nonaka found a willing audience in the wake of the downsizing craze that followed the initial round of business process reengineering. At the time, Eisenberg (1997) lamented the loss of knowledge that accompanied the early investments in enterprise systems that ignored the human aspects of knowledge. Nonaka extended Nelson and Winter's ideas about tacit knowledge by revisiting Polanyi's distinction between tacit and explicit knowledge.

He emphasized the importance of the tacit dimension and, more importantly, pointed out that not all knowledge content can be readily communicated as information, and therefore some knowledge resists capturing in information systems. At the time, this simple distinction between tacit and explicit knowledge explained the loss of organizational capability felt in organizations trying to navigate the transition to an informational economy. Nonaka's distinction between tacit and explicit knowledge and the social interaction process that changed knowledge from one type or location to another established the field of knowledge management. Instantly, personnel management became human resource management and information management became knowledge management. The focus shifted from information to knowledge and marks the start of managerial reflection about the relationship between data, information, and knowledge. To understand this shift in emphasis, we must first take a step back and look at how information theorists thought about information and knowledge in earlier developments that happened in parallel to the history of the economic and management sciences described above.

2.4 Information Theory

Information theory conceives of information primarily in terms of messages. In fact, Shannon and Weaver's (1949) mathematical theory of communication aimed to solve the technical problem of transmitting messages over a channel in the presence of noise. In the preamble to their theory, they took care to delimit the scope of their endeavor by separating the information from meaning: "The fundamental problem of communication is … reproducing in one point … a message selected at another point. [The] semantic aspects of communication are irrelevant to the engineering problem" (Shannon & Weaver, 1949, p. 31). This goes against the common understanding of information as meaningful messages. For them, however, information is a physical pattern in a medium carrying the message, but the meaning does not travel along with the message itself; it must be reconstructed through a process of decoding and information processing. Meaning therefore results from the interpretation of the symbols transmitted as a message, and this interpretation is dependent on the background knowledge of and the context assumed by the receiver.

Shannon and Weaver (1949, p. 4) distinguished three levels of communication problems to separate the technical problem they sought to solve from the broader conceptual problems related to information. The first level concerns the technical question of whether the message received is identical to the one sent. The second level concerns the semantic question of whether the message is understood by the receiver. The third level concerns the pragmatic question of effectiveness, whether the understood message produced the desired behavior. Shannon and Weaver (1949, p. 4) saw the semantic problem as "a very deep and involved situation" since it concerned the identity of the receiver and their interpretation of meaning, which could differ significantly from the sender's intended meaning. Therefore, they limited themselves to the technical level and worked on the engineering problem of accurately encoding, transmitting, and decoding the transmitted pattern, leaving the semantic and effectiveness problems to social science.

To solve the technical problem of replicating the sent message at its destination, Shannon and Weaver had to estimate the required number of symbols needed to encode a message so that it could be transmitted over a noisy channel and successfully decoded at the receiving end. This is the basis of their claim that the technical measure of information is best understood as the number of bits (binary digits) required to faithfully communicate a pattern. The counter-intuitive result is that one needs more information to communicate an unordered random state than an ordered determined state because more bits are needed to accurately transmit a particular message as the number of possible messages increases. In other words, the information measure of any transmitted message is contingent upon the extent to which the message's content is unexpected. Messages about highly likely events are less informative than messages about unlikely events. Information theory thus sees information as a "measure of the amount of uncertainty dispelled (= the amount of information gained) when the message is received" (Arbib, 1964, p. 64).

Information theory is useful for a stable definition and a precise measure of information, but the technical definition of information is less useful to describe what humans do when they search for and use information to act in the world. Application of information is clearly about the content and meaning of messages and not about their transmission. Moving from the technical level of Shannon and Weaver's framework to the semantic and effectiveness levels requires consideration of the recipient's pre-existing knowledge, cognitive abilities, personal identity, social context, motivation, and values.

2.5 Data, Information, and Knowledge

From the foregoing, it is clear that information theory has a very specific, albeit narrow, definition of information as the physical form of messages. In the other disciplines, there seems to be quite a lot of variety regarding the nature of information. Some of the neoclassical economists used knowledge and information interchangeably without making strict distinctions. Others seem to associate information closely with data, while management scholars tend to associate information closely with knowledge.

In information science and knowledge management, the three concepts are usually depicted as a hierarchy of data, information, and knowledge (while some variations of the hierarchy also include wisdom at the apex). However, the relation between data, information, and knowledge remains contested, and according to Bratianu and Bejinaru (2023, p. 197), the hierarchy does not provide a definitive answer to the relationship between levels, nor does it explain the transitions between levels. Spender (2008, p. 163) does not consider the nesting of the hierarchical levels (where data given meaning becomes information and information related to the wider context becomes knowledge, etc.) to be helpful for understanding knowledge and learning in organizations. Zins (2007) mapped 130 different definitions of these concepts and categorized them in five versions, depending on whether the concept is seen as an objective external feature of the world or a subjective internal quality of a person. They found that some scholars considered all three to be external, while others considered all three to be in principle internal, and various possibilities between.

The mainstream view, however, sees data and information as closely coupled external phenomena and knowledge as a subjective property of a person processing the information. In this view, knowledge is the framework for interpreting and making information actionable (Zins, 2007, p. 483). It implies that knowledge precedes data and information, and without the appropriate prior knowledge, the data and information might be meaningless. Weick (1995, pp. 109–110) applies a sensemaking perspective to these distinctions, where observable stimuli are data, selected cues are information, and the frame connecting the cues in a sensible way is knowledge. In Weick's view, knowledge is less a stock to be accumulated and stored as information but is rather a process of collective interpretation and embedding.

2.6 Knowledge Management

Now we can return to knowledge management. Nonaka and Takeuchi (1995, p. 61) claimed that "knowledge is created and expanded through social interaction between tacit knowledge and explicit knowledge". This distinction between the two types of knowledge comes from the philosopher Polanyi (1967) via Nelson and Winter (1982) to the work of Nonaka. According to Nonaka (1991, p. 98), explicit knowledge is easily communicable through words or numbers, in other words readily expressible as information, whilst tacit knowledge is deeply personal, attainable only through experience, and hard to express in language. Nonaka's distinction is explained by Weggeman (1997), who sees knowledge as the product of information, experience, skills, and attitude that a person needs to act at a particular moment. He equates the information component with explicit knowledge. Instead of a formal definition of information, he sees it as knowledge that can, in principle, be written down and thus become person-independent or disembodied and therefore easily communicated. The experience, skills, and attitude components of knowledge are equated with Nonaka's tacit knowledge (Weggeman, 1997, p. 34). Decoding explicit knowledge (or information) requires a tacit knowledge base, as past experience, skill levels, and attitude toward the information all color the interpretation. Of course, once interpreted, that information has the potential to update the tacit knowledge because it counts as a new experience to be integrated, and it may improve skill or alter attitude. The implication of this view of knowledge as an interpretive framework means that information is not the same for actors with different experience, skills, and attitude (which incidentally equates with "different information" as a cause of asymmetry in Bergh et al. (2019, p. 129)).

In Nonaka's (1991) theory, knowledge conversion happens in four modes: socialization converts tacit knowledge to tacit knowledge during co-located social interaction (Nonaka, 1994, p. 19), and externalization converts tacit knowledge to explicit knowledge through figurative language (Nonaka, 1994, p. 19), which can then be shared beyond the people originally involved in the interaction. Combination converts it from newly explicit knowledge to established explicit knowledge (Nonaka, 1994, p. 19) by integrating it with the existing knowledge base of the organization. Then, internalization converts it from explicit knowledge back to tacit knowledge as people use the explicit knowledge (Nonaka, 1994, p. 19) and then absorb it through a process of learning-by-doing. These four modes form a spiral process whereby the cycle continues to convert knowledge as it moves from intersubjective interaction to team, organizational, and interorganizational levels (Nonaka, 1994, p. 20).

From the outset, Nonaka's distinction between tacit and explicit knowledge has been widely criticized, either because Nonaka supposedly misunderstood Polanyi (Tsoukas, 2003), or the labels of tacit and explicit were misleading (Gourlay, 2004), or there are more kinds of knowledge than these two (Blackler, 1995), or the idea that one kind of knowledge can be converted into another seemed at odds with our experience (Cook & Brown, 1999; Gourlay, 2006). Broadly speaking, however, all researchers share Nonaka's fundamental assumption that organizational knowledge is of more than one kind. This is of course a radical idea, because ever since The Enlightenment, the scientific view of knowledge has been decidedly monist as justified true belief arrived at by the procedures of the scientific method. However, in organizations, managers see different types of knowledge applied to work practices. Whereas information theorists and economists tried to maintain an objective measure of information, knowledge managers embraced subjective plurality, perhaps because their pluralist epistemology fits an established management paradigm called contingency theory very well. In its original version, proposed by Lawrence and Lorsch (1967), contingency theory held that the best way to manage is contingent upon the environmental context, so that firms in stable environments can pursue machine-like efficiency while firms in changeable environments are better off with organism-like adaptability. In other words, there is no one best way to manage; what is best depends on the wider organizational context. The knowledge management version of this contingency approach holds that one's strategy for managing knowledge depends on the type of knowledge content and where it is held in the organization. A firm with an emphasis on leveraging existing explicit knowledge should aim for a knowledge externalization strategy where employees are connected to documents via repositories; in contrast, a firm with an emphasis on creating new knowledge should aim for a knowledge exploration strategy where people are connected to other experts via management mechanisms (Hansen et al., 1999). Good knowledge management then depends on aligning the primary knowledge purpose with the appropriate knowledge processes and fostering a technical and organizational context conducive to knowledge of that kind (Newell, 2009, p. 26).

Early knowledge management emphasized knowledge creation over information processing since it was born out of the failure of business process reengineering (Eisenberg, 1997) to capture tacit knowledge in the pursuit of codifying information. However, over time, knowledge management largely moved into the effective use of information technology to make the knowledge of experts productive by connecting them to each other in project teams and updating the organization-wide knowledge base in the form of databases. Fuller (2014, p. 75) points out that, while institutional economists regard knowledge creation as the spontaneous variation of routines in an evolutionary process, knowledge management tries to tame the information overload caused by the information systems meant to manage that overload. As a result, mainstream knowledge management is far more focused on capturing and applying knowledge than producing it (Fuller, 2014, p. 76).

Knowledge management systems show great variety. Ruggles (1998) found that initially firms spent their knowledge management budgets on intranets, data warehousing, decision support, and collaborative work systems. Blackler (1995, p. 1030) shows that in typical bureaucracies, the focus is on the development of computer-integrated work systems; in professional firms, the focus is on education and training, knowledge-intensive firms concentrate on expert systems, and communication-intensive adhocracies rely on sensemaking processes and cooperative work systems. Where the emphasis is on explicit knowledge and connecting employees with documents, effort goes into knowledge management systems. Where the emphasis is on tacit knowledge and connecting experts with each other, the effort goes into human resource mechanisms. Expertise results from specialization, and this means that experts cannot be productive without collaboration. However, this division of labor is at the root of the knowledge management problem faced in organizations today because specialization means that people possess different knowledge with different information needs. Spender (2006, p. 4) distinguishes various types of knowledge management projects addressing this unequal distribution. Where data are incomplete, the organization is faced with an innovation problem, in particular the problem of translating newly created knowledge into products and services. Where data are complete but not available where it is needed, the organization faces a communication problem of having to move data from where it is available to where it is needed when it is needed. Where data are seen as a resource, the organization confronts a pooling problem, that is, experts need to be encouraged to contribute their knowledge to the benefit of all. He notes that managers mostly overestimate the benefit of communications and pooling-type projects (Spender, 2006, p. 5), because they fail to understand that what is important is the meaning of the data to the people using it to act and that meaning is closely related to human practices (Spender, 2006, p. 9). Spender (2006, p. 15) concludes that "behind data always lies the complex of meanings people attach to the data, and when these are unclear or contested, data projects need supporting by meaning management projects". Managing meaning turns out to be much harder than managing information because people arrive with meanings and their views are tied to their practices and identities.

The increased complexity that arises from people's interpretations, practices, and interests highlighted by Spender belongs to the semantic and effectiveness problems of communication that Shannon and Weaver excluded from their narrow information concept. Carlile (2004, p. 557) uses Shannon and Weaver's three levels of communication to develop a framework for knowledge boundaries that must be overcome in collaborative work (see Table 2.1). The first boundary is what Carlile (2004, p. 558) calls the syntactic or information-processing boundary that can be overcome through sharing or transfer of commonly understood information. The second boundary is semantic in nature and requires translation because it involves different interpretations of the information (p. 558). The third boundary is pragmatic and involves competing interests, which can be overcome through the transformation of knowledge and practices (p. 559).

Newell (2009, p. 18) draws on the work of Shannon and Carlile in comparing different perspectives on the nature of knowledge and its implications for knowledge management. Table 2.1 summarizes how Shannon and Weaver's (1949) levels of communication problems were appropriated and modified in

Table 2.1 Comparison of the levels in information theory and knowledge management

Communication Problems (Shannon & Weaver, 1949)	*Knowledge Boundaries (Carlile, 2004)*	*Knowledge Management Perspectives (Newell, 2009)*
Technical problem: Reproduction of symbols	Syntactic boundary: Knowledge transfer	Structural perspective: Knowledge as content
Semantic problem: Understanding messages	Semantic boundary: Knowledge translation	Process perspective: Knowledge as socially constructed
Effectiveness problem: Leading to desirable action	Pragmatic boundary: Knowledge transformation	Practice perspective: Knowing as part of practice

the domain of knowledge management. What Newell (2009, p. 18) calls the structural perspective corresponds to Shannon's technical level and Carlile's syntactic level and sees knowledge as content that can be captured, stored, and transmitted. From this perspective, the task of knowledge management is primarily a logistical exercise of transforming knowledge from one type or location to another (Newell, 2009, p. 18). The process perspective corresponds to what both Shannon and Carlile call the semantic level and sees knowledge as a social construct that is continually enacted during intersubjective interactions. Here, the task of knowledge management is to translate and legitimize knowledge between interacting groups (Newell, 2009, p. 18). The practice perspective corresponds to Shannon's effectiveness level and Carlile's pragmatic boundary and sees knowing as part of practice and mediated through material practices and technology. The task of knowledge management in this case is to transform knowledge and transcend the boundaries of communities of practice through boundary spanners (Newell, 2009, p. 18). In summary, the latter two perspectives move away from knowledge as a kind of content that can be possessed and consider it as an active process that is part of people's ability to act in the world and, through their collective interpretations and actions, they enact the social reality that forms the context of future interactions (Weick, 1995, p. 30).

2.7 Organizational Learning

Over time, the interaction of information and knowledge drives a learning process. There are two approaches to learning in management science: The organizational learning approach starts from the model of individual learning and tries to achieve this on a collective level (Kim, 1993, p. 37). The learning organization approach asks which organizational design features create the enabling conditions for shared learning (Levitt & March, 1988, p. 336). Organizational learning has a much longer history than knowledge management, with Argyris (1977, 1991) and Schön (1983, 1987) writing about learning in organizations for at least a decade earlier than Nonaka (1991). Argyris (1977) launched the field with the distinction between single- and double-loop learning. Others later refined this original distinction by adding loops or reverting to an earlier conception called deutero-learning; see Visser (2007) for a conceptual analysis of the related terms. However, the key difference is between simple learning, which only processes information, and meta-learning, which updates the framework used for future rounds of processing.

Organizational learning views organizational change as adaptation through deliberate learning, which differs from the previously described institutional perspective (Nelson & Winter, 1982), which views organizational change as evolution through variation and selection. Research on dynamic capabilities (Teece & Pisano, 1994; Zollo & Winter, 2002) refers to the meta-capabilities required for the development of new routines but remains an evolutionary rather than learning approach.

From a knowledge management perspective, the updating of operating procedures fits well with the mainstream view of the interaction between information and knowledge outlined above, where explicit knowledge is communicated and *shared* as information, but its successful *transfer* depends on the absorptive capacity provided by the tacit knowledge that the recipient already has. Learning occurs when this tacit knowledge base is sufficiently updated to influence future rounds of information interpretation.

Interpretive approaches to organizing, such as Weick (1995), describe this process at the organizational level using the social psychological concepts of frames and cues that form the basis of organizational sensemaking. In the social sensemaking process, previous rounds of sense made ossify into relatively stable frames with which stimuli are noticed and picked out of the flow of experience to become cues that are connected to other cues and interpreted as coherent and meaningful (Weick, 1995, p. 111). At the organizational level, this occurs through interactions that create an intersubjective sense for the participants (Weick, 1995, p. 71). Only when those framings become generically available (Weick, 1995, p. 71) to other organizational members who were not part of the original interaction does the experience become an organizational memory. In this mode of explanation, double-loop organizational learning happens when such frames are temporarily malleable to be updated.

Boisot's (1999, p. 41) information space refines the distinction between tacit and explicit knowledge by mapping it onto three dimensions: codification (coding phenomena into categories), abstraction (reducing the categories to the relevant features), and diffusion (sharing the abstracted and codified knowledge). Inside this three-dimensional space, concrete, uncodified, personal experience is codified and abstracted before it is diffused and then internalized by recipients. Boisot (1999, p. 59) describes this as a social learning cycle that starts with scanning for problems and solving them. This includes the codification of knowledge about the solution, the generalization of the codified knowledge in an abstraction process, its sharing with others in the diffusion phase, before it is absorbed when applied in concrete situations, and, finally, there is impacting when the absorbed knowledge is embedded in practices (which are a combination of technological, organizational, and behavioral patterns).

These examples show how organizational learning depends on the interaction between information and knowledge and on the understanding of the information specified by knowledge.

2.8 Conclusion

What we learn from knowledge management is that the information processing view of the organization focuses too much on information as ordered data and that information is not simply a resource available in repositories. The information problem is complex in that there may be too little or too much information, it may be contradictory or ambiguous, or it may simply be the wrong information for the situation.

The common view of knowledge management that what counts as information shifts depending on the recipient's pre-existing knowledge would be anathema to information theorists because solving the technical problem of information measurement requires a stable concept of information. What we need from our concepts depends, of course, on what we want to achieve with them when we think about the world. If our primary concern is not with measuring the amount of information, but rather with how people learn from information and apply it at work, the interpretive and pragmatic views of information and knowledge are more appropriate.

When thinking about the difference between knowledge and information, the common belief is that background knowledge ascribes meaning to information and data. Knowledge management and organizational learning show that the semantic and effectiveness aspects of information depend on knowledge, not only explicit knowledge understood as content that can be communicated as information but also tacit knowledge understood as skill, capability, and value. Once we accept that knowledge is not just a kind of content that has not yet been represented as information but a process of sensemaking linked to actions in the world, issues such as identity, mental models, trust, absorptive capacity, and learning must also be taken into account.

We are now a long way from the predominantly economic research field on information asymmetry, which is either game theory or case study-oriented. However, implications for information asymmetry can be drawn. While much knowledge management research is concerned with knowledge sharing (focusing on individual behavior on the supply side), the broader view of knowledge transfer moves to a collective level of analysis and considers both supply and demand (Lakomski, 2005). We know from Szulanski (1996) that even in contexts where participants want to share information, translation into capability fails for epistemological rather than motivational reasons. It appears that lack of absorptive capacity, causal ambiguity, and difficult interpersonal relationships contribute far more to transfer failure than willingness and intent to share.

Against this background, we can observe that information asymmetries are likely to be compounded as we move from information to capability via knowledge. The higher we climb from the technical to the semantic and effectiveness levels of Shannon and Weaver's framework, the more acute these issues are likely to become. At the semantic level, there is no escaping the interpretation problem of how people make collective sense given their different viewpoints, and at the effectiveness level, we must face the problem of transforming practice and the identity and trust aspects that go with it. The upside is that there is much scope for future research on information asymmetry in supply chains that takes the interplay of information, knowledge, and learning seriously.

References

Akerlof, G. A. (1970). The market for 'lemons': Quality uncertainty and the market mechanism. *Quarterly Journal of Economics*, *84*(3), 488–500. DOI:10.2307/1879431

Arbib, M. A. (1964). *Brains, machines, and mathematics*. McGraw-Hill.

Argyris, C. (1977). Double loop learning in organizations. *Harvard Business Review, Sep-Oct*, 115–125.

Argyris, C. (1991). Teaching smart people how to learn. *Harvard Business Review, May-Jun*, 99–109.

Arrow, K. J. (1984). *The economics of information*. Blackwell.

Arrow, K. J. (1996). The economics of information: An exposition. *Empirica*, *23*(2), 119–128. DOI:10.1007/bf00925335

Bergh, D. D., Ketchen, D. J., Orlandi, I., Heugens, P. P. M. A. R., & Boyd, B. K. (2019). Information asymmetry in management research: Past accomplishments and future opportunities. *Journal of Management*, *45*(1), 122–158. DOI:10.1177/0149206318798026

Blackler, F. (1995). Knowledge, knowledge work and organizations: An overview and interpretation. *Organization Studies*, *16*(6), 1021–1045. DOI:10.1177/017084069501600605

Boisot, M. (1999). *Knowledge assets: Securing competitive advantage in the information economy*. Oxford University Press.

Bratianu, C., & Bejinaru, R. (2023). From knowledge to wisdom: Looking beyond the knowledge hierarchy. *Knowledge*, 3(2), 196–214. DOI:10.3390/knowledge3020014

Carlile, P. R. (2004). Transferring, translating, and transforming: An integrative framework for managing knowledge across boundaries. *Organization Science*, 15(5), 555–568. DOI:10.1287/orsc.1040.0094

Chen, F. (2003). Information sharing and supply chain coordination. In S. C. Graves & A. G. De Kock (Eds.), *Supply chain management: Design, coordination and operation* (pp. 341–421). Elsevier.

Cook, S. D., & Brown, J. S. (1999). Bridging epistemologies: The generative dance between organizational knowledge and organizational knowing. *Organization Science*, *10*(4), 381–400. DOI:10.1287/orsc.10.4.381

Eisenberg, H. (1997). Reengineering and dumbsizing: Mismanagement of the knowledge resource. *Quality Progress*, *30*(5), 57.

Fuller, S. (2014). *The knowledge book: Key concepts in philosophy, science and culture*. Routledge.

Gourlay, S. (2004). Knowing as semiosis: Steps towards a reconceptualization of 'tacit knowledge'. In H. Tsoukas & N. Mylonopoulos (Eds.), *Organizations as knowledge systems: Knowledge, learning and dynamic capabilities* (pp. 86–105). Palgrave Macmillan UK. DOI:10.1057/9780230524545_5

Gourlay, S. (2006). Conceptualizing knowledge creation: A critique of Nonaka's theory. *Journal of Management Studies*, *43*(7), 1415–1436. DOI:10.1111/j.1467-6486.2006.00637.x

Hansen, M. T., Nohria, N., & Tierney, T. J. (1999). What's your strategy for managing knowledge? *Harvard Business Review*, *Mar-Apr*, 106–116.

Hayek, F. (1945). The use of knowledge in society. *The American Economic Review*, *35*, 519–530.

Hurwicz, L. (1969). On the concept and possibility of informational decentralization. *The American Economic Review*, *59*(2), 513–524. www.jstor.org/stable/1823704

Kim, D. (1993) The link between individual and organizational learning. *Sloan Management Review*, Fall, 37–50.

Kuhn, S. (2019). Prisoner's dilemma. In E. N. Zalta (Ed.), *The Stanford encyclopedia of philosophy (Winter 2019)*. Metaphysics Research Lab, Stanford University. https://plato.stanford.edu/archives/win2019/entries/prisoner-dilemma/

Lakomski, G. (2005). Moving knowledge: What is transfer? In *Managing without leadership* (pp. 99–116). Elsevier.

Lamberton, D. M. (1998). Information economics research: Points of departure. *Information Economics and Policy*, *10*(3), 325–330. https://doi.org/10/drznp5

Lawrence, P. R., & Lorsch, J. W. (1967). Differentiation and integration in complex organizations. *Administrative Science Quarterly*, *12*(1), 1–47. DOI:10.2307/2391211

Levitt, B., & March, J. G. (1988). Organizational learning. *Annual Review of Sociology*, 14(1), 319–338 DOI:10.1146/annurev.so.14.080188.001535

Mycielski, J. (1992). Games with perfect information. In *Handbook of Game Theory with Economic Applications* (Vol. 1, pp. 41–70). Elsevier (Chapter 3). DOI:10.1016/S1574-0005(05)80006-2

Nelson, R. R., & Winter, S. G. (1982). *An evolutionary theory of economic change*. Harvard University Press.

Newell, S. (2009). *Managing knowledge work and innovation*. Palgrave Macmillan.

Nightingale, P. (2003). If Nelson and Winter are only half right about tacit knowledge, which half? A Searlean critique of 'codification'. *Industrial and Corporate Change*, 12(2), 149–183. DOI:10.1093/icc/12.2.149

Nonaka, I. (1991). The knowledge-creating company. *Harvard Business Review*, *Nov-Dec*, 96–104.

Nonaka, I. (1994). A dynamic theory of organizational knowledge creation. *Organization Science*, *5*(1), 14–37. DOI:10.1287/orsc.5.1.14

Nonaka, I., & Takeuchi, H. (1995). *The knowledge creating company*. Oxford University Press.

Polanyi, M. (1967). *The tacit dimension*. Anchor Books.

Ren, Z. J., Cohen, M. A., Ho, T. H., & Terwiesch, C. (2010). Information sharing in a long-term supply chain relationship: The role of customer review strategy. *Operations Research*, 58(1), 81–93. DOI:10.1287/opre.1090.0750

Ruggles, R. (1998). The state of the notion: Knowledge management in practice. *California Management Review*, *40*(3), 80–89. DOI:10.2307/41165944

Schön, D. A. (1983). *The reflective practitioner: How professionals think in action*. Basic Books.

Schön, D. A. (1987). *Educating the reflective practitioner: Toward a new design for teaching and learning in the professions*. Jossey-Bass.

Shannon, C. E., & Weaver, W. (1949). *The mathematical theory of communication*. Univ. of Illinois Press.

Shen, B., Choi, T.-M., & Minner, S. (2019). A review of supply chain contracting with information considerations: Information updating and information asymmetry. *International Journal of Production Research*, 57(15–16), 4898–4936. DOI:10.1080/00207543.2018.1467062

Simon, H. A. (1978). Information-processing theory of human problem solving. In *Handbook of Learning & Cognitive Processes: V. Human Information* (pp. 271–295). Lawrence Erlbaum.

Spender, J.-C. (2006). Getting value from knowledge management. *The TQM Magazine*, *18*(3), 238–254. DOI:10.1108/09544780610659970

Spender, J.-C. (2008). Organizational learning and knowledge management: Whence and whither? *Management Learning*, 39(2), 159–176. DOI:10.1177/1350507607087582

Stiglitz, J. E. (2000). The contributions of the economics of information to twentieth century economics. *The Quarterly Journal of Economics*, *115*(4), 1441–1478. https://doi.org/10.1162/003355300555015

Szulanski, G. (1996). Exploring internal stickiness: Impediments to the transfer of best practice within the firm. *Strategic Management Journal*, *17*(S2), 27–43. https://doi.org/10.1002/smj.4250171105

Teece, D., & Pisano, G. (1994). The dynamic capabilities of firms: An introduction. *Industrial and Corporate Change*, *3*, 537–556. DOI:10.1093/icc/3.3.537-a

Teece, D., Pisano, G., & Shuen, A. (1997). Dynamic capabilities and strategic management. *Strategic Management Journal*, *18*(7), DOI:10.1002/(sici)1097-0266(199708)18:7<509::aid-smj882>3.0.co;2-z

Tsoukas, H. (2003). Do we really understand tacit knowledge? In M. Easterby-Smith & M. A. Lyles (Eds.), *The Blackwell handbook of organizational knowledge management* (pp. 410–427). Blackwell.

Visser, M. (2007). Deutero-learning in organizations: A review and a reformulation. *The Academy of Management Review*, *32*(2), 659–667. DOI:10.5465/amr.2007.24351883

Vosooghidizaji, M., Taghipour, A., & Canel-Depitre, B. (2020). Supply chain coordination under information asymmetry: A review. *International Journal of Production Research*, *58*(6), 1805–1834. DOI:10.1080/00207543.2019.1685702

Weggeman, M. (1997). *Kennismanagement: Inrichting en besturing van kennisintensiewe organisaties*. Scriptum.

Weick, K. E. (1995). *Sensemaking in organizations*. SAGE.

Williamson, O. E. (1985). *The economic institutions of capitalism: Firms, markets, relational contracting*. Free Press.

Zins, C. (2007). Conceptual approaches for defining data, information, and knowledge. *Journal of the American Society for Information Science and Technology*, *58*(4), 479–493. DOI:10.1002/asi.20508

Zollo, M., & Winter, S. G. (2002). Deliberate learning and the evolution of dynamic capabilities. *Organization Science*, *13*(3), 339–351. DOI:10.1287/orsc.13.3.339.2780

3 Information Asymmetry as a Challenge in Chain Governance

Michał Pietrzak,[1] Joanna Domagała,[1] and Wojciech Florkowski[2]

[1]Warsaw University of Life Sciences – SGGW, Poland
[2]University of Georgia, USA

3.1 Introduction

Let's take a bird's eye view of the agri-food sector, assuming it is instrumentally rational in the Weberian sense (Weber, 2019). Instrumental action denotes using means that work as tools/instruments.

> Instrumental action is rooted on the one hand in desired outcomes and on the other hand in beliefs about cause/effect relationships. Given a desire, the state of man's knowledge (…) dictates the kinds of variables required and the manner of their manipulation to bring that desire to fruition.
>
> (Thompson, 2008, p. 14)

This brings us to the notion of technology. Technology is often connoted in a narrow manner to the manufacturing processes, but we prefer the broader meaning. According to the "*Summa Technologiae*", technology means the way in which any group pursues its goals, conditioned by its own knowledge and social skills (Lem, 2020).

Therefore, it will be useful to refer to the very general typology of technologies proposed in the seminal work of Thompson (2008), who distinguishes: the long-linked technology, the mediating technology, and the intensive technology. Long-linked technologies involved sequentially interdependent linear processes that begin with X, then, after successful completion of X proceed toward Y, which, after completion, in turn proceed toward Z. For example, the process starts with raw materials, then proceeds toward a semi-finished product and, finally, turns into a finished product ready for consumption, as it is typically in manufacturing assembly lines or in continuous processing in chemicals. Mediating technologies are those used in transactions between parties that are or wish to be interdependent. For example, banks link depositors with borrowers, employment agencies mediate job seekers with employers, etc. Also, modern internet platforms and marketplaces fall into that kind of technology. The third category, intensive technologies, uses a variety of techniques to modify some object, e.g.

DOI: 10.4324/9781032633725-4

to heal a man or construct a complex product or create a sophisticated, unique service. Thus, the examples of using intensive technology could refer to a hospital, or construction company, which built the big ship or bridge, or NASA, which prepared a special space mission.

A bird's eye view of the agri-food sector through the lens of Thompson's typology easily finds that from a very general perspective, it falls into the long-linked technology category, starting from crop and livestock production, through trading and collecting agricultural products, then processing them, towards wholesaling and retailing, and final consumption in households or HoReCa. Consequently, the sequential interdependence of these processes hinges on the successful completion of upstream activities. This poses significant challenges, particularly in agri-food chains where perishability is a concern. For instance, products requiring refrigeration or freezing necessitate an uninterrupted cold chain. Any deviation from optimal temperatures at any stage can compromise the efforts invested in other links of the chain. Therefore, effective coordination is critical to ensuring food quality and safety.

Stanisław Lem states that "every technology is essentially an artificial extension of the natural tendency, inherent in all living things, to control the environment (…). In this way, islands of decreasing entropy have been created in a world of its universal increase" (Lem, 2020, p. 7). The obvious way to decrease entropy is to somehow close the system of action (technology) and, therefore, separate it from the increasing entropy of the external environment, which creates uncertainty. "The essence of the instrumental question is whether the specified actions do in fact produce the desired outcome, and the instrumentally perfect technology is one which inevitably achieves such results" (Thompson, 2008, p. 14). Striving to such inevitability, there is a need not only for the knowledge of relevant cause-and-effect relationships leading to the desired outcome but also the power to control environment and its impact – "under norms of rationality, organizations seek to seal off their core technologies from environmental influence" (Thompson, 2008, p. 19). In the agri-food sector, such seal-off is particularly challenging due to the determination of agricultural production by nature.

The primary challenges associated with the dependence on nature include perishability, seasonality, randomness, and variability. Perishability arises from the organic origin of materials, leading to issues such as decomposition, spoilage, and rot. Seasonality in agricultural production causes timing conflicts across supply chain stages, resulting in significant temporal imbalances. Moreover, the unpredictability of nature introduces occasional shocks in production output quantities, alongside qualitative challenges due to variability in organic raw materials. Premium brands face the critical task of transforming heterogeneous and uncertain raw materials into consistent products of regular quality (Raynaud et al., 2009, p. 836).

There is another significant indirect consequence of nature dependence: the predominant structure of agricultural production worldwide, which is characterized by family farming. For a more detailed discussion on this topic, see other sources (cf. Allen & Lueck, 1998, 2002; Pietrzak & Ziętara, 2022). Here, it is important to highlight that family farming tends to result in dispersed and atomistic production, leading to batch fragmentation. This fragmentation poses substantial challenges for chain governance.

The seal-off could take the form of buffering, smoothing, anticipating and adapting, and, finally rationing. Buffering implies surrounding the technology and securing it from uncertainty by stockpiling and absorbing environmental fluctuations. Smoothing, on the other hand, attempts to reduce those fluctuations. If those environmental fluctuations could be predicted, they could be treated as constraints. Thus, the technological core could be adjusted. When buffering, smoothing, and anticipating fail, rationing is the final resort (Thompson, 2008, pp. 18–23). All of these means are widely used in agri-food chains.

So far, the discussion is based not only on taking an aerial view of the agri-food sector but also on treating it as a unity. In reality, it is split into multiple pieces due to functional and geographical division of labor. This atomization causes a striving for the instrumental rationality complex and raises tensions between the rationality of subsystems and that of the whole system. Recognizing these tensions invokes the concept of a supply chain.

This chapter aims to explore the issue of informational asymmetry as a significant challenge in supply chain governance, especially regarding agri-food chains in particular. We will investigate this issue through the lens of aligning physical flows of agricultural products and food, as well as ensuring quality assurance and maintenance.

3.2 Framework

In the agri-food chains, two problems challenge the instrumental rationality: the fluctuations of quantity and variation of quality. Those challenges are at the core of this book, namely (cf. Figure 3.1):

- mutual alignments in the physical flow of goods;
- coping with differences in quality, particularly if they are difficult to verify in advance.

The ideal performance of the supply chain would require suppliers sharing information about their own capabilities and inventories, 3PL companies processing conditions and locations of products in stock and transit, all international shipments, tariffs, and modalities, and buyers communicating about their exact needs and delivery timing. For those reasons, the primary motive for chain integration is to streamline information flow and uncertainty reduction through

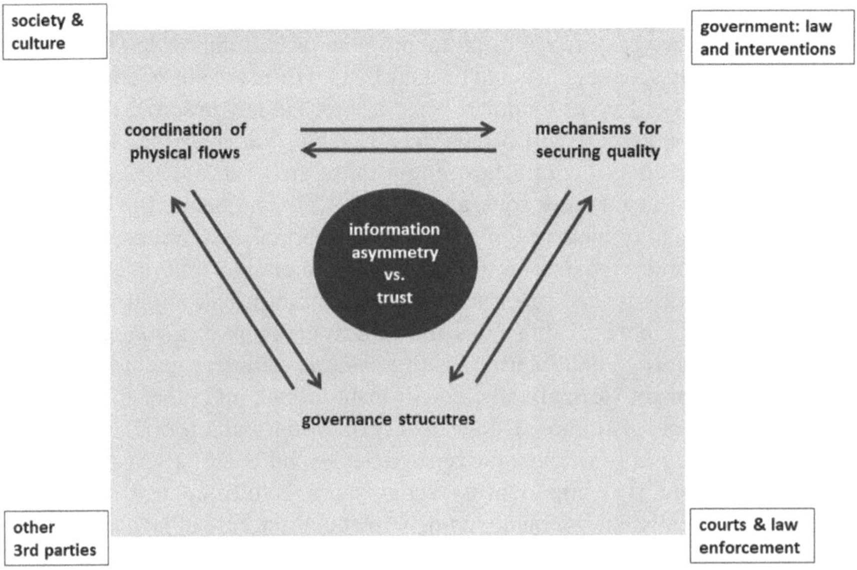

Figure 3.1 The general framework.

Source: Own work.

information sharing. The result is cost reduction and enhanced resilience of the entire supply chain.

Apart from the cost optimization through information sharing, there is information asymmetry regarding quality. If differences in quality are difficult to verify in advance, there is an incentive to deliver low-quality products (so-called lemons). The buyer could experience difficulties distinguishing a quality product from a poor one, which creates problems in quality assurance through the supply chain. The upstream transmission of end-user quality expectations could substantially improve the performance of the whole supply chain.

Despite the huge progress in digital connectivity and data standardization, economic agents are still reluctant to share information. People are limited in cognition and rationality (bounded rationality) and susceptible to opportunism, and information asymmetry aggravates the problem in supply chains.

Sharing information fails due to the lack of incentives. The better-informed party gains by lowering product quality, avoiding punishment. Such behavior disrupts different activities in the chain. As a result, the functioning of the whole supply chain could be distorted. A non-trivial number of opportunistic agents, difficult to recognize in advance, creates risk for transacting across the supply chain. Therefore, the aim of integrated chain governance takes effort to implement. There are benefits from cooperation, however, the temptation to defect is still possible.

Accordingly, we have to confront the problem of willingness to share information. Generally speaking, it could be done by two forms of contracting: formal contracts and self-enforcing contracts (trust-driven, namely based on the expectation that the counterpart will behave in a reliable, fair manner). The effectiveness of both forms of contracts strongly relies on what is defined here as a context (depicted in the gray square in Figure 3.1). The context of any inter-organizational relation consists of formal and informal institutions, following North (2011), or external (enforced by state sanctions) and internal (e.g., enforced by private formal rules or social sanctioning) institutions, following Voigt (2019). As Figure 3.1 illustrates, the context encompasses society and culture (creating informal and internal institutions), government, including courts and law enforcement (formal and external institutions), and other third parties (formal and internal institutions). "The quality of formal and informal institutions likely plays a role in how cooperative societies A and B are" (Servátka, 2019, p. 266). Therefore, it is important to recognize the role of context in creating cooperation-friendly environment[1], namely trust culture, rule of law, and private ordering[2]. Except of spot markets – both types of contracts, in the pure or mixed form, are building blocks of governance structures (cf. Figure 3.1) of dyadic relations in the supply chain: specification contracts, captive contracts, equity-based contracts, relational contracts, and full vertical integration (cf. Gereffi et al., 2005, pp. 83–84; Peterson et al., 2001, pp. 150–156; Raynaud et al., 2005, p. 63).

3.3 The supply chain and the role of feedback and information sharing

According to the system theory firm consists of three components (systems): causal, response, and normative (Bossel, 2007). The causal system (also called a physical system) is "composed of those processes representing the material functioning of the system" (Bossel, 2007, p. 58). In the causal system, instructions originating from the response system are converted into internal processes or actions influencing the environment. The response system is "an information processing system combining the processes of situation perception and classification, state analysis, problem-solving, policy synthesis, the assessment of outcomes of alternatives and the decision" (Bossel, 2007, p. 58). The response system, in performing its tasks, has to refer back to the normative system. The normative system provides "normative references" such as values, attitudes, and preferences (Bossel, 2007, p. 58). By its actions, the causal system effects the business environment, and a firm gains the information feedback. The information feedback enables the learning process, which could take the form of single-loop (Figure 3.2A) or double-loop learning[3] (Figure 3.2b).

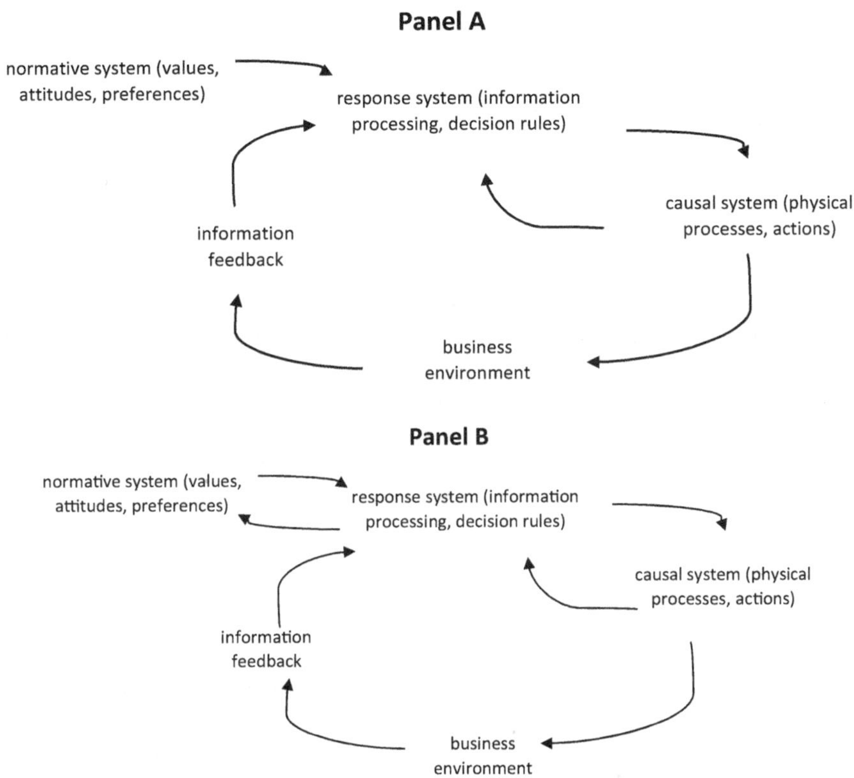

Figure 3.2 Single-loop (a) and double-loop (b) learning in the business firm.

Source: Own work.

Sterman (2000, p. 664) defines the supply chain as consisting of both a structure of stocks and flows for the acquisition, storage, and conversion of inputs into outputs and the decision rules governing these flows. Van der Vorst defines the supply chain in a very similar vein (2004, p. 105). Chains consist of cascades of companies, each receiving orders and adjusting production to meet changes in demand and each maintaining and controlling inventories of material and finished product (Sterman, 2000, p. 666).

In the case of many actors involvement in the chain, the multiple sub-structures of stocks and flows act to some extent separately. The same independence concerns sub-structures of decisions governing the flows, including rules for ordering, scheduling, shipping, etc. (Sterman, 2000, p. 664). In the non-integrated supply chain, each actor performs at the interface between two successive stages and is decoupled from them so it can optimize locally without hindering by problems of other stages (van der Vorst, 2004, p. 106).

The described mode of operation necessitates buffering each link in the chain with the inventory stocks due to the difficulty of reciprocal synchronization of the supply flow with the demand flow. Poor synchronization creates the uncertainty in the upstream links about the size of orders from the downstream links and in the downstream links with availability and stability of supply. Thus, such independent behavior patterns are the endogenous sources of oscillation (Sterman, 2000, p. 686) known as the bull whip effect (van der Vorst, 2004, pp. 107–109), first described by Forrester (1961, pp. 21–42). As it was explained by Sterman: "As customer requirements change, the managers of the supply chain respond by adjusting rate at which resources are ordered and used. Supply chains are thus governed primarily by negative feedback. Because supply chains typically involve substantial time delays, they are prone to oscillation – production and inventories chronically overshoot and undershoot the appropriate levels. (…) Typically, the amplitude of fluctuations increases as they propagate from the customer to the supplier, with each upstream stage in a supply chain tending to lag behind its immediate customer" (2000, pp. 664–665). Lack of information is part of the problem. However, another difficulty is also to see the issue at the proper level of aggregation. An individual actor in the chain tends to overlook his own input to problems and treats it as a part of the business environment, namely exogenous (Sterman, 2000, p. 697). Unless a firm recognizes it is a part of the problem, which is endogenous due to the interrelations among chain partners, the double-loop learning will be difficult. Thus, the normative system (values, attitudes, preferences) would likely remain unchanged.

We can use the triple systemic structure of the firm (cf. Figure 3.2) to depict the supply (value) chain. In the simplest, dyadic model of the chain, there are two firms (A and B), each consisting of its CS – causal system, RS – response system, and NS – normative systems (Figure 3.3). The crucial feature of the chain is the way in which information flows are arranged. In the neoclassical competitive market, there is no private information, thus anyone could gain the same information feedback from the business environment, assuming symmetry between information stock in A and B in the chain. However, in opposition to the standard assumption of neoclassical economics, the information stocks vary among different agents. Under the information asymmetry condition, the information feedback gained by A and B about their interrelations could differ substantially. Thus, firms (links in the chain) can benefit from taking action to overcome this asymmetry. One approach is to disclose and share private information benevolently (Figure 3.3). Sharing and disclosures allow to improve the learning process about the chain dynamics and, therefore, a part of the problem, which is internally generated.

Examples of solutions in this regard include Collaborative Planning, Forecasting and Replenishment (CPFR), Co-Managed Inventory (CMI, and

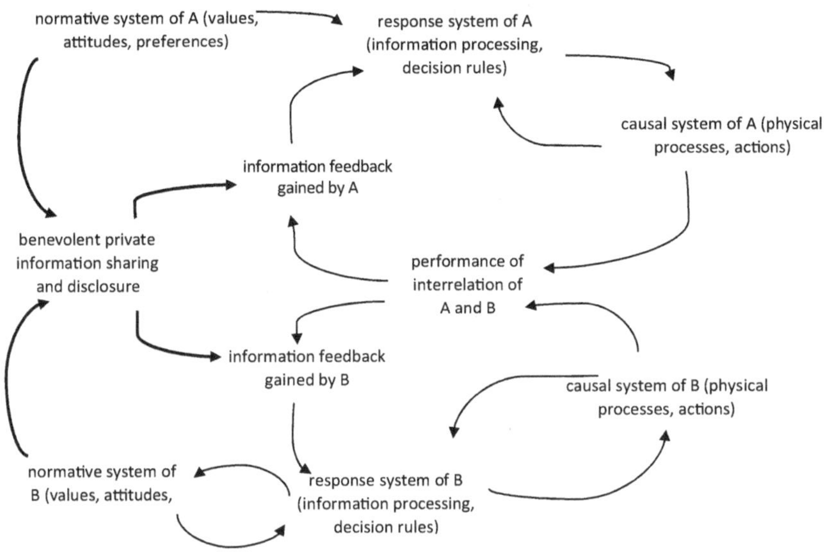

Figure 3.3 The supply chain as a learning system.

Source: Own work.

Vendor Managed Inventory (VMI). CPFR is an in-depth collaborative concept based on joint business planning, demand and order forecasting, and replenishment to increase forecast accuracy and improve supply organization, thereby reducing global logistics chain costs. The key to success with CPFR is to establish a common set of processes within which to support the exchange of information. CPFR in the US is used by Wal-Mart with Warner Lambert and Procter & Gamble, while in Europe CPFR is used by Eroskiz with Henkel; Sainsbury's with Unilever; Veropoulosz with Elgeka and Procter & Gamble (Tenhiälä, 2003). In the Co-Managed Inventory (CMI) model, on the other hand, trading partners exchange and discuss information on sales forecasts and promotional plans. In this way, they reduce inventory levels, maintaining and developing product availability in the supply chain.

On the other hand, Vendor Managed Inventory (VMI) changes the traditional rules of the purchasing department and creates a novel approach to inventory management. In the production planning process, the buyer of the material is responsible for arranging its own supply continuity. VMI works in a completely different way. The burden of responsibility for delivering material in a timely manner is shifted to the supplier, who – with access to current information at the customer's site – monitors changes in current inventory levels and, with knowledge of inventory requirements, organizes and delivers material at the right time. The effectiveness of VMI requires the provision of information about the current level of inventory and necessitates full transparency of the customer's material consumption. The information thus obtained is used to implement the procurement process.

A well-known illustration of the CPFR model is the collaboration between the retail chain Wal-Mart and the cosmetics and personal care products manufacturer Procter & Gamble (P&G). Using modern ICT technologies, Wal-Mart made data on the inventory and turnover of P&G products available directly from the points of sale (shops). P&G gained direct (via satellites) access to information on consumer purchase behavior. It allowed to base production and distribution plans not on error-laden demand forecasts but on the realized demand in real time. The approach eliminated much of the inventory buffer resulting from forecast unreliability (van der Vorst, 2004, p. 121).

The management methods mentioned above (CPFR, CMI, VMI) in food supply chains are typically implemented for processed products. For instance, the Campbell Soup Company, a multinational corporation, introduced VMI to reduce supply chain inventories among certain buyers (Post, 2020). Similarly, CPFR has been implemented by Nabisco and Wegmans Food Markets. Nabisco is a prominent global manufacturer of biscuits, snacks, and premium grocery products, while Wegmans operates a chain of 58 supermarkets across New York and Pennsylvania. CPFR is employed by these companies to enhance inventory management through accurate collaborative demand forecasting. This approach aims to ensure products are available in optimal condition, minimize warehouse shortages or overstocking, and reduce overall operational costs (Fang et al., 2009). However, in the food industry, few suppliers match the size and influence of Nabisco and Wegmans. Most suppliers are smaller organizations that lack the resources to initiate extensive improvement processes like VMI or CPFR.

3.4 Information asymmetry and trust in coordination of physical flows

Agriculture is the oldest segment of the economy that provides food and non-food goods to society. As society developed, it became increasingly important not only to produce agricultural commodities but also to process them, store (warehouse), and ship (transport) to the right place at the right time, ensuring the quality of the products and the information associated with the flow. Thus, a certain system has taken shape, linking the various stages from the production and processing of agricultural raw materials to the trade of raw materials and processed products. Food supply chains include all entities involved in the production of food and its delivery to consumers.

Physical flows of raw materials and agri-food products are characterized by certain specificities. These specificities are mainly due to the transfer of living organisms, organic raw materials, or their products. Therefore, the main challenge is to ensure the quality of fresh products, which are easily subjected to decomposition, spoilage, or other forms of deterioration during the flow. The utility of space and time is therefore extremely relevant in this context. For products that do not spoil or ripen quickly, time requirements for their flow are less critical. For perishables, the importance of the time regime determines production and economic rewards. For example, milk must be cooled immediately after milking a cow and taken for processing expeditiously. Failure to cool milk or delayed collection from the farmer compromises milk processing worthiness but also risks contamination with harmful substances leading to disposal.

The availability of agri-food products at a specific place and time is also particularly important due to the temporal imbalance of supply and demand for agri-food products (for example, due to crop production seasonality, and effects such industries as grain, fruit, and vegetable processing). Although many agricultural products are prone to seasonality (strawberries – early summer, cereals – summer, apples – mainly in autumn[4], etc.), the demand is quite stable throughout the year. Seasonality of production can have economic consequences. In order to synchronize the physical flows of raw materials from producers (farmers) to processors and consumers, it is necessary to buffer processes through stockpiling and warehouse construction. Storage space must assure specific temperature, humidity, or air flow requirements (silos for grain, coolers/cellars for potatoes, beets, etc.) and involve the maintenance cost. Inventories held by agricultural enterprises and agri-food processors include opportunity or real costs by freezing cash (lost interest on capital, or the cost of servicing loans financing the purchase of raw materials for production). However, storage of agricultural products ensures continuity of production for many processors.

Another challenge that arises within the physical flows of food chains is the low ability of many agricultural products to transport and store. This is both due to the economic (bulkiness) and technical reasons (perishability). Products such as milk, meat, fruits, and vegetables often contain a large amount of water, and are often very fragile. For example, raspberries or strawberries lose consumer visual appeal and value if they are improperly transported. In addition, physiological processes such as fermentation or rotting can occur, causing further losses.

A way to increase the ability to transport and store agricultural raw materials and food is to use various methods of preservation. Preservation of food can be achieved mainly[5] by the concentration[6] or by thermal methods (through the action of high temperature, namely pasteurization[7], and sterilization[8], or just the opposite – through its reduction, namely cooling and freezing[9]). The proper preservation of raw and processed agricultural products enables longer storage and transport over longer distances. This makes it possible to supply and feed the population normally, regardless of the regionalization and seasonality of agricultural production[10]. For example, transporting milk powder from Europe to China by sea can take more than 30 days and by rail 14–18 days, and this doesn't affect the quality of the product due to the proper preservation.

Concentration, pasteurization, and sterilization are typically integrated parts of food processing and are not especially challenging from the agri-food chain management perspective. However, cooling and freezing can pose challenges when the governance of the chain is imperfect.

Refrigerated or deep-frozen food products must be maintained at the correct temperature throughout their whole journey from production to consumption. The cold chain begins when the raw material is sourced (sea fishing, plantations, slaughtering), through production, storage, refrigerated transport, and finally delivery to the consumer. Any deviation from the recommended temperature range at any point in the cold chain can lead to diminished product quality. Therefore, each link in the cold chain determines the quality assurance of food commodities and health safety, and the various links in the chain should work together as one system.

This is determined by the private information sharing and disclosure and by trust. When some link in the agri-food chain interrupts through negligence or out of greed (desire to save costs) the continuity of the cold chain, it is not motivated to admit. When the responsibility in the chain is divided between many partners and special procedures are not introduced, the information asymmetry could incentivize negligence or shirking of the common efforts to maintain the continuity of the cold chain.

On the other hand, the preservation of agri-food products means that the consumer receives not a fresh product. This raises the question of whether, and to which extent, the consumer prefers to consume fresh product or to enjoy the extended shelf life. This is an important trade-off because it has potential to impact the whole chain design (Esteso et al., 2021).

Generally speaking, the more preserved agri-food products are, the more inventories could be stored and longer transport routes could be considered; thus, the role of orchestrating the whole chain governance is not so crucial. However, if the products are perishable, the uncertainty due to information asymmetry could cause high waste and cost accordingly. Therefore, in such cases, chains should be more coordinated or just will remain quite short. This issue is interestingly depicted in Chapter 7, where chains for different cheeses are compared. For example, while in the cases of long-ripening cheeses (Parmigiano Reggiano and Comté), the milk production, processing, and ripening cheese are executed by separated links in the chain, in the case of short-ripening Koryciński Swojski cheese, all three stages are executed under one organizational umbrella, namely at farms, and the export share is very low. Moreover, the scale of production and sales in this scenario tends to be small, which need not be the case. An alternative solution would involve a reorganization of the supply chain, emphasizing rapid and reliable information flow and cold chain logistics. This reasoning aligns with the results of Esteso et al. (2021), which show the impact of product shelf life on agri-food supply chain designs. Thus, taking into account perishability issues promotes the chain design based on flawless information flow that better adjusts to the nature of products to be placed on the final consumer market.

From this point of view, the stocks allowed by the preservation of agri-food products could be seen, at least in some cases, as a cover, which hides the problems with information flow and chain governance. Let's consider the case of the Polish apple chain described in Chapter 8. Poland is one of the biggest apple producers and exporters in the world. Around one-half of the apples produced in this country are processed into concentrated juice. This high percentage is due to problems with information asymmetry and chain governance (cf. Pietrzak et al., 2020). Therefore, growers are forced to put a high volume of their production into processing towards low-priced commodities because most of them are not able to create or participate in a tightly coordinated chain, which would be indispensable to offering value-added products (like club varieties, e.g., Pink Lady) for final consumers.

Another issue arises in the case of the treatment of fragile fruits and vegetables. The continuity of very careful, delicate, and gentle treatment from harvesting through storage, transportation, and each time handling in all intermediary links is hard to maintain when there are many independent agents involved between the farmer's field and the consumer's table. Tracking responsibility is then very tough due to delays between poor product handling and visual symptoms of it.

The additional challenge in the physical management of product flows in food supply chains can be the high dispersion of small farms, which have a small scale of production and deliver relatively small batches to further stages in the supply chain. Firstly, such atomization causes problems for quality standardization. Secondly, when quality is difficult to measure and verify and reliable tracking methods are not easily available, this dispersion creates opportunities for mixing poor-quality products with good ones or for food counterfeiting.

3.5 The role of information asymmetry and trust in securing quality

The abovementioned issues with physical flows of agricultural products and food are usually connected or supplemented with problems with securing quality[11]. Information asymmetry offers an advantage to the better-informed party. The asymmetry undermines business relations related to quality assurance within the supply chain.

Nelson (1970) differentiated between two sets of attributes of a good: search attributes and experience attributes. Search attributes buyers could assess prior to purchase. Acquiring information about those attributes could be sometimes costly. However, knowledge about them can be obtained by searching before buying. Such activities generate search costs. If the cost of the search is relatively low compared to the consumer's surplus, consumers will prefer to gather information about many goods simultaneously before deciding to buy. If the cost of the search is relatively high compared to the consumer's surplus, consumers will prefer to search for information sequentially, due to the considerable time and travel (Besanko et al., 2017).

For example, one could easily assess the size, shape, color, and general appearance of an edible agricultural product such as tomato. Furthermore, it is not costly to gain information on the taste or other traits of any tomato variety or a brand name (if any exists). However, it is not possible to assess the real taste and aroma, texture, crispness, etc., of any particular tomato before eating it. Experience attributes are those which buyers could assess only after purchase—by using a particular product or service (Nelson, 1970). Tirole (1988, p. 95) states that "the main issues in regard to such goods [goods with experience attributes] are whether there are incentives for firms to supply quality".

Nelson's classification was extended by Darby and Karni (1973), who added a third category, namely, credence attributes. These are attributes valuable to a buyer, though she cannot evaluate them by normal use. Typical examples relate to medical treatment and business consulting. In agriculture, this concept is illustrated by issues such as product adulteration (e.g., counterfeiting of honey and beehive products, as discussed in Chapter 13) or the blending of organic or GMO-free raw materials with conventional ones in final products.

Pietrzak et al. (2020) provide a simple illustration of this categorization on the example of a horticultural product. Size, shape, color, and general appearance of an apple are search attributes. Also, general knowledge about the taste and other specific traits of any variety or brand name belongs to this category. However, the real taste of any particular piece, its aroma, texture, and crispness are possible to assess only after eating it; thus, they belong to experience attributes. The existence of pesticide residues on apples cannot be assessed even after buying and eating. This can be evaluated only through laboratory tests, which are not typically available to the everyday buyer. Therefore, it is a credence attribute.

When the features of any product are impossible to assess before buying, then the complexity arises and challenges supplier-buyer relations. What are, if any, the incentives for suppliers to disclose accurate information about product quality? What are, if any, barriers against the temptation to deliver low-quality goods ('lemon') to the market? The presence of unfair suppliers contributes to market inefficiency, as buyers face the risk of purchasing low-quality goods. Trust emerges as a crucial factor in mitigating the information asymmetry, enabling effective communication, and maintaining quality along the agro-food chains.

Consumer trust in the quality of agri-food products can be partially assured by the introduction of quality regulations. Initially, food laws were directed at protecting against food fraud and adulteration. Ancient Egypt regulated the labeling of certain foods; ancient Athens checked the purity and integrity of beer; and ancient Rome had a well-organized system of official food inspections to protect consumers from adulterated or unsafe food (Understanding The

Codex…, 1999). During the Middle Ages, individual European countries issued regulations on the quality and safety of eggs, cured meats, cheese, beer, wine, and bread (MacMaolain, 2007). From the 19th century onward, sanitation issues gained prominence, and modern food law today seeks to protect human health, economic interests, livestock welfare, plant health, and the environment. This law normalizes the various stages of food production, processing, and distribution. Food producers and processors in the EU are obliged to operate in accordance with the legislation in operation regarding food safety and quality. The law regulates, among other things, food labeling, food additives, plastics, and other items in contact with food, certification of products of a special nature, official inspection of food products, hygiene of food products, or processing methods. As a result of regulations on the quality of raw materials and agri-food products, consumer trust in food quality is increasing. For example, concerning dairy products, minimum requirements for the quality of raw milk (including microbial and somatic cell content) contribute to enhanced trust in the overall quality of processed products.

3.6 Governance structures

Sharing and disclosing the information among supply chain links (Figure 3.3) is crucial for smoothing physical flows as well as assuring and maintaining quality. Relations between seller and buyer contain cooperative as well as antagonistic and competitive aspects. Hence, the situation is somehow similar to the prisoner dilemma (cf. discussion about it in Chapter 4). By focusing on the antagonistic aspect of relationships, each party can strive to maximize its benefits, regardless of the interests of the other party (opportunism). Such behaviors represent the expectation of obtaining a "payoff of temptation", ignoring the fact that it is accompanied by a "sucker's payoff" for the for the transaction partner (cf. Axelrod, 2006). However, the trap of the prisoner's dilemma implies that – if both sides act as maximizers of individual utility – they both are punished for mutual opportunism. In our context, this "punishment for opportunism" translates into high costs of stocks and flows coordination and quality issues. The trap of prisoner dilemma arises from the issue of seeing the problem as exogenous while being part of the problem (cf. Figure 3.2 vs. Figure 3.3), which means it should be resolved collectively by cooperation. Confrontation, competition, and win-lose market struggles become costly and inefficient, thus giving way to deliberate win-win cooperative play (Kempny, 1998).

There are three general approaches to avoid the trap of a prisoner's dilemma: changing the structure of payoffs in the game, establishing lasting long-term relationships, and socialization and learning (Axelrod, 2006; Kay, 1993). The payoffs could be changed by creating credible formal contracts. An additional approach involves self-enforcing contracts, which are based on enlarging the impact of the future on present decisions, thus establishing long-lasting relations. Both depend strongly on the general social norms and values gained in the socialization process as well as on the ongoing learning process (cf. deeper discussion about this issue in Chapter 4).

Forms of contracts differ according to dimensions such as mutual dependency, time horizon, and strength of social ties. Based on these three dimensions, some basic governance structures of dyadic relations in supply chains could be differentiated (Table 3.1). The degree of dependency of partners is important because, due to the possibility of mutual control, it introduces the ability to change the payoffs. For example, a specification contract allows the definition of basic terms of trade as regards quantitative and qualitative information disclosure to enable better planning of physical flows and to assure stable quality. If the institutional environment offers proper contract law, efficient courts, and law enforcement, such a governance structure could be a valid solution for many problems in the agri-food chain provoked by information asymmetry. This solution could also be a starting platform for the further development of governance modes. It could be developed into longer engagement and higher commitment of the parties as it is observed in equity-based contracts. Thus, the scope of changes in payoff is even broader due to the higher stakes of the parties and the bigger threat of termination relationships.

Another typical solution is represented by a relational contract, which is a form of self-enforcing contracting (Furubotn & Richter, 2011, pp. 258–265). Relational contracts are often used when business relationships encounter unexpected contingencies that cannot be foreseen and therefore put in the contract. They are based on trust, defined as the expectation that the counterpart will behave in a reliable, predictable, and fair manner (Zaheer et al., 1998). Relationships between supply chain participants based on trust lead to better communication, contribute to constructive conflict resolution, reduce uncertainty and risk, and enable synergistic effects (Kwon & Suh, 2004, p. 27). If a party can trust a counterpart, rather than completely rely on formal contract safeguards, the cost of governance is much reduced when unexpected contingencies are severe. Trust allows the party to be confident about the positive intentions of the other party, and this way to economize on formal safeguards every time they consider an interaction with the exchange partner (Rousseau et al., 1998).

3.7 Summary and conclusions

Information asymmetry in conjunction with a lack of trust has substantial consequences on how supply chains operate in regards to both physical flows of goods and quality of them. Due to the functional and geographical division of labor, agri-food chains are split into multiple pieces. Specialization and division of labor imply that there are many separate links in supply chains. This raises the problem of proper coordination of all agents within the chain. The

Table 3.1 Governance structures of dyadic relations in supply chain

Item				*STRENGTH OF SOCIAL TIES*		
				None/weak	*Medium*	*Strong*
DEPENDENCY	Weak	TIME HORIZON	Short	Spot Market		
	Medium		Medium	Specification Contract	Specification Contract	Relational contract
				Captive Contract	Equity-based contract	Relational contract
	Strong		Long		Hierarchy/full vertical integration	

Source: Adapted from classifications of governance structures compiled from Gereffi et al. (2005, pp. 83–84), Peterson et al. (2001, pp. 150–156), and Raynaud et al. (2005, p. 63).

atomization raises tensions between the rationality of subsystems and that of the whole system. The literature sometimes presents an overly idyllic vision of partnerships in supply chains. It assumes that all participants in the supply chain gain and there are no losers. In practice, however, some companies abuse their bargaining power. Moreover, many companies are also reluctant to share data and information for fear of unfair competition. Although the benefits of sharing and disclosing information generously could be substantial, the barriers against it could be overwhelming. This makes coordinating supply chains very challenging and often leads to suboptimized physical flows of goods and inferior quality. Trust is referred to as a "soft" coordination mechanism and is pointed out as an alternative mechanism to those based on safeguards that emanate from formal contracts. Both issues will be deeply discussed in the following chapters: trust in inter-organizational relations in Chapter 4 and solutions for overcoming Information Asymmetry, with special emphasis on forms of contracts in Chapter 5.

Notes

1 For discussion on this issue, see, for example, Acemoglu & Robinson (2012).
2 For example, "merchant communities enforce agreements without relying on state-sponsored courts" (Richman 2004, p. 2338).
3 According to Argyris and Schön (1978), in single-loop learning, the theory (here: values, attitudes, and preferences, namely the normative systems), which steers of actions, remains exogenous and unchanged. Under double-loop learning, the theory (the normative system) could not be treated as being graven on tablets of stone. On the contrary, it is the subject of validation, adaptation, and rethought. In this way, it becomes an endogenous category from the learning process point of view.
4 From the perspective of the northern hemisphere
5 There are also some other methods, such as acidification, drying, and addition of osmotic or other chemical substances.
6 Concentration is a process that reduces the water content in products with a liquid consistency. It is used, for example, in dairy (condensed milk, milk powder, whey powder), fruits and vegetables (fruit juice concentrates, tomato concentrates), and food concentrates (nutritional supplements, protein and vitamin concentrates, tea and coffee extracts).
7 Pasteurization is a thermal treatment of food products at a temperature below 100°C to destroy or inhibit the growth of pathogenic microorganisms or enzymes while preserving the taste of the products and avoiding a reduction in their nutritional value. It is commonly used in milk and milk products, wine, beer, jams, marmalades, fruit juices, vegetable products, and meat products.
8 A high-temperature sterilization process – UHT (Ultra High Temperature) – is typically used for milk. UHT involves heating milk to 135-150°C for at least 2 seconds. Thanks to pasteurization and sterilization, products can be protected against microorganisms, and their shelf life can be extended, facilitating storage and transport processes even over long distances.

9 Cooling and freezing preserve the natural properties of food, i.e., its composition and nutritional value, while don't significantly restricting its use for processing, culinary, and consumption purposes.

10 On the other hand, the preservation of agri-food products means that the consumer receives a processed product rather than a fresh one. This raises the question of whether the consumer prefers to consume, for example, raw raspberries or raspberry jam.

11 Here, quality is understood in a comprehensive sense, encompassing all non-price attributes of agricultural products or foods, including the reliability of the type of production (e.g. organic, GMO-free) as well as the product's origin, etc.

References

Acemoglu, D., & Robinson, J. (2012). *Why nations fail: The origins of power, prosperity, and poverty*. The Crown Publishing Group. ISBN: 030771929.

Allen, D. W., & Lueck, D. (1998). The nature of the farm. *Journal of Law and Economics*, *41*(2), 343–386. DOI: 10.1086/467393.

Allen, D. W., & Lueck, D. (2002). *The nature of the farm: Contracts, risk, and organization in agriculture*. The MIT Press.

Argyris, C., & Schon, D. (1978). *Organizational learning: A theory of action perspective*. Addison-Wesley.

Axelrod, R. (2006). *The evolution of cooperation*. Revised ed. Basic Books. ISBN 978-0-465-00564-2.

Besanko, D., Dranove, D., Shanley M., & Schaefer S. (2017). *Economics of strategy*. 7th ed. Wiley & Sons. ISBN: 9781119378761.

Bossel, H. (2007). *Systems and models. Complexity, dynamics, evolution, sustainability*. Books on Demand.

Darby, M. R., & Karni, E. (1973). Free competition and the optimal amount of fraud. *Journal of Law and Economics*, *16*(1), 67–88. DOI: 10.1086/466849

Esteso, A., Alemany, M. M. E., & Ángel Ortiz, A. (2021). Impact of product perishability on agri-food supply chains design. *Applied Mathematical Modelling*, *96*, 20–38, DOI: 10.1016/j.apm.2021.02.027

Fang, X., Leung, S. C.H., Zhang, J. L., & Lai, K. K. (2009), Procurement of agricultural products using the CPFR approach. *Supply Chain Management: An International Journal*, 14 (4), 253–258.

Forrester, J. W. (1961). *Industrial dynamics*. MIT Press.

Furubotn, E. G., & Richter, R. (2011). *Institutions & economic theory. The contribution of the new institutional economics*. 2nd ed. The University of Michigan Press. ISBN: 978-0-472-03025-5.

Gereffi, G., Humphrey, J., & Sturgeon, T. (2005). The governance of global value chains. *Review of International Political Economy*, *12*(1), 78–104, DOI: 10.1080/09692290500049805

Kay, J. (1993). *Foundations of corporate success: How business strategies add value*. Oxford University Press. ISBN 0-19-828781-X.

Kempny D. (1998). Co-markership: Zarządzanie dostawami w biznesie przyszłości [Co-markership: Supply management in the business of the future]. In: *Supply chain management*, Conference materials, Vol. 1, Katowice.

Kwon, I-W. G. & Suh, T. (2004). Factors affecting the level of trust and commitment in supply chain relationships. *Journal of Supply Chain Management*, *40*(2), 4–14.

Lem, S. (2020). *Summa Technologiae*. Wydawnictwo Literackie. ISBN: 978-83-08-07333-9.

MacMaolain, C. (2007). *EU food law, protecting consumers and health in common market*. Oxford.

Nelson, P. (1970). Information and consumer behavior. *Journal of Political Economy*, *78*, 311–329.

North, D. C. (2011). *Institutions, institutional change and economic performance*. 31st printing. Cambridge University Press. ISBN: 978-0-521-39734-6.

Peterson, H. C., Wysocki, A. F., & Harsh, S. B. (2001). Strategic choice along the vertical coordination continuum. *International Food and Agribusiness Management Review*, *4*(2), 1–18. DOI: 10.22004/ag.econ.34469

Pietrzak, M., Chlebicka, A., Kraciński, P., & Malak-Rawlikowska, A. (2020). Information asymmetry as a barrier in upgrading the position of local producers in the global value chain – Evidence from the apple sector in poland. *Sustainability*, *12*(19), 7857. DOI: 10.3390/su12197857

Pietrzak, M., & Ziętara W. (2022). Beyond the black box: Towards a systems theory of farming family and family farm. *Problems of Agricultural Economics*, *370*(1), 42–86. DOI: 10.30858/zer/143079

Post, R. (2020). *Vendor-managed inventory in fresh-food supply chains*. University of Groningen, SOM Research School. DOI: 10.33612/diss.130028783

Raynaud, E., Sauvee, L., & Valceschini, E. (2005). Alignment between quality enforcement devices and governance structures in the agro-food vertical chains. *Journal of Management & Governance*, *9*(1), 47–77. DOI: 10.3920/JCNS2014.0004

Raynaud, E., Sauvee, L., & Valceschini, E. (2009). Aligning branding strategies and governance of vertical transactions in agri-food chains. *Industrial and Corporate Change*, *18*(5), 835–868. DOI: 10.1093/icc/dtp026

Richman, B. D. (2004). Firms, courts and reputation mechanisms: Towards a positive theory of private ordering. *Columbia Law Review*, *104*, 2328–2368.

Rousseau, D. M., Sitkin, S. B., Burt, R. S., & Camerer, C. (1998). Not so different after all: A cross-discipline view of trust. *Academy of Management Review*, *23*(3), 393–404.

Servátka, M. (2019). How do experiments inform collective action research? In C. Ménard & M. M. Shirley (Eds.), *A research agenda for new institutional economics*. Edward Edgar Publishing, p. 260–268. ISBN: 978 1 83910 269 1.

Sterman, J. D. (2000). *Business dynamics. systems thinking and modeling for a complex world*. McGraw-Hill.

Tenhiälä, A. (2003). *Collaborative planning, forecasting, and replenishment in European grocery retail*. Seminar in Industrial Management, Helsinki University of Technology.

Thompson, J. D. (2008). *Organizations in action. Social science bases of administrative theory. With a new preface by Mayer N. Zald and a new introduction by W. Richard Scott*. Transaction Publishers. ISBN: 978-0-7658-0991-9.

Tirole, J. (1988). *The theory of industrial organization*. The MIT Press. ISBN 978-0-262-20071-4.

Understanding The Codex Alimentarius, Codex Alimentarius. (1999). Joint FAO/WHO Food Standards Programme. www.fao.org/docrep/W9114E/W9114E00.htm (accessed April 15, 2024).

Van der Vorst, Jack G. A. J. (2004). Supply chain management: Theory and practices. In T. Camps, P. Diederen, G. J. Hofstede, and B. Vos (Eds.), *Chains and networks. Bridging theory and practice*. Reed Business Information.

Voight, S. (2019). Internal institutions: The major unknowns in institutional economics. In C. Ménard & M. M. Shirley (Eds.), *A research agenda for new institutional economics* (pp. 145–152). Edward Edgar Publishing. ISBN: 9781 83910 269 1.

Weber, M. (2019). *Economy and society*. Harvard University Press.

Zaheer, A., McEvily B., & Perrone, V. (1998). Does trust matter? Exploiting the effects of interorganizational and interpersonal trust on performance. *Organization Science*, *9*(2), 141–159.

4 Fundamentals of Trust in Interorganizational Relations

Michał Pietrzak

Warsaw University of Life Sciences – SGGW, Poland

4.1 Introduction

The supply chain in its simplest form is the dyadic relation between supplier and buyer. Typically, any real-world chain is, in fact, a whole set or sequence of such supplier–buyer connections. Nevertheless, a simple dyadic relation could serve as a convenient generalization of some problems by which value chains are plagued. One such crucial challenge is the one signaled in the title of this book, namely information asymmetry.

From the neoclassical economic perspective, perfectly competitive markets are efficient due to the equimarginal principle. Taking into account the task of dividing resources among a number of possible and competing uses, the term efficiency means that each unit of resources is allocated in such a way that the benefits of transferring such a unit into one use are equal to the harms involved in withdrawing it from another use (Blaug, 1985). In other words, the results of the exchange conditions on the competitive markets are Pareto optimal. Pareto optimality „occurs when no possible reorganization of production or distribution can make anyone better off without making someone else worse off" (Samuelson & Nordhaus, 2010, p. 160).

Nevertheless, markets could fail due to market imperfections such as market power (imperfect competition), externalities, and imperfect information (Samuelson & Nordhaus, 2010). In fact, the structure of information is extremely complex and intricate, yet neoclassical economics describes a system that is governed, in a completely reliable way, by only one signal – prices (Kornai, 1977). Typically, this is not the case in the real world. This is certainly not the case for agro-food chains with challenging flows of goods and differences in their quality, which are further affected by fluctuations due to weather and other natural conditions.

4.2 Problem statement

The assumption about asymmetrical information has substantial consequences on how supplier–buyer relations operate in regards to both physical flows of

DOI: 10.4324/9781032633725-5

goods and their quality (cf. the general framework in Chapter 3 – Figure 3.1). Let's start with the physical flow of goods. When there are many different players operating independently in the supply chain, they make decisions about ordering, planning, and shipping – optimizing locally without paying attention to the problems of other players. Stocks play an important function here, namely to smooth production or consumption under fluctuations in inflows and outflows, which are subject to a certain degree of uncertainty. The upstream links of the chain are uncertain about the volume of orders from the downstream links, while the downstream links are concerned about the availability and stability of supply. This independent action is the source of the internal oscillations, called the bullwhip effect (cf. Forrester, 2013; Sterman, 2000; van der Vorst, 2004). If particular links in the chain will share information about their capabilities and inventories, conditions and locations of products in stock and transit, about what they exactly need and when they need it – then we can reach much smoother physical flows of goods with much less uncertainty[1]. However, despite great progress in digital connectivity and data standards, firms in the chain are often not willing to share information.

The necessity of obtaining resources (financial, physical, information) from the environment made organizations potentially dependent on the sources of these resources (Pfeffer & Salancik, 2003). As Thompson (2008) explains, "since the dependence of an organization on its task environment introduces not only constraints but also contingencies, both of which interfere with the attainment of rationality[2], we would expect organizations subject to norms of rationality to attempt to manage dependency" (p. 30). According to Kornai (1977), the possession by one organization of the information necessary for the functioning of another organization is a source of power of the former over the latter. In the case of a monopoly of indispensable information, this power may even be stronger than the hierarchical power, which is based on the issuing of directives and orders. This reasoning is in line with Thompson (2008): "an organization has power, relative to an element of its task environment, to the extent that the organization has capacity to satisfy needs of that element and to the extent that the organization monopolizes that capacity" (p. 31). Therefore, information could be seen as a source of power, and the need for it as a source of dependency – dependence can be perceived as the obverse of power (cf. Thompson, 2008).

Thus, it is not surprising that particular firms in the supply chain could be reluctant to disclose and share information voluntarily. Typically, in any dyadic connection in the supply chain, the informational dependency is mutual. For example, buyers want to know suppliers' capabilities and inventories, while suppliers want to know what buyers need exactly and when they need it. This kind of keeping each other in check brings to mind the Galbraithian[3] notion of countervailing power (cf. Pfeffer & Salancik, 2003; Thompson, 2008). Although the mutual benefits of sharing information may be obvious, it could be difficult

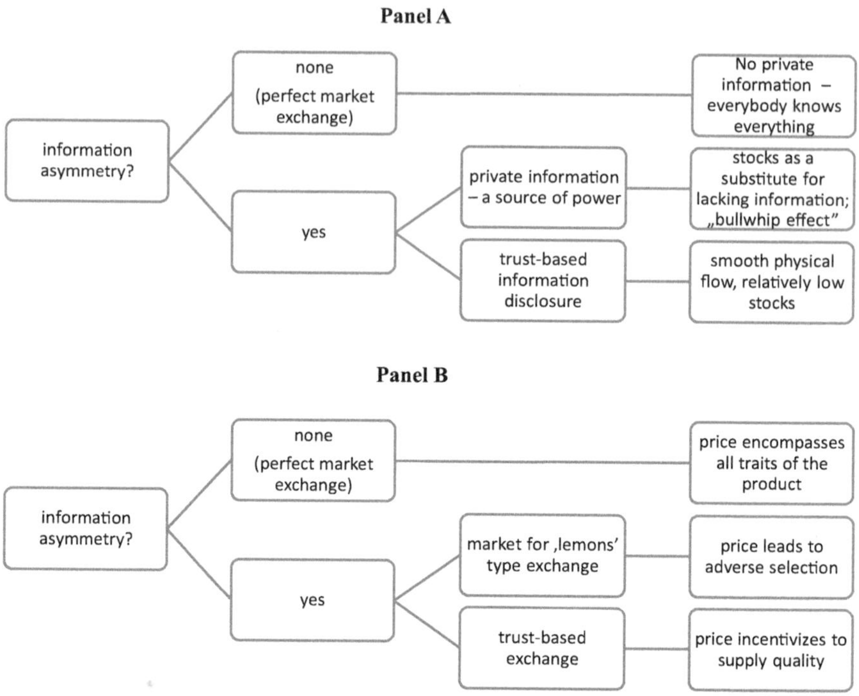

Figure 4.1 The impact of information asymmetry and the role of trust in supplier–buyer relations with regard to both: physical flows of goods (A) and their quality (B).

Source: Own work.

to give up the potential source of power. This is the moment when trust comes onto the scene (see panel A in Figure 4.1).

Arrow calls trust "an important lubricant of the social system" (Arrow, 1974, p. 23). According to Coleman (1990), trust can be seen as a relationship of mutual calculation between an individual placing trust and the individual being trusted. It is similar to the decision to place a bet. Sztompka (1999) defines trust in a similar vein: "trust is a bet about the future contingent actions of others" (p. 25). According to Hardin (1992), "trust is a three-part relation: A trusts B to do X" (p. 154). Thus, trust is particularly important in conditions of uncertainty regarding others' actions (Gambetta, 1988). "Since other people have their own first-hand access to the world and can experience things differently they may consequently be a source of profound insecurity to me" (Luhmann, 1979, p. 6). Trust could be defined as "a subjective probability with which one agent assesses that another agent or group of agents will perform a particular action, both before he can monitor such action (or independently of his capacity to monitor it) and in a context in which it affects his own action" (Gambetta, 1988, p. 217).

An individual rationally places trust if the chance of winning relative to the chance of losing is bigger than the value of loss relative to the value of gain. Thus, the condition for trusting could be operationalized as follows (Coleman, 1990, p. 99; Gabbay & Leenders, 2002, pp. 3–4; Paliszkiewicz, 2013, p. 18; Ritzer-Angerer, 2018, p. 3):

$p/(1-p) > L/G$ (or $pG > (1-p)L$[4]), where: p denotes the chance of winning (receiving gain) or the chance of credibility of trustee, L – possible loss (given an untrustworthy trustee), G – possible gain (given a trustworthy trustee).

Typically, the trustor knows the value of gain (G) and loss (L), but the issue is the probability of the trustee's credibility (Coleman, 1990, p. 102). We will discuss this in the following section.

Let's go now to the issue of quality of goods. Neoclassical perfect competition theory assumes that buyers and sellers have complete information about the goods and services they exchange, and "consumers are presumed to be perfectly knowledgeable about the quality" (Samuelson & Nordhaus, 2010, p. 164). However, in the real world, the information available to the buyers and sellers is neither perfect nor costless (Stiglitz, 2000). This leads us to the so-called "shopping problem" – that is, to find the seller's offer that best meets the consumer's needs (Besanko et al., 2017, pp. 320–321).

Generally speaking, buyers buy goods looking for the benefits that they expect to derive from a product or a service. The valuation of these benefits is a consumer's willingness-to-pay. If his/her willingness-to-pay exceeds the price of the goods, the consumer's surplus is created. However, to properly assess such a surplus, the consumer needs to know the quality attributes of any product or service.

According to Nelson (1970) and Darby and Karni (1973), three kinds of quality attributes could be distinguished: search (possible to verify before buying), experience (those which the consumer can learn only after purchasing – by using a particular product or service), and credence (features valuable for a buyer but not possible to evaluate even after buying and normal use).

When the features of any product are impossible to assess before buying, then the issue arises whether there are incentives for the supplier to undertake efforts towards quality and to disclose information about the true quality. In other words, under the condition of information asymmetry, there are two problems in supplier–buyer relations, namely the hidden action problem (moral hazard) and hidden information problem, which leads to adverse selection (Wilkin, 2016; Pietrzak, 2022). If there are no incentives for the seller to supply quality, one could easily imagine that, regarding information asymmetry, a temptation occurs to deliver low-quality goods ('lemons') to the market (moral hazard).

Therefore, unfair suppliers do not like to disclose information about quality, while fair suppliers have trouble carrying out reliable disclosures. It is a tough task for the seller to convince the buyer that just his/her particular offer is of high quality in a market populated by opportunistic, unfair suppliers. Thus, buyers presuppose a risk of purchasing 'lemons', which leads to a market price reduction. At the end of the day, the fair sellers (who offer high quality, but difficult to verify in advance) will either accept the inadequately low price or refrain from supplying the market at all. Subsequently, adverse selection arises (Akerlof, 1970). "In a Coasean perspective[5], the lemon problem identified by Akerlof (1970) leaves 'money on the table' because valuable transactions are not implemented due to the lack of support devices" (Raynaud et al., 2009, p. 840). And again, this is the moment when trust comes onto the scene (Figure 4.1B).

If a buyer trusts that a seller will deliver proper quality, and, on the other hand, if the supplier trusts that the buyer will warrant proper terms of trade (including) price, then the problem of hidden action and hidden information could be overcome. Ultimately, the crucial issue for the value chains in the real world (plagued with more or less severe information asymmetry) is how to build and maintain trust between parts involved, and therefore assure information disclosures between partners and maintain quality along the chain. The issue of quality is particularly challenging in agri-food chains according to three particular features.

Firstly, in agriculture, we observe the natural heterogeneity of raw materials due to the fluidity of bio-climatic conditions of production. Turning "heterogeneous and uncertain raw materials into homogeneous products with regular quality" is a burdensome task (Raynaud et al., 2009, p. 836). Secondly, agri-food chains becoming nationwide and global were getting longer and longer, with more and more narrowly specialized firms among them. On the whole, final quality depends on efforts possible to be carried out on many different stages of the value chain, from breeding and propagation and other input suppliers, through farmers and processors, to wholesalers and retailers (Pietrzak et al., 2020; Raynaud et al., 2005; Raynaud et al., 2009). For example, the final quality of parmesan depends on the breed of cattle, a special type of feed, hygienic milking, collecting and processing, and the duration of the cheese maturing stage[6]. Thirdly, this complementary impact of many agents throughout the chain on final quality is combined with the strong fragmentation observed at some stages, particularly farming. A largely fragmented supply of naturally heterogeneous raw agricultural products "can pose serious problems for evaluating and assessing each firm's separate contribution to the final quality or individual responsibility in case of food-related diseases[7]" (Raynaud et al., 2005, p. 56). Therefore, if building and maintaining trust is a challenge in the dyadic exchange, it is even more challenging along the whole agri-food chain.

We follow Coleman (1990) in treating trust as a kind of bet with known gain and loss but with an unknown probability of the trustee's credibility, so it seems reasonable to study this problem from a game-theoretic point of view. The aims of this chapter are twofold. The first objective is to recognize the essence of the challenge of trusting in the environment, where incentive structure pushes actors to follow their selfish interests rather than to care about common gains. The second objective is to define and discuss possible approaches to overcome traps caused by information asymmetry and to enhance trust as well. Both aims are pursued regarding the reasoning rooted in game theory. These objectives are relevant to create the context for both the discussion of solutions for the trust problem in Chapter 5 and the practical implication of this problem presented in the II section of the book.

4.3 Game theory framework

In a perfectly competitive market (including perfect information conditions), exchange could not be harmful. Gains from trade, the fundamental idea of neoclassical economics, means that the opportunity to be involved in a voluntary exchange is mutually beneficial for the engaged parties by increasing both consumer surplus and producer surplus. If price does not warrant such a surplus for a given agent, he or she will just not engage in the trade.

Under information asymmetry, the picture is not so obvious. Exchange could be harmful in terms of potential abuse due to the possibilities of hidden action/hidden information. Because there is a space for the discretionary behavior of each party (to behave trustfully or opportunistically), the buyer-seller relations contain both cooperative as well as antagonistic aspects. In the seller's case, the scope of their behavior is spanned between to-do or not efforts towards a mutual beneficial ends (e.g., high quality), which are not easily observable. Similarly, in the buyer's case, they could offer terms of trade that are adequate for the seller's efforts (e.g., toward a quality product) or he/she could offer a price matched to the lemon. Ultimately, these relations could evolve both into a win-win or lose-lose solution, and therefore they could be modeled from a game theory perspective as the non-zero-sum games.

Non-zero-sum games could be considered both non-cooperative games (with 2 players) and cooperative games (with n>2 players, which allows the creation of coalitions). Let's consider a non-cooperative version of the game commonly known as the prisoner's dilemma. The invention of the structure of this game in 1950 is attributed to Dreher and Flood from the RAND Corporation and was named the prisoner's dilemma after Tucker, who supplemented this game with a story about two arrested criminals (Dixit & Nalebuff, 2008; Straffin, 2004). This story is widely presented elsewhere (Dixit & Nalebuff, 2008; Kay, 1993; Straffin, 2004, Tirole, 1988), so we will focus here not on the criminal story but on the generalized structure of this game and its consequences (Figure 4.2A).

The payoff structure shown in Figure 4.2A (please refer to the explanation of the payoffs denoted by the letters P, S, T, and R below the graph) means that what

Panel A – static game, decisions are made simultaneously

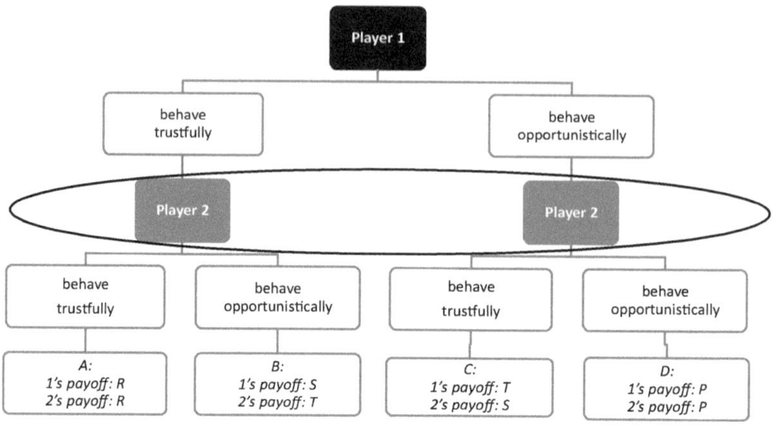

Panel B – dynamic game, decisions are made sequentially (the trust-abuse game)

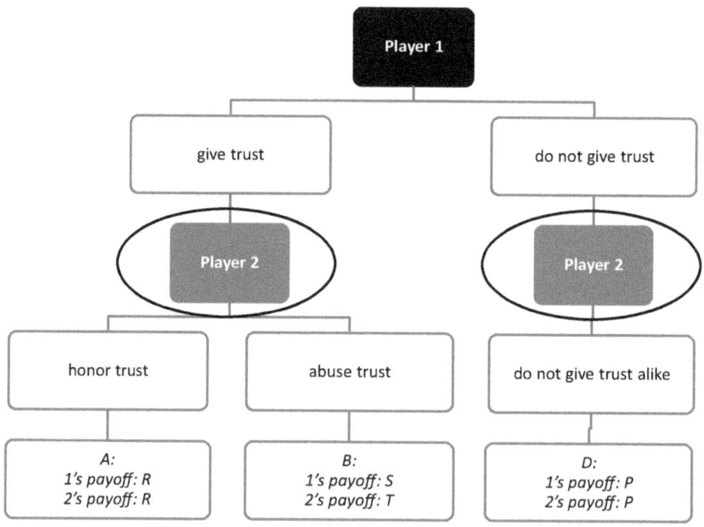

Figure 4.2 Extensive form of the prisoner's dilemma game and its mutation (the trust-abuse game).

Notes: Ovals which surround Player 2 denote the same information set; R – denotes reward for trustful cooperation, S – denotes sucker's payoff, T – denotes temptation to take advantage over partner, P – denotes punishment for opportunism or distrustful behavior; Conditions: T > R > P > S.

Source: Own work based on ideas from existing literature (Axelrod, 2006, p. 8; Baron & Kreps, 2015, p. 555; Kreps, 2001, p. 100; Miller, 2006, p. 200; Straffin, 2004, p. 95, Tirole, 1988, p. 424).

is best for each player individually has become a trap, according to which both parties end up in a position that is not preferred for both. In other words, striving for individual interests ends in a collectively inefficient result (Axelrod, 2006). The basic game-theoretic rule for decision-making is the dominance criterion. According to Straffin (2004), strategy A dominates strategy B if every outcome given by A is at least as favorable as the corresponding outcome given by B and at least one outcome given by A is more favorable than the corresponding outcome given by B. In other words, the dominant strategy means the optimal option for a rational decision-maker, no matter how the second party may play.

Thus, one could easily find that in a prisoner's dilemma game, the dominant strategy for Player 1 is to behave opportunistically (because T is better than R – if Player 2 chooses to cooperate trustfully, as well as P is better than S – if Player 2 chooses to behave opportunistically). On the other hand, the dominant strategy for Player 2 is also to behave opportunistically (for the very same reasons). In other words, the solution of the game is the mutual punishment of opportunism (P, P) – Figure 4.2A. This solution represents the Nash equilibrium, which means that no player can do better by changing his/her strategy unilaterally. In other words, in a Nash equilibrium, with the second party's strategies fixed, it does not pay for either player to change their strategy. That is exactly the case of outcome D (P, P), and that is exactly why this is the trap. What is more, even knowing the second party's choice, every player prefers not to switch his/her decision.

If the game has only one Nash equilibrium, this equilibrium will be the only possible solution for rational players. However, in the prisoner's dilemma, the Nash equilibrium is a Pareto-inefficient outcome. Pareto-optimality (compare definition in 4.1. section) is the basic condition for collective rationality. The Pareto-optimal solution of the prisoner's dilemma is the mutual reward for trustful cooperation, namely outcome A (R, R). However, it is hardly achievable by individually rational self-interest seekers.

In its canonical form, the prisoner's dilemma is considered a static game, where the decisions of players are made simultaneously (Figure 4.2A). However, it could also be considered a dynamic game, where the decisions of players are made sequentially. One such mutation is the trust-abuse game, which could be seen as a one-sided version of the prisoner's dilemma (Baron & Kreps, 2015; Kreps, 2001). In our dyadic generalization, Player 1 (P1 or just One) is playing against Player 2 (P2 or just Two) and has to choose whether or not to trust P2 (Figure 4.2B). If P1 trusts P2, Two has the option either to honor or to abuse the given trust. When both parties choose trust, both get R, and thus both are mutually rewarded for trustful cooperation – outcome A(R, R). If Two chooses to abuse trust, he or she gets the temptation payoff and One gets the sucker's payoff – outcome B (S, T). If no one trusts the other, both players end with a punishment for distrustful behavior – outcome D (P, P). In this sequential version of the prisoner's dilemma, outcome C (T, S) can be rejected as irrelevant.

Absent other considerations, P1 would not willingly trust P2 because since One trusts Two, when the game is played once, a rational Two should choose the best for themselves, namely abuse trust (because T > R). Knowing that, One will not give trust to Two (because P > S). Even in the sequential variant of the prisoner's dilemma, both players end up in the trap, namely with the outcome D, which represents the Nash equilibrium but is Pareto-inefficient. Thus, what can be done to promote trust, achieve an efficient cooperative solution, and therefore overcome information asymmetry?

4.4 Approaches to overcoming information asymmetries and promoting trust

4.4.1 Search

The most obvious method of overcoming information asymmetry is to obtain the necessary data directly. The second one is to approach researchers, experts, etc. with the problem of lacking information (Png & Lehman, 2007). Acquisition of information should be the first-choice approach against informational asymmetry. It was described in the seminal paper of Stigler (1961), which gives insights on how to economize on the search for information. Generally speaking, the key is the relation between marginal gains from accruing additional information and marginal costs of such a search. Along similar lines should be assessed the rationale for paying for informational services of researchers or appraisers, etc.; the expert's fee should not be larger than potential gain from their expertise for marginal users (Png & Lehman, 2007). According to Stigler (1961), information asymmetry possible to solve by searching could be treated analogously to the subzero weather – "by a sufficient expenditure its effects upon people can be kept within tolerable or even comfortable bounds" (p. 224).

However, the search approach is adequate only for some classes of information asymmetry, which could be overcome by costly, but possible to conduct, accruing of objective information. In such cases, trust does not play a crucial role, but this is a limited possibility. Consider a supplier who wants to establish plans regarding their production capacity and stock levels. The precise knowledge about buyers' future orders is strongly desired by them. However, the only information that typically could be accrued are rough estimations and forecasts, unless buyers want to voluntarily share information about their inventories and production plans, but this would be possible only in trustful relations. Consider a buyer who wants to find the best suppliers offering the highest value (benefits minus price). Let's assume most benefits are tied to product features, which are experience or credence attributes. Product traits, which are searchable attributes, could play only a marginal role in creating buyer satisfaction. In such a situation, a search approach to information asymmetry is clearly insufficient. The seller knows all important attributes, but how could the buyer induce them to disclosure? Situations where trust is an important factor of an efficient exchange could be depicted by the prisoner's dilemma (and trust-abuse game in particular) presented in the previous section. Thus, the possible approaches here could be found through further analysis of this game.

4.4.2 Changing the payoffs

Let's start with the notion of strategic move. According to Dixit et al. (2015), "Unless the rules of a game are fixed by an outside authority, each player has the incentive to manipulate them to produce an outcome that is more to his own advantage. Devices to manipulate a game in this way are called strategic moves" (p. 343). A strategic move means that one player does something outside of the scope of defined decisions in the game in advance. This move gives them a strategic advantage by commitment (unconditional move) to some course of action or by threats and promises (conditional moves). However, the key point is the credibility of strategic moves (Dixit et al., 2015).

Consider the history of William the Conqueror landing with Normans in England in the XI century. He could have announced that he would never retreat, regardless of the outcome of the battle at Hastings. The incentive of such a move is obvious. If King Harold believed such an announcement, there would be a chance that the English would capitulate immediately. However, King Harold would probably have disregarded the announcement and treated it as a bluff. Action speaks louder than words, and thus, according to the legend, William the Conqueror burnt the Normans' boats after they invaded England. By doing that, he engaged in credible commitment: we will certainly not retreat (Kay, 1993).

Due to their nature, it is also hard to make credible threats or give credible promises. The threat is a declaration on the conditional move (regarding what the other party of the game will be doing), which will be (1) costly for the other party as well as (2) costly for the player on its own (Straffin, 2004). What is particularly important is point (2), which makes the difference between just warning and the true threat. This point also makes the threat hard to believe in. If your threat has been disregarded, it is not worthwhile for you to carry it out, as the move by the other party against which it was intended to protect has already been made anyway. So, by fulfilling the threat, you would lose doubly; firstly, through this move by the other party, and secondly, by fulfilling a threat which is costly to you and which has no chance of helping you anyway.

The promise is a declaration on the conditional move (regarding what the other party of the game will be doing), which will be (1) beneficial for the other party as well as (2) costly for the player on its own (Straffin, 2004). Again, what is particularly important is point (2), which makes the difference between just assurance and a true promise, as well it also makes the promise hard to believe in. If the move for which you promised a reward was already made, it does not pay off to fulfill the promise because the move of the other player you wanted to obtain has already been made anyway. So, by fulfilling the promise, you would incur an unnecessary cost of reward for something you had already received anyway.

Consider the trust-abuse game (Figure 4.2B). As Player 2, you can promise Player 1 that you will reward them for trusting you. But after P1 trusts you, you can gain doubly; firstly, by taking T for abusing trust, and secondly, by not paying the promised reward. Thus, your promise would not be credible. If you are P1, you can threaten P2 that you will punish her/him for abusing your trust. But if P2 already abused you, you will not want to be even worse off by not only receiving a "sucker's payoff" – S, but also by bearing additional costs of fulfilling your threat.

How could players of the trust-abuse game (Figure 4.2B) be able to change the payoffs? Parties could write the contract that would change the initial incentives. For example, P2 could promise to honor trust under the sanction of penalty for abusing trust. The penalty should be large enough, namely it should cover at least the difference T – R. An important success condition of such a solution is the effective execution of the contract; otherwise, P2 will have an incentive to violate (Kay, 1993; Kreps, 2001; Miller, 2006). Thus, the transaction costs of enforcing the contract could be taken into account (cf. Williamson, 1975, 1985).

Let's recall the general framework from Chapter 3. Now we can see the importance of the context of the information asymmetry and trust issue, for example: government, courts, and law enforcement, other third parties (cf. Figure 3.1). One and Two could hire some third party as a credible contract enforcer unless it creates prohibitively high transaction costs (Miller, 2006). Axelrod (2006) emphasizes the role of government in dealing with changing the payoffs in prisoners' dilemmas, including laws passed to cause people to honor contracts. Thus, effective courts and law enforcement will also be crucial. Moreover, the additional role of government could be a direct intervention. It could take the form of incentives for players to cooperate and thus to value more trustful behavior. For example, in Poland, the government supports[8] establishing and maintaining producer organizations (POs) in agriculture (for more details, see Chlebicka & Pietrzak, 2018). Government intervention could also take the form of subsidizing other third parties to push down transaction costs of using them as credible contract enforcers.

In the framework proposed in this book (cf. Figure 3.1 in Chapter 3), the context is also created by society and culture. Due to the process of socialization and learning (which will be discussed further in this chapter), the norms of society and cultural patterns create attitudes and expectations of the parties playing the trust-abuse game. Moreover, society uses additional means, such as social sanctioning (e.g., ostracism), to assure the obedience of norms. For this reason, the normative system (Bossel, 2007), which provides normative references such as values, attitudes, or preferences of any decision-maker (cf.

Figure 3.2 in Chapter 3) should be considered to have been impacted by society and culture. However, an "oversocialized" conception of social action is not the cure (cf. Coleman, 1988; Granovetter, 1985). Let's try to follow Coleman's (1988) advice and borrow from both economics and sociology. Therefore, accepting the principle of purposive and rational action, we should not neglect its social context. All in all, there is a trade-off built-in pursuit of self-interest or other normative values promoted by society and its culture, e.g., altruism and trustworthiness.

The choice between them can be expressed as a function with a negative slope (Figure 4.3). Considering altruism and trust as a social norm, and therefore as a value in one's actions, it has a relative "price" as measured by self-interest needed to give up for the increase of this value. If this price is relatively low (cf. curve A in Figure 4.3), trust will play a significant role in the decision-making. However, if it is relatively high (cf. curve B in Figure 4.3), trust's influence will be smaller as compared to the role of selfishness, but it will not be neglected completely.

Game theory assumes that rational players will behave by pursuing their own interests, although it is debatable if narrowly defined selfishness represents their utility function. If following internalized norms creates psychological

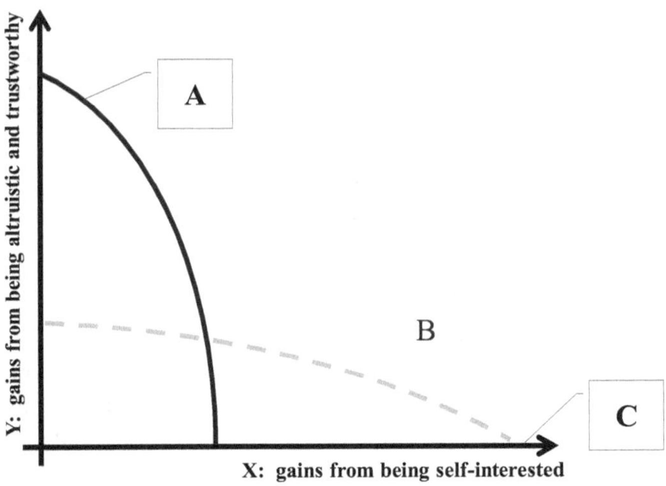

Figure 4.3 Possible trade-off functions between selfishness and altruism.

Notes: A negative slope of curves A and B reflects the relative "price" of being altruistic and trustworthy as measured by self-interest needed to give up for the increase of this value; In the case of curve A this "price" is relatively low, while in the case of curve B it is relatively high. In the case of curve C this "price" is infinitive, therefore altruism could be not considered at all in this case and decision-making will be based solely on self-interest.

Source: Own work.

satisfaction, it should be included in the utility function. If breaking social rules meets social ostracism and leads to psychological dissatisfaction, it should be included as well. Thus, an extreme case, when the only value taken into account is self-interest (cf. C curve, namely „X" axis in Figure 4.3), which means that the cost of considering altruism and trust is infinite, is… just an extreme case. It could be possible in the case of a sociopathic individual or in the case when society does not value altruism and trust, or when it is unable to punish breaking these values by its members. This discussion brings us to the conclusion that a society and its culture could play a substantial role in overcoming information asymmetry problems (cf. Figure 3.1).

4.4.3 Enlarging the impact of the future on the present moves

Let's abandon the world of one-shot games and move out into the repeated games world. Consider now that players are able to establish long-term, lasting relationships. What would be changed in a trust-abuse game? In the one-shot prisoners' dilemma game, players could achieve cooperation according to social sanctioning or by contracts, which are externally enforced. However, "The legal system may be imperfect or the relevant information may not be verifiable by the courts" (Furubotn & Richter, 2011, p. 170). "Enlarging the shadow of the future" (Axelrod, 2006, p. 126) in repeated games allows new kinds of contracts to emerge, namely self-enforcing contracts. In self-enforcing contracts, "the only recourse of the party who discovers a violation of the contract terms by the other side is to terminate the agreement. No third party intervenes, no public reaction of disapproval is necessary" (Furubotn & Richter, 2011, p. 170).

Consider the possibility that the players might meet each other again. This possibility changes how the choices are perceived. Choices made today determine not only the present payoffs but also impact the choices made tomorrow or sometime in the future and their outcomes accordingly. "The future can therefore cast a shadow back upon the present and thereby affect the current strategic situation" (Axelrod, 2006, p. 12).

How strong will this influence of the future on the present moves be? Let's call such importance of the future the weight (w) of the next choice relative to the current choice. In other words, it shows why the future is less important than the present (namely $w < 1$) in decision-making (Axelrod, 2006). The parameter w could be interpreted in three ways. One of them is the probability (p) of meeting again. We will start with this interpretation (namely $w = p$); others will be discussed later.

Repeated game assumption means the possibility that the players might meet each other; however, $p < 1$ means that the interaction may not continue. In this way, we can consider outcomes of any repeated game an infinite geometric series: initial game payoff + initial game payoff times p + initial game payoff times p^2 + … .

If s denotes the starting quantity and r denotes the common ratio, for $r < 1$, the sum of the infinite geometric series will be: $s/(1-r)$. Thus, assuming fixed choices of the first player, the other party of the repeated game should consider any choice outcome as: initial game payoff/(1-p). Therefore, p "must be large enough to make the future loom large in the calculation of total payoffs" and if it is "sufficiently high, there is no best strategy independent of the strategy used by the other player" (Axelrod, 2006, p. 15). In other words, the outcome D (P, P), namely double punishment (cf. Figure 4.2), is no longer an inevitable trap with no escape, even for fully self-interested players without external enforcers.

For better illustration, let's assume that T, R, P, and S denote real numbers, namely 5, 3, 1, and 0 points of utility, respectively (cf. Axelrod, 2006, p. 8). Let's assume for a while that Player 1 will choose the ALWAYS TRUST (or NICE GUY) strategy. Consider now Player 2's options. P2 could choose the ALWAYS ABUSE strategy. In the one-shot game, P2 will receive 5 points. If in a repeating game P1 continues his/her naïve strategy, the total of P2's payoff will be: 5/(1-p) points. In the case of $p = 0.5$, it will be 10 points. Now assume P1 plays the GRIM COOPERATION strategy, namely starting with giving trust and continuing this as long as P2 reciprocates by doing the same, and otherwise withdrawing trust forever (cf. Baron & Kreps, 2015). Then, the total of P2's payoff of ALWAYS ABUSE will be: 5 + 1/(1-p) points. In the case of $p = 0.5$, it will be: 5 + 2 = 7 points. If P2 plays GRIM COOPERATION, then their payoff will be: 3/(1-0.5) = 6 points. Still, ALWAYS ABUSE will be more profitable for P2. However, when p, for example, is 0.8, then GRIM COOPERATION outbids ALWAYS ABUSE[9]. In general, if the other player is playing GRIM COOPERATION, you are better off choosing cooperation (to honor trust) as well, when $p > (T-R)/(T-P)$[10].

The same results as above will be achieved if P1 plays the TIT FOR TAT strategy, while P2 considers playing the TIT FOR TAT versus ALWAYS ABUSE strategy. "TIT FOR TAT is merely the strategy of starting with cooperation, and thereafter doing what the other player did on the previous move" (Axelrod, 2006, p. viii). Thus, starting with cooperation gives the same results as GRIM COOPERATION if both sides continue to cooperate. However, TIT FOR TAT is forgiving, while GRIM COOPERATION is not. Essentially, the former offers more flexibility, which is advantageous in situations when some process of learning about mutual expectations and attitudes is needed or in cases when some kind of noise about the behavior of the other side is present.

The TIT FOR TAT strategy was invented by Anatol Rapoport, who designed it especially for playing repeated prisoner's dilemmas (Axelrod, 2006; Straffin, 2004). According to Axelrod (2006), "What accounts for TIT FOR TAT's robust success is its combination of being nice, retaliatory, forgiving, and clear" (p. 54). Being nice is a trait, which means never being the first who defects (who abuses trust from our perspective). What is crucial, however, is how quickly and reliably to respond to the unprovoked opportunistic behavior of the other side who abuses trust. Thus, being retaliatory is the property of implementing immediate punishment in the form of withdrawal of cooperation (trust-based behavior). Clarity means that strategy is understandable to the other player, namely once encountered, it should be easy to recognize. Due to its niceness (nonexploitability), TIT FOR TAT is easy to appreciate, thereby engendering a long-term cooperation based on trust (cf. Axelrod, 2006).

Let's discuss the forgiveness property more deeply. The undesired side effect of being retaliatory is the risk of an echo effect, when a single defection (abusing trust) episode can provoke some kind of chain reaction with a long string of allegations, recriminations, counter-recriminations, etc. (Axelrod, 2006; Dixit & Nalebuff, 2008). To stop such a chain reaction, the bygones be bygones approach is needed. Forgiveness means the propensity to trust again even after the other party abused the trust. Dixit and Nalebuff (2008) argue that sometimes TIT FOR TAT is not forgiving enough to prevent the echo effect. In such cases, TIT FOR TWO TATS would be a more preferable strategy (Axelrod, 2006; Dixit & Nalebuff, 2008). In a more generalized form, Nowak (2006) calls such a strategy GENEROUS TIT FOR TAT.[11] Forgiveness is important because it helps not to break the potential of successful cooperation too easily by the echo effect due to inadvertent slip-ups.

"Because enforcement is by punishment when the contract is broken, we must be able to observe compliance" (Kreps, 2001, p. 105). Up to now, in our game-theory consideration, it was taken for granted that any deviation from cooperation (abusing trust) will be recognized and dealt with. In real situations, players often have only a rough idea of what others are doing because they are based on "noisy" signals about the other party's behavior. As Baron and Kreps (2015) explain: "participants can try to implement certain action, but sometimes (against their will) what is realized is other than what is intended" (p. 558). Let's assume that with the probability n, action that takes place is the reverse of what was intended (and as such represents noise); therefore, $(1 - n)$ means the probability that what is intended is what transpires, and even if P2 intends to honor trust, P1 with probability n could perceive P2's behavior as abusive. "The more noise there is, the harder it will be to sustain cooperation" (Baron & Kreps, 2015, p. 558). The problem of noise is particularly severe in agriculture. This is due to the production embedded in the natural processes, which translates directly into high variability in the quantity and quality of agricultural products. Thus, the trade partner of the farmers could have difficulties in assessing if discrepancies between contracted volume and quality are due to the noise disturbing the honest intentions of the farmer or are just a result of intended cheating.

One could find that the effect of noise is analogous to the effect of the probability factor. Increasing noise is equivalent to the decreasing probability (p) of meeting again because, according to Baron and Kreps (2015), "when noise rises, the future becomes less a product of the player's intentions" (p. 558), and therefore "there is less in the future to trade off against short-term gains" (pp. 558–559). For this reason, the unimportance of noise could be the second interpretation of the weight factor (w), namely the weight of the next choice relative to the current choice ($w = 1 - n$).

The third interpretation of weight factor (w) is as a discount factor ($1 - d$), namely $w = (1 - d)$. "Players tend to value payoffs less as the time of their obtainment recedes into the future" (Axelrod, 2006, p. 12). Thus, the present value of future payoffs should be found by discounting them using discount rate d. According to Ostrom (2011): "individuals discount future benefits – how severely depends on several factors" (p. 34). The discount rate is affected inter alia by "the general norms shared by individuals (…) regarding the relative importance of the future as compared with the present" (Ostrom, 2011, p. 35). Once again, the importance of social context in building trust and dealing with information asymmetry is highlighted.

To sum up, the w factor could be interpreted threefold as a probability (p) of meeting again, as an unimportance of noise ($1 - n$), and as a discount factor ($1 - d$). For explanatory purposes, it could be useful to treat these interpretations separately. In practice, however, they play jointly in taking into account the future as making decisions in the present. Thus, the weight factor should be interpreted as: $w = p\,(1 - n)\,(1 - d)$. Ultimately, the higher the weight of the future, the more likely the cooperation would be achieved and sustained, namely the lower the noise and the lower the discount rate, the more probable continuing the relation is. To put it simply, one must always have some important stake in the future if one wants to sustain trustful cooperation (cf. Kreps, 2001, p. 102)

Up to now, we have considered the role of enlarging the impact of the future on the present moves in creating bilateral reciprocity, and therefore enhancing trust and cooperation. If the shadow of the future (expressed as w) is large enough and player 1 plays GRIM COOPERATION or TIT FOR TAT, player 2's response should be to honor trust (Figure 4.2B), and therefore P1 could trust P2 and sustained cooperation could start. This conclusion is due to the involvement of P2 in a relationship with a single P1. But is such a condition inevitable?

What about the case of an extended dyadic relation, when P2 meets many P1s (namely many representatives of a given stage in the supply chain), with no guarantee to meet any particular one again? For example, P2 can meet $P1_1$ at time t_1, $P1_2$ at time t_2, $P1_3$ at time t_3, …, and so on. Such a structure of relationships is quite common in agro-food chains, where some links in the chain are highly fragmented and others are highly concentrated. Consider farmers vs. brokers or food processors as well as individual consumers vs. retailers or food processors. The crucial feature of such a case will be the ability of P1s to be informed of how P2 behaved in the past with previous representatives of P1's stage in the chain. This is where the notion of reputation comes onto the scene. A person or a firm that cheats takes the risk of losing future gains from deals with other players (Tirole, 1988). Cumulatively, the past behavior of P2 creates their bad reputation (when he/she abuses trust) or good reputation (when he/she honors trust). Therefore, any P1 could adopt a modified version of GRIM COOPERATION: trust P2 as long as P2 has never abused trust given by earlier representatives of P1; otherwise, refuse to give trust to P2 (Baron & Kreps, 2015).

As trusting due to the long-lasting relationship could be seen as a form of direct reciprocity, trust based on reputation could be perceived as a form of indirect reciprocity. Both are considered by evolutionary biologists to be the rules for cooperation, which is necessary "for evolution to construct new levels of organization. Genomes, cells, multicellular organisms, social insects, and human society are all based on cooperation" (Nowak, 2006, p. 1560). Direct reciprocity means cooperation between individuals according to the rule: if I meet you, I will play cooperatively, hoping that you will also play cooperatively the next time I meet you. Thus, direct reciprocity strongly relies on the probability of meeting again. "This is one reason why cooperation emerges more readily in small towns than in large cities" (Axelrod, 2006, p. 130). Direct reciprocity with its principle of 'favor for favor' is somewhat reminiscent of an economy based on barter exchange. Just as the invention of money was a quantum leap in economic development, an analogous breakthrough in the evolutionary mechanisms of cooperation is indirect reciprocity, specific to the human species and distinguishing us from animals. A role analogous to money is played here by reputation (cf. Nowak, 2006). "Knowing people's reputation allows you to know something about what strategy they use even before you have to make your first choice" (Axelrod, 2006, p. 151).

Cooperation based on reputation involves other parties (outside bilateral relations), rewarding individuals with a reputation for altruism (Fehr & Fischbacher, 2003). In other words, helping someone builds a reputation that is rewarded by others, who do not necessarily observe the interaction directly, but who have the possibility to obtain this information from observers. Cooperation based on reputation is an evolutionary stable strategy when: $q > c/b$ (Nowak, 2006, p. 1561), where q denotes the probability of knowing about someone's reputation, c denotes the cost of cooperation for Player 1, and b denotes the benefits of Player 2 for the cooperative behavior of Player 1. The careful reader easily finds that factor q is equivalent to factor p (probability of meeting again directly) discussed above, and thus as such it builds up the factor w, namely the weight of the future in making present decisions.

Note that due to the development of humans and human society with gossip, shared morality, and culture, with the socialization and the creation of institutions (Dunbar, 2014; Fehr & Fischbacher, 2003), it can be assumed that $q > p$. What is more, nowadays, with the development of mass media, internet, social media, etc., it can be assumed that $q >> p$, which significantly increases the effectiveness of the indirect reciprocity mechanism. Nevertheless, one should also note that the overall factor w is still prone to noise (n). The discount factor (d) should also be taken into consideration. For example, in regards to the quality, the longer the time lag between sales and the moment when a consumer is able to observe the quality of an item bought, the larger the discount rate per period given the same *d* factor per unit of time (Tirole, 1988). However, it is typically not a big issue in most agro-food consumables due to their limited durability.

A characteristic form of bearing "reputational capital" in agro-food chains is through a brand (Raynaud et al., 2005). "It is the threat of termination of the relationship by the consumer, and the corresponding loss of reputation that makes the implicit 'trademark contract' self-enforcing" (pp. 50–51). To create a significant stake located in the future, branding involves substantial investments in a brand, which could be perceived as a signaling strategy.

Producers of high-quality goods may seek an observable signal in order to manipulate it, and therefore to demonstrate their superior quality, unobservable in advance (if quality substantially relies on experience attributes). To signal quality effectively, the costs of the signal have to be negatively correlated with the capability to offer quality products (cf. Spence, 1973). For producers which are able to supply high-quality food, it will be less costly to invest in the brand than for the producers of poor-quality food, which could hardly hope to be sustained in business long enough to receive payback from investments in the brand. Thus, the logic of signaling by using the brand as a signal could be depicted by the course of iterative runs of the following feedback loop: (1) The consumer belief in the conditional probability of quality -> (2) offered price premium as a function of signal -> (3) producers' decisions about branding -> (4) purchase, observation of links between brand and quality -> (1) the consumer belief in the conditional probability of quality, and so on (cf. Spence, 1973).

4.4.4 Socialization and learning

The third piece of advice (after changing the payoffs and enlarging the shadow of the future on the present decisions) from Axelrod (2006) on how to extend and sustain propensity for mutual cooperation is: "teaching the players values, facts and skills that will promote cooperation" (p. 126). Baron and Kreps (2015) emphasize the role of alignment of mutual expectations in achieving the desired equilibrium outcome in the trust-abuse game. They find that "when one side expects that any attempt at trust (…) will be met with a sneer (…), then the first party will behave accordingly" (p. 75). This brings us again to the role of socio-cultural context (cf. Figure 3.1 in Chapter 3). According to Coleman (1988), there are two streams in the description and explanation of social action: economics and sociology. Economics perceives the individual "as having goals independently arrived at, as acting independently, and as wholly self-interested" (p. S95). However, such a view contradicts empirical reality: "persons' actions are shaped, redirected, constrained by the social context; norms, interpersonal trust, social networks, and social organization are important in the functioning not only of the society but also of the economy" (p. S96).

Human actions take place in complex fields of actions such as groups, communities, associations, organizations, and societies. Sociologists see such interactional fields as having some synthetic qualities. They are typically addressed in metaphorical terms, such as collective morale, social moods, social climate, etc. Taking the bet to trust or not occurs in the pre-existent context. In this context, norms push toward or away from giving and honoring trust (Sztompka, 1999). From this point of view, trust could be perceived as the property of social wholes, which could be termed as trust culture. It could be defined as: "a system of rules – norms and values – regulating granting trust, and meeting, returning, and reciprocating trust" (Sztompka, 1999, p. 99).

Socio-cultural identity and continuity are attained by socialization. Socialization is the process of individuals internalizing the norms of society and cultural patterns. In this process, an individual acquires the skills to adapt to a society or to a particular group by learning to conform to the approved behaviors and norms of that group or society. Socialization is a lifelong learning process that affects both children and adults throughout their entire life course. Therefore, it would be useful to distinguish between primary and secondary socialization. While the first one occurs during early childhood and is typically facilitated by the family, the second one is facilitated by formal education, media, religious institutions, and other types of social wholes, such as groups, professional associations, organizations, etc. Agents of socialization other than family provide additional layers of social understanding (cf. Berger & Luckman, 1991).

The discussion above makes it clear that trust culture is not unconditionally functional. It is functional only if "the rules are two-sided" as Sztompka (1999, p. 111) claims. Furthermore, he finds that "When the culture of trust is one-sided (…), it is in fact a culture of naiveness and has highly dysfunctional consequences" (p. 112). One could claim that the low level of generalized trust may be a result of bad experiences in a nation's history or in a particular social group's history. Chlebicka and Pietrzak (2018) give Poland as an example of low generalized trust among citizens as well as among farmers, resulting from the heritage of communism. Thus, culture could still be dysfunctional even if it loses real ground and exists by inertia (Sztompka, 2007). In such situations, the role of changing attitudes and building trust culture from scratch cannot be overemphasized.

As was already mentioned, a trust-oriented social climate or collective morale could encompass whole societies as well as smaller social wholes, such as groups or organizations. Society is not a monolith; it consists of groups, which could be delineated through many criteria. Such groups and their subcultures' identity and continuity are attained through secondary socialization (cf. Berger & Luckman, 1991). For example, if the participant of the supply chain learns trustworthy behavior and starts benevolent information sharing and disclosure (cf. Figure 3.3 in Chapter 3), it could be perceived as a result of secondary socialization inside the group built-up by supply chain participants. If the ties binding them are strong enough, one could argue that in such a case the supply chain is a kind of hybrid[12] organization. Thus, the notion of organizational learning (cf. Chapter 2) could be applied to such a mode of coordination (Pietrzak & Domagała, 2022). From this perspective, the supply chain could be perceived as a learning system (cf. Chapter 3), in which learning that only processes information (single-loop learning) is extended by meta-learning or double-loop learning. In this last one, the framework responsible for future processing of information is updated, namely tacit knowledge capacity is enlarged, and therefore can reshape the future rounds of information interpretation (cf. Chapter 2).

According to Baron and Kreps (2015), the manner in which parties play the prisoner's dilemma depends on their expectations, which, in turn, are driven inter alia by "the history of relations between the two parties themselves" (p. 75). Sterman (2000) claims that effective learning involves continuous experimentation. Thus, one could expect some more or less complicated process of learning before mutual trustful cooperation in the supply chain could be effectively conducted. Expectations, values, and attitudes (normative system) could be seen as an espoused theory in Argyris's and Schon's (1978) learning model. Such a theory steers the response system (cf. Chapter 3), which is responsible for information processing and interpretation. In a simple single-loop learning cycle, the espoused theory is not questioned (cf. Figure 3.2a in Chapter 3). However, the espoused theory should not be treated as being etched on stone tablets; it could be tested through the actions of the causal system (cf. Figure 3.2b in cf. Chapter 3). As additional information feedback inflows into the response system, it could be interpreted as a need to update the theory (normative system), and therefore be a base for double-loop learning.

A learning mechanism in which expectations, values, and attitudes are no longer treated as being etched in stone makes it possible to iteratively build up a supply chain that could be more resilient and viable against the turbulent environment. Normative systems frame how the system and its environment are perceived, and therefore are the basis of the process of "deciphering" the real world (cf. North, 2011, p. 20). "Deciphering" business systems like supply chains means that we perceive them through filters, and we are more cautious about hearing the messages we are structured to hear (Hoverstadt, 2010). Such structurization, namely normative systems, could change as we learn (cf. Sterman, 2000).

Essentially, even in the poor scenario of the dominance of a society-wide distrust culture, the learning process within the chain may be able to change the initial expectations through positive experience gained due to an iterated trust-abuse game. As a result, a trust sub-culture among chain partners could be built under the condition of proper governance of the relations within the chain. These issues will be discussed in the next chapter.

4.5 Summary and conclusions

Opposite to the neoclassical economics' view, markets are not perfectly efficient and often are plagued by market power, externalities, and information asymmetry. The assumption about asymmetrical information has substantial consequences on how supplier–buyer relations in supply chains operate in regard to both physical flows of goods and their quality. Although the mutual benefits of sharing and disclosing information could be obvious for smoothing flows and reducing inventories as well as for enhancing the quality and safety of food, it could be difficult to give up the potential source of power and short-term gains, namely private information. In order to disclose and share private information with a trade partner, mutual trust is needed. Trust is fragile and can easily be abused, which could be illustrated by the prisoner's dilemma and trust-abuse game in particular. In such games, the Nash equilibrium, which represents a stable outcome of individual rationality of players, is a Pareto-inefficient outcome, namely it is not rational from the collective standpoint.

There are three complementary approaches to overcoming this problem: changing payoffs, enlarging the impact of the future on the present choices, and socialization and learning. The payoffs could be changed by making credible strategic moves (such as threats and promises), for example, by creating contracts. Due to transaction costs associated with contracts, the role of government and courts in facilitating contract enforcement cannot be neglected. Also, societal and cultural factors should not be underestimated.

An additional approach to facilitating trustful cooperation involves self-enforcing contracts, which are based on enlarging the impact of the future on present decisions. When a gainful agreement governing repeated transactions is possible, then any party could terminate such an agreement in the case of contract violation. Therefore, if the gains of future cooperation are large enough, the agreement would be self-enforced without external intervention. How much the future gain weighs against present profit from abusing trust depends on the probability of meeting again, noise, and the discount factor. Repeated interactions create an environment in which reputational concerns could occur. Reputation is a mechanism for facilitating and sustaining trust, which is based on indirect reciprocity. Indirect reciprocity arises due to the development of human society and its culture and institutions. One of the possible strategies based on reputational capital is branding. Branding could be perceived as a form of signaling strategy when producers invest in brands to signal high quality. The logic of signaling through branding is based on a feedback loop involving consumer beliefs, price premiums, producers' decisions about branding, and the observation of links between brand and quality.

Axelrod (2006) recommends teaching players values, facts, and skills to promote cooperation. In this way, socialization and learning could foster and sustain mutual trust. Through socialization, individuals internalize societal norms and cultural patterns. Normative systems are frameworks deciding how the world is perceived, acting as filters through which business systems, such as supply chains, are deciphered. The notion that normative systems can change as learning occurs should be emphasized. Expectations, values, and attitudes are driving factors in prisoner's dilemma scenarios and are influenced by the history of relations between the parties. Thus, they could be changed according to the double-loop learning process involving continuous experimentation. The significance of the socio-cultural context, particularly trust culture, should be explored as an attribute of social wholes such as nations and societies as well as groups and organizations. On the whole, even in a society-wide distrust culture, it would be possible to change attitudes and to build up a trust sub-culture from scratch through the process of secondary socialization inside an organization or among interconnected supply chain participants. The secondary socialization could be regarded as organizational learning and be applied to the supply chains, which could be treated as learning systems.

One could easily find that the usefulness of the three complementary approaches discussed above strongly relies on what was defined as a context in Chapter 3 (formal and informal, external and internal institutions). Namely, context covers: society and culture (which creates informal and internal institutions), government, as well as courts and law enforcement (formal and external institutions), and other 3rd parties (formal and internal institutions). Recognizing the role of context in creating a cooperation-friendly environment, we will focus in the following chapters of this book, mainly on solutions to overcoming the lack of trust applicable on the supply chain level.

Last but not least, the limitations of this study should be mentioned. It is based on a game-theoretic approach, in which information is treated somehow as the raw material. This kind of input is used in the process of decision-making. Thus, in this approach, conceptual differences between categories such as data, information, and knowledge are not seriously taken into account. Information is perceived as disembodied content or a message, and issues such as emotions, cognitive biases, or other behavioral factors are not considered as deeply as they deserve due to their role in the interpretation and application of information. Nevertheless, I am convinced that game theory could effectively grasp some important issues and challenges regarding information asymmetry and trust crucial for participants of agro-food chains. All in all, it could offer fruitful context for the discussion of solutions for these problems (Chapter 5), as well as for the case studies and practical implications of this problem (II section of this book). Readers interested in issues not discussed here, such as differentiation between data, information, and knowledge, interpretation problems, causal ambiguity, absorptive capacity, collective sense giving and learning, as well as translation of knowledge into capability and practice, may find an overview of these in Chapter 2.

Notes

1 The case of cooperation between Procter & Gamble and Wal-Mart described in Chapter 3 is an insightful example of it.
2 Compare discussion on rationality in Chapter 3.
3 Cf. Galbraith (2014).
4 In Humprey and Schmitz's (1996) adaptation, the condition is modified: $p(G\text{-}S) > (1\text{-}p)L$, where S denotes costs of monitoring and enforcing sanctions (pp. 5–6).
5 Coase (1937) was the first to notice that using the market incurs various costs beyond just the price of a good or service. These costs, called later the transaction costs, include search and information costs, bargaining costs, policing and enforcement of the contract costs, etc. Here we refer to the information asymmetry (Akerlof 1970). One who can mitigate the "lemon" problem is one who is able to decrease the transaction costs and therefore enhance the market exchange and gain from it.
6 A more detailed analysis of the complementary impact of different stages in the apple value chain split into search, experience, and credence attributes one could find in (Pietrzak et al., 2020).
7 Just to continue the parmesan example. During the EAAE (European Association of Agricultural Economists) Congress 2017 in Parma, the author of this chapter visited one of the small cooperatives producing parmesan. The whole milk collecting and processing processes were designed and organized according to the ability to evaluate each farmer's separate contribution to the final quality and individual responsibility for it. The cooperative consisted of 15 members, and thus the milk-collecting tank was split to allow the collection of milk separately. Then, the milk was processed in separate 15 tubs in a way that the final block of cheese could be attributed to the milk obtained from a particular member.
8 After the transition to a free market economy in Poland in 1989, farmers' producer organizations had to be built almost from scratch. The formation of producer organizations began in 2000, following the introduction of comprehensive legal regulations. Poland's accession to the EU improved support conditions for these organizations. Joining the Common Agricultural Policy created further opportunities for investment and public funding for POs.
9 In GRIM COOPERATION, the payoff will be 15 points (because 3/(1-0.8) = 15) versus 10 points (because 5 + 1/(1-0.8) = 5 + 5 = 10) in the case of ALWAYS ABUSE. For $p = 0.9$, the advantage in payoffs will be even more overwhelming: 30 points (3/(1-0.9) = 30) versus 15 points (5 + 1/(1-0.9) = 15) points.
10 Using this rule in the examples used above, one could find that 0.5 = (5-3)/(5-1) = 2/4=1/2. Therefore, for the $p = 0.5$, the condition of viable cooperation is not met. However, 0.9 > 0.8 > (5-3)/(5-1), and thus for $p = 0.8$ and even more for $p = 0.9$, the condition of viable cooperation is met.
11 In this strategy, with some probability, the reaction to the other player's defection (abusing trust) could be cooperation (continuing trust). This probability is defined as $p_c = 1 - (c/b)$, where p_c denotes the probability of cooperative reaction regardless of defection, c denotes the cost of cooperation for player 1, and b denotes benefits for

player 2 for the cooperative behavior of player 1 (Nowak, 2006, p. 1560). It should be noted that this probability is lower the higher the cost of cooperation (granting trust).

12 By hybrid, I mean something between atomistic and fully autonomic parties and hierarchical organizations (namely bureaucracy).

References

Akerlof, G. A. (1970). The market for "lemons": Quality, uncertainty and the market mechanism. *The Quarterly Journal of Economics*, 3(84), 488–500.

Argyris, C., & Schön, D. A. (1978). *Organizational learning: A theory of action perspective*. Addison -Wesley.

Arrow, K. J. (1974). *The limits of organization*. W.W. Norton & Company.

Axelrod, R. (2006), *The evolution of cooperation*. Basic Books.

Baron, J. N., & Kreps, D. M. (2015). *Strategic human resources. Frameworks for general managers*. Wiley India.

Berger, P., & Luckmann, T. (1991). *The social construction of reality: A treatise in the sociology of knowledge*. Penguin.

Besanko, D., Dranove, D., Shanley, M., & Schaefer, S. (2017). *Economics of strategy*. Willey.

Blaug, M. (1985). *Economic theory in retrospect*. Cambridge University Press.

Bossel, H. (2007). *Systems and models. Complexity, dynamics, evolution, sustainability*. Books on Demand.

Chlebicka, A., & Pietrzak, M. (2018). Size of membership and survival patterns of producers' organizations in agriculture – Social aspects based on evidence from Poland. *Sustainability*, 10(7), 2293. https://doi.org/10.3390/su10072293.

Coase, R. H. (1937). The nature of the firm. *Economica*, 4(16), 386–405. doi:10.1111/j.1468-0335.1937.tb00002.x

Coleman, J. S. (1988). Social capital in the creation of human capital. *American Journal of Sociology*, *94*(Supplement: Organizations and Institutions: Sociological and Economic Approaches to the Analysis of Social Structure), S95–S120.

Coleman, J. S. (1990). *Foundations of social theory*. The Belknap Press.

Darby, M. R., & Karni, E. (1973). Free competition and the optimal amount of fraud. *Journal of Law and Economics*, *73*(16), 67–88.

Dixit, A. K., & Nalebuff, B. J. (2008). *The art of strategy: A game theorist's guide to success in business and life*. W. W. Norton & Company.

Dixit, A. K., Skeath, S., & Reiley, D. (2015). *Games of strategy*. W. W. Norton & Company.

Dunbar, R. (2014). *Human evolution*. Pelican.

Fehr, E., & Fischbacher, U. (2003). The nature of human altruism. *Nature*, *425*(23), 785–791.

Forrester, J. W. (2013). *Industrial dynamics*. Martino Publishing.

Furubotn, E. G., & Richter, R. (2011). *Institutions and economic theory. The contribution of the new institutional economics*. The University of Michigan Press.

Gabbay, S. M., & Leenders, R. T. A. J. (2002). *A perceptional view of the Coleman model of trust. Working paper*. University of Groningen, Groningen, NL.

Galbraith, J. K. (2014). *American capitalism. The concept of countervailing power.* Transaction Publishers.

Gambetta, D. (1988). Can we trust trust? In D. Gambetta (Ed.), *Trust: Making and breaking cooperative relations* (pp. 213–237). Basil Blackwell.

Granovetter, M. (1985). Economic action and social structure: The problem of embeddedness. *American Journal of Sociology*, *91*(3), 481–510.

Hardin, R. (1992). The street-level epistemology of trust. *Analyse & Kritik*, *14*(2), 152–176.

Hoverstadt, P. (2010). The viable system model. In M. Reynolds and S. Holwell (Eds.), *Systems approaches to manage change: A practical guide* (pp. 87–133). Springer.

Humprey, J., & Schmitz, H. (1996). *Trust and economic development* (Discussion paper 355). Institute of Development Studies, University of Sussex.

Kay J. (1993). *Foundations of corporate success. How business strategies add value.* Oxford University Press.

Kornai, J. (1977). *Anti-equilibrium*. PWN.

Kreps, D. M. (2001). Corporate culture and economic theory. In J. E. Alt & K. A. Shepsle (Ed.), *Perspectives on positive political economy*. Cambridge University Press.

Luhmann, N. (1979). *Trust and power*. Wiley.

Miller, G. J. (2006). *Managerial dilemmas. The political economy of hierarchy.* Cambridge University Press.

Nelson, P. (1970). Information and consumer behavior. *Journal of Political Economy*, *78*, 311–329.

North, D. C (2011). *Institutions, institutional changes and economic performance.* Cambridge University Press.

Nowak, M. A. (2006). Five rules for the evolution of cooperation. *Science*, 314, 1560–1563.

Ostrom, E. (2011). *Governing the commons. The evolution of institutions for collective action*. Cambridge University Press.

Paliszkiewicz, J. (2013). *Zaufanie w zarządzaniu* [Trust in management]. Wydawnictwo Naukowe PWN.

Pfeffer, J., & Salancik G. R. (2003). *The external control of organizations. A resource dependence perspective.* Stanford University Press.

Pietrzak, M. (2022). *Fenomen spółdzielni rolników. Pomiędzy rynkiem, hierarchią i klanem* [The phenomenon of farmers' cooperatives: Between market, hierarchy, and clan]. CeDeWu.

Pietrzak, M., Chlebicka, A., Kracinński, P., & Malak-Rawlikowska, A. (2020). Information asymmetry as a barrier in upgrading the position of local producers in the global value chain-evidence from the apple sector in Poland. *Sustainability*, 12, 7857. DOI:10.3390/su12197857

Pietrzak, M., & Domagała J. (2022). A strategy map as a framework of a shared mental model for interactive control systems. *Economics and Organization of Logistics*, *7*(2), 67–96. DOI: 10.22630/EIOL.2022.7.2.13

Png, I., & Lehman, D. (2007). *Managerial economics*. 3rd ed. Wiley-Blackwell.

Raynaud, E., Sauvée, L., & Valceschini, E. (2005). Alignment between quality enforcement devices and governance structures in the agro-food vertical chains. *Journal of Management and Governance*, *9*, 47–77.

Raynaud, E., Sauvée L., & Valceschini, E. (2009). Aligning branding strategies and governance of vertical transactions in agri-food chains. *Industrial and Corporate Change*, *18*(5), 835–86.

Ritzer-Angerer, P. (2018). *Digital transformation and trust (dis)intermediation – Coleman's models thirty years on. Working paper*. Leibniz Information Centre for Economics, Kiel, Germany.

Samuelson, P. A., & Nordhaus W. D. (2010). *Economics*. The McGraw-Hill.

Spence, M. (1973). Job market signaling. *The Quarterly Journal of Economics*, *87*(3), 355–374.

Sterman, J. D. (2000). *Business dynamics. Systems thinking an modeling for a complex world*. Irwin McGraw-Hill.

Stigler, G. J. (1961). The economics of information. *Journal of Political Economy*, *69*, 213–225.

Stiglitz, J. (2000). The contributions of the economics of information to twentieth century economics. *The Quarterly Journal of Economics*, *4*(115), 1441–1478.

Straffin, P. D. (2004). *Teoria gier* [Game theory]. Wyd. Naukowe Scholar.

Sztompka, P. (1999). *Trust. A sociological theory*. Cambridge University Press.

Sztompka, P. (2007). *Zaufanie. Fundament społeczeństwa* [Trust. The foundation of society], Wyd. Znak.

Thompson, J. D. (2008). *Organization in action. Social science bases of administrative theory*. Transaction Publishers.

Tirole, J. (1988). *The theory of industrial organization*. The MIT Press.

van der Vorst, Jack G. A. J. (2004). Supply chain management: Theory and practices. In T. Camps, P. Diederen, G. J. Hofstede, & B. Vos (Eds.), *The emerging world of chains and networks. Bridging theory and practice* (pp. 105–128). Reed Business Information.

Wilkin, J. (2016). *Instytucjonalne i kulturowe podstawy gospodarowania. Humanistyczna perspektywa ekonomii* [Institutional and cultural foundations of economy: A humanistic perspective of economics]. Wydawnictwo Naukowe Scholar.

Williamson, O. E. (1975). *Markets and hierarchies: Analysis and antitrust implications. A study in the economics of internal organization*. The Free Press.

Williamson, O. E. (1985). *The economic institutions of capitalism*. The Free Press.

5 Solutions for Overcoming Information Asymmetry and Enhancing Trust in Supply Chains

Aleksandra Chlebicka
Warsaw University of Life Sciences – SGGW, Poland

5.1 Introduction

The agro-food sector is facing progressively complex coordination challenges arising from regulatory, technological, and socio-economic factors that shape final products and the way transactions are orchestrated. These challenges, as described by Ménard and Valceschini (2005) and Bijman et al. (2014), frequently relate to information asymmetry, particularly within the context of globalized supply chains. For example, regulations pertaining to traceability contribute to transaction complexity by necessitating the documentation of information about the product's origins, characteristics, processing, and handling throughout the supply chain. Technologies enabling tailored products for specific end-users introduce relationship-specific investments, creating the potential for opportunistic behavior. Changes in consumer preferences, driven by lifestyle shifts, elevate the demand for specific product attributes, intensifying the need for information about product quality. Beyond basic quality in food production, consumers now seek assurance regarding ethical practices, animal welfare, and environmental stewardship, shifting the focus from observable to nonobservable experience and credence attributes (Raynaud et al., 2009). Heterogeneous consumer preferences in international markets further drive product differentiation, steering the sector away from its traditional commodity orientation.

Consequently, a multitude of institutions and organizational approaches have emerged to address information asymmetry issues within agrifood systems (Martino, 2010; Pascucci et al., 2012). Among these approaches, closer vertical coordination stands out as an important strategy. Vertical coordination refers to the means by which products move through the supply chain from production to consumption. It encompasses a continuum of possibilities from open market spot transactions at one extreme through to full vertical integration at the other, but includes intermediate forms such as contracting and hybrid organizations based on contracts (cooperatives, strategic alliances, licensing, etc.). Additional solutions involve enhancing knowledge about products and processes through

DOI: 10.4324/9781032633725-6

comprehensive data collection, testing, and vigilant monitoring (as discussed in Chapter 6). Another viable strategy entails the adoption of food standards and certification systems overseen by third parties to mitigate information asymmetry in agrifood systems (illustrated in Part II of the book).

While some of the solutions mentioned above heavily rely on formal arrangements, trust remains a critical element for initiating and sustaining long-term relationships among actors in the supply chain. While trust is often viewed as an interpersonal phenomenon (refer to Chapter 4 of this book), it can also be conceptualized as interorganizational trust within economic transactions, as outlined by Zucker (1986) and Sztompka (1999). In this perspective, trust is positioned as the adhesive that binds partners in inter-organizational relationships. Some authors go so far as to consider trust a distinct governance mechanism because the investments made by partners to cultivate trust go beyond minimizing transaction costs, creating economic value in the exchange relationship (Dyer & Chu, 2003; Lui & Ngo, 2004).

This chapter delves into a detailed exploration of solutions pertaining to vertical coordination that address the information asymmetry issue within the supply chain. We adopt a universal perspective based on Williamson's continuum, drawing specific references to the agribusiness sector, as certain solutions and the driving forces behind them are inherently intertwined with its unique characteristics. Within our discussion, we aim to highlight two critical issues. The first pertains to the significance of trust and other informal mechanisms and their relations with formal arrangements. In this context, we pose the question of whether trust operates as a substitute or a complementary element to traditional formal agreements. The second issue relates to dependencies and power dynamics in relationships between supply chain actors. Here, we inquire about how the distribution of power among partners may influence the form of agreements between them. This latter aspect is particularly crucial concerning relationships where agricultural producers, typically situated in a less advantageous position, constitute one of the parties involved.

5.2 Adapting to Information Asymmetry via Vertical Coordination in the Supply Chain

The pivotal role of addressing and mitigating information asymmetries among actors in the market is assumed by the continuum of vertical coordination strategies, defined as "the alignment of direction and control across segments of a production/marketing system" (King, 1992).The factors aligned and controlled within vertical coordination include price, quantity, quality, and other terms of exchange (Sporleder, 1992). Scholars have delineated a continuum of coordination strategies within the agrifood chain, building on Williamson's (1975) conceptualization. The continuum, as illustrated in Figure 5.1, spans from spot markets, specification contracts, and relations-based alliances to equity-based

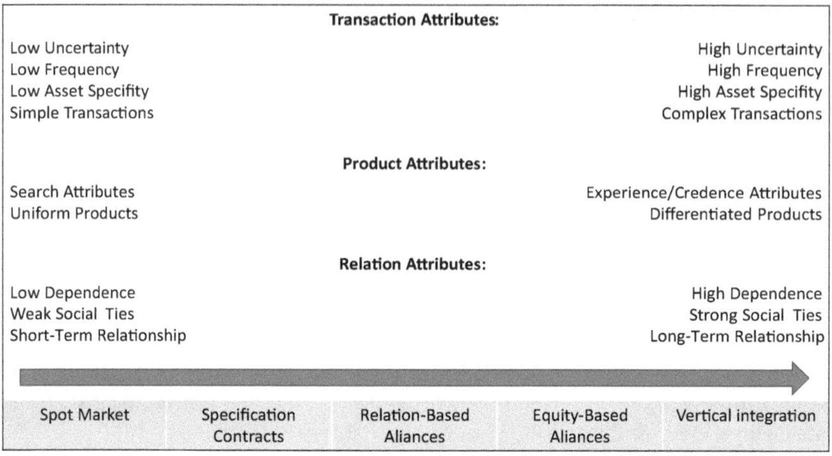

Figure 5.1 Factors influencing the selection of vertical coordination strategies.

Source: Own elaboration.

alliances and complete vertical integration, as articulated by Peterson et al. (2001).

At one end of the spectrum of vertical coordination are spot markets that operate with decentralized transactions where the invisible hand of the market determines prices and standards. This decentralized nature exacerbates information asymmetries, as participants lack knowledge about each other's capabilities and intentions. Participants prioritize independence, engaging in simple transactions with limited information sharing. The product specifications within the spot market are uncomplicated, facilitating easy supply by sellers with minimal information input from buyers. This market structure enables the swift and direct exchange of goods or services at current prices, rendering the identity of the parties involved irrelevant due to the low switching costs associated with finding new partners.

Contracts that fall in the middle of the continuum combine elements of spot market and integrated solutions. Specification contracts involve mutual promises outlining a specific course of action, marked by a scope of obligations within a legally enforceable framework. Relational contracts rely less on legal enforcement and more on reputation and social ties. Within an equity-based contract, one firm holds stock in its partner while maintaining legal independence.

A considerable share of agricultural transactions is conducted through contractual arrangements (Hendrikse, 2007)[1]. Noteworthy examples include

France's poultry industry, where over 80 percent of growers operated under contracts in 1994, and the U.S. pork industry, where marketing contracts facilitated the sale of approximately 72 percent of total hogs in 2001 (Bellemare & Lim, 2018). The typology of contracts in agri-food chain, as well as their specific provisions and terms, exhibits considerable variation across commodities and even among producers involved in the production of the same commodity (Rehber, 2018). In broad terms, there are three principal categories of contracts: market-specific contracts, production-management contracts, and resource-providing contracts.

Market-specific production contracts are formal arrangements established between a buyer and a seller situated at distinct points along the value chain. In practical terms, this could involve a farmer committing to supplying a predetermined quantity of animals to a meatpacker at an agreed-upon future date. These contracts are distinguished by their predetermined delivery schedules, offering the crucial benefit of ensuring a consistent and uniform supply for buyers. This predictability not only streamlines operations but also contributes to cost reduction in processing. Moreover, market-specific contracts may entail premium payments to farmers that surpass prevailing spot-market prices. Importantly, these contracts allow farmers to maintain control over their production practices.

Production-management contracts, on the other hand, introduce a more extensive transference of control and risk across various stages of the value chain. Such contracts commonly materialize when the actions of one party significantly impact an attribute deemed valuable to the other. Consequently, buyers gain additional control over decision-making aspects that were traditionally the prerogative of sellers. For instance, these contracts may encompass the timing of planting schedules or the choice of seed varieties, input usage, etc.

Resource-providing contracts represent a variant of production-management contracts in which a contractor, positioned at one stage of production, retains ownership of a key input that is subsequently transferred to another stage. For instance, a poultry processor may maintain ownership of chicks as they are raised by a farmer. These contracts are generally adopted when specialized inputs and management practices are indispensable to inculcate specific attributes into the final product. Resource-providing contracts represent the greatest level of control for buyers, who provide a market outlet, supervise production practices, and supply key inputs. In doing so, the buyer usually assumes a greater proportion of the risk and may retain ownership of the product, with the farmer, in effect, paid a management fee.

All three contract types mentioned above share a common trait—they are characterized by formal agreements and specific terms and conditions between parties, aligning them with specification contracts. However, certain conditions underpin this classification. In the case of specification contracts, the primary emphasis lies on the explicit, legally binding agreement that delineates obligations, responsibilities, and expectations. The interaction between parties is transactional, with the involved parties entering into agreements to fulfill specific functions or exchanges. In contrast to specification contracts, relation-based alliances rely on enduring, collaborative ties among involved parties. These alliances transcend mere formal contracts, placing emphasis on elements such as trust, shared values, and aligned objectives. While many alliances do incorporate some contractual framework, the presence of a contract is just one element of the partnership. The focal point is not the legal agreement itself, but mutual control, with a fallback reliance on a contract as a minimum standard for the exchange relationship. This mutual control involves extensive communication and collaboration, fostering a relationship where information asymmetries can be more effectively addressed (Peterson et al., 2001).

Equity-based alliances, in turn, introduce a formal organizational structure with shared equity capital between exchange actors. A formal organization with an identity distinct from the exchange actors serves as their joint agent in coordinating transactions. Unlike relation-based alliances, the center of control is established through a formal organizational structure. This allows the implementation of formal policies and procedures for the exchange between parties. An equity commitment in this context provides a clearer delineation of decision rights and responsibilities compared to relation-based alliances.

Relation-based alliances and equity-based alliances are considered to be organizational hybrids. The concept of hybrids is extremely broad and includes various forms of relationships between firms, such as subcontracting, chains, franchises, joint brands, partnerships, cooperatives, and alliances between firms, joint ventures, licensing, and trade associations. Despite the extensive variety, hybrids involve two or more partners pooling strategic decision rights and some property rights while maintaining distinct ownership of key assets (Ménard, 2004). This unique setup necessitates specific mechanisms to coordinate joint actions and allocate payoffs. The complex balance of autonomy and cooperation within hybrids is often based on relational contracts. However, effective governance relies on a combination of devices, with contracts representing a significant, albeit not sole, element in this framework (Ménard, 2013).

Hybrid organizations specific to agribusiness, are exemplified by entities such as agricultural cooperatives, Protected Geographical Inidications (PGI) or Protected Destination of Origin (PDO), alliances/consortia, or club varieties. Farmer cooperatives take center stage as equity-based alliances, often playing a crucial role in specific agri-food sectors. A notable instance of their significance is observed in the dairy industry, where these cooperatives manage a substantial 64% of cow's milk deliveries in the European Union alone (EUROSTAT, 2021). Ménard (2004) identifies three recurring features common to hybrid forms: the bundling of resources, the importance of contractual safeguards, and the maintenance of competitive pressure. These characteristics, as noted by Pietrzak (2022), are evident in cooperatives. For instance, in a traditional dairy processing cooperative, members not only pool their milk resources but also accumulate capital to finance joint endeavors, internalizing transactions that might be exposed to opportunistic risks under market exchange conditions. Contractual safeguards play a pivotal role, particularly when transactions necessitate close coordination of activities or quality control. Despite cooperation, cooperative members continue to function as competitors.

Pietrzak (2022) emphasizes the unique character of cooperatives by underlining their ability to combine the benefits of collective action with the advantages of economic independence. When forming a cooperative, members organize certain activities jointly, like making purchases through a collectively owned enterprise, thereby internalizing market transactions within the cooperative. While collaboration exists in specific areas, members refrain from consolidating all activities into a single large company. Instead, they engage with the broader economic landscape through the market, maintaining their economic independence.

In the context of agricultural cooperatives and their unique organizational hybridity, the significance of social capital becomes particularly evident. As discussed by Hendrikse and Bijman (2002), the dual nature of cooperatives involves the interaction of farms owned by cooperative members and the cooperative business itself. Social capital acts as a cohesive force within these dual layers, fostering trust, cooperation, and effective communication. Members engage in a threefold relationship with the cooperative, encompassing transactions, control, and finance. The strong social ties built through social capital contribute to the cooperative's success by enhancing trust among members, facilitating information sharing, and promoting commitment. This social cohesion is pivotal in aligning the cooperative's interests with those of member farms, ensuring that cooperative members play a proactive role in the decision-making process and contribute to the cooperative's financial stability. Therefore, selecting partners in agricultural cooperatives and other hybrid organizations is one of the key success factors. The identity of partners is significant; it helps in aligning interests, fostering trust, and reducing the likelihood of opportunistic behavior. Equally important are shared planning (expenditures, quantities, prices, quality standards, training) and information exchange – as tools for coordination and the foundation for monitoring the activities of partners.

Agricultural cooperatives share several common traits with other hybrid models in the agri-food sector. A notable example is found in alliances primarily formed to efficiently signal high-quality food products to consumers. One specific strategy involves consortia or associations dedicated to marketing products distinguished by labels such as PGI/PDO or products with private brands, as demonstrated by club varieties. A comprehensive exploration of these hybrid organizations is detailed in the second section of the book.

Finally, at the far end of the continuum, we encounter vertical integration, which represents the highest level of coordination. Vertical integration leads to the consolidation of the two parties in a transaction into one entity, thereby achieving true or complete hierarchy. This consolidation can arise through the merger of the two parties, the acquisition of one party by the other, or one party internally dedicating resources to supplant the market function of the other party. For the first time in the continuum, control is conceptualized as centralized, with no separate parties to the transaction retaining independent decision rights. Similar to an equity-based alliance, the focal point of control is defining the property rights of key stakeholders, but now these rights are consolidated within a single surviving entity rather than in a distinct limited entity. Moreover, vertical integration addresses the need for extensive contractual agreements and negotiations between separate entities, thereby streamlining coordination. With all stages under one umbrella, there may occur a potential reduction in information asymmetry, as the integrated entity has direct access to information at every step. Full vertical integration offers enhanced control over the entire supply chain.

5.3 Factors Affecting the Choice of Vertical Coordination Strategy

Transaction Cost Economics (TCE) acts as a theoretical framework guiding our exploration of the evolving dynamics of closer vertical coordination in the supply chain. TCE acknowledges that economic transactions encounter challenges and come with costs due to factors like information asymmetry, bounded rationality, and opportunism (Eggertsson, 1990; Williamson, 1986). These costs, which we break down into information or sorting costs, negotiation costs, monitoring, and enforcement costs, shape how closely different components of the supply chain work together. In the context of rising transaction costs, we can expect a shift towards enhanced vertical coordination, involving different types of contracts or full vertical integration (Williamson, 1975).

Governance structures within supply chains vary based on many factors (Figure 5.1). First, expanding on the insights shared by Williamson (1979), we recognize that certain characteristics of transactions influence how vertical coordination is organized or the choice of a "governance structure" through their influence on transaction costs. Williamson suggests that the choice between market and hierarchy depends on the levels of uncertainty, frequency, and asset specificity involved in a transaction. High uncertainty, high frequency, and high asset specificity typically favor hierarchical coordination, while low uncertainty, low frequency, and low asset specificity favor market coordination.

At one end of the continuum, where uncertainty is high, Williamson suggests that hierarchical governance structures, such as internalization within a firm, are more efficient. This is because a firm can coordinate activities and adapt to unforeseen changes more effectively than relying on external market mechanisms. High uncertainty implies that the future state of the market or the transaction is unpredictable, making it challenging to establish clear and complete contracts. In such situations, a firm's internal hierarchy can provide better coordination and control. Breaking down uncertainty into its components provides us with a clearer picture. For instance, there is uncertainty for the buyer regarding the quality of the product, leading to sorting costs as they try to determine the true quality (Barzel, 1982). Similarly, both buyers and sellers face uncertainty about the reliability of the supply in terms of timeliness and quantity. Consider a NFC (Not From Concentrate) juice manufacturer needing timely supplies of fresh fruit to meet regular contracts with clients. Price uncertainty is a long-term planning challenge, adding another layer of complexity to the decision-making process. Sellers may face uncertainty in finding a buyer, especially if their product has unique qualities, increasing their information or search costs. As uncertainty levels rise, we anticipate a preference for closer forms of vertical coordination over open market transactions due to the associated increase in information and monitoring costs.

The frequency of transactions is somewhat self-explanatory, with occasional transactions tending to occur in the spot market (Williamson, 1979). The concept of relationship-specific investment, where one party invests in a production process tailored to a specific buyer or seller, presents another layer of consideration. Transactions involving such specific assets make firms vulnerable to opportunistic behavior, increasing the likelihood of opting for more complex contractual solutions present in hybrid models enhanced by trust or vertical integration as the chosen governance structure.

In addition to uncertainty, frequency, and asset specificity, another pertinent transaction characteristic to consider is the complexity of transactions. With increasing complexity, a range of outcomes becomes possible, discouraging spot market transactions. Dealing with complexity might require a more detailed contract with a greater number of contingencies to handle the added dimensions of the transaction. Alternatively, vertical integration becomes a feasible option, and the transaction is managed through within-firm managerial orders. A hybrid organization, such as a strategic alliance, which offers flexibility to navigate complexities, emerges as a further possibility.

These specific features of transactions are shaped by particular characteristics of the products, as argued by Hobbs and Young (2000). Take product perishability (typical for agrifood chains), for instance, which introduces uncertainty for the buyer regarding both the quality and reliability (quantity) of supply. For sellers, perishable products create uncertainty in finding a buyer because they must be quickly moved to the marketplace to prevent deterioration, leaving sellers with no option to store the product while waiting for favorable market conditions. This immediacy also leads to frequent transactions. The perishability of products adds complexity to the transaction as the quality can deteriorate, imposing sorting and information costs on buyers. Additionally, negotiation costs increase as procedures are needed to determine the party responsible for product quality at different stages of the transaction. For example, should the processor take ownership of the product upon collection from the farm, upon delivery to the processing plant, or during storage, and so forth. This situation is common in the production and processing of fresh fruit and vegetables.

As agricultural products become more diverse and are no longer considered uniform basic commodities, buyers face heightened uncertainty about the quality and reliability of supply because sellers are less interchangeable. Price uncertainty grows, mainly because product quality can vary and prices are linked to quality. Often, the parties involved in the transaction have made an asset-specific investment. Sellers put effort into differentiating their product to meet the specific requirements of an individual buyer, while buyers tailor their production or distribution practices to the products of specific sellers. When clear variations in quality exist among products before purchase, there is buyer uncertainty about finding sufficient supplies of the good, although not about the quality received, as this can be determined. However, price uncertainty arises when prices are tied to quality. In such cases, buyers and sellers cannot be sure of the prices they will pay or receive for a commodity in advance because they do not know the quality in advance. This adds complexity to the transaction. If quality differences cannot be detected before purchase (experience or credence attributes – cf. Chapter 4 for definitions and examples), buyers face additional uncertainty about product quality. This is often the case for livestock sold on a "liveweight" basis, where processors cannot accurately determine the eating qualities of the meat solely based on the characteristics of the live animal. In other cases, consumers seek reassurance about the product's production practices, such as animal welfare, environmental impacts, child labor practices, no pesticide residue, etc. These characteristics are often not easily detectable before purchase. Buyer uncertainty about quality and sometimes availability of supplies, price uncertainty, uncertainty for the seller in finding a buyer, asset specificity, and complexity all define transactions.

Expanding on earlier discussions of trust in Chapter 4, the framework depicted in Figure 5.1 introduces attributes of relations between parties that shape transactions, including dependency and time horizon. The degree of dependency among partners is a critical factor because it introduces the potential for mutual control, thereby influencing the ability to alter payoffs. For instance, a specification contract enables the definition of fundamental trade terms, encompassing both quantitative and qualitative information disclosure. This facilitates improved planning of physical flows and ensures stable quality. When supported by a robust institutional environment with proper contract laws, efficient courts, and effective law enforcement (cf. context in framework in Chapter 3 – Figure 3.1), such a governance structure can serve as a viable solution to numerous challenges in the agro-food chain arising from information asymmetry. Additionally, it can provide a foundational platform for the subsequent evolution of governance modes, potentially transitioning into longer-term engagements with higher commitments, as observed in equity-based contracts. Consequently, the scope of changes in payoffs becomes even more extensive, reflecting the heightened stakes of the involved parties and an increased threat of relationship termination.

5.4 Formal versus Informal Governance in Supply Chains

The question of determining the optimal approach for governing inter-organizational relations has captivated the attention of many scholars. Initially, the question was posed in terms of depending on formal approaches like contracts as opposed to relying on informal methods such as trust (for instance, Deakin & Wilkinson, 1998; Poppo & Zenger, 2002; Ring & Van de Ven, 1992; Sitkin & Roth, 1993).

Economists often work with the assumption that the contracts they describe will take on a formal, written structure. However, formal contracts come with certain limitations that warrant consideration (Hennart, 2008). To begin with, they rely on external enforcement, introducing uncertainty for the parties involved regarding their ability to demonstrate a breach and obtain the expected compensation. This uncertainty arises because the legal system's intervention is necessary for enforcement. Therefore, the effectiveness of formal safeguards is tied to the reliability of the court system (cf. Figure 3.1). In the presence of a robust judicial framework, when the parties involved are identifiable, there might emerge an incentive to adhere to the contractual clauses. North (1990) extensively explores enforcement mechanisms in this context.

Additionally, formal contracts require that all potential contingencies and necessary adaptations be predetermined before they actually occur. This becomes challenging when dealing with high levels of non-indexable uncertainty and longer contract durations. Simply resorting to incomplete or shorter contracts is not a viable solution, as it exposes parties to the risk of opportunistic behavior from their partners, as emphasized by Williamson (1975). Lastly, the more constraints formal contracts impose on behavior, the more they tend to diminish incentives for parties to maximize their output, potentially encouraging slacking.

Under such conditions, formal contracts offer limited assistance, often leaving informal devices such as trust and reputation as the primary means of effectively conducting exchanges. Trust and reputation form the bedrock of self-enforcing mechanisms (cf. Chapter 4), as shown by Klein (1992). The relationships rely on trust in the other party's commitment to fulfilling the explicit clauses of the contract, essentially filling in the gaps of formal contracts and using trust as the foundation for a set of implicit agreements. This interpersonal trust, developed over repeated interactions, becomes a crucial determinant in the success of ongoing relationships. Simultaneously, reputation serves as a tangible manifestation of trustworthiness, amplifying the self-enforcing nature of the contractual relationship. The anticipation of future interactions, often referred to what Axelrod (1984) termed a "shadow of the future", shapes the behaviors of parties involved, influencing their decisions to abide by contractual terms to safeguard not only immediate gains but also the prospect of sustained collaboration. In Klein's conceptualization, the self-enforcing mechanism is predicated on the notion that parties, cognizant of the potential rewards and punishments in the future, are incentivized to comply with the contract without the need for external enforcement.

Bachmann and Zaheer (2008) emphasize that the role of trust does not become significant only when the business relationship has no extension beyond the present moment. They argue that in cases where the risks associated with a single decision are relatively easily quantifiable, it is possible to employ calculative reasoning rather than having to depend on trust. They refer to this type of relationship as "classical contracting". However, many relationships do not fit within the classical contracting framework. Numerous long-term partnerships in supply chains tend to align more with the model of so called relational contracts. These contracts differ from conventional legal agreements in that they are defined by the central role that the ongoing relationship between the parties plays in shaping the contract's terms and ultimate outcomes (Michler & Wu, 2020). The relationship between formal, informal, and relational contracts is depicted in Figure 5.2.

Consider, for example, a longstanding agreement between a family-owned farm and a local grocery store. While their agreement may lack legal clauses, both parties maintain the relationship – the farm consistently supplies fresh produce, and the store, in turn, provides a steady market for the farm's products. When unforeseen challenges like bad weather occur, these parties do not rush to the courtroom. Instead, they rely on their trust and understanding to find mutually agreeable solutions, such as adjusting delivery schedules or prices, reinforcing the power of their longstanding 'handshake' agreement. Similarly, imagine a procurement agent for a supermarket chain and a cooperative of fruit growers. The agent places orders on their standard forms, but intriguingly, the purchaser's and the supplier's terms do not align, and no attempt is made to align them. While legal experts might find this informality surprising, it does not bother these parties – they have been working together for years, and their shared belief is that if any issues were to arise, they could address them amicably.

Relational contracts do not necessarily entail complete informality. Rather, they can encompass a combination of formal, legally enforceable obligations and informal elements or tacit understandings layered upon the formal contract. For example, in certain transactions between processors and farmers, a written contract may outline specific terms such as payments per unit, quality or quantity obligations, and reject standards. However, this written contract

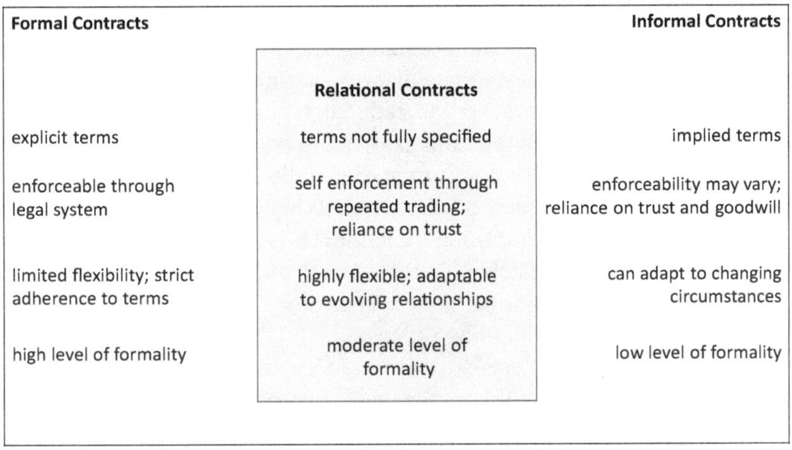

Figure 5.2 The relationship between formal, informal and relational contracts.

Source: Own elaboration.

often functions as a baseline, providing the parties with discretion to make payments beyond the specified amounts to reward exceptional performance or adapt to evolving market conditions. Additionally, the buyer might accept deliveries that fall below the written reject standards, either as a form of recognition for outstanding producers or as a remedy for exemplary past performance. The flexibility inherent in informal agreements allows trading parties to adjust aspects such as the timing of deliveries in response to seasonal factors or market dynamics. The way parties handle orders is very often a blend of formality and informality.

There is an ongoing debate on how formal contracts, designed to mitigate relational risks through their controlling function, interact with trust (Mellewigt et al., 2007). One viewpoint suggests that trust and formal contracts are substitutes, while the other perspective considers them as complements. There are at least two arguments supporting the notion that trust and formal contracts may act as substitutes. Firstly, trust, by diminishing relational risk, economizes on costly contracts. The expectation of reduced opportunistic behavior associated with trust relaxes the need for protective governance mechanisms. Individuals who trust each other are more open, reducing the necessity for stringent control. Consequently, the presence of trust may render detailed contracting unnecessary (Uzzi, 1997). Secondly, detailed contracting might even diminish the level of trust in parties. Some argue that formal contracts emphasize the (subjective) relational risk attributed to a specific partner through the contract (Sitkin, 1995).

In this sense, formal contracts sow seeds for mutual suspicion, leading to a decline in mutual trust.

On the contrary, some authors contend that trust and formal contracts, as control mechanisms, are complementary. Contracts, firstly, reduce the scope and severity of risks in inter-organizational relationships (Poppo & Zenger, 2002). Thus, formal contracts enable partners to commit to small and calculable risks as an initial step in building trust. Secondly, clauses in formal contracts meant to control the partner, such as specifying monitoring procedures and reporting duties, serve an additional function. Only by monitoring and reporting behaviors can the parties establish a record of their (trustworthy or not) conduct (Mellewigt et al., 2007). Formal contracts enhance transparency in the partnership and facilitate mutual learning processes (cf. Chapters 2–4).

A third perspective suggests an alternative way in which trust can affect control concerns and contractual completeness. Instead of a direct effect, trust has a moderating influence on the relationship between control concerns and contractual completeness (Dekker, 2004). As discussed earlier, trust alters the willingness of the trusting party to assume risks, allowing commitment to higher risks through its risk absorption capacities. However, trust does not reverse the conventional relationship between transaction hazards and the need for control. High transaction hazards still entail high risks that are typically addressed through formal contracts.

Highlighting the importance of trust in networks where formal contracts coexist, scholars emphasize that while contracts effectively address the transfer of tangible assets, trust remains crucial, especially in situations involving intangible aspects like brand loyalty (Gnyawali & Madhavan, 2001). This observation resonates with the challenges in the agri-food industry, where quality assurance and information asymmetry often prevail, as illustrated in Section II of this book.

Specification and relational contracts can coexist and function as either complements or substitutes based on contextual factors. This complexity is supported by empirical evidence from various studies. Beckmann and Boger (2004) found that in situations where relationship value is low, parties may resort to formal contracts and seek court mediation. Goodhue (2000) and Leegomonchai and Vukina (2005) provide evidence that, in specific settings, formal contracts serve as fallback options for relational contracts. Ness and Haugland (2005) establish that the presence of formal controls strengthens trust development among involved parties. In regions marked by intense competition, Macchiavello and Morjaria (2015) reveal that formal and relational contracts act as substitutes. Furthermore, Michler and Wu (2020) explore how the quality of third-party enforcement influences the use of formal and relational contracts.

Trust is intricately linked to social capital in interorganizational relations. It constitutes a fundamental element of social capital and plays a pivotal role in shaping its formation in interorganizational contexts. As noted by Putnam (2000), social capital is based on networks, shared norms, values, and understandings facilitating cooperation within or among groups. Gulati and Garguilo (1999), in their study of different firms, discovered interpersonal relationships extending beyond organizational boundaries, laying a solid foundation for increased trust dependence. Social capital plays a crucial role in establishing reputation, as actors' reputations are constructed partly from the identities of their associates. This role becomes particularly salient in scenarios where discerning the quality of potential partners is challenging or largely unknown. In such contexts, lacking direct experience or a track record with one another, the prominence and status of associates and partners serve as proxy measures for assessing quality and the potential for success (Nahapiet 2008). The emphasis on social capital aligns with findings in agri-food chain studies related to producers' organizations, highlighting the role of trust in initiating and succeeding in collective actions among farmers. Notable studies include Fulton (1999), Hansen et al. (2002), Karantininis (2007), Nilsson et al. (2009), Martino (2010), Fałkowski et al. (2017), and Chlebicka et al. (2017).

The theoretical and empirical research also highlights the limits of relational-based governance. Relational contracts, while valuable in imperfect information and costly enforcement settings, incur costs related to relationship building and persistent imperfections in enforcement.

5.5 Power Imbalance in Relations in Agri-food Chains

Understanding the dynamics of power is fundamental to comprehending buyer–supplier relationships in supply chains. In this context, power represents the capacity of one channel member to influence another, compelling them to act differently than they might have otherwise. Emerson's (1962) theory closely associates power with dependence, asserting that A's influence over B grows as B's reliance on A deepens. Dependence, as outlined by Buchanan (1992), pertains to the extent to which a trade partner furnishes critical resources with limited alternative sources.

Switching costs, identified as the latent expenses incurred if a relationship were to terminate (Scheer et al., 2015), play a pivotal role in perpetuating dependency and, consequently, power imbalances. This dependency renders the weaker firm vulnerable to potential opportunism and unethical behavior.

The concept of interdependence asymmetry, introduced by Kumar et al. (1995), underscores the variations in partners' levels of dependence. Symmetrical interdependence arises when parties are equally reliant, whereas asymmetric interdependence empowers the independent partner, creating the potential for exploitation. Power imbalances within buyer–supplier relationships can lead to unproductive partnerships and diminished economic benefits (McDonald, 1999). Such imbalance not only causes dissent but may also lead to low performance by the aggrieved partner, deteriorating the social capital built within the relationship. On the other hand, asymmetric interdependence, where one party holds more power, can lead to sensible standards, unity, and efficiency. From a game theory perspective, the stronger party can achieve socially desirable outcomes. While benefit distribution may not always be fair, integration can still lead to overall gains for all involved, offering a way out of the prisoner's dilemma.

In agri-food systems, especially within emerging and developing economies, agricultural producers frequently find themselves in a precarious position, heavily reliant on larger buyers and input suppliers. This dependence results in substantial switching costs, effectively making farmers "captive", i.e., bound or trapped in a relationship where their options are constrained (Cox et al., 2000). The power dynamics in such relationships are prone to misuse, leading to exploitative practices (Abosag et al., 2016).

In captive contracting, where one party has limited freedom to choose alternative partners, the genuine voluntary nature of trust is compromised. Trust only emerges when individuals have the freedom to make choices. In any transaction, both parties must possess the liberty to engage in voluntary cooperation. Imposing cooperation under unequal circumstances diverges significantly from cooperation rooted in trust. Lorenz (1999) argues that for actions based on trust, and the associated risks of potential misuse, it is crucial that individuals perceive the ability to avoid such interactions. The fundamental concept lies in the capacity to opt out of the relationship; otherwise, individuals might find themselves in a position where they feel compelled to trust without an alternative. When choice is absent, there is no necessity to invoke trust to elucidate behavior. Therefore, trust is intricately tied to the anticipation of a specific future action by another party and is evident in an agent's decision to expose themselves to the risks and uncertainties associated with that action.

As stressed by Gereffi et al. (2005), the dynamics that lead to captive contracting become particularly pronounced when the ability to articulate detailed instructions and the complexity of product specifications both reach a high level, yet supplier capabilities remain low. In these instances, the governance of the value chain tends to assume a captive form. The limited competence of suppliers in handling intricate products and specifications necessitates extensive intervention and control by the lead firm. Consequently, this fosters the development of transactional dependence as lead firms seek to lock in suppliers, excluding others from benefiting from their collaborative efforts. In turn, suppliers face formidable switching costs, further solidifying their 'captive' status.

Captive suppliers often find themselves confined to a narrow range of tasks, primarily engaged in simple activities like agricultural production or sometimes a part of this process, as their limited capabilities restrict their involvement in more complex and value-added aspects of the supply chain. They become reliant on the lead firm for essential complementary activities, including branding, logistics, and process technology upgrading. These captive inter-firm linkages serve the dual purpose. They allow lead firms to maintain control, prevent opportunistic behavior, and simultaneously provide support to subordinate firms, creating a situation where leaving the relationship is not an attractive option for the subordinates.

Larger firms, wielding substantial negotiating power, often dictate contract terms that favor their interests over smaller agricultural producers. This inequity may manifest in pricing structures, payment terms, and distribution agreements, leaving smaller entities at a disadvantage. Power imbalances can also manifest in the limited decision-making autonomy afforded to smaller suppliers. Larger buyers, due to their dominant position, may exert significant control over production practices, quality standards, and even the choice of crops cultivated. This lack of autonomy can hinder the ability of smaller suppliers to innovate, adopt sustainable practices, and respond dynamically to market demands, stifling long-term competitiveness.

The pervasive issue of power imbalances in contracts entered by farmers is further exacerbated by the influence of information asymmetry. Larger buyers and input suppliers, equipped with superior access to market information intelligence, exploit this information advantage to consolidate their negotiating power. This information asymmetry not only deepens the economic disparities within the agri-food chain but also significantly contributes to the creation of contracts that effectively render smaller agricultural producers "captive" to the decisions and terms dictated by more powerful counterparts. The consequences of this information asymmetry are profound, as smaller entities may unwittingly agree to suboptimal conditions, perpetuating the unequal distribution of power and exacerbating the challenges faced by these suppliers.

Power imbalances contribute to a dependency relationship wherein smaller suppliers rely heavily on larger buyers for market access (Di Marcantonio et al., 2020). This reliance can lead to a situation where smaller entities have limited alternatives and are vulnerable to the whims of larger partners. The restricted market access faced by smaller suppliers can stifle diversification, hinder growth, and limit the economic prospects of these entities within the agri-food system (Hobbs & Goddard, 2015). Consequently, power imbalances extend beyond economic implications, affecting the overall sustainability and viability of smaller suppliers within the agri-food chain.

Therefore, the introduction of legal regulations very often becomes necessary to establish a framework that ensures fairness and mitigates exploitation of smaller entities in the agri-food sector. Examples of EU initiatives related to addressing power imbalances in the agri-food chain include the EU Directive on Unfair Trading Practices that aim to combat unfair trading practices, such as late payments, retroactive changes to contracts, and unilateral changes to delivery and payment terms. Under this regulation, the Office of Competition and Consumer Protection in Poland took decisive actions in 2022 against five major retail networks operating domestically, initiating proceedings over suspected exploitation of their contractual advantage against suppliers of fresh fruit and vegetables and dairy products. These retailers amassed approximately 1.3 billion dollars annually from fees imposed on suppliers. Notably, some of these fees accounted for a significant percentage, exceeding even a dozen, of the value of goods purchased from suppliers. Subsequently, in 2023, UOKiK imposed a fine of 22 million dollars on Auchan for imposing fees for transporting goods from the central warehouse to network stores, essentially placing the financial burden of internal logistics of a supermarket chain on food suppliers.

5.6 Conclusions

Transaction cost economics provides useful insights into understanding the alignment of direction and control across the supply chain. This approach explicitly recognizes that economic transactions do not occur in a frictionless vacuum but that buyer and seller incur costs in conducting a transaction. These costs emerge due to information asymmetry, bounded rationality, and opportunism when we depart from the neoclassical assumption of perfect information.

This chapter emphasizes the need for coordinated efforts to address information asymmetry in supply chains. Building upon Williamson's continuum from spot markets, through contracts, to vertical integration, the typical solutions operating in the agri-food chain are clarified. Certain transaction characteristics affect the choice of coordination solution through their influence on transaction costs. They encompass uncertainty, frequency, asset specificity, and complexity, largely determined by the product attributes. The choice of a particular solution is also influenced by factors pertaining to the relationship between the transaction parties, such as the duration of the relationship, dependence of partners, and social ties between them.

The role of trust, both as a standalone mechanism and in conjunction with formal contracts, is recognized as pivotal for building and sustaining relationships in supply chains. Formal solutions are indispensable for establishing clear expectations and rules governing transactions. They provide a structured and enforceable foundation for the parties involved in the agrifood chain. However, they may not comprehensively address every aspect of these transactions. Informal solutions, relying on interpersonal relationships, trust, and reputation, can fill the gaps left by formal mechanisms, offering adaptability in situations where strict adherence to contracts or regulations may be impractical. In practice, the interaction between formal and informal solutions is fluid. However, power imbalances, particularly in captive contracting scenarios, pose significant threats to genuine trust. This chapter calls for a nuanced understanding of power dynamics, emphasizing the importance of choices and voluntary engagement to foster authentic trust and cooperation within agri-food supply chains.

The recognition that economic transactions incur costs due to factors like information asymmetry and opportunism underscores the need for effective coordination mechanisms. Hybrid organizations, such as agricultural cooperatives, stand out as useful solutions operating within the continuum proposed by Williamson, offering benefits of spot markets and vertical integration. These entities serve as a bridge between formal and informal solutions, providing a structured framework through contracts while leveraging interpersonal relationships and trust to address the inherent limitations of purely formal mechanisms. In the upcoming Part II of the book, these theoretical concepts will be vividly illustrated with insightful examples, providing a practical understanding of how hybrid organizations navigate the complexities of information asymmetry and contractual relationships within the dynamic landscape of agri-food supply chains.

Note

1 Given that a significant proportion of contractual agreements within the agrifood chain pertains to agriculture, this section focuses on the contractual arrangements entered into by farmers.

References

Abosag, I., Yen, D. A., & Barnes, B. R. (2016). What is dark about the dark-side of business relationships? *Industrial Marketing Management*, *55*, 5–9.

Axelrod, R. (1984). *The evolution of cooperation*. Basic Books.

Bachmann, R., & Zaheer, A. (2008). Trust in interorganizational relations. In S. Cropper, M. Ebers, C. Huxham, & P. Smith Ring (Eds.), *Handbook of inter-organizational relations* (pp. 566–593). Oxford University Press. DOI: 10.1093/oxfordhb/9780199282944.003.0020

Barzel, Y. (1982). Measurement cost and the organization of markets. *Journal of Law and Economics, 25*(1), 27–48. doi:10.1086/467005

Beckmann, V., & Boger, S. (2004). Courts and contract enforcement in transition agriculture: Theory and evidence from Poland. *Agricultural Economics*, *31*(3), 251–263.

Bellemare, M. F., & Lim, S. (2018). In all shapes and colors: Varieties of contract farming. *Applied Economic Perspectives and Policy*, *40*, 379–401.

Bijman, J., Hanisch, M., & van der Sangen, G. (2014). Shifting control? The changes of internal governance in agricultural cooperatives in the EU. *Annals of Public and Cooperative Economics*, *85*(4), 641–661.

Buchanan, L. (1992). Vertical trade relationships: The role of dependence and symmetry in attaining organizational goals. *Journal of Marketing Research*, *29*(1), 65–75. DOI:10.2307/3172493

Chlebicka, A., Fałkowski, J., & Łopaciuk-Gonczaryk, B. (2017). Horizontal integration between farmers – Governing cooperation through different enforcement mechanisms. In G. Martino, K. Karantininis, S. Pascucci, L. Dries, & J. M. Codron (Eds.), *It's a jungle out there – The strange animals of economic organization in agri-food value chains* (pp. 85–104). Wageningen. DOI:10.3920/978-90-8686-844-5_4

Cox, A., Sanderson, J., & Watson, C. (2000). *Power regimes: Mapping the DNA of business and supply chain relationships*. Earlsgate Press.

Deakin, S., & Wilkinson, F. (1998). Contract law and the economics of inter-organizational trust. In C. Lane & R. Bachmann (Eds.), *Trust within and between organizations: Conceptual issues and empirical applications* (pp. 146–172). Oxford University Press.

Dekker, H. C. (2004). Control of inter-organizational relationships: Evidence on appropriation concerns and coordination requirements. *Accounting, Organizations and Society*, *29*(1), 27–49.

Di Marcantonio, F., Ciaian, P., & Fałkowski, J. (2020). Contracting and farmers' perception of unfair trading practices in the EU dairy sector. *Journal of Agricultural Economics*, *71*(3), 877–903.

Dyer, J. H., & Chu, W. (2003). The role of trustworthiness in reducing transaction costs and improving performance: Empirical evidence from the United States, Japan, and Korea. *Organization Science*, *14*(1), 57–68.

Eggertsson, T. (1990). *Economic behavior and institutions*. Cambridge University Press.

Emerson, R. M. (1962). Power-dependence relations. *American Sociological Review*, *27*(1), 31–41. DOI:10.2307/2089716

EUROSTAT. (2021). Milk and milk product statistics. European Commission. https://ec.europa.eu/eurostat/statistics-explained/index.php?title=Milk_and_milk_product_statistics

Fałkowski, J., Chlebicka, A., Łopaciuk-Gonczaryk, B. (2017). Social relationships and governing collaborative actions in rural areas: Some evidence from agricultural producer groups in Poland. *Journal of Rural Studies*, *49*, 104–116. DOI:10.1016/j.jrurstud.2016.11.010.

Fulton, M. (1999). Cooperatives and member commitment. *The Finnish Journal of Business Economics*, *4*, 418–437.

Gereffi, G., Humphrey, J., & Sturgeon, T. (2005). The governance of global value chains. *Review of International Political Economy*, *12*(1), 78–104 DOI:10.1080/09692290500049805

Gnyawali, D. R., & Madhavan, R. (2001). Cooperative networks and competitive dynamics: A structural embeddedness perspective. *Academy of Management Review*, *26*(3), 431–445. DOI:/10.2307/259186

Goodhue, R. (2000). Broiler production contracts as a multi-agent problem: Common risk, incentives, and heterogeneity. *American Journal of Agricultural Economics*, *82*(3), 606–622.

Gulati, R., & Gargiulo, M. (1999). Where do interorganizational networks come from? *American Journal of Sociology*, *104*(5), 1439–1493.

Hansen, M. H., Morrow, J. L. Jr., & Batista, J. C.(2002). The impact of trust on cooperative member retention, performance and satisfaction: an exploratory study. *International Food and Agribusiness Management Review*, *5*, 41–59.

Hendrikse, G. W. J. (2007). On the co-existence of spot and contract markets: The delivery requirement as contract externality. *European Review of Agricultural Economics*, *34*(2), 257–282. doi:10.1093/erae/jbm019

Hendrikse, G. W. J., & Bijman, J. (2002). On the emergence of new growers' associations: Self-selection versus countervailing power. *European Review of Agricultural Economics, 29*(2), 255–269. doi: 10.1093/erae/29.2.255

Hennart, J.-F. (2008). Transaction costs perspectives on inter-organizational relations. In S. Cropper, Ch. Huxham, M. Ebers, & P. S. Ring (Eds.), *The Oxford handbook of inter-organizational relations* (pp. 339–365). Oxford University Press. DOI:10.1093/oxfordhb/9780199282944.003.0013

Hobbs, J. E., & Goddard, E. W. (2015). Consumers and supply chains: How consumers shape the future of agriculture. Oxford University Press.

Hobbs, J. E., & Young, L. M. (2000). Closer vertical co-ordination in agri-food supply chains: A conceptual framework and some preliminary evidence. *Supply Chain Management: An International Journal*, *5*(3), 131–143. DOI: 10.1108/13598540010338884

Karantininis, K. (2007). The network form of cooperative organisation. In K. Karantininis & J. Nilsson (Eds.), *Vertical markets and cooperative hierarchies* (pp. 19–34). Springer.

King, R. P. (1992). Management and financing of vertical coordination in agriculture: An overview. *American Journal of Agricultural Economics*, *74*(5), 1217–1218.

Klein, B. (1992). The self-enforcing range of contracts. *Economic Inquiry*, *30*(2), 278–293.

Kumar, N., Scheer, L. K., & Steenkamp, J.-B. E. M. (1995). The effects of perceived interdependence on dealer attitudes. *Journal of Marketing Research*, *32*(3), 348–356. doi: 10.2307/3151986

Leegomonchai, P., & Vukina, T. (2005). Dynamic incentives and agent discrimination in broiler production tournaments. *Journal of Economic Management and Strategy*, *14*(4), 849–877.

Lorenz, E. (1999). Trust, contract and economic cooperation. *Cambridge Journal of Economics, 23*(3), 301–315. doi:10.1093/cje/23.3.301

Lui, S. S., & Ngo, H.-Y. (2004). The role of trust and contractual safeguards on cooperation in non-equity alliances. *Journal of Management*, *30*(4), 471–485.

Macchiavello, R., & Morjaria, A. (2015). The value of relationships: Evidence from a supply shock to Kenyan rose exports. *American Economic Review*, *105*(9), 2911–2945.

Martino, G. (2010). Trust, contracting, and adaptation in agri-food hybrid structures. *International Journal of Food System Dynamics*, *4*, 305–317.

McDonald, F. (1999). The importance of power in partnership relationships. *Journal of General Management*, *25*(1), 43–59.

Mellewigt, T., Madhok, A., & Weibel, A. (2007). Trust and formal contracts in interorganizational relationships: Substitutes and complements. *Managerial and Decision Economics*, *28*(8), 833–847. www.jstor.org/stable/25151570 (accessed December 20, 2023).

Ménard, C. (2004). The economics of hybrid organizations. *Journal of Institutional and Theoretical Economics (JITE)*, 160(3), 345–376. https://doi.org/10.1628/0932456041960605

Ménard, C. (2013). Hybrid modes of organization: Alliances, joint ventures, networks, and other strange animals. In R. Gibbons & J. Roberts (Eds.), *The handbook of organizational economics* (pp. 1066–1106). Princeton University Press (Chapter 26). DOI:10.1515/9781400845354-028

Ménard, C., & Valceschini, E. (2005). New institutions for governing the agri-food industry. *European Review of Agricultural Economics*, *32*(3), 421–440.

Michler, J. D., & Wu, S. Y. (2020). Relational contracts in agriculture: Theory and evidence. *Annual Review of Resource Economics*, *12*(1), 111–127. DOI:10.1146/annurev-resource-101719-034514

Nahapiet, J. (2008). The role of social capital in inter-organizational relationships. In S. Cropper (Ed.), *The Oxford handbook of inter-organizational relations* (2nd ed.; online ed., p. 22). Oxford Academic. DOI:10.1093/oxfordhb/9780199282944.003.0022

Ness, J., & Haugland, S. A. (2005). Formal controls and trust development in strategic alliances. *International Journal of Strategic Business Alliances*, *1*(1–2), 70–90.

Nilsson, J., Kihlen, A., & Norell, L. (2009). Are traditional cooperatives an endangered species? About shrinking satisfaction, involvement and trust. *International Food and Agribusiness Management Review*, *12*(4), 101–121.

North, D. C. (1990). *Institutions, institutional change, and economic performance.* Cambridge University Press.

Pascucci, S., Gardebroek, C., & Dries, L. (2012). Some like to join, others to deliver: An econometric analysis of farmers' relationships with agricultural co-operatives. *European Review of Agricultural Economics*, *39*(1), 51–74.

Peterson, H. C., Wysocki, A. F., & Harsh, S. B. (2001). Strategic choice along the vertical coordination continuum. *International Food and Agribusiness Management Review*, *4*(2), 1–18. DOI: 10.22004/ag.econ.34469

Pietrzak, M. (2022). *Fenomen spółdzielni rolników. Pomiędzy rynkiem, hierarchią i klanem* [The Phenomenon of Agricultural Cooperatives: Between Market, Hierarchy, and Clan]. 2nd ed. CeDeWu.

Poppo, L., & Zenger, T. (2002). Do formal contracts and relational governance function as substitutes or complements? *Strategic Management Journal*, 23, 707–725 DOI:10.1002/smj.249

Putnam, R. D. (2000). Bowling alone: The collapse and revival of American community. Simon & Schuster.

Raynaud, E., Sauvee, L., & Valceschini, E. (2009). Aligning branding strategies and governance of vertical transactions in agri-food chains. *Industrial and Corporate Change*, *18*(5), 835–868. DOI:10.1093/icc/dtp026.

Rehber, E. (2018). *Contract farming in practice: An overview*. University of Connecticut, Charles J. Zwick Center for Food and Resource Policy. Research Reports No. 290069. DOI:10.22004/ag.econ.290069

Ring, P. S., & Van de Ven, A. H. (1992). Structuring cooperative relationships between organizations. *Strategic Management Journal*, *13*, 483–498. DOI:10.1002/smj.4250130702

Scheer, L. K., Mio, C. F., & Palmatier, R. W. (2015). Dependence and interdependence in marketing relationships: Meta-analytic insights. *Journal of the Academy of Marketing Science*, *43*, 694–712.

Sitkin, S. (1995). The rhetoric and reality of total quality management. *Academy of Management Review*, *20*(3), 579–604.

Sitkin, S., & Roth, N. L. (1993). Explaining the limited effectiveness of legalistic "remedies" for trust/distrust. *Organization Science*, *4*(3), 367–392.

Sporleder, T. L. (1992). Managerial economics of vertically coordinated agricultural firms. *American Journal of Agricultural Economics*, *74*(5), 1226–1231.

Sztompka, P. (1999). *Trust: A sociological theory*. Cambridge University Press.
Uzzi, B. (1997). Social structure and competition in interfirm networks: The paradox of embeddedness. *Administrative Science Quarterly*, *42*(1), 35–67.
Williamson, O. E. (1975). *Markets and hierarchies*. Free Press.
Williamson, O. E. (1986). *Economic institutions of capitalism: Firms, markets, relational contracting*. Free Press.
Zucker, L. G. (1986). Production of trust: Institutional sources of economic structure, 1840–1920. In B. M. Staw & L. L. Cummings (Eds.), *Research in organizational behavior* (Vol. 8, pp. 53–111). JAI Press.

6 The Use of Information Technology to Mitigate the Problem of Information Asymmetry in Supply Chains

Monika Roman,[1] Konrad Michalski,[1] and Zdeňka Žáková Kroupová[2]

[1]Warsaw University of Life Sciences – SGGW, Poland
[2]Czech University of Life Sciences Prague, Czechia

6.1 Introduction

In the age of the knowledge economy, information, information systems that it co-creates, and related information technology (IT), are particularly vital to business competitiveness. The rapid development of IT, along with communication technology in supply chain management (SCM), is playing a major role in optimizing decisions on cargo flow in the chain, bringing such benefits as improved service levels, organizational competitiveness, reduced inventory, supply chain costs, and electronic risk (e-risk) (Varma & Khan, 2014). Information technology also provides an opportunity to mitigate sources of discontent in supply chains. These include divergent goals, disintegrated performance measures, unsynchronized decision-making, information asymmetry, misaligned incentives, and fragmented business processes (Alkhudary et al., 2022). All of these sources contribute to reducing the total benefit in the potential of supply chain collaboration (Simatupang & Sridharan, 2005). Indeed, information technology can effectively mitigate the discontent associated with information asymmetry in the supply chain.

Many publications address the issue of mitigating supply chain information asymmetry. For example, Li et al. (2012) and Chung et al. (2011) used numerical analysis tools to derive results from models built by researchers. Further, some scholars use econometric analysis tools to reduce information asymmetry in the supply chain (Lodree & Taskin, 2008). Others highlight the role of personal ties in reducing information asymmetry and improving operational efficiency in the supply chain (Chen et al., 2021) or analyze how the ways contracts are made and information is used affect each other in the supply chain (Shen et al., 2019). Nevertheless, few of them address the use of information technology.

DOI: 10.4324/9781032633725-7

Therefore, the chapter aimed to identify information technologies used in mitigating information asymmetry in supply chains. The beginning of the chapter attempts to identify the most commonly used information technologies for mitigating information asymmetry in the supply chain. For this purpose, a synthetic literature review indexed in the Scopus and Web of Science databases containing such solutions was performed. Then, systems dedicated to supply chain management (SCM) and technologies supporting monitoring of flow in supply chains (such as traceability, but also blockchain) were indicated as key in mitigating information asymmetry between supply chain participants. The next part of the chapter focuses on the benefits and limitations of using the information technologies mentioned above. The last section of the chapter discusses the challenges of using information technology in the supply chain. The results of this study can serve as a guide and reference for further parts of the book, which present empirical illustrations of the issues of information asymmetry and trust in the agri-food chains.

6.2 Literature review on systems dedicated to supply chain management and technologies supporting the monitoring of flow in supply chains

To identify the contribution of information technology usage to mitigate the problem of information asymmetry in the supply chain, a systematic review following the PRISMA protocol (Page et al., 2021; Shamseer et al., 2015) was conducted. Searches for studies were performed using the Web of Science and SCOPUS databases. In the identified literature, as the result of the literature review, the most widely described solutions for mitigating supply chain information asymmetry are blockchain, the Internet of Things (IoT), and traceability. These technologies are described later in this chapter.

6.2.1 Supply chain management and its IT components

Supply chain management means the integration of the activities that procure materials and services, transform them into intermediate goods and final products, and finally deliver them to customers through a dedicated system. These activities include purchasing and outsourcing activities, plus many other important functions to maintain the relationship with suppliers and distributors (Heizer & Render, 2004). There are two areas of supply chain management: planning and execution. Orders, advanced scheduling and manufacturing, demand, distribution, and transportation are the main capabilities of supply chain planning. Capabilities of supply chain execution include order commitments, final production, replenishment, distribution management, and reverse distribution (Laudon & Laudon, 2004). Information technologies support all these tasks. It is possible

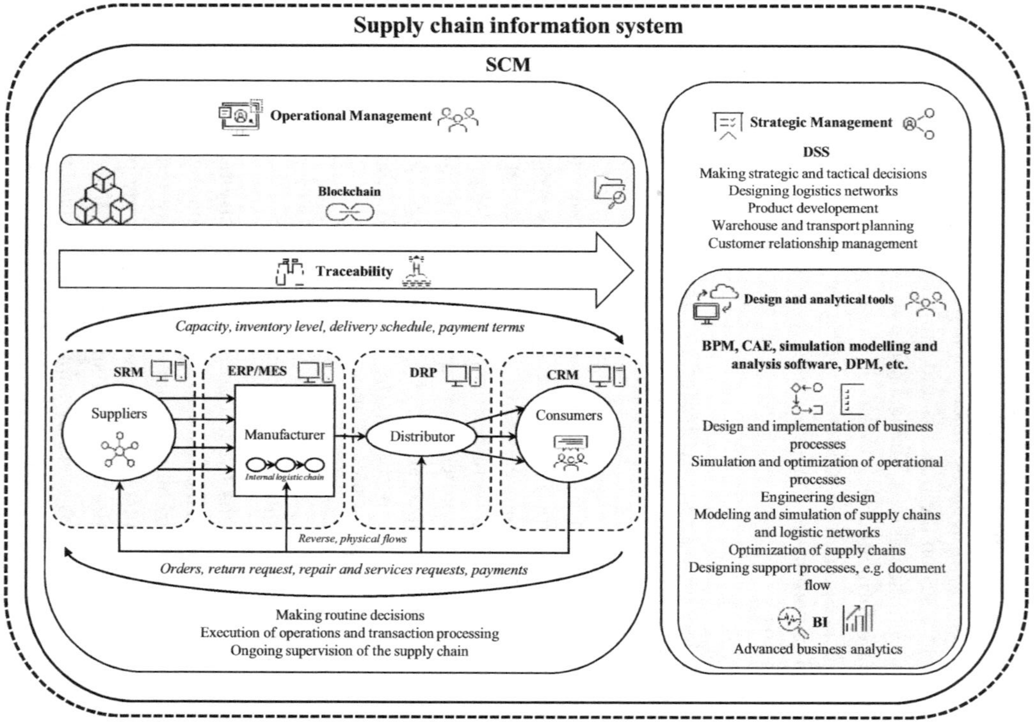

SCM – Supply Chain Management; **SRM** – Supplier Relationship Management; **ERP/MES** – Enterprise Resource Planning or Manufacturing Execution System; **CRM** – Customer Relationship Management; **BPM** – Business Process Management; **BI** – Business Intelligence; **CAE** – Computer-Aided Engineering; **DPM** – Document Process Management; DPM – Distribution Resource Planning.

Figure 6.1 The key classes of IT systems and information technologies in the supply chain information system.

Source: Own work.

to create a map of the key information systems and technologies covering the supply chain in many areas: designing, planning, execution, and optimization (Figure 6.1).

All levels of supply chain management can be supported with IT tools, from strategic planning through operational management to analysis of performance and improvement of operations. Below is a description of the most important groups of IT solutions from the point of view of mitigating the information asymmetry among supply chain participants.

6.2.2 IT tools for design

Supply chain management starts with its design. The flow of information, undisturbed, efficient, transparent, ensuring equal access to information for all participants of the supply chain, and limiting the phenomenon of information asymmetry should be the goal chosen already at the stage of designing the network of connections in the supply chain. Effective support for these activities is provided by a range of dedicated utility applications that are used in different functional and management areas of the supply chain, i.e.:

- BPM (Business Process Management) – to design and implement effective, efficient, flexible business processes,
- CAE (Computer Aided Engineering) – a subcategory of computer-aided tools that includes, i.e:, CAD (for engineering design) and CAM (for manufacturing system design),
- Simulation modelling and analysis software – to simulate and optimize operational processes in the supply chain and logistic network,
- DPM (Document Process Management) – to design key support processes, in the area of document flows.

The above-specified IT tools are only selected ones, and their scope of application and detailed use at the supply chain design stage should result from the analysis of the goals set for those designing the network of connections. Strategic analysis, user business analysis, and analysis of constraints, including bottlenecks, are just some of the design stages. The more details about the expectations and requirements of supply chain participants are taken into account at the stage of planning flows and their modeling and simulation to the expected configuration of relationships, the lower the risk of information asymmetry. Obviously, it is not possible to plan and configure an "ideal" supply chain, but the use of the advanced IT support at the design stage can prevent disruptions in flows and misunderstandings among its participants.

6.2.3 SCM systems

SCM systems are the basic class of IT solutions for the supply chain, which are assumed to cover all operational and information connections between the chain participants. These systems have already been developed in the 21st century on the basis of the earlier ERP (Enterprise Resource Planning) solutions; they are a younger but more developed generation of integrated systems than ERP. In practice, SCM systems complement ERP.

SCM systems are treated as integrated ones, along with ERP and CRM (Customer Relationship Management) (Szmelter, 2019; Szymonik, 2012). SCM systems were developed on the basis of the ERP class and enable support for the management of many company functions. The development of integrated systems enabled the rapid development of the Internet and mobile computers. These systems are focused on inter-organizational cooperation, further globalization, and virtualization (Michalski, 2023a). General characteristics of SCM systems include:

- supply chain planning and execution is a priority implementation goal,
- integration of business processes within the organization and in the supply chain,
- involving suppliers and customers in planning and execution of the supply chain,
- the ability to handle transactions in real time,
- high complexity of supported transactions,
- a high degree of use of the Internet as the basic channel of information flow,
- synchronization of activities with cooperators,
- efficient work in real time,
- an already working ERP system is needed for implementation,
- integration with electronic markets,
- high technical requirements (Mindur & Norek, 2017; Szmelter, 2019).

In practice, SCM systems are a set of many modules or complete domain systems such as SRM (Supplier Relationship Management), MES (Manufacturing Execution System), DRP (Distribution Requirement Planning), CRM, and others. SCM systems also contain many smaller components and applications that primarily enable the synchronization of material flows between partners in the supply chain, which allows all participants to adapt to specific market demand. According to Mindur & Norek (2017), SCM solutions are used in the product design phase, selection of supply sources, forecasting demand for products, and distribution control.

Cooperation in the supply chain is the most difficult area to manage, for example, due to the different positions held by participants in the chain, their power and influence on others, and, finally, different access to information and the phenomenon of asymmetry. SCM systems support cooperation in the field of cooperation thanks to various dedicated applications, i.e., for the following concepts:

- CPFR (Collaborative Planning, Forecasting, and Replenishment) – for manufacturers who want to cooperate with their strategic retail clients in the field of joint planning, forecasting, and replenishment "on the shelf",
- VMI (Vendor Managed Inventory) – management of the recipient's inventories by the supplier,
- SMI (Supplier Managed Inventory) – management of the supplier's inventories by the recipient.

One of the biggest global IT providers offers the following SCM solutions dedicated to:

- supply chain planning (including, among others: SAP Integrated Business Planning for Supply Chain),
- supply chain logistics (including, among others: SAP Extended Warehouse Management),
- manufacturing (including, among others: SAP Digital Manufacturing),
- product life management (including, among others: SAP Enterprise Portfolio and Project Management),
- enterprise resource management (including, among others: SAP Asset Performance Management) (SAP, 2023).

From the perspective of the manufacturer, who is by definition the strongest link in the supply chain, it should not be forgotten that suppliers in particular can disturb the flow of information in the network and, as a result, have a negative impact on the final profits (Shultheis & Summer, 1989). It is obvious that suppliers should be included in the production planning process already at the product design stage. Suppliers can provide valuable knowledge that the manufacturer does not have (Schroeder, 1993). Next, at the production stage, reliable communication with suppliers using EDI (Electronic Data Interchange) standards and the creation of an EDI-based purchasing system on this basis is a key element of the so-called inbound logistics (Zwass, 1992).

Currently, the role of more advanced data exchange standards in the supply chain (e.g., XML language) is growing, but EDI still remains a standard solution. Further electronization of flows, or more broadly, digitization of processes, is possible thanks to the increasing role of the Internet in servicing supply chains. For this reason, eSCM (electronic SCM) is implemented, which enables the handling of even single transactions (so-called instantaneous supply chains). After concluding a transaction, such a chain simply ceases to exist (Stanisławski, 2013; Tundys & Sowa, 2010).

6.2.4 Blockchain

SCM systems also absorb innovative technologies already present in supply chains. This ability requires companies to be willing to reconfigure their business models in a way that places technology at the heart of their operations. One such technology is blockchain. A blockchain network is a set of interconnected computers (nodes) that use a common protocol to verify and store the same information in a peer-to-peer (P2P) network. Information saved in each node is shared with other computers in the network, and new data saved on each device is sent in encrypted form throughout the network for individual verification (Berdik et al. 2021). Blockchain enables a distributed system with real-time communication between supply chain participants, making it possible to reduce many of the disruptions associated with distorted or asymmetric supply chain information (Liu et al., 2019; Notheisen et al., 2017). Thanks to this, the whole system does not require a central computer for authentication, providing a higher level of security (which works very well, e.g., in logistics) and also enabling cooperation between links of the supply chain through the so-called smart contracts (Michalski & Ochnio, 2023).

While blockchain was initially used in the financial sector, today many enterprises have also seen the potential of using this technology. Examples include agriculture, healthcare, logistics, manufacturing, and supply chain management by logistic operators. Blockchain is already used in many management processes (Rossi et al., 2019; Pandl et al., 2020; Jarka et al., 2022). Alkhudary et al. (2022) investigated what supply chain disruptions can be mitigated with blockchain. They believe that blockchain does not mitigate internal supply chain risks (process and control risks). In their view, blockchain is useful with respect to such supply and demand risks as behavioral uncertainty, low information security, fraud and forgery risk, data loss and human error, operational risk, transaction risk, and information asymmetry. They also point to a research gap regarding the blockchain structure. The literature lacks a description of different consensus algorithms, which lead to various models of supply chain management (Alexandridis et al., 2021). In their article, Fu et al. (2020) analyzed the link between a blockchain-based digital system and the agri-food supply chain. Additionally, using the example analyzed, they concluded that the proposed system based on this technology could lead to a groundbreaking transition in agri-food supply chain management in China. They also noted that blockchain technology, the Internet of Things, and big data are transforming the agri-food supply chain into an expansive smart network, poised to overcome information limitations. Singh & Kumar (2022) explored the potential of blockchain technology in the context of Smart Contracts applications and supply chain management in the construction sector. They proposed mitigating information asymmetry by distributing information to enable decentralized consensus building among the various parties involved. Choi et al. (2020) point out that blockchain technology use has positive applications for information disclosure in supply chains involving rental service platforms. Modern solutions such as blockchain are moving towards cloud data processing, but work is still underway to increase the availability of this technology; it may soon become one of the most powerful technologies used in supply chains. Chapter 13 presents a case study of the use of blockchain technology in the agri-food chain.

6.2.4.1 Internet of Things

A popular way to mitigate supply chain information asymmetry is to combine blockchain and IoT technologies (Fu et al., 2020; Liu et al., 2021). One of the areas for applying these technologies is supply chain finance (SCF), which is increasingly becoming a multidisciplinary field at the junction of logistics, supply chain management, and finance (Hofmann & Johnson, 2016). For example, IoT can improve the ability of traditional banks to extract information, and blockchain can facilitate reliable information transformation by enabling banks to obtain knowledge from collateral. Thus, an e-platform combining these two technologies would increase banks' involvement to reduce storage risk (Liu et al., 2021). Network management based on a platform utilizing such a new architecture could also integrate operations and finance in supply chain management to address information asymmetry, costly monitoring, insufficient qualified collateral, and mitigate credit rationing, among other things (Chen et al., 2019). In their research, Agrawal et al. (2021) indicate that one industry that requires the implementation of traceability to address the prevailing issues of information asymmetry and low visibility is the textile and apparel industry. Using the example of organic cotton supply, they point out that implementing a blockchain-based traceability system would give all partners the flexibility and power to track their supply networks and create a transparent and sustainable supply chain.

6.2.5 Traceability

The key technology implemented in supply chains is TCC (Track, Trace, Control). This means traceability of any item in the supply chain, made possible by integrated system solutions such as SCM. Traceability makes possible:

- tracing the product's path from the moment it is manufactured from raw materials until it reaches the point of final consumption,
- registration of parameters identifying these goods and all locations covered by the flow (Szymonik & Nowak, 2018).

The use of TTC systems is applicable wherever, due to the object of the flow, e.g., food products with a limited date of consumption or medicines (e.g., vaccines), tracked for supervisory, regulatory, or safety reasons, it is necessary to track each batch, and even each cargo unit, along its entire route. From the final recipient`s point of view, the key attribute and the goal of implementing information flows based on the traceability systems is consumer security. Defective goods can be quickly and precisely identified, not only in which link of a chain is located but also in which location is stored, thanks to integration with the appropriate domain system (in this case, in WMS – Warehouse Management System) (Michalski, 2021). In relation to goods requiring specific conditions of transport, storage, distribution, and final consumption, the traceability system monitors detailed parameters related to the flow object (temperature, lighting, pressure, etc.).

The most advanced traceability systems are implemented in industry. The flow of information is based on electronic data exchange (EDI) using various information technologies (barcodes, RFID), from devices integrated with automation (code readers, temperature or light sensors, motion detectors, optical identifiers), through local systems integrated with production, to comprehensive systems collecting data (ERP/MES).

Traceability software is integrated, apart from the MES system (basic in a manufacturing environment), also with the WMS (in what location the goods are stored), and with the TMS (Transport Management System), at what stage of the flow is the tracked good. At the transport stage, the most detailed information is provided by telematics solutions that track the flow object (vehicle, container, pallet, etc.). Telematics elements used to track a flow object include, i.e., sensors, detectors, cameras, radars, navigation systems, geographic databases, road databases, weather monitoring devices, traffic monitoring devices, and wireless communication devices. According to the assumptions, full information about the location and condition of the flow object is provided by the SCM system.

Researchers note that traceability systems combined with blockchain technology effectively mitigate information asymmetry. For example, Balzarova (2021) discusses the case of the organic food chain. In her analysis, she points to the importance of these technologies in the effectiveness of ecolabels. Gachukia (2015) highlights that adopting traceability systems offers numerous benefits in agri-food chains. According to him, one of these benefits is the confidence gained by third-party certification agencies in the origin of the traced products, which helps reduce costs and non-transparency. Such a system also helps to promote supply chain integration of suppliers, products, processes, and customers and to transition from loose contractual relationships to formal short-term agreements based on a large information base and lean processes in value chain management.

6.2.6 IT tools for analytics

Nowadays, the analytical base for supply chain managers is an environment using Business Intelligence (BI) tools. The term “BI” was first used in 1958

(IBM Journal), and the current meaning of this concept was given by Howard Dresner from Gartner in 1989, who described BI as an "umbrella" covering many methods, technologies, and applications focused on real business decision support. BI is a user-centric process of collecting, exploring, interpreting, and analyzing data that leads to improved and rationalized decision-making. BI supports managers in making business decisions in order to create organizational value (Surma, 2009).

IT solutions that support the processing of large data sets (Big Data), aimed at supporting business decisions, are referred to as BI systems. These systems are assigned the role of secondary data processing (collected and pre-processed by domain systems such as MES, TMS, WMS, CRM, etc.) and from external sources and are classified as information and analytical solutions.

The key analytical processing layer for the BI system (the system usually contains four layers) includes the following tools dedicated to:

- basic reporting,
- graphic data visualization,
- multidimensional OLAP (On-Line Analytical Processing) analyses,
- advanced data mining and text mining analytics,
- analytical applications, for a given domain (e.g., logistics), for the type of problems to be solved (e.g., the analysis of material losses), for a given industry (e.g., agricultural), complex (e.g., for Balanced Scorecard concept) (Michalski, 2023b).

BI solutions are usually associated with the implementation of ERP systems and complement them. Advanced BI solutions are equipped with many decision support functions, including simulation and forecasting, using AI mechanisms, primarily machine learning (Jurek, 2016). The use of advanced data analytics, supported by AI technologies, to correct and improve the operation of the supply chain may not only have a positive impact on mitigating the consequences of information-related misunderstandings between the chain participants. Supporting the supply chain design stage with the BI-based solutions may eliminate the occurrence of negative phenomena in the operational or post-operational phase of flows.

6.3 Supply chain information system

The goal of creating a comprehensive supply chain information system should be to achieve high intelligence of the entire system. Today we talk about intelligent IT systems, which constitute a key element of information systems. The definition of intelligent systems is very broad; however, from a computational perspective, the intelligence of a system can be understood as its flexibility, adaptability, memory, learning, temporal dynamics, reasoning, and the ability to deal with uncertain and imprecise information (Rudas & Fodor, 2008). It is assumed that intelligent systems are those that support the decision-making process or make such decisions independently.

Artificial intelligence (AI) is the basis for building intelligent systems. For their construction, self-learning and self-adapting systems are used, e.g., neural networks, genetic (evolutionary) algorithms, machine learning, deductive databases, or automatic reasoning. These methods are also mixed to obtain hybrid systems. Approximative modeling of the environment in conditions of uncertainty, incomplete knowledge, inaccurate measurements, and unclear concepts (fuzzy logic) is also applicable. Intelligent systems were originally one of the stages of creating an artificial brain; however, they did not solve this problem and only contained elements imitating the brain, which can be called intelligence (Sakamoto et al., 2019).

AI-based management systems are built on the basis of intelligent systems, which monitor and collect data on an ongoing basis, then analyze it in real time and correct their operation in accordance with the results of the analyses performed (Michalski & Ochnio, 2023). The next step in the use of advanced IT systems is their synchronization and gradual automation of processes occurring between these systems. All concepts with "smart" in their name (e.g., smart factory) operate through highly advanced architecture and connected systems, using automated networks of sensors to transmit, integrate, and process data (Mehdipour, 2016). Thanks to such integration of intelligent systems and analysis of collected data, information about a given situation is immediately provided, or even independent decisions are made by the system (it is so called the golden loop). As a result, a quick response is made to changed or permanent operating conditions.

Finally, it is worth mentioning the concept of the Internet of Things (IoT), i.e., a network enabling mutual communication between various electronic devices. The first devices that meet the definition of IoT were already in operation at the end of the 20th century. In the 1980s, scientists from the American University of Carnegie Mellon developed a drinks machine that connected to the Internet, allowing users to remotely check the availability of drinks (Gokhale et al., 2018). The idea of the IoT is not new, just like BI. But the IoT differs from the standard Internet in that the connection does not concern people but objects, e.g., the sensor is controlled by an application on a smartphone. Therefore, in the IoT there are networked devices that collect information and perform immediate, advanced analyses based on the received data, which is used to solve business problems. Thanks to these analyses, it can be quickly made accurate management decisions in real time. Therefore, the IoT consists of devices with sensors that constantly monitor the state of some parameter (e.g., temperature or pressure) and can send a message to the decision-making mechanism, i.e., issue a command to perform a given task. Then, through a wireless connection, the data is usually sent to the cloud. Such a system requires a user interface, usually in the form of a mobile or web application, which helps in interacting with the entire information system (Michalski & Ochnio, 2023).

The supply chain information system should be complemented by a dedicated management structure that develops draft decisions of tactical and strategic importance. This structure is based on the DSS (Decision Support Systems) class of computer systems. The DSS class are computerized information systems that allow users to analyze, process, and present data in a way that facilitates the decision-making process at a high management level (Bozarth & Handfield, 2007). Examples of decision-making areas of tactical importance for the supply chain will be, e.g., budgeting or operational risk analysis. Strategic decisions will concern, e.g., planning a new product or introducing new technology.

DSS class systems are not the most technologically advanced solutions to support decisions made in the supply chain. More advanced classes of systems are expert systems (ES) and artificial neural networks (ANN). In both cases, knowledge, also obtained through the use of AI mechanisms, is a key resource.

6.4 Discussion

In general, IT systems can help participants in the supply chain in:

- deciding when and what to produce, store, and move,
- rapid communicating orders,
- tracking the status of orders,
- checking inventory, transportation, and warehousing costs,
- tracking shipments,
- planning production based on actual customer demand,
- rapid communicating changes in product design (Laudon & Laudon, 2004).

In the context of reducing the phenomenon of information asymmetry in the supply chain, Mindur and Norek (2017) identify the following benefits of implementing SCM systems:

- possibility of global planning of demand for products,
- possibility of optimizing supply sources,
- simultaneous planning of specialized material needs and determining production capacity,
- ensuring transparency of interdependencies between links in the supply chain,
- creating collective plans related to the supply, storage, production, and transport of manufactured goods,
- defining constraints in the supply network.

To maximize the benefits resulting from covering the supply chain with one IT system, information technologies complementary to this system are necessary. The purpose of implementing new technologies is the desire to change: the organization or nature of work, relationships with partners, business goals. Technology management in the supply chain area should concern activities that determine the application of policy, goals, and responsibilities and their implementation in the organization in terms of planning, resource allocation, organizing, and ensuring results that improve the processes performed (Kabanda, 2019). In modern business, dematerialization, disintermediation, i.e., the elimination of intermediaries, and the design and production of goods on demand are important (Kumar et al., 2022).

In addition, in order to maximize the benefits resulting from the implementation of modern and innovative information systems, it is first necessary to take into account the strength and direction of changes taking place in the environment of modern supply chains. It's not just about technological trends. Obviously, it should also be taken into account that IoT is becoming more and more common and will most likely become a necessity in a few years for companies that want to stay on the market. But Subic et al. (2018) stated that the modern organization paradigm is moving from a hierarchical model to a self-organizing model. For this reason, autonomous operation of management support systems will be a strong trend in the coming years. Due to the enormous pace of creation of new solutions based on AI, new methods and techniques of activities, especially analytical ones, acceleration of calculations, management systems are constantly being evaluated and enriched with new functionalities. The AI-based models are becoming more and more complicated and can learn better on their own using Internet resources. The growing autonomy of IT systems raises concerns about the possibility of a "moment" of losing control over the systems. If a human allows a given intelligent model to be "overtrained", it may start using various data, not always of high quality, unreliable, or even fictitious (fake data). These are real security problems that modern supply chain owners already face.

Adapting organizational structures using IT systems consisting of flexible and fast-learning teams and experts is also important. A related topic is ensuring high-quality digital competencies of information systems users. Regarding analytical workers and decision-makers consuming the results of their work, high computational and managerial intelligence is needed. For the above-mentioned reasons, the issues of high quality, not only of data, but of entire information systems and their computerized parts, become exceptionally important. The rapid development of information technologies means that in order to use the current systems for management, it is necessary to constantly adapt, develop, and improve the technology before it becomes obsolete, as Asaul et al. underline (2019).

Today, the integration of the economy into the global information space is one of the determinants of its competitiveness and efficiency. One of the most important elements of contemporary innovative changes are information systems and technologies that are able to produce large amounts of information and knowledge resources, transmit them remotely, collect, store, and create new intellectual products both within national and international economic systems, including supply chains.

6.5 Conclusions

This chapter aimed to identify information technologies used to mitigate supply chain information asymmetry. This was achieved through an in-depth analysis of the relevant literature. The most common solutions explored in research publications were blockchain technology, the Internet of Things, and traceability systems. However, it must be noted that the number of publications in this field was small. Further, the search for publications was limited to English-language scientific articles only. Limitations concerning the data exchange and utilization of information systems and technology in mitigating information asymmetry in the supply chain belong to data quality and integrity in the supply chain, incompatible systems, problems with trust, security, and relational barriers, high cost of implementation, technological, cultural, or organizational barriers. Considering the growing interest in these technologies in the economy, a rising trend in the number of publications in this field is to be expected. One particularly interesting research area could be the analysis of the limitations and benefits of introducing information technology in the supply chains of various products.

At the strategic level of the supply chain functioning, many potential areas for further research can also be identified: in terms of the security of the information system of supply chains of various products, the resistance of these chains to various disruptions (including information asymmetry), their management models, roles, and their competences in these chains, etc. These are important areas of modern supply chain management, because their environment is called VUCA (volatility, uncertainty, complexity, ambiguity). The final effectiveness of the supply chain and the quality of the products delivered by itself are determined by the success of design work in the area of information supply provided by IT systems. But this is not a sufficient condition. Effective, flexible, and self-learning IT systems and complementary information technologies, such as traceability, are a condition for high-quality functioning of the chain. The information system built around the supply chain must also be open to newer, breakthrough technologies. This is what blockchain is today.

References

Agrawal, T. K., Kumar, V., Pal, R., Wang, L., & Chen, Y. (2021). Blockchain-based framework for supply chain traceability: A case example of textile and clothing industry. *Computers & Industrial Engineering*, *154*, 107130, 1–12. https://doi.org/10.1016/j.cie.2021.107130

Alexandridis, A., Al-Sumaidaee, G., Alkhudary, R., & Zilic, Z. (2021). Making case for using RAFT in healthcare through hyperledger fabric. *2021 IEEE International Conference on Big Data*, 2185–2191. DOI: 10.1109/BigData52589.2021.9671934
Alkhudary, R., Queiroz, M. M., & Fenies, P. (2022). Mitigating the risk of specific supply chain disruptions through blockchain technology. *Supply Chain Forum: An International Journal*, *25*(1), 1–11. https://doi.org/10.1080/16258312.2022.2090273
Asaul, A., Voynarenko, M., Dzhulii, L., Yemchuk, L., Skorobohata, L., & Mykoliuk, O. (2019). The latest information systems in the enterprise management and trends in their development. In *Ninth international conference on advanced computer information technologies (ACIT)* (pp, 409–412). IEEE. DOI: 10.1109/ACITT.2019.8779874.
Balzarova, B. (2021). Blockchain technology – A new era of ecolabelling schemes? *Corporate Governance*, *21*(1), 159–174. https://doi.org/10.1108/CG-08-2020-0328.
Berdik, D., Otoum, S., Schmidt, N., Porter, D., & Jararweh, Y. (2021). A survey on blockchain for information systems management and security. *Information Processing & Management*, *58*(1), 102397. https://doi.org/10.1016/j.ipm.2020.102397
Bozarth, C., & Handfield, R. B. (2007). *Wprowadzenie do zarządzania operacjami i łańcuchem dostaw* [Introduction to operations and supply chain management]. Helion.
Chen, T., Levy, H., Martin, X., & Shalev R. (2021). Buying products from whom you know: Personal connections and information asymmetry in supply chain relationships. *Review of Accounting Studies*, *26*, 1492–1531. https://doi.org/10.1007/s11142-020-09578-1
Chen, Z., Chen, J., Zhang, Z., & Zhi, X. (2019). Does network governance based on banks' e-commerce platform facilitate supply chain financing? *China Agricultural Economic Review*, *11*(4), 688–703. https://doi.org/10.1108/CAER-06-2018-0132
Choi, T., Feng, L., & Li R. (2020). Information disclosure structure in supply chains with rental service platforms in the blockchain technology era. *International Journal of Production Economics*, *221*, 107473. https://doi.org/10.1016/j.ijpe.2019.08.008
Chung, W., Talluri, S., & Narasimhan, R. (2011). Price markdown scheme in a multi-echelon supply chain in a high-tech industry, *European Journal of Operational Research*, *215*(3), 581–589. https://doi.org/10.1016/j.ejor.2011.07.002
Fu, H., Zhao, C., Cheng, Ch., & Ma, H. (2020). Blockchain-based agri-food supply chain management: Case study in China. *International Food and Agribusiness Management Review*, *23*(5). DOI: 10.22434/IFAMR2019.0152
Gachukia, M. K. W. (2015). Moderating effect of traceability on value chain governance of credence goods: A perspective of the New Institutional Economics framework. *Studies in Agricultural Economics*, *117*, 102–110. DOI: 10.22004/ag.econ.208885
Gokhale, P., Bhat, O., & Bhat, S. (2018). Introduction to IOT. *International Advanced Research Journal in Science, Engineering and Technology*, *5*(1), 41–44. DOI: 10.17148/IARJSET.2018.517
Heizer, J., & Render, B. (2004). *Principles of operations management*. Pearson Education.
Hofmann, E. & Johnson, M. (2016). Supply chain finance – Some conceptual thoughts reloaded. *International Journal of Physical Distribution and Logistics Management*, *46*(4), 1–8.
Jarka, S., Biernat-Jarka, A., & Gębska, M. (2022). *The role of trust in modern food production through blockchain and related technologies*. In J. Paliszkiewicz & K. Chen (Eds.), *Trust, organizations and the digital economy. Theory and practice*. Routledge.

Jurek, J. (2016). *Wdrożenia informatycznych systemów zarządzania* [Implementation of IT management systems]. PWN.

Kabanda, G. (2019). *Trends in information technology management.* GRIN Verlag. Retrieved from www.grin.com/document/491408 (accessed November 5, 2023).

Kumar, S., Lim, W. M., Sivarajah, U., & Kaur, J. (2022). Artificial intelligence and blockchain integration in business: Trends from a bibliometric-content analysis. *Information Systems Frontiers*, *25*, 871–896. DOI: 10.1007/s10796-022-10279-0.

Laudon, K. C., & Laudon, J. P. (2004). *Management information systems. Managing the digital firm.* Prentice Hall.

Li, Y., Xu, X., Zhao, X., Yeung, J. H. Y., & Ye, F. (2012). Supply chain coordination with controllable lead time and asymmetric information. *European Journal of Operational Research*, *217*(1), 108–119. https://doi.org/10.1016/j.ejor.2011.09.003

Liu, L., Li, F. & Qi, E. (2019). Research on risk avoidance and coordination of supply chain subject based on blockchain technology. *Sustainability*, *11*(7), 2182. DOI: 10.3390/su11072182.

Liu, L., Zhang, J. Z., He, W. & Li, W. (2021). Mitigating information asymmetry in inventory pledge financing through the Internet of things and blockchain. *Journal of Enterprise Information Management*, *34*(5), 1429–1451. DOI: 10.1108/JEIM-12-2020-0510

Lodree Jr, E. J., & Taskin, S. (2008). An insurance risk management framework for disaster relief and supply chain disruption inventory planning. *Journal of the Operational Research Society*, *59*(5), 674–684. https://doi.org/10.1057/palgrave.jors.2602377

Mehdipour, F., Rahman M. F., & Murakami K. J., (2016). *Intelligent wireless sensor networks (iWSNs) in cyber-physical systems.* In S. Zeadally & N. Jabeur (Eds.), *Cyber-physical system design with sensor networking technologies.* Retrieved from https://digital-library.theiet.org/content/books/10.1049/pbce096e_ch10 (accessed November 13, 2023). DOI: 10.1049/PBCE096E_ch10.

Michalski, K. (2021). *Nowoczesne technologie informatyczne w logistyce* [Modern information technologies in logistics]. In B. Klepacki (Ed.), *Logistyka.* CeDeWu.

Michalski, K. (2023a). *Systemy informatyczne i ich zarządcze wykorzystanie w przedsiębiorstwie* [IT systems and its management use in the enterprise]. In W. Pizło (Ed.), *Cechy funkcjonalne przedsiębiorstw.* CeDeWu.

Michalski, K. (2023b). *Systemy i technologie informatyczne w zarządzaniu organizacją* [Information systems and technologies in organization management]. In K. Michalski & A. Werenowska (Eds.), *Najnowsze trendy, koncepcje i metody w zarządzaniu.* CeDeWu.

Michalski, K., & Ochnio, L. (2023). *Rozwój informatyki we wsparciu decyzyjnym organizacji* [Development of IT in decision-making support of organizations]. In K. Michalski & A. Werenowska (Eds.), *Najnowsze trendy, koncepcje i metody w zarządzaniu.* CeDeWu.

Mindur, M., & Norek, T. (2017). *Informatyka w logistyce* [Informatics in logistics]. In M. Mindur (Ed.), *Logistyka. Nauka-Badania-Rozwój.* ITE-PIB.

Notheisen, B., J. B. Cholewa, & Shanmugam. A. P. (2017). Trading real-world assets on blockchain: An application of trust-free transaction systems in the market for lemons. *Business & Information Systems Engineering*, *59*(6), 425–440. DOI: 10.1007/s12599-017-0499-8.

Page, M., McKenzie, J., Bossuyt, P., Boutron, I., Hoffmann, T., Mulrow, C., Shamseer, L., Tetzlaff, J., Akl, E., Brennan, S., Chou, R., Glanville, J., Grimshaw, J., Hróbjartsson, A., Lalu, M., Li, T., Loder, E., Mayo-Wilson, E., & McDonald, S. (2021). The PRISMA 2020 statement: An updated guideline for reporting systematic reviews. *BMJ*, 372. https://doi.org/10.1136/bmj.n71

Pandl, K. D., Thiebes, S., Schmidt-Kraepelin, M., & Sunyaev, A. (2020). On the convergence of artificial intelligence and distributed ledger technology: A scoping review and future research agenda. *IEEE Access*, *8*, 57075–57095. https://doi.org/10.1109/ACCESS.2020.2981447

Rossi, M., Mueller-Bloch, C., Thatcher, J. B., & Beck, R. (2019). Blockchain research in information systems: Current trends and an inclusive future research agenda. *Journal of the Association for Information Systems*, *20*(9), 1388–1403. https://doi.org/10.17705/1jais.00571

Rudas I. J., & Fodor J. (2008). Intelligent Systems. *International Journal of Computers, Communications & Control*, *3*, 132–138.

Sakamoto, S., Barolli, A., Barolli, L., & Okamoto, S. (2019). Implementation of a Web interface for hybrid intelligent systems: A comparison study of two hybrid intelligent systems. *International Journal of Web Information Systems*, *15*(4), 420–431.

SAP. (2023). www.sap.com/poland/products/scm/solutions.html (accessed November 12, 2023).

Schroeder, R., G. (1993). *Operations management. Decision making in the operations functions*. McGraw-Hill.

Shamseer, L., Moher, D., Clarke, M., Ghersi, D., Liberati, A., Petticrew, M., Shekelle, P., & Stewart, L. (2015). Preferred reporting items for systematic review and meta-analysis protocols (PRISMA-P) 2015: Elaboration and explanation. *BMJ*, *350*, 7647. https://doi.org/10.1136/bmj.g7647

Shen, B. Choi, T.M. & Minner S. (2019). A review on supply chain contracting with information considerations: Information updating and information asymmetry. *International Journal of Production Research*, *57*(15–16), 4898–4936. DOI: 10.1080/00207543.2018.1467062

Shultheis, R. M., & Sumner, M. (1989). *Management information systems. The managers view*. Irwin.

Simatupang, T. M., & Sridharan, R. (2005). Supply chain discontent. *Business Process Management Journal*, *11*(4). 349–369. DOI: 10.1108/14637150510609390

Sing, A. K., & Kumar, V. R. P (2022). Smart contracts and supply chain management using blockchain. *Journal of Engineering Research*, ACMM Special Issue, 1–11. https://doi.org/10.36909/jer.ACMM.16307

Stanisławski, K. (2013). *Infrastruktura informatyczna wspierająca logistykę przedsiębiorstw* [IT infrastructure supporting enterprise logistics]. In R. Kozłowski & A. Sikorski (Eds.), *Nowoczesne rozwiązania w logistyce*. Wolters Kluwer SA.

Subic, A., Xiang, Y., Pai, S., de La Serve, E. (2018). *Blockchain and Industry 4.0: Why blockchain is at the heart of the Fourth Industrial Revolution and Digital Economy*. Capgemini. Retrieved from www.swinburne.edu.au/media/swinburneeduau/research/research-centres/capgemini-swinburne-blackchain-coe/swinburne-capgemini-blockchain-brochure.pdf (accessed November 14, 2023).

Surma, J. (2009). *Business intelligence. Systemy wspomagania decyzji biznesowych* [Business intelligence. Business decisions support systems]. PWN.

Szmelter, A. (2019). *Informatyka w logistyce* [Informatics in logistics]. In S. Wrycza & J. Maślankowski (Eds.), *Informatyka ekonomiczna. Teoria i zastosowania*. PWN.
Szymonik, A. (2012). *Logistyczny system informacyjny przedsiębiorstwa* [Enterprise logistic information system]. In A. Szymonik (Ed.), *Logistyka produkcji. Procesy, systemy, organizacja*. PWN.
Szymonik, A., & Nowak, I. (2018). *Współczesna logistyka* [Contemporary logistics]. *Difin*.
Tundys, B., & Sowa, M. (2010). *Wpływ informatycznego wsparcia procesów logistycznych na konukrencyjność łancucha dostaw* [The impact of IT support for logistics processes on the competitiveness of the supply chain]. In M. Chaberek & A. Jezierski (Eds.), *Informatyczne narzędzia procesów logistycznych*. CeDeWu.
Varma, T. N., & Khan, D. A. (2014). Information technology in supply chain management. *Journal of Supply Chain Management Systems*, *3*(3). https://ssrn.com/abstract=2921128
Zwass, V. (1992). *Management information systems*. Wm. C. Brown Publishers.

PART II

Empirical Illustrations of Information Asymmetry and Trust in Agri-Food Chains

7 Food Labelling as a Way to Address Trust and Information Asymmetry Issues in Premium Cheese Supply Chains

Agata Malak-Rawlikowska,[1]
Edward Majewski,[1] *Filippo Arfini,*[2] *and*
Valentin Bellassen[3]

[1]*Warsaw University of Life Sciences, Poland*
[2]*University of Parma, Italy*
[3]*National Research Institute for Agriculture, Food and Environment – INRAE, France*

7.1 Introduction

Food quality certification is one of the measures to deal with the problems of trust and information asymmetry in food supply chains. The label, which is provided with every product, provides information about ingredients and the designation of product origin, but quality certificates add proof of compliance with the quality standard, which in turn increases the product's credibility and level of trust in the supply chain. It is specifically important for high-value-added products, food based on traditional recipes, and emphasizing regional features, of which credence attributes are difficult to assess even after the purchase.

However, as it was emphasized in Chapter 5 of this book (*Solutions for Overcoming Information Asymmetry and Enhancing Trust in Supply Chains*), supply chains of certified quality products are particularly vulnerable to problems with information asymmetry, especially when they are unproperly managed. The recognition of food quality certificates (geographical indications – GI) among consumers is low (European Commission, 2022; Hartmann et al., 2019), which causes low understanding of their price, especially in foreign markets (Monier-Dilhan et al., 2021). Although European GI achieve a median 29–38% price premium, sufficient to generate a 11% higher margin, some producers do not manage to create these more profitable market niches (Monier-Dilhan et al., 2021). The information asymmetry along the food supply chains may result in worsening product quality, e.g., due to improper storage in downstream segments of the chain, which destroys their reputation. In the area of legitimacy and enforcement, the information asymmetry facilitates indirect and illicit use

DOI: 10.4324/9781032633725-9

of the protected names by counterfeit products, which also reduces trust in these products along the chain.

In this chapter, we analyse the importance of product certification to increase the level of trust and reduce information asymmetry in the food chains on the example of three cheese supply chains registered as the EU Food Quality Schemes (Regulation (EU) No 1151/2012, 2012) – Italian Parmigiano Reggiano (Protected Designation of Origin – PDO), French Comté Cheese (PDO), and Polish Koryciński Swojski Cheese (Protected Geographical Indication – PGI). Each of these chains has a different scale of operation and struggles with various aspects related to trust and information asymmetry. Italian Parmigiano Reggiano is a worldwide known cheese with a broad international chain and over 30% export share in production. Comté Cheese is recognized as ripened cheese representing mountainous heritage in French cuisine with a more modest 10% export share (CIGC, 2022), and Koryciński Swojski Cheese is locally produced short-ripened cheese with a regional chain and brand known in Poland. They are also characterized by a different level of integration and the specificity of solutions that increase trust in these chains. The research purpose was to exploit the general role of information asymmetry and trust in the coordination of physical flows of certified products, mechanisms of securing quality as well as governance structures, and legitimacy and enforcement challenges of these products and methods to overcome them.

Data for the case studies were collected within the EU H2020 Strenth2Food project (Arfini & Bellassen, 2019) in the years 2018–2019 in Poland, Italy, and France by personal interviews with case study representatives (mainly producers and processors of cheese) and were updated by authors based on the desk-research study and available secondary sources.

7.2 Overview of the studied chains

7.2.1 Product and producers

Koryciński Swojski Cheese is a Polish, short-ripening cheese made from raw whole cow's milk with the use of the enzyme rennet and the addition of table salt. Different herbs and spices might be added. The ripening time is quite short – 2 up to 14 days. Its name indicates the region where it is produced. The area covers three communes of the Podlaskie Province, in the district of Suchowolski: Korycin, Suchowola, and Janów. The Koryciński Swojski Cheese is a unique regional product, and it is worth emphasizing its presence in the region's culinary heritage. Koryciński Swojski Cheese was registered as a PGI in June 2012 by a group of 30 producers who created the Koryciński Swojski Cheese Producers Association. In 2024, only nine remained in the system (GIJHARS, 2024). All the producers of Koryciński Swojski Cheese run family farms. Cheese is produced at the farm level.

Comté is a French PDO-labelled cheese produced from raw milk, usually from Montbéliarde or French Simmental breeds, cooked and pressed. It is produced in the Jura Mountains, in the Jura region, and Doubs, a portion of Ain (department of the Auvergne-Rhône-Alpes region). The Comté heritage is based on local processing and ripening know-how and grassland-based production. This PDO cheese is highly recognized by consumers, and its yearly production ranges 72,000 tonnes in 2022 (CIGC, 2022). The Comté chain comprises 2,400 PDO milk producers, 140 cheese manufactures, "fruitières", and 14 ripeners (Comté webpage, accessed 04/04/2024). Only a few processors perform both processing and ripening; the others deliver their preripened cheeses to ripening firms. The cheese is ripened in cellars for about 8 months (minimum 4 up to 24 months).

Parmigiano Reggiano, often referred to as Parmesan, is a prestigious and traditional Italian cheese with the Designation of Origin (DO) label since 1957 and the Protected Designation of Origin (PDO) label since 1992. The production of Parmigiano Reggiano is strictly regulated, and it can only be produced in specific provinces of Italy, which are Parma, Reggio Emilia, Modena, and parts of Bologna and Mantua. The cheese is made from raw cow's milk, partially skimmed through a natural creaming process, typically from two daily milkings. Traditional production methods involve using calf rennet to coagulate the milk, and the cheese is aged usually for 24 months but is controlled and labelled as PDO at the 12th month of maturation. Parmigiano Reggiano is a symbol of Italian culinary excellence, cherished worldwide for its exceptional taste and quality. Its yearly production ranges 152.543 tonnes in 2023. Parmigiano Reggiano chain consists of 2600 PDO milk producers and 319 cheese manufacturers.

7.2.2 Chain structures and governance

As indicated in Chapter 3 of this book (*Information Asymmetry as a Challenge in Chain Governance*), the chain structure and its governance type can be characterized by features, such as the length of the relationship, the degree of formalization of relations, the strength of social ties, or the level of dependency in the chain. Table 7.1 shows the characteristics of the supply chain of individual cheeses and their synthetized governance structures.

Koryciński Swojski cheeses are processed and ripened by farmers themselves at the farm level, representing full integration of the production and processing stage of the value chain. After short-ripening, the cheese is sold using various distribution channels. In short chains, we may observe mainly spot market governance structures or relational (informal) contracts that characterize on-farm sales (on-farm shops), sales at fairs (such as the Cheese Festival in Koryciński Swojski, or the Dominican Fair in Gdańsk), and farmers' markets, which include direct delivery by farmers to consumers and internet sales. The

Table 7.1 Characteristics of the supply chain of selected cheeses

Cheese	*Koryciński Swojski (Poland)*	*Comté Cheese (France)*	*Parmigiano Reggiano (Italy)*
Production of milk	8 farms	2400 breeding farms	2600 breeding farms
Processing into cheese	At the farm level – 8 farms	140 dairies "fruitières" 80% cooperatives, 20% farms with own processing	319 dairies (59% cooperatives, 21%, private dairies, 20% farms with own processing)
Ripening	At the farm level – 8 farms	14 ripeners	
Distribution chain	Short chains: on farm sales, fairs and farmers' markets, direct delivery to consumers, internet sales, Longer chains as: sales to intermediaries (wholesalers), sales to retail,	Direct selling by fruitières, wholesale to mass retail	Short chains: dairy shop, farmers' markets, internet sales Longer chains as: traders/wholesalers or directly to retail
Export share	Small 1–2%	10%	20–30%
Stakeholders	Group of producers, an association that registered PDO	Comité Interprofessionnel de Gestion du Comté	Consortium of Parmigiano Reggiano PDO (CFPR)
Value chain governance	Farm/processing: hierarchical/full integration Distribution: spot-market, relational or less frequently captive governance	Farm/processing: hierarchy or captive Processing/ripening: hierarchy or relational contracts; Retail: spot-market, specification contract or captive.	Farm/processing: hierarchy or captive; Processing/ripening: hierarchy or relational contracts; Wholesale/Retail: spot-market, relational or, specification contract, less frequently captive.

Source: Own elaboration.

latter is an intensively developing distribution channel, which reduces the time producers spend on selling, but it is associated with the quality-related risk of storage conditions during transport via couriers. In the case of sales via longer chains, we observe mostly relational contract governance type when selling to intermediaries (wholesalers) or with retail. Mid- or long-time relations are mainly not formalized. Moreover, there is competition for buyers/traders of cheese and price competition between different producers living in the same region. Less commonly, specific contracts are implemented in the captive relation form, mainly in the case of sales to large retail chains, which represent high purchasing power and require specific adjustments in product labelling or packing. Although the producers are affiliated with an association, they do not jointly sell a certified product. Most producers sell their cheeses individually, under individual farm logos and PGI labels.

Comté cheese chain has three main stages. Cheese is being produced in dairy processing plants (fruitières), which are mainly cooperatives, with farmers being their members. Relations have some typical long-term hierarchical character based on how much milk each farmer delivers as well as on social relations between members, or in the case of private firms collecting milk, rather captive relationships based on long-term contracts. Then, in the second stage, cheese ripening is carried out by 16 companies, partly owned by processors and partly by private firms. Close ties and historical trust underpin the interactions between fruitières and ripeners, which usually have close hierarchical or relational contract character, characterized by complex ties between fruitières and ripeners involving the exchange of tacit knowledge and a high level of investment in specific assets. In terms of social cost, switching ripeners is quite costly for a fruitière, which makes it uncommon. The wholesaling and retailing of cheese is mainly based on specification contracts or captive relations (in the case of large retailers/wholesalers). The bargaining power is quite evenly distributed since there are only 14 ripeners, which may be serious partners for large-scale wholesalers and retail traders. The chain is supported by the official interbranch organization CIGC (Comité Interprofessionnel de Gestion du Comté), created in 1963 and registered by the European Union system in 1996. Spreading accurate information in the GI, managing volume and contracts, allocating revenues, and advertising are all important tasks performed by CIGC. It also does research for marketing and innovation. The CIGC spends over half its money on advertising (Arfini & Bellassen, 2019).

The Parmigiano Reggiano PDO supply chain is complex, with three essential participants: dairy farmers, processors and ripeners, and wholesalers/retailers, all involved in close trust-based cooperation, strongly rooted in the territorial context (Arfini et al., 2019). Universities and other organizations, including the Emilia Romagna regional government and local Chambers of Commerce, assist the chain by encouraging research on it to improve marketing and manufacturing and to support the necessary governmental interventions. There is also a

Consortium CFPR that provides support and governance assistance for members of the cheese chain. The Parmigiano Reggiano production structure is based on a tightly connected system of farms that provide milk to cooperative and/or private dairies located within the geographical borders specified in the code of practice. The relations of farmers with dairies are based on the classical hierarchical/ or hybrid governance type, characteristic for cooperatives or captive relations, when farm–processor relations are based on contracting arrangements. Mutual trust and loyalty to the cooperative processor are core social relations on which the cooperation is based (De Roest, 2000). The cheese ripening until 12 months is still done mainly at the dairy processor level, where we can observe hierarchical (with ripeners) or relational contracts (with traders), due to the strong integration and high level of asset specificity as well as volumes traded. Finally, cheese ripeners, who process the cheese for 24 months or longer, keep spot market relationships and/or specification contract type governance, with relatively less-stable relationships with strong bargaining positions of large-scale traders (mainly for export).

7.3 Results – main challenges of the cheese chains related to information asymmetry and trust

The problem of information asymmetry and distrust in quality certified food products may manifest itself in three areas: quality attributes and specificity of the product, market relevance and recognition of the product, governance structures and management of the products' chain, and legitimacy and enforcement regarding protection against fraud and falsification (Barjolle & Sylvander, 2000). In the following paragraphs, we present the main challenges related to trust and information asymmetry in these areas, on example of selected cheeses.

7.3.1 Quality attributes and specificity of the product

Quality attributes of PDO and PGI-certified cheeses are related not only to easy-to-assess visual features (appearance, color, size) or sensory features (taste, smell) but, above all, to their credence attributes such as the region and method of production, method of obtaining raw materials (milk), food security in the supply chain, and, finally, the originality of the certified product (Table 7.2). These quality features, which are difficult to detect for the consumer, are guaranteed by independent certification bodies and special product marking with the PDI/PGI logo.

The existence of un-experimental/credence features in the case of GI (Geographical Indications) products is associated with the need to build trust in producer-customer relationships. All supply chain actors participate in building this relationship based on trust and quality labels. Many GI products are sold through short supply chains characterized by close relational contact between

Table 7.2 Certified cheese quality attributes from the consumer perspective and location of efforts to shape them in the value chain

Quality Attributes		*Type*	*Stages (Activities) in the Value Chain*			
			Inputs Provision (Milk)	*Cheese Production (Ripening, Processing)*	*Transport/ Trading Intermediaries*	*Wholesaling and Retailing*
Visual	Appearance/Shape	Search	0	+++	0	++
	Colour	Search	0	+++	+	+
	Size	Search	0	+++	+	+++
Other Sensory	Smell	search/experience	0	+++	+++	+++
	Taste	experience	++	+++	+	++
	Consistency	experience	0	+++	+	++
Health	Health security	credence	+	+++	++	++
	Conditions for breeding cows (animal welfare/pasture/other)	credence	+++	++	0	+
	Crop production practice/ fertilization	credence	+++	++	0	+
	Manufacturing practices/ Production process	credence	+++	+++	0	+
Symbolic	Indication of place of origin/ geographical area	credence	++	+++	+++	+++
	Brand/Labels	search	0	creation	0	+
Others	Durability (shelf life)	search/experience	++	+++	+++	+++
	Quality stability	search/experience	+	+++	+++	+++
	Convenience[a]	search	0	++	++	+++
	Complaints, guarantees, etc.	search/ experience	0	+	+	+++

Source: Own elaboration.

[a] Convenience to buy, convenience to transport, convenience to eat, convenience to prepare or to process; 0 denotes marginal or none; +, ++, and +++ denote, respectively, weak, medium and strong influence and responsibility.

the producer and the consumer and a limited number of intermediaries. In this type of chain, transmitting information to the consumer, as well as receiving feedback on the quality attributes of the product, is easier due to the organizational and social proximity of short food supply chains (Malak-Rawlikowska et al., 2019; Vittersø et al., 2019).

Producers processing cheese on a larger scale, like in the case of Parmigiano Reggiano or Comté, are forced to use long supply chains, where the consumer buys a product that has passed through several stages in the supply chain. In this case, the role of chain integration and trust built between individual stages cannot be overestimated. The certificate, which strengthens the added value of these products, is one of the key guarantees of quality that the customer cannot experience. In the case of a longer supply chain like Comté, or Parmigiano cheese, intermediaries play a significant role in transmitting information about the quality certificate to the customer, building consumer trust in the product's credence features. They are also responsible for the product's search/experience attributes in the chain (size, smell, appropriate storage of cheese, and therefore its taste, shelf life, and quality stability); thus, mutual, trust-based, relational contacts are essential in keeping the product quality along the distribution stages.

In the case of a shortly ripened type of cheese, as Koryciński Swojski, the appropriate temperature in the cold chain and packaging are critical factors in maintaining product quality. This is also one of the biggest problems with maintaining its quality because these cheeses cannot be stored in a foil package in wholesalers/stores for too long. If a consumer loses trust by purchasing a spoiled product once, he or she will not come back for such a product again. Therefore, selling this type of product in a long distribution chain is very difficult. Unfortunately, in a long chain, the risk of opportunistic behaviour of intermediaries is high, and if the contracts are weak (not detailed enough) and not based on trust and social relations, this may affect or even destroy the product's reputation. Therefore, farmers often choose to deepen vertical integration in the chain and distribute their perishable product via short food supply chains, which they might control. Thus, it is extremely important to develop a high level of mutual relations (formal or not-formal) between producers and distribution chain actors.

7.3.2 Market relevance

Building trust and complete information about the product in the GI system is based on the recognition of the PDO/PGI label. While certification is intended to alleviate information asymmetry, the challenge lies in discerning specific product features, potentially exacerbating the issue. Despite the assurance of intrinsic, unobservable quality features through labels, products that closely resemble others may lack consumer trust (Filipovic, 2019). This observation aligns with findings described in the Eurobarometer 520 Report (European Commission, 2022), which reports that only 22% of respondents in the EU recognize PGI and 16% PDO labels. In the countries with the highest number of GI products in the EU, like France, Italy, or Spain, the level of recognition reaches only a maximum of 33% for PGI (in Italy and France) and 30% PDO in Italy. It points to a significant information asymmetry in most of the EU GI chains, although this indication is nuanced by the much higher level of recognition of more specific and national labels (Hartmann et al., 2019). For example, Comté and Parmigiano Reggiano have their own labels, which are likely much better recognized in their respective countries than the generic PDO label. Market relevance and product recognition issues are also reiterated in three EU reports: European Commission, 2021, 2021a, 2021b, evaluating the GI functioning in the European Union. It is emphasized that GI products often have a local dimension (both in terms of production and their sales range) and are recognized only regionally. Smaller producer groups do not have the resources to promote and protect their products against unfair practices in the supply chain.

The recognition of the certificate, transmitting the information about the product and its values, and therefore building trust in the product and its search and credence features, is built throughout the entire distribution chain. It starts at the production stage, where it is extremely important to have uniform packaging and a uniform manufacturer's logo. This is not a problem in the case of larger, integrated, and experienced processors or ripeners with a history of cooperation, supplied by dozens or hundreds of producers who are often members of cooperatives, such as in the case of Parmigiano Reggiano or Comté. Here, labelling is used in accordance with the policy imposed by an organization associating producers or a given large-scale processing/ripening entity or trader. For example, The Consortium of Parmigiano Reggiano PDO (CFPR) establishes "common rules for all members of the supply chain, and exercises control over and promotion of the product in the market" (Giacomini et al. 2011/12, p. 139 onwards). It safeguards the designation of origin and oversees the manufacture and marketing of Parmigiano Reggiano PDO cheese. The Consortium additionally promotes cheese consumption in Italy and abroad by developing and supporting any commercial or consumer education initiative aimed at improving the image and reputation of Parmigiano Reggiano PDO, such as participation in and establishment of consortia companies or organizations (Arfini & Bellasen, 2019). A similar organization is acting on behalf of Comté cheese producers – CIGC. In the case of smaller GI products, such as Koryciński Swojski Cheese, the ripening and processing stage of the cheese takes place on individual farms. Since the history of this GI is not long enough, cooperation on packaging standardization is not sufficient. The Koryciński Swojski cheese producers lack a unified logo or certified product label (Kamińska et al., 2021). The only consistent feature on the cheese labels is the PDO symbol, facilitating the identification of the GI certificate. Instead of a shared label, each producer employs a distinct one highlighting the product's specific attributes. However, these labels vary significantly from one another, making it challenging to recognize the producer GI certificate effectively.

Another issue of building trust in the area of market relevance is effective and appropriate promotion along the food chain, transmitting complete information about the product's unique features from producer to final consumer. Results reported for consumers in Poland, similar to those at the European level, indicated that their recognition of GI products is very low, and according to Eurobarometer, it amounts to 16% for PGI and 10% for PDO labels (European Commission, 2022). Research conducted on Koryciński Swojski cheese specifically shown slightly better results; however, the recognition is limited to the regional scale where the product is produced or sold (Malak-Rawlikowska et al., 2023; Borowska, 2017). Nevertheless, the overall low recognition of GI means failed information flow in the value chain, at least in the case of small GIs'. It results in losing the product's added value and forcing producers to sell their unique products outside the certificate without adequate added value. This additionally worsens the product's reputation and trust in the certificate among consumers.

Promotional activities and nationwide campaigns are effective in the case of larger, large-scale, and powerful products protected by producers' organizations, such as the previously mentioned Parmigiano Reggiano or Comté Cheese. These GIs are also efficient in encouraging local stakeholders like Chambers of Commerce, local governments, or universities to promote research on the product and introduce appropriate policy support. On the other hand, small GIs, like Koryciński Swojski cheese, do not have enough resources to create strong organizations to defend the rights along the chain and promote the product to consumers. They often use ineffective, traditional forms of promotion like printed materials or farm displays, and their promotion activities are unprofessional and dispersed, not focused on specific market segments (Kamińska et al., 2021). This is hardly surprising because small producers, usually farmers, do not have efficient promotion skills and cannot afford to employ people to build the reputation of their product. Thus, in the countries with a small number of GI products, like Poland with its 37 GIs (a small number of GI have almost all EU countries except Italy, France, Spain, Portugal, and Greece), umbrella organizations should be established at the national level that will act, support, and promote products on behalf of all producers certified in the food quality system in the country (Malak-Rawlikowska et al., 2023).

7.3.3 Governance structures

One way to deal with information asymmetry in the food supply chain, loss of quality, and unfair practices is close cooperation and vertical integration (European Commission, 2021; Hofmeier et al., 2023; Newman et al., 2014). Many authors point out that cooperation in the field of promotion, distribution, and sales strategies, as well as cost sharing, is particularly important in the case of GI products, which are usually created by small groups of entities (European Commission, 2021a; Belletti, Marescotti, & Brazzini, 2017; Belletti, Marescotti, & Touzard, 2017; Sellers-Rubio & Mas-Ruiz, 2015).

As described in Section 2.2., integration in the supply chain of the case study of cheeses takes different forms at subsequent stages of the chain. Although the scale of production is very different, pure market exchange occurs mainly at retail sales in stores to consumers or through intermediaries or traders for export (in the case of Parmigiano Reggiano or Comté). In all three cases, manufacturers use various forms of deeper integration in the chain. Full integration occurs in the case of milk production and processing on farms producing Koryciński Swojski cheese, but also in numerous smaller producers of Parmigiano Reggiano or Comté cheese, who ripen the cheese on their own farms and sell it directly to consumers. As a rule, however, most farmers supply milk to cooperative processors, with which they are linked through capital shares or long-term contracts specifying the parameters of the transaction and the quality of the supplied milk. Usually they also have quite close social relations with cooperatives, based on mutual trust, which additionally integrates them with each other. In both the cases of Parmiggiano and Comté, close ties and historical trust underpin the interactions between processors and ripeners. Due to these close formal and informal ties, switching ripeners is quite difficult for a processing plant, making it uncommon.

Producing ripened cheese requires specific knowledge and technology, which binds the cooperating entities in a long-lasting relationship. As the research results indicate (Muller et al., 2020), most GIs have the ability to reach a fair distribution of bargaining power. Bargaining power is distributed evenly in the production-processing-ripening part of the chain, both for Parmigiano Reggiano and Comté cheese; however, downstream segments tend to dominate slightly due to their smaller number and cooperation within the branch organizations. However, because the production and sale of Parmigiano and Comté generate appropriate and satisfactory added value and profit margin for all segments of the supply chain (1), the participants of these chains feel a specific sense of community of interest. The long-standing tradition of cooperation has developed protective mechanisms that enable the fight against unfair practices and free-riding problems in the chain. In the case of Comté and Parmigiano Reggiano, a strong industry organization defends the interests of the product and supports chain participants in promoting GI and building consumer trust. Its strength lies in a large scale of cooperation and funds in membership fees. Such organizations can represent manufacturers in court against unfair practices and effectively promote the product on a large scale. On the other hand, the processing and ripening industry is highly concentrated, which makes them able to compete with aggressive price policies of retail chains and non-GI processors penetrating the market.

However, such examples of exemplary cooperation are few among GI products. Most of the smaller groups producing GI products face various problems related to chain governance. Finding the right balance between cooperation and competition is a challenge, particularly at the sales stage in the supply chain. While at the production level, it is easier to find good examples of cooperation between producers because the registration and certification of the product itself require it, the sale and promotion of products on the market create many problems with cooperation (Mancini et al., 2019; Hofmeier et al., 2023). Only a group of producers may request to have the name of an agricultural product or food item registered under the certification regulations. It may be a newly established organization or one that already exists with the sole intent of participating in the GI registration procedure. These organizations typically do not become marketing groups after registering with the European Commission, so they are less likely to effectively promote the product and safeguard the reputation of the registered names by engaging in joint distribution and other collective actions.

Such a negative example may be the cooperation of Koryciński Swojski cheese producers in terms of sales and promotion. Our research shows that producers sell cheese through their own sales channels, often competing with each other for the same trader or retail customer. They do not use common packaging or product labelling and have little trust in each other regarding quality and billing. They also poorly evaluate the group's joint activities, such as promotion, cooperation, information sharing, and leadership. At the same time, they notice it as a problem that has not yet been efficiently solved. The lack of cooperation and joint control of the supply chain creates problems with the distribution of the product in terms of its quality and labelling, destroying the reputation of this product among consumers. Frequent practices of falsification or unfair behaviour of intermediaries are known, but it is difficult to fight them alone. One of the standard practices is selling certified and non-certified products together under the GI logo or selling non-certified products with the suggestion of being certified or with a similar name to the certified product. More than 63% of Koryciński Swojski Cheese producers encountered unlawful use of the registered name, and they observe that these practices are growing. Manufacturers are helpless against such practices; they often do not even report them because their competitors are their neighbours who do not have the certificate. This indicates that the problem lies not only in the area of chain governance but also in the area of legitimacy and enforcement.

7.3.4 Role of legitimacy and enforcement

An efficient control system, which includes monitoring the use of registered names like PDO and PGI, and controlling production process compliance with specifications, is one of the fundamental components guaranteeing the protection of registered names and reliability of unexperimental product features for the consumer. Even though only about 22% of EU consumers recognize the PGI certificate and 16 PDO certificates, as many as 80% of them declare that having a specific label ensuring their quality is an important factor in their decision to buy food products (European Commission, 2022). The structure and execution of the system of controls are the responsibility of the EU Member States, even if the broad guidelines are outlined in EU legislation. Nevertheless, the effectiveness of the counterfeit control system in the downstream supply chain segments is low in the majority of EU countries (European Commission, 2021). Unlawful use of the product logo and name, sales of similar products under the GI sign, and using a similar name to the GI product are only examples of unlawful practices. This is misleading customers, causing them to believe they are purchasing a certified product even though the counterfeit goods lack the PGI or PDO label. Despite this, the product loses its distinctiveness since consumers are misled and certified manufacturers become less credible and trustworthy.

In general, tighter control over the counterfeiting of the logos of the enterprises engaged in the GI schemes can only be achieved by joint, solidary, management of goods and, more importantly, the value chain, with agents sharing obligations and responsibilities. Fighting against counterfeiting cannot be left only for institutions but should be a solidarity shared between the governmental institutions and stakeholders in the food supply chain. This mechanism of self-defending chain, supported by the institutional structures, is working efficiently in the case of Parmigiano Reggiano and Comté but fails in the case of Koryciński Swojski cheese due to a lack of cooperation within the chain.

Governmental control bodies should effectively regulate and execute manufacturers' intellectual property rights, but chain participants should make counterfeiting more challenging. GI producers in the food chain should work together to create marketing plans that will help each producer within the group establish a unique identity and educate consumers about the distinctive features of the product. The government's and producers' combined commitment is required to accomplish these goals.

7.4 Conclusions

Although quality certification aims to alleviate information asymmetry, practice shows that the specific nature of GI products has the potential to exacerbate the problem. The research results on three case studies of cheeses produced under EU quality certificates (Protected Designation of Origin, Protected Geographical Indication), characterized by distinctiveness and credence attributes, indicate that in general GI chains encounter information asymmetry issues, facing low levels of recognition among consumers. They result from dysfunctions of GI products in the areas of quality assurance and market relevance, chain governance and legitimacy, and enforcement. The existence of un-experimental/

credence features of GI products is associated with the need to build trust relationships in producer-customer relationships. Thus, the role of chain integration and relational capital built between individual stages of the food chain cannot be overestimated. Intermediaries play a significant role in transmitting information about the quality attributes to the customer, building consumer trust in the product's credence features. In all three cases described, manufacturers use various forms of deeper integration in the chain. Full integration occurs in the case of milk production and processing on farms producing Koryciński Swojski cheese, but also in numerous smaller producers of Parmigiano Reggiano or Comté cheese. As a rule, however, in larger groups such as Parmigiano or Comte, most farmers supply milk to cooperative processors, with which they are linked through capital shares or long-term contracts. Usually they also have quite close social relations in the chain, based on mutual trust, which additionally integrates them with each other. However, most of the smaller groups producing GI products face various problems related to and chain governance related to distrust and lack of cooperation. Finding the right balance between cooperation and competition is a challenge.

One of the biggest challenges of the GI system is the fight against counterfeiting, which cannot be left only for public institutions but should be solidarity shared between the governmental institutions and stakeholders in the food supply chain. This mechanism of self-defending chain, supported by the institutional structures, is working efficiently in the case of Parmigiano Reggiano and Comté but fails in the case of Koryciński Swojski cheese due to a lack of cooperation within the chain and the small market power of the group. In the countries with a small number of GI products, umbrella organizations should be established at the national level that will act, support, and promote products on behalf of all producers certified in the food quality system in the country.

References

Arfini, F., Antonioli, F., Cozzi, E., Donati, M., Guareschi, M., Mancini, M.C., & Veneziani, M., (2019). Sustainability, innovation and rural development: the case of parmigiano reggiano PDO. *Sustainability* 11 (18). DOI:10.3390/su11184978

Arfini, F., & Bellassen, V. (Eds.), (2019). Sustainability of European Food Quality Schemes: Multi-Performance, Structure, and Governance of PDO, PGI, and Organic Agri-Food Systems. Springer International Publishing, Cham. DOI:10.1007/978-3-030-27508-2

Barjolle D., & Sylvander B., (2000). Some Factors of Success for "Origin Labelled Products" in Agri-Food Supply Chains in Europe: Market, Internal Resources and Institutions. In B. Sylvander; D. Barjolle, & F. Arfini (Eds.). *The Socio- Economics of Origin Labelled Products in Agro-Food Supply Chains: Spatial. Institutional and Coordination Aspect.* vol. 1–2. Proceeding of 67th EAAE Seminar. Paris:INRA. ISBN: 9782738009500

Bellassen V., Drut M., Hilal M., Bodini A., Donati M., de Labarre M., Filipović J., Gauvrit L., Gil J., Hoang V., Malak-Rawlikowska A., Mattas K., Monier-Dilhan S., Muller P., Napasintuwong O., Peerlings J., Poméon T., Tomić Maksan M., Török Á., Veneziani M., Vittersø G., & Arfini F. (2022) The economic, environmental and social performance of European certified food, *Ecological Economics*, vol. 191, 1–11, DOI:10.1016/j.ecolecon.2021.107244

Belletti, G., Marescotti, A., & Brazzini, A. (2017). Old world case study: the role of protected geographical indications to foster rural development dynamics: the case of Sorana Bean PGI. In W. Vancaenegem & J. Cleary (Eds.), *Ius Gentium-Comparative Perspectives on Law and Justice. Importance of place: geographical indications as a tool for local and regional development*, 58, 253–276. DOI: 10.1007/978-3-319-53073-4_10

Belletti, G., Marescotti, A. & Touzard, J. M. (2017). Geographical Indications, Public Goods, and Sustainable Development: The Roles of Actors' Strategies and Public Policies. *World Development* 98, 45–57. DOI:10.1016/j.worlddev.2015.05.004

Borowska, A. (2017) *Uwarunkowania ekonomiczne i pozaekonomiczne konsumpcji żywności wysokiej jakości w Polsce* [Economic and non-economic determinants of high-quality food consumption in Poland], Wydawnictwo SGGW. ISBN 978-83-7583-745-2.

CIGC (2022). Rapport d'activité, Comité Interprofessionnel de Gestion du Comté, 2022 (60 pages).

Comté cheese webpage, www.comte.com/portrait-dun-grand-fromage/, accessed 04/04/2024.

De Roest, K. (2000). T*he production of Parmigiano-Reggiano cheese: the force of an artisanal system in an industrialised world*. Uitgeverij Van Gorcum. Assen.

Drut M., Antonioli F., Böhm M., Brečić R., Dries L., Ferrer-Pérez H., Gauvrit L., Hoàng V., Steinnes K., Lilavanichakul A., Majewski E., Napasintuwong O., Nguyễn A., Mattas K., Ristic B., Schaer B., Tangeland T., Maksan M., Csillag P., Török Á., Tsakiridou E., Veneziani M., Vittersø G., & Bellassen V. (2020). Foodmiles: The Logistics of Food Chains Applied to Food Quality Schemes, *Journal of Agricultural and Food Industrial Organization, Walter de Gruyter GmbH*, 19, (2), 127–143, DOI:10.1515/jafio-2019-0040

European Commission (2010). Impact Assessment on Geographical Indications. Accompanying Document to the Proposal for a Regulation of the European Parliament and of the Council on Agricultural Product Quality Schemes. COM733 final 2010/0353 (COD). Commission staff working paper: 83. www.europarl.europa.eu/registre/docs_autres_institutions/commission_europeenne/sec/2010/1524/COM_SEC(2010)1524_EN.pdf, access 01/02/2024.

European Commission (2020). Communication from the Commission to the European Parliament, the Council, the European Economic and Social Committee and the Committee of the Regions – A Farm to Fork Strategy for a fair, healthy and environmentally-friendly food system (COM/2020/381 final), Brussels, 20.05.2020.

European Commission (2021). Commission Staff Working Document Evaluation of Geographical Indications and Traditional Specialities Guaranteed Protected in the EU SWD/2021/0427 final Brussels, 20.12.2021 commission staff working document evaluation of geographical-PART-2021-846550V1.pdf

European Commission (2022). Europeans, Agriculture and the CAP. Special Eurobarometer 520/Wave EB88.4 – TNS Opinion & Social, June 2022, Europeans, Agriculture and the CAP – czerwiec 2022 – Eurobarometer survey (europa.eu)

European Commission, Directorate-General for Agriculture and Rural Development (2021a). Evaluation support study on geographical indications and traditional specialities guaranteed protected in the EU: final report, Publications Office, 2021, https://data.europa.eu/doi/10.2762/891024

European Commission, Directorate-General for Agriculture and Rural Development (2021b). Study on economic value of EU quality schemes, geographical indications (GIs) and traditional specialities guaranteed (TSGs): final report, Publications Office, 2021, https://data.europa.eu/doi/10.2762/396490

Filipovic, J. (2019). Market-oriented sustainability of sjenica sheep cheese. *Sustainability* 11 (3). doi:10.3390/su11030834.

Giacomini, C., Arfini, F., & de Roest, K. (2011/12). Interprofession and typical products: The case of Parmigiano Reggiano cheese. *Sviluppo Locale XV*, 37–38, 125–150.

GIJHARS (2024). Wykaz producentów ChNP, ChOG, GTS – Wykaz producentów ChNP, ChOG, GTS – Inspekcja Jakości Handlowej Artykułów Rolno-Spożywczych – Portal Gov.pl (www.gov.pl), access 01/02/2024.

Hartmann, M., Yeh, C.H., Amilien, V., Csillag, P., Filipovic, J., Giraud, G., Kuč, V., Menozzi, D., Poschwatta, O., Roos, G., Saïdi, M., Tocco, B., Veneziani, M., & Vreden, T. (2019). Report on quantitative research findings on European consumers' perception and valuation of EU food quality schemes as well as their confidence in such measures.

Hofmeier M., Menapace L., & Rahbauer S. (2023). Adoption of Geographical Indications and origin-related food labels by smes – A systematic literature review, *Cleaner and Circular Bioeconomy*, 4, 100041, ISSN 2772-8013, DOI: 10.1016/j.clcb.2023.100041

Kamińska I., Majewski E., Malak-Rawlikowska A., Obydź D., & Arfini F. (2021). Report evaluating the pilot initiative on improving food quality schemes sales in Poland" Strength2Food, Deliverable n. 9.3. www.strength2food.eu/2021/02/08/report-evaluating-the-pilot-initiative-on-improving-food-quality-schemes-sales-in-poland/.

Malak-Rawlikowska A., Majewski E., & Kamińska I. (2023): Unlocking the potential of the European Union Quality Schemes for Polish regional and traditional food products. Problems of Agricultural Economics. *Institute of Agricultural and Food Economics National Research Institute* (Zagadnienia Ekonomiki Rolnej, Instytut Ekonomiki Rolnictwa i Gospodarki Żywnościowej – PIB), 375(2), 5–124, DOI:10.30858/zer/168871

Malak-Rawlikowska, A., Majewski, E., Wąs, A., Borgen, SO., Csillag, P., Donati, M., Freeman, R., Hoàng, V., Lecoeur, J-L., Mancini, M.C,. Nguyen, A., Saïdi, M., Tocco, B., Török, Á., Veneziani, M., Vittersø, G., & Wavresky, P. (2019) Measuring the Economic, Environmental, and Social Sustainability of Short Food Supply Chains. *Sustainability*. 11(15):4004. DOI:10.3390/su11154004

Mancini, M.C., Menozzi, D., Donati, M., Biasini, B., Veneziani, M., & Arfini, F., (2019). Producers' and Consumers' Perception of the sustainability of short food supply chains: the case of parmigiano reggiano PDO. *Sustainability* 11 (3). DOI: 10.3390/su11030721.

Monier-Dilhan, S., Poméon, T., Böhm, M., Brečić, R., Csillag, P., Donati, M., Ferrer-Pérez, H., Gauvrit, L., Gil, J., Hoàng, V., Lilavanichakul, A., Majewski, E.,

Malak-Rawlikowska, A., Mattas, K., Napasintuwong, O., Nguyễn, A., Nikolaou, K., Papadopoulos, I., Pascucci S., Peerlings, J., Ristic, B., Steinnes, K., Stojanovic Z., Tomić Maksan M., Török Á., Veneziani M., Vittersø G., & Bellassen V. (2021). Do Food Quality Schemes and Net Price Premiums Go Together?, *Journal of Agricultural and Food Industrial Organization* 19, (2), 79–94, DOI:10.1515/jafio-2019-0044

Muller, P., Böhm, M., Csillag, P., Donati, M., Drut, M., Ferrer-Pérez, H., Gauvrit, L., Gil, J., Hoang, V., Malak-Rawlikowska, A., Mattas, K., Napasintuwong, O., Nguyen, A., Papadopoulos, I., Ristic, B., Stojanovic, Z., Török, Á., Tsakiridou, E., Veneziani, M., & Bellassen, V. (2020). Are Certified Supply Chains More Socially Sustainable? A Bargaining Power Analysis, *Journal of Agricultural and Food Industrial Organization,* Walter de Gruyter GmbH, 19, (2), 177–192, DOI:10.1515/jafio-2019-0039

Newman, C.L., Turri, A.M., Howlett, E., & Stokes, A., (2014). Twenty years of country-of-origin food labeling research: a review of the literature and implications for food marketing systems. *J. Macromark.* 34 (4), 505–519. DOI:10.1177/0276146714529306.

Regulation (EU) No 1151/2012 of the European Parliament and of the Council of 21 November 2012 on quality schemes for agricultural products and foodstuffs. Regulation (EU) No 1151/2012 of the European Parliament and of the Council of 21 November 2012 on quality schemes for agricultural products and foodstuffs (europa.eu)

Sellers-Rubio, R., & Mas-Ruiz, F.J., (2015). Economic efficiency of members of protected designations of origin: sharing reputation indicators in the experience goods of wine and cheese. *Rev. Manag. Sci.* 9 (1), 175–196. DOI:10.1007/s11846-014-0124-x.

Vittersø G, Torjusen H, Laitala K, Tocco B, Biasini B, Csillag P, de Labarre M D, Lecoeur J-L, Maj A, Majewski E, Malak-Rawlikowska A, Menozzi D, Török Á & Wavresky P (2019). Short food supply chains and their contributions to sustainability: Participants' views and perceptions from 12 European cases. *Sustainability* 11, 1–33. DOI:10.3390/su11174800.

8 Club Varieties and Geographical Indications as Mechanisms Mitigating Information Asymmetry in the Apples' Supply Chain

Aleksandra Chlebicka,[1] Michał Pietrzak,[1] and Pavel Kotyza[2]

[1]Warsaw University of Life Sciences – SGGW, Poland
[2]Czech University of Life Sciences Prague, Czech Republic

8.1 Introduction

The majority of agri-food products are characterized by the dependence on experience or credence attributes in quality assessment by consumers. Given the inherently unobservable nature of these attributes, the predicament known as the "lemons problem", elucidated in Chapter 3 of this book, may manifest. Spence's seminal signaling theory (1973) offers a theoretical framework, advocating the use of observable signals to convey information pertaining to unobservable characteristics. Signaling serves as a means to mitigate information asymmetry in transactions, where one party possesses proprietary information inaccessible to the other. Shapiro (1983) posits that signaling quality and fostering repeat consumer engagements can mitigate the adverse impacts of the lemons problem.

Nevertheless, the effective implementation of quality signals within the agri-chain presents formidable challenges. First of all, signals must exhibit correlation with the underlying characteristic they aim to represent, ensuring their effectiveness in facilitating trust and reducing uncertainty in economic interactions. Secondly, the credibility of a quality signal, and consequently the perceived quality by consumers, is entwined with earlier stages involving processors, farmers, and, at times, input suppliers. As a result, effective signaling requires collaborative efforts across the entire supply chain, necessitating vertical coordination. Vertical integration may take various forms of cooperation among supply chain actors, often requiring classical and/or relational contracting that frames the business architecture of hybrid organizations (for a more detailed discussion, see Chapter 5 in the first section). The reputation of a quality signal becomes a unique asset, bringing quasi-rent to its owner, such as a price premium for their products. However, sharing a quality signal among independent entities poses challenges in creating an effective incentive system.

DOI: 10.4324/9781032633725-10

This chapter aims to unravel the efficacy of governance structures in addressing information asymmetries concerning the quality of fresh apples. Two governance solutions, namely the Protected Geographical Indication (PGI) alliance and the club variety, are presented, each striving to mitigate information asymmetries linked to quality, albeit through divergent quality signals and vertical coordination solutions. We discuss two cases: Jabłka Grójeckie (JG) as an illustration of the PGI and Pink Lady (PL) as a representative of the club variety. Despite the global implementation of these two models, the absence of club varieties in Poland, a nation recognized as a leader in apple production and export, raises intriguing questions. Utilizing the Polish apple sector as a background, the discussion expands to encompass the contextual conditions under which these governance models operate effectively.

In the initial part of the chapter, we introduce the structure of the apple supply chain and explore the interdependencies among different actors. Moving to the next section, we address the matter of product quality and chain governance, analyzing the specific experience and credence attributes associated with fresh apples. The subsequent part focuses on two particular solutions employed to coordinate transactions in the apple chain, with the aim of effectively communicating quality signals. We showcase two cases exemplifying these solutions – Jabłka Grójeckie PGI and a club variety with the brand Pink Lady. Subsequently, we discuss the outcomes of a comparative analysis within the context of the Polish apple sector. Finally, we offer concluding remarks

8.2 Apples' supply chain based on evidence from Poland

Poland holds a prominent position in the global apple sector, ranking as the largest producer in the European Union (EU) and third globally, trailing China and the USA. Its annual apple production averages 3.3 million tons, representing approximately 4% of the world's total (Kraciński, 2018~~2019~~). Despite this, Poland's share in global apple exports is substantial, reaching 11% by volume, indicating a strong export orientation (cf. Figure 8.1) and integration into the global value chain. However, in terms of export value, Poland's share drops to 4%. In comparison to key competitors in the EU, such as Italy and France, as well as global players like the USA, Chile, and China, Poland's emphasis on price competition is evident. While it holds a robust position in export volume, the lower share in export value highlights potential challenges in offering high-quality apples.

A significant shift occurred with the negative impact of the Russian import embargo imposed in 2014. This embargo had a profound effect on the trade dynamics for apple producers in the EU, particularly in Poland. The unexpected consequence was the loss of Poland's largest export market for apples. In 2013, Poland exported a substantial 600 thousand tons of apples to Russia, representing about half of its total fresh apple exports (Klepacka & Florkowski,

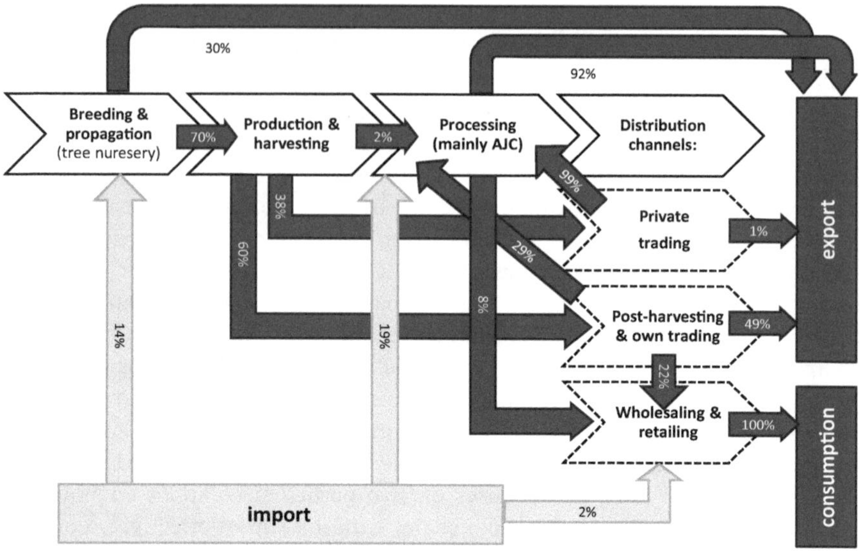

Figure 8.1 The key components and flow of the apple supply chain in Poland.

Note: Arrows emanating from the white boxes represent the total output (100%) at that stage of the supply chain. The amounts shown by arrows entering the export and consumption boxes do not add up to 100%. Similarly, the arrows exiting the import box also do not sum to 100%.

Source: Own elaboration.

2016). Efforts to explore new markets in Europe, Southeast Asia, North Africa, and the Middle East became crucial. Finding alternative markets for Polish apples proved challenging due to the fact that Poland predominantly exported apples of relatively low quality to Russia, particularly varieties that are not highly regarded on more discerning markets.

In 2004, Poland's accession to the European Union marked a transformative milestone, leading to the opening of new exporting markets and crucial financial support for apple growers under the common market organization. The primary focus of this financial aid was on the modernization of orchards and fortifying the organizational structure of the market. This involved initiatives such as establishing producer organizations and investing in essential production and marketing infrastructure, including cool storage, sorting, and packing facilities (cf. Figure 8.1; stage D2). The overarching goal was to strengthen grower organizations, a strategic move considering the tarnished reputation of agricultural cooperatives in post-communist Poland. As a result of these changes, albeit without delving into specific details, producer organizations currently account for approximately 35% of the total produce, primarily in the fresh apple segment. Figure 8.1 illustrates the key components and flow of the apple supply chain in Poland.

However, not all turning points were positive. Another significant shift occurred with the negative impact of the Russian import embargo imposed in 2014. This embargo had a profound effect on the trade dynamics for apple producers in the EU, particularly in Poland. The unexpected consequence was the loss of Poland's largest export market for apples. Efforts to explore new markets in Europe, Southeast Asia, North Africa, and the Middle East became crucial. Finding alternative markets for Polish apples proved challenging due to the fact that Poland predominantly exported apples of relatively low quality to Russia, particularly varieties that are not highly regarded on more discerning markets.

The production is based on an apple-growing area of approximately 177 thousand hectares (Nosecka & Bugała, 2019). Over the last decade, it has witnessed an upward trend in harvests, primarily driven by orchard modernization, resulting in the harvesting of about 3,300 thousand tons (cf. Figure 8.1; stage B). A distinctive feature of the apples' supply chain is its fragmented production, characterized by diverse grower groups based on orchard size and expertise. With approximately 109 thousand apple growers, producers can be segmented into four groups, each facing unique challenges and contributing differently to the overall output. The first group consists of approximately 77 thousand small farms (up to 1 hectare), often serving semi-subsistence purposes. In the second group, nearly 20 thousand producers with orchards ranging from 1 to 5 hectares face challenges due to inadequate infrastructure and lack of expertise, resulting in an average yield of about 16 tons per hectare. The majority of their harvest (approximately 0.8 million tons) is directed to apple juice concentrate (AJC) processing companies, though profitability has diminished over time. Moving to the third group, about 9 thousand growers with holdings of 5 to 10 hectares achieve an average yield of about 22 tons per hectare. They contribute approximately 1.2 million tons to the overall output, primarily sold to AJC processing companies. Some within this group manage to market a portion (around 0.4 million tons) as dessert apples. The fourth group, representing orchards with higher productivity (around 30% of the total growing area), boasts average yields of 24 to 50 tons per hectare. Approximately 3.3 thousand specialized producers in this group, equipped with necessary infrastructure, belong to producer organizations (POs). They contribute an estimated 1.3 million tons to the overall output, with about 1 million tons being high-quality dessert apples. A significant proportion of their produce is exported, with about 30% directed to processing due to natural quality fluctuations.

In terms of post-harvest and trading activities (cf. Figure 8.1; stage D), the agri-food system significantly influences the processes. Producer organizations (POs) engage in pre-sale activities, including sorting, grading, and packing. However, a portion of post-harvesting and own trading is conducted individually by large orchardists and export companies that are not producer organizations (cf. Figure 8.1; stage D2). Large retail chains, particularly discount chains, dominate domestic apple wholesaling and retailing (cf. Figure 8.1; stage D3). They account for about 50% of the retail trade in fresh apples. The wholesaling and retailing stage mainly sources from stage D2 (producers' organizations or major individual growers) and also imports small amounts of premium products.

The sector faces challenges in adapting to changing consumption patterns. Despite a 3% annual growth in global apple consumption, Poland experienced a decline in domestic consumption, linked to a preference for citrus fruits and the perceived lower quality of fresh apples in retail stores.

Over 50% of Poland's total apple output is directed towards processing due to quality concerns and market dynamics. Apple Juice Concentrate (AJC) dominates processed products, constituting about 90% of the processed apples (cf. Figure 8.1; stage C). This phenomenon is particularly pronounced due to the unsatisfactory quality of dessert apples produced in small orchards, coupled with challenges arising from the Russian embargo mentioned earlier in this text. The surplus of dessert apples, characterized by insufficient quality for direct sale and limited opportunities for domestic consumption, creates a favorable scenario for processors. Prices of apples destined for processing are typically three times lower than those intended for the dessert market, occasionally failing to cover even variable costs. Notably, recent years have witnessed extremely high fluctuations in prices received by growers, ranging from 0.04 to 0.13 EUR/kg for industrial apples and 0.22 EUR/kg to 0.66 EUR/kg for dessert apples (Nosecka & Bugała, 2019). Processors source only a small amount directly from growers, while the main input comes from intermediaries represented by private trading (cf. Figure 8.1; stage D1). The need to use intermediaries comes from the strong dispersion of the orchards.

Large retailers, acting as gatekeepers, significantly impact domestic consumer perceptions of apple quality. However, a divergence between consumer expectations and retailer criteria, driven by factors like shelf life and durability, exacerbates information asymmetry. The pursuit of lower purchase prices by retailers may compromise formal quality requirements, influencing the overall quality of apples available to consumers. Moreover, growers, especially non-members of producer organizations (POs) selling to intermediaries, very often face unfair quality assessments in an opaque grading process, making them vulnerable to accepting lower prices for apples destined for processing despite meeting higher quality criteria. On the other hand, catering to distant markets, ensuring prolonged shelf life, transport resilience, and collecting adequate volumes of apples with uniform quality and specific varieties that align with foreign market demands pose considerable challenges.

Efforts to differentiate high-quality apples are currently underway, primarily led by hypermarket chains and discount networks through initiatives such as private labeling, as seen in brands like "Produced for Biedronka[1]" or "The Selection of Auchan[2]". This practice is widespread, with nearly every retail chain (cf. Figure 8.1; stage D3) introducing its own private label for domestically produced fresh fruits, including apples, pears, plums, and strawberries, among others. While the largest producer organizations (cf. Figure 8.1; stage D2) utilize branding based on their company names for packed apples, the impact of these brands is somewhat limited. This limitation is attributed to the predominant export-focused approach of these organizations, which does not prioritize local supermarkets in Poland. Presently, there are four Geographical Indications (GIs) registered for domestically sold apples – Jabłka Grójeckie (JG), Jabłka Łąckie, Jabłka Lubelskie, and Jabłka Wielkopolskie. Further details on JG, the largest regional brand, are outlined later in this chapter. Jabłka Łąckie, Jabłka Lubelskie, and Jabłka Wielkopolskie exist, albeit with marginal market shares. It is noteworthy that Poland has yet to introduce any club varieties, and foreign club varieties are notably absent from supermarket shelves.

8.3 Product quality and the governance of the chain

The coordination of food quality in supply chains affects the choice for contractual arrangements. First, the inherent characteristics of technology and products play a role in determining the nature and intensity of credibility issues. For instance, products like fresh fruit, influenced by climatic uncertainties and perishability constraints, pose challenges for the quality signal owner[3]. These challenges introduce uncertainty and a form of asset specificity (Williamson, 1985), such as temporal specificity (Masten et al., 1991; Williamson, 2004).

Moreover, food quality is multidimensional and consists of different quality attributes (Raynaud et al., 2005). Quality consists of search, experience, and credence attributes (Darby and Karni, 1973). Search attributes are those that consumers can assess before purchasing the product. In the context of fresh apples, visual aspects such as size, color, and general appearance fall into this category. Consumers can visually inspect these attributes at the point of purchase, allowing them to make informed decisions based on observable characteristics. Experience attributes are qualities that consumers can only evaluate during or after consumption. In the case of apples, sensory characteristics like smell, flavor, and texture are considered experience attributes. Consumers can fully appreciate these qualities only when they consume the fruit. Credence attributes are those that consumers cannot directly assess, even after consumption, and must rely on external information sources as a proxy for the quality. In the context of apples, health safety, pro-health features, production methods (e.g. lack of residues), and place of origin are classified as credence attributes. These attributes often necessitate reliance on trust in quality assurance devices, such as the brand, certificates, or other labeling practices.

Significantly, the responsibility for ensuring these quality attributes extends across the entire supply chain, involving not just producers but also intermediaries and retailers. A noteworthy observation, as highlighted by Pietrzak et al.

(2020), is the fluidity in the classification of attributes into search, experience, and credence along the supply chain. For instance, what may be considered a credence attribute demanding trust from consumers might be perceived as a search attribute by retailers or shippers, who can employ tangible methods like product sampling and testing. Drawing from Pietrzak et al. (2020), who analyzed quality attributes important from the point of view of consumers, we present Figure 8.2, delineating fresh apple quality attributes and the corresponding distribution of responsibilities in shaping them throughout the supply chain.

The interdependence of behavior of supply chain actors to achieve the desired food quality and the unobservability of credence attributes lead to information asymmetries and uncertainty about the quality performance of partners. Transaction partners often invest in specific assets to comply with quality standards. Such investments increase dependency and create the risk of hold-up. Transaction cost economics predicts that if quality requirements go up, transaction costs go up (owing to higher uncertainty and asset specificity). Consequently, it leads to a shift from market-type to hierarchy-type contract arrangements (Ménard & Valceschini, 2005).

Through transmitting information on the product and production process, quality indications such as quality standards, certificates, and different types of brands provide credible quality signals, which reduces buyers' search and measurement costs, particularly for credence attributes. This, in turn, minimizes the efforts and costs associated with buyers searching for and evaluating products, especially when it comes to attributes that are challenging to assess directly (Raynaud et al., 2005). Creating an effective quality signal in hybrid organizations (see Chapter 5 for a detailed explanation of hybrid organizations) poses challenges due to the shared nature of the signal among legally independent actors. Collective reputation, wherein independent firms unite under a common brand to enhance product recognition and perceived quality, is a notable strategy in the agricultural sector (Zago, 2015).

Examples like Protected Designations of Origins (PDO) and Protected Geographical Indications (PGIs) illustrate the application of collective reputation. In such scenarios, each producer has the incentive to encourage others to invest in maintaining quality. However, there is a simultaneous risk of producers aiming to minimize their individual efforts while capitalizing on the collective reputation. This individualistic approach, driven by profit maximization, may lead to conflicts among producers sharing the same quality signal. Consequently, the pursuit of personal gains can have adverse effects on the overall effectiveness of the collective reputation strategy within hybrid organizations. Geographical indications establish a nexus between a product's origin and its unique qualities, often referred to as terroir, signifying the influence of agronomic conditions and craftsmanship on flavor and quality (Giovannucci et al., 2009; Teuber et al., 2011). GIs function akin to brands or certification labels, addressing market

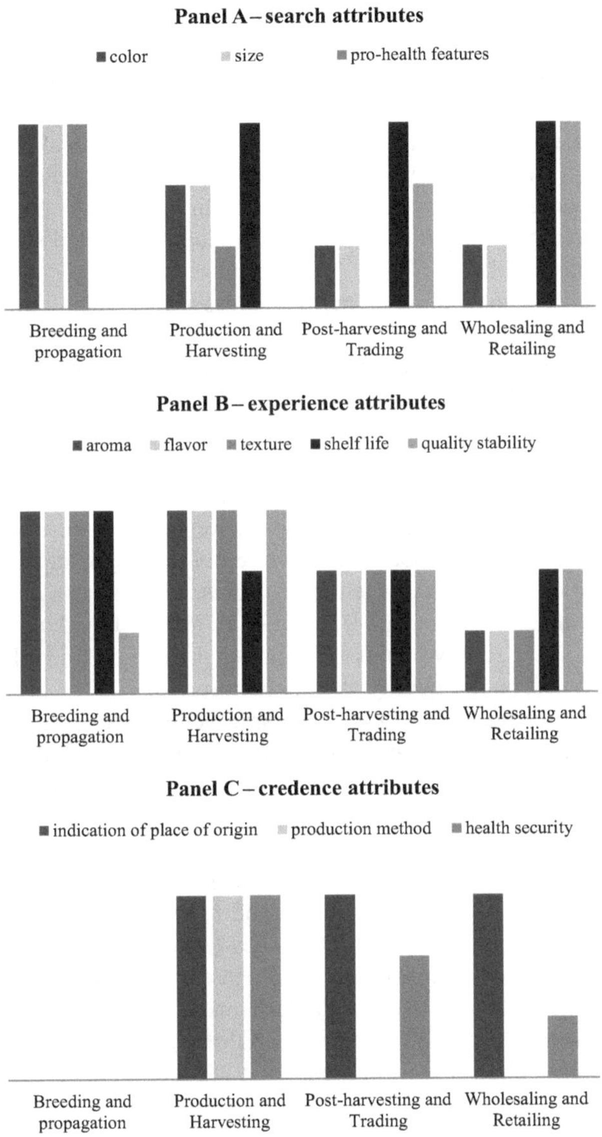

Figure 8.2 Delineating fresh apple quality attributes and the corresponding distribution of responsibilities in shaping them throughout the supply chain.

Note: A lack of a bar denotes marginal or no influence and responsibility; a short bar indicates weak influence and responsibility; a medium bar signifies medium influence and responsibility; a long bar represents strong influence and responsibility. * Suggesting freshness; ** convenience for buying, transporting, eating, preparing or processing.

Source: Own elaboration based on Pietrzak et al. (2020, p. 12).

failures due to information asymmetry by providing consumers with verifiable origin information.

Another approach to brand as signaling quality is so-called club varieties. In contrast to the GIs, club apples signify a closed network where owners have exclusive rights over varieties, ensuring control over propagation, production, and marketing (Legun, 2015). This exclusivity allows breeders to recover investments efficiently while catering to evolving consumer preferences through intentional variety design (Di Fonzo et al., 2019). Both approaches highlight the importance of leveraging origin and quality attributes to create distinctive products in a competitive market.

The impact of quality signals on uncertainty and asset specificity, however, remains uncertain. In particular, empirical studies reveal that public and private quality standards influence contract arrangements differently. Public standards are governed and regulated by public authorities, typically at the national or regional level. These authorities set specific criteria and rules that producers must adhere to, for example, in order to use the PGI designation. In contrast, private standards are established by non-governmental entities – companies, industry associations, or private certification bodies. Regarding public quality standards, Raynaud et al. (2005) observed that the region-of-origin standard in three European agri-food supply chains led to an increase in market-type contract arrangements. Similarly, Fernandez-Barcala et al. (2017) found a similar outcome in European meat supply chains adhering to the same standard. The authors demonstrated that public quality standards introduce additional layers of control in the supply chain, allowing contract arrangements to specialize in quality control through monitoring and motivating compliance. Additionally, adherence to public standards falls under the responsibility of individual actors, eliminating the requirement for additional coordination in more hierarchical contract arrangements (Trienekens and Wognum, 2013).

Private quality standards decrease uncertainty but simultaneously increase asset specificity, leading to bilateral dependency and higher transaction costs. Consequently, as found by Raynaud et al. (2005), they lead to more hierarchical arrangements when associated with private brand names. This aligns with the findings of Ghozzi et al. (2016, 2018) and Banterle and Stranieri (2008), who observed that non-genetically modified organism (GMO) standards in Europe and voluntary traceability standards in Italy resulted in more hierarchical contract arrangements, respectively.

8.4 The case of GIs – Jabłka Grójeckie

8.4.1 Unique attributes of products and quality specification

Jabłka Grójeckie is a regional brand encompassing 27 varieties of apples and their cultivars grown in the area of Grójec[4], located in central Poland.

The most important varieties marked as Jabłka Grójeckie include 6 varieties, namely: Gala, Gloster, Jonagold, Golden Delicious, Red Jonaprince, and Ligol, which account for 70% of the offer. In addition to popular varieties, the offer also includes so-called "old varieties", grown in Poland on a small scale, as well as newly introduced varieties, such as Chopin. The brand was introduced to the market with the registration as a Protected Geographical Indication (PGI) granted by the European Union in 2011. The Grójec region is the largest apple production region in Poland and even in the European Union – it produces 20% of apples produced in the European Union and nearly 40% of domestic production. The region can also boast the longest, 500-year-old tradition of orchard cultivation in Poland. The unique microclimate of Grójec, characterized by large temperature variations between day and night from mid-September to the end of October, fosters the development of apples with distinctive qualities. The region's nighttime temperature drops, coupled with ground frosts, contribute to the apples' intense coloration and superior taste. Apples from this region are characterized by higher acidity than the average for a given variety, on average by 5%.

Jabłka Grójeckie are exclusively premium-class apples (extra and I), meeting detailed requirements regarding color, size, and firmness of the flesh – specific for each variety.[5] Additionally, since 2021, JG has met more stringent requirements regarding pesticide residue levels. Only residues of 5 pesticides from the permitted group may be present in them. The allowable level of each of these substances in JG is a maximum of 50% of the norm established in the generally applicable regulations of the European Union. Jabłka Grójeckie meeting the requirements regarding variety, size, firmness, and coloration but bearing clear signs of frost damage or scarred hail damage covering no more than 20% of the total fruit surface may be directed to processing, contributing to the expansion of the range of products from JG. The Main Inspectorate of Trade Quality of Agricultural and Food Products in Poland oversees the certification process of products with a Protected Geographical Indication (PGI), as well as controls compliance of production with this specification.

The regional brand aims at capitalizing on the consumer belief that a product's origin is pivotal in endowing it with unique qualities valued by consumers. However, disseminating this connection to consumers, even on a national scale, proves to be a prolonged endeavor. Despite the region's status as a major apple production hub, it lacks distinctive attributes that could substantially bolster its recognition, even within Poland. Despite being on the market for a decade, Jabłka Grójeckie initially faced constrained distribution channels.

It should be noted here that Jabłka Grójeckie can potentially benefit from the strength of the EU geographical indication, which has already established a strong market position over the years as a symbol of high European quality built by leading food brands recognized worldwide, such as Prosciutto ham or Parmesan cheese. Moreover, JG holds the distinction of being the first apple brand with a geographical indication in the Polish market. However, awareness of the EU PGI certificate remains limited in the country yet.

It is also challenging to evoke specific organoleptic associations among consumers related to the purchase of JG due to the brand's extensive variety of apple cultivars. Despite the variety being indicated on the packaging of Jabłka Grójeckkie (such as Gala), consumers must possess a discerning understanding of the differences between cultivars to derive the greatest satisfaction from their purchase. This challenge is non-existent in the case of Pink Lady and other club apples (see sub-chapter 8.5).

8.4.2 Brand – safeguarding, custodians and partnerships

Brands serve as invaluable representations not only of products or services but also as promises of quality, reliability, and trustworthiness to consumers. Therefore, implementing safeguarding measures is crucial to shield these assets from unauthorized use, imitation, or dilution, all of which could undermine consumer confidence and tarnish the brand's reputation. Through legal protection mechanisms such as trademarks, copyrights, or geographical indications, brands can establish their distinct identity and thwart competitors from leveraging their goodwill or reputation.

The Jabłka Grójeckie brand could leverage the established mechanism of geographical indications within the Common Agricultural Policy of the European Union. However, it should be noted that the procedure associated with the recognition of Jabłka Grójeckie by the European Commission as a product with a protected designation of origin was not easy, and the process of preparing and reviewing the application lasted for three years. In addition to the name Jabłka Grójeckie, the brand also utilizes a logo featuring a black-and-white woodcut of a woman, inspired by the image of Queen Bona Sforza from the 16th century, who initiated apple production in the Grójec region. Part of the visual branding of Jabłka Grójeckie also includes the EU graphical symbol for protected geographical indication.

The custodian of the Jabłka Grójeckie brand is the Sady Grójeckie Association, founded in 2007 by three young orchardists from the Grójec region. Inspired by the success of the Italian Südtirol brand, their vision was to establish a regional brand that could compete on a broader scale. The association's primary objective was to garner support and participation from partners in pursuing an EU geographical indication certificate. This milestone was achieved in 2011 under Commission Implementing Regulation (EU) No. 981/2011, officially recognizing Jabłka Grójeckie as a protected geographical indication. Presently, the Sady Grójeckie Association boasts a membership of 414 producers and serves as the exclusive distributor of apples bearing the Jabłka Grójeckie PGI designation. The Association assigns an identification number to a producer intending to produce apples marked with the protected geographical indication "Jabłka

Grójeckie", ensuring, among other things, traceability, i.e., the ability to reconstruct the product's history. In order to obtain an identification number, a producer intending to produce JG is obliged to specify the estimated production volume for a given year with a breakdown of varieties, undertake to comply with the product specification, attach valid Global G.A.P. or Integrated Production certificates, as well as a positive opinion (recommendation) from two other association members. The Main Inspectorate of Trade Quality of Agricultural and Food Products oversees the certification process of products with a Protected Geographical Indication (PGI), as well as controls compliance of production with this specification. The Sady Grójeckie Association has the right to conduct annual inspections on 10% of producers holding a Compliance Certificate. These inspections entail verifying compliance with product specifications and mass balance.

Notably, a considerable number of certified orchardists (around 120) are affiliated with RAJPOL, one of Poland's largest producer organizations, while the remaining members are part of 13 other producer organizations. The association's alliance with RAJPOL in 2017 significantly bolstered the brand's presence, doubling production capacity and opening up new sales channels for Jabłka Grójeckie. The statutory objectives of the association include, in particular, the integration and coordination of marketing activities of fruit producers from the Grójec region and other entities associated with the fruit growing industry, especially activities aimed at promoting and increasing recognition among consumers and producers of the name Jabłka Grójeckie, providing support to fruit producers from the Grójec region who want to use the protected geographical indication JG, organizing and supporting promotional activities for fruits from the Grójec region, as well as promotional and development-supporting activities for the Grójec region itself, promoting high standards of fruit production and distribution in the region. Acting on the basis of the Promotion Plan for Jabłka Grójeckie, the Association continuously implements, plans, coordinates, and supervises marketing activities related to JG.

Initially, Jabłka Grójeckie were sold in the Lidl discount chain[6] and were only available in the largest cities in Poland. This retailer was interested in introducing regional products in the fresh fruit category. After the successful first stage of cooperation, Lidl introduced Jabłka Grójeckie for distribution throughout the country and in neighboring countries such as the Czech Republic and Slovakia. Currently, the apples are also available in four other retail chains.

8.5 The case of club variety – Pink Lady

8.5.1 Unique attributes of products and quality specification

Pink Lady apples epitomize the trend towards private branding in the apple industry. Pink Lady was one of the first apples to be marketed under a specific brand name rather than by its variety name; however, the source of the unique quality signal in this case lies in breeding – unique traits of the variety aligned with consumer preferences shaped during the breeding process. Under the Pink Lady brand, apples of the Cripps Pink variety and its sports[7] – Rosy Glow and Lady in Red – are marketed. Cripps Pink, a hybrid of Golden Delicious and Lady Williams, was developed in 1973 by John Cripps as part of the Western Australian research program conducted at the Department of Agriculture West Australia (DAWA). The new apple variety displayed a distinctive pink blush against a green backdrop with a firm, crisp texture and an appealing sweet-tart taste. Both the appearance and flavor of the new variety received acclaim from consumers (Cripps et al., 1993). The variety requires a very long growing period and a hot climate, and hence is only grown in the warmer apple-growing regions (South Africa, USA, southern Europe, and of course Australia). Since its introduction, several sports or variants have been discovered. Technically, these are separate cultivars, but because of the strength of the Pink Lady brand, many of them (with the agreement of the trademark owners) are marketed as Pink Lady and consumers are not likely to be aware of the difference.

To ensure consistent taste, texture, and appearance of Pink Lady apples worldwide, a Global Pink Lady Quality Specification was developed. This standardized quality specification is applicable across all production regions. As emphasized by Apple and Pear Australia Limited (APAL), the Pink Lady quality specification prioritizes key consumer-centric attributes, often referred to as eating quality, determined by brix content[8], apple firmness, and color. For Pink Lady apples, it is precisely this combination of characteristics that defines their uniqueness. To aid suppliers/exporters/importers in meeting the requirements of the international Pink Lady quality specification, a Pink Lady Quality Manual has been devised. Alongside the specification, the manual includes a photo guide, a description of inspection methods, and food safety requirements. The manual is distributed to all licensed exporters, importers, and retailers of Pink Lady. Producers, exporters, and importers are obliged to adhere to the specification requirements[9]. Fruit not meeting these specifications (about 65% of the production) is marketed as Cripps Pink.

In contrast to the Jabłka Grójeckie in the Pink Lady case, there exists a clear relationship between the brand and specific product attributes. Pink Lady apples represent only one variety that is easily discernible from other varieties. Pink Lady apples stand out distinctly against other varieties to the extent that the average consumer would be able to distinguish them solely based on appearance (color and shape) even without the Pink Lady logo sticker. This level of consumer recognition and association is not feasible with Jabłka Grójeckie, which relies on the most popular cultivars. The clarity of identity combined with consistent quality assurance (65% rejection rate in selection) contribute to Pink Lady's strong consumer recognition. Additionally, Pink Lady boasts unique organoleptic properties that have been refined through consumer testing, a process that is only conducted to a limited extent for open cultivars, which form the basis of the Jabłka Grójeckie brand.

8.5.2 Brand – safeguarding, custodians, and partnerships

At its inception, Pink Lady faced significant challenges in safeguarding its brand identity and reproductive material while navigating the complexities of commercialization. The solutions devised as part of the commercialization strategy were groundbreaking, constituting a notable organizational innovation within the global industry. This approach involved acquiring exclusive rights to the variety (PBR, Plant Breeder Rights) and subsequent trademark registration. Furthermore, it included implementing a licensing system for the trademark, targeting entities engaged in the production and introduction of fruits to the market. In addition to the verbal identifier "Pink Lady", the trademark incorporated a logo featuring a "flowing heart", complemented by national symbols, including the kangaroo. Notably, Pink Lady marked the first instance of a trademark-protected apple. While the primary financial return for cultivators of the new fruit variety stemmed from trademark usage fees, those based on PBR licenses remained modest.

The Cripps Pink variety was initially made available to orchardists in Australia. However, DAWA did not apply for PBR in Australia, nor did it register the Pink Lady trademark in the country. Nevertheless, the Department of Agriculture obtained PBR in other apple-producing countries and a patent in the USA. Attempts were also made to register the Pink Lady trademark in key export markets. However, in countries such as Argentina, France, the United Kingdom, and the United States, it turned out that other applicants had registered the Pink Lady trademark earlier than DAWA. Over time, negotiations successfully transferred the Pink Lady trademark to DAWA in Argentina, France, and the United Kingdom, although this achievement could not be replicated for the trademark registered in the USA.

In 1998, the Department of Agriculture transferred Pink Lady trademark rights to the Australian Apple and Pear Growers' Association Inc (AAPGA), an association of apple and pear producers. The current custodian of the Pink Lady brand is Apple and Pear Australia Limited (APAL). It is a non-profit industry organization and advocates for commercial apple and pear producers in Australia. APAL assumes the legal responsibilities of AAPGA and serves as the primary representative of apple and pear producers in Australia. APAL globally extends licenses for the Pink Lady trademark, generating substantial revenues. Simultaneously, the Department of Agriculture West Australia (AGWEST) accrues licensing fees for the sale of Cripps Pink apple tree varieties (PBR license). Conversely, AGWEST does not derive any revenue from the international use of the Pink Lady trademark. The department facilitates the sale of Cripps Pink trees through licensed nurseries, enabling nursery owners to sublicense rights to the variety. Mandatory annual reporting and payment of license fees are in place, and licensees maintain records of tree sales, overseeing the legality of plantings in their respective areas.

APAL's statutory responsibilities span the implementation of the Future Orchards advisory program, creation of export opportunities, promotion of sector interests in collaboration with various stakeholders, and data collection and analysis. APAL manages programs financed by fees levied by the Australian government on orchardists, transferred to the organization Hort Innovation. Collaborating with growers, Hort Innovation identifies strategic investments in research, development, and marketing programs.

APAL oversees a meticulous licensing system, ensuring the production of high-quality fruits and comprehensive brand support throughout the supply chain. Key collaborators for APAL include Master Licensees and Territory Managers, tasked with licensing, Pink Lady apple trade development, and brand promotion. Producers of Pink Lady apples are required to obtain a license, pay fees based on sales volume, and adhere to specified quality standards outlined in the licensing agreement. The Pink Lady trademark's licensing system encompasses three key components: exclusive licenses with Master Licensees, licenses for the production and sale of apples with orchardists, and export and import licenses in the "pier-to-pier" system.

8.6 Success factors for PGI and club variety – lessons learned from comparison of Jabłka Grójeckie PGI and Pink Lady Club Apples

Jabłka Grójeckie, introduced to the market in 2011, represents a relatively younger brand primarily focusing on establishing its presence within the domestic market. In contrast, Pink Lady, established in 1992, stands as a pioneer in the industry, having made significant strides to solidify its position as a global leader in apple branding. The annual sales volume of Jabłka Grójeckie in the years 2018–2022 amounted to 70,000 tons of apples with average annual revenue of $54 million, primarily directed towards the domestic market (70% of sales). In contrast, Pink Lady's well-established presence on the international stage is evidenced by its global reach, with annual volumes nearly about 650,000 tons and an estimated retail value of approximately $2 billion. It means that the difference is slightly more than 9 times in volume, while 37 times in value. One could note that the value in the case of JG is on the wholesaling, while in the case of PL, the value is on the retailing; nevertheless, the difference is really striking. The level of prices per 1 kg in retail for Pink Lady is 80%-100% higher than the same variety without a brand logo, whereas in the case of Jabłka Grójeckie, the price differential is only 10%–20% higher (and the prices of dessert apples in Poland are relatively low in general).

Given the fundamental characteristics outlined in the comparative analysis of Pink Lady and Jabłka Grójeckie, it appears that the approaches of club apples and Geographical Indications (GI) diverge across various elements. Club varieties, exemplified by Pink Lady, are distinguished by their refined attributes crafted through meticulous breeding, prioritizing consumer-centric qualities. These apples undergo exhaustive research and development endeavors to harmonize their characteristics with evolving consumer preferences. Robust research and development capabilities within breeding programs are imperative prerequisites for pursuing this option of branding apples. Another key factor contributing to the success of Pink Lady lies in brand recognition, meticulously cultivated through targeted marketing endeavors and strategic market positioning. Securing and perpetuating such recognition necessitates substantial investments in branding and promotional activities. Legal protection for Pink Lady and similar club varieties typically relies on trademark and plant variety protection mechanisms, safeguarding the intellectual property of breeders and brand owners.

In contrast, successful regional brands of apples rely on the unique attributes derived from the terroir, encompassing soil composition and climate conditions related to geographical location. These elements contribute to the distinctly noticeable product properties appreciated by consumers. Consumer recognition of PGI apples stems from awareness of their regional origin, often supported by government initiatives aimed at promoting and protecting regional identity. Collaboration among supply chain actors is crucial for maintaining regional characteristics and implementing marketing strategies that highlight the unique attributes associated with the region of origin. Geographical indication regulations provide legal protection for PGI apples, ensuring compliance with regulatory requirements and quality standards. The main distinctions visible in the comparative analysis of Pink Lady (as an example of club apples) and Jabłka Grójeckie (as an illustration of PGI) are depicted in Table 8.1.

Jabłka Grójeckie epitomizes the efforts of Polish apple growers, who have been pioneers in the domestic industry, realizing the importance of branding apples to move beyond mere price competition and ensure fair compensation for products of superior quality. However, considering the prices achieved in trade, production scale, and export share, the success of the Jabłka Grójeckie brand should be regarded as modest. Several factors likely contribute to this.

Firstly, considering the cases presented earlier, there may be doubts about whether Jabłka Grójeckie can distinguish themselves with exceptional qualities compared to competing products, prompting consumers to pay a significantly higher price. The association between brand and unique product qualities is not as clear-cut as in the case of Pink Lady. Even more – contrary to expectations, from a branding perspective, the addition of new distinguishing factors can potentially disrupt the coherence of the promotional message, which has thus far been based on exceptional taste. While the introduction of stricter quality specifications, such as reduced pesticide content, may be aimed at enhancing the

Table 8.1 Key contrasts between club apples and apples under PGI

Factor	*Pink Lady (Club Apples)*	*Conditions for Successful Club Apples*	*Jabłka Grójeckie (PGI)*	*Conditions for Successful PGI for Apples*
Source of Unique Quality Signal	Breeding Focus on only one specific variety Strict selection of producers' output	Strong research and development capabilities in breeding programs; unique traits of the variety aligned with consumer preferences Clear, easy to communicate, and understand unique selling proposition (USP) Warranty of superior quality stable quality	Terroir	Unique attributes from the region of origin conducive to apple cultivation, influencing distinctly noticeable unique product properties
Consumer Recognition	Brand recognition	Promotion campaigns targeting brand awareness	Regional origin awareness	Promotion campaigns targeting awareness of GI certification and the region
Legal Protection	Trademark and plant variety protection	Strong intellectual property laws and enforcement mechanisms	Geographical indication regulations	Compliance with regulatory requirements and quality standards

Source: Own elaboration.

perceived healthiness of Jabłka Grójeckie, it could dilute the emphasis on their unique flavor profile, which has been a cornerstone of their marketing strategy. This shift in focus from taste to health attributes might introduce confusion among consumers and weaken the brand's identity.

Another challenge is the recognition of the region itself and its association with the unique characteristics of Jabłka Grójeckie. While "Grójec" is already familiar to most consumers in central Poland as a region of orchards, according to research by Ahrendsen and Majewski (2017), it does not enjoy the same recognition nationwide. There is still much work to be done in this regard, and despite many initiatives undertaken jointly with local authorities, it seems to be just the beginning of the journey.

Certainly, the Jabłka Grójeckie brand benefits from a certain premium, firstly due to the use of the EU geographical indication, although its recognition in Poland is not yet at a sufficiently high level. Moreover, only 22% of consumers recognized Jabłka Grójeckie with PGI, yet 70% of consumers indicated they would be willing to pay more (Ahrendsen & Majewski, 2017). For those willing to pay more, the average premium they are willing to pay was 32%, which aligns with the prices currently achieved by Jabłka Grójeckie. However, barriers to paying more may still exist due to the lower affluence of domestic consumers (average for EU countries) or inadequate value proposition, stemming from the previously mentioned weaknesses of the brand. The EU certification can certainly facilitate apple exports to markets where origin labeling from the European Union is seen as synonymous with luxury. Additionally, the brand may still benefit from a novelty effect – being the first regional brand with an EU PGI designation sold nationwide.

On the other hand, club varieties of apples, such as the renowned Pink Lady brand, represent the epitome of apple cultivation, characterized by distinct quality, flavor, and branding. While these varieties have achieved global recognition and success in developed markets, their implementation in countries like Poland, positioned between developing and most developed, faces numerous challenges. Referring to the column from Table 8.1 listing conditions for successful club apples, it becomes evident that meeting these conditions poses a significant challenge for the Polish apple sector. Firstly, the source of unique quality signal, which in the case of club varieties relies on breeding to align traits with consumer preferences, demands robust research and development capabilities. While Poland has made strides in agricultural research, achieving the level necessary for consistently producing competitive club varieties remains elusive. Moreover, building consumer recognition akin to that enjoyed by brands like Pink Lady requires substantial investment in branding and promotional activities, often spearheaded by private initiatives. The Polish apple sector struggles to muster the financial resources required for such endeavors and very often depends on public support that is accessible for supporting PGI granted by the EU but not for private brands.

Furthermore, high investments and risks are inherent for growers seeking to join a club. These commitments stem from the necessity to establish new orchards for the club variety, the market success of which may not be guaranteed. Establishing orchards for club varieties requires substantial upfront investments in land, infrastructure, and specialized cultivation practices tailored to the specific requirements of the chosen variety. Moreover, growers face the risk of market acceptance and consumer demand, particularly for varieties that lack established consumer recognition and may not align with prevailing market trends. Furthermore, legal protection for club varieties typically relies on trademark and plant variety protection mechanisms. While Poland has regulatory frameworks in place, enforcing these protections effectively against unauthorized propagation and marketing may prove challenging. Moreover, the initiative behind club varieties primarily stems from private endeavors, necessitating collaboration among supply chain actors and a proactive approach to marketing and distribution. Yet, the fragmented nature of the Polish apple sector and the weak position of producer organizations may hinder the establishment of successful club varieties or joining an existing one. These are some of the reasons that explain not only the absence of Polish growers initiatives to establish a club variety but also the absence of foreign clubs offering cooperation to Polish growers.

Additionally, another significant challenge lies in the willingness of Polish consumers to pay a significantly higher price for club varieties, which must compensate producers for elevated costs and risks associated with their cultivation. While research indicates a willingness among some consumers to pay more for premium products like Pink Lady apples, it remains uncertain whether this sentiment is widespread enough to support the sustained demand necessary for profitability. Also, the role of premium segments in the strategies of Polish supermarkets presents a complex dynamic. Historically focused on price competition, supermarkets and discounts may be hesitant to allocate shelf space and resources to higher priced club varieties without assurance of sufficient consumer demand. Convincing retailers to embrace premium products amidst their traditional focus on affordability poses an additional challenge for the widespread adoption of club varieties in Poland.

Despite the challenges outlined, the pursuit of such initiatives by the Polish sector appears imperative. Firstly, there is room for club brands in the Polish market, especially considering the size of the market and the growing consumer interest in premium products. Moreover, as Polish growers aspire to compete in increasingly demanding export markets, the need for high-quality produce that is adequately signaled and protected becomes paramount. Therefore, while the path may be fraught with obstacles, the endeavor to introduce club varieties into the Polish market seems not only necessary but also strategically vital for the long-term competitiveness and sustainability of the Polish apple industry.

8.7 Conclusions

The coordination of fresh apple quality within the supply chain significantly influences the selection of contractual arrangements. This is due to the multidimensional nature of quality, which encompasses various attributes. Apples possess not only observable attributes such as color or size but also intangible characteristics such as flavor profile or nutritional value. Furthermore, consumers increasingly seek attributes related to production methods, environmental impact, and ethical considerations. As such, coordinating quality signals across the supply chain becomes crucial for meeting consumer expectations and maintaining market competitiveness.

To effectively signal the high quality of apples that is very often based on experience and credence attributes, chain actors apply different strategies. The challenge here is that the quality signal is shared by many actors across the supply chain. The solutions used to deal with information asymmetries chosen by chain actors more frequently resemble hybrid organizational modes. This is not surprising since we know from transaction costs theory that assuring high level of quality usually requires tighter vertical coordination as a means to deal with high transaction costs stemming from bounded rationality and opportunism.

We discussed two solutions to information asymmetry concerning quality: geographical indication and club variety. The comparative analysis of Pink Lady and Jabłka Grójeckie revealed significant divergences in their approaches, with club varieties emphasizing meticulous breeding and consumer-centric qualities, while regional brands rely on unique terroir attributes and geographical indications (GI). It also revealed some weaknesses of Jabłka Grójeckie PGI in comparison to the Pink Lady club variety. Pink Lady's success is attributed to robust research and development capabilities, brand recognition, and legal protection mechanisms. In contrast, Jabłka Grójeckie's moderate success is caused by challenges in distinguishing themselves based on unique attributes and limited recognition.

Meeting the conditions for successful club apples, such as breeding capabilities and brand recognition, presents formidable hurdles for Polish growers. High investments and risks associated with club varieties demand financial resources and proactive marketing strategies, which may be hindered by the sector's fragmented nature and weak organizational structure. Moreover, persuading Polish consumers to pay premium prices for club varieties poses a significant challenge amid the predominance of price competition. Nevertheless, the endeavor to introduce club varieties seems essential, given the potential for market differentiation and the necessity to compete in more demanding markets.

Notes

1 Which means "produced for Biedronka". Biedronka is a Portuguese-origin retail chain in Poland belonging to Jeronimo Martins (in fact, Biedronka generates two-thirds of the total sales of this holding). In Poland, it is a leader in food retailing with around 3,500 discount outlets. Its revenues in 2023 were 85 billion PLN (approximately $21 billion).

2 Which means "selected for Auchan". Auchan is a French-origin retail chain operating in 13 countries. In Poland, it holds third place in food retailing. It owns 106 outlets, mainly hypermarkets (70), and collaborates with another 99 outlets through franchising or other partnerships. Recently, Auchan plans to form an alliance with the chain Intermarche for joint procurement. Their combined sales are estimated at 20 billion PLN (approximately $5 billion).

3 It's important to note here that the management of supply, quality, and quantity issues differs when dealing with processed products (juices, dried fruit, etc.)
4 In fact, "Jabłka Grójeckie" means apples from Grójec.
5 Extra class apples are apples of the highest quality, with characteristics such as uniform size, shape, and color. They are typically free from defects and blemishes, presenting an optimal appearance for retail and export markets. Class I apples include apples that are slightly less uniform or may have minor defects that do not significantly affect their overall quality. Class I apples are still of good quality and suitable for retail markets, though they may not meet the stringent criteria of extra class.
6 Lidl is a German-origin retail chain operating in 31 countries (mainly in Europe). In Poland, it is the second largest player in food retailing, with more than 850 discount outlets. Its revenues in 2023 were 33 billion PLN (about $8 billion).
7 A variety in apple cultivation refers to a distinct type of apple that has been deliberately bred or selected for specific characteristics such as flavor, color, size, and disease resistance. Varieties are typically propagated through controlled breeding methods to maintain their unique traits. Sports are spontaneous genetic mutations within existing varieties that may or may not stabilize into new cultivars.
8 Brix is a measure of the amount of dissolved solids in a liquid via its specific gravity, and is used especially to measure dissolved sugar. One degree Brix is 1 gram of sucrose in 100 grams of solution.
9 Firmness: an average of 6.5 kg/cm^2, brix (a measurement of sugar content): an average of 13%, coloring: > at least 40% colored surface on the same side with a "bold pink to red" intensity (>60% for Asia), damage: <3% (including internal damage <1%).

References

Ahrendsen, B. L., & Majewski, E. (2017). Protected geographical indication recognition and willingness to pay: A case of Grojec apple. *Applied Studies in Agribusiness and Commerce APSTRACT, 3–4*(11). doi10.19041/APSTRACT/2017/3-4/11

Banterle, A., & Stranieri, S. (2008). The consequences of voluntary traceability system for supply chain relationships: An application of transaction cost economics. *Food Policy, 33*(6), 560–569. doi:10.1016/j.foodpol.2008.06.002

Cripps, J. E. L., Richards, L. A., & Mairata, A. M. (1993). 'Pink Lady' apple. *HortScience, 28*(10), 1057. doi: 10.21273/HORTSCI.28.10.1057

Darby, M. R., & Karni, E. (1973). Free competition and the optimal amount of fraud. *The Journal of Law and Economics, 16*(1), 67–88. doi:10.1086/466756

Di Fonzo, A., Nardone, V., Fathinejad, N., & Russo, C. (2019). The Impact of plant variety protection regulations on the governance of agri-food value chains. *Social Sciences, 8*(3), 91. doi:10.3390/socsci8030091

Fernandez-Barcala, M., González-Díaz, M., & Raynaud, E. (2017). Contrasting the governance of supply chains with and without geographical indications: Complementarity between levels. *Supply Chain Management: An International Journal, 22*(4), 305–320. doi:10.1108/SCM-05-2016-0161

Ghozzi, H., Platoni, S., Tillie, P., & Soregaroli, C. (2018). TCE determinants and governance forms in the EU "Non-GMO" soybean supply chain. *Food Policy, 78*, 68–80. doi:10.1016/j.foodpol.2018.02.011

Ghozzi, H., Soregaroli, C., Boccaletti, S., & Sauvée, L. (2016). Impacts of non-GMO standards on poultry supply chain governance: transaction cost approach vs resource-based view. *Supply Chain Management: An International Journal*, *21*(6), 743–758. doi:10.1108/SCM-03-2016-0089

Giovannucci, D., Josling, T., Kerr, W. A., & Yeung, M. T. (2009). Guide to geographical indications – Linking products and their origins. International Trade Centre.

Klepacka, A. M., & Florkowski, W. J. (2016). Poland's apple sector and the embargo on fruit exports to Russia. *Acta Horticulturae*, *1132*, 31–38. https://doi.org/10.17660/ActaHortic.2016.1132.5

Kraciński, P. (2018). Pozycja konkurencyjna Polski na światowym rynku zagęszczonego soku jabłkowego. *Zeszyty Naukowe Szkoły Głównej Gospodarstwa Wiejskiego. Ekonomika i Organizacja Gospodarki Żywnościowej, 121*, 71–81. doi:10.22630/EIOGZ.2018.121.5

Legun, K. A. (2015). Club apples: A biology of markets built on the social life of variety. *Economy and Society*, *44*(2), 293–315. doi:10.1080/03085147.2015.1013743

Masten S. E., Meehan J. W., & Snyder E. A. (1991), The costs of organization, *Journal of Law, Economics and Organization*, *7*(1), 1–25.

Ménard, C. (2005). New institutions for governing the agri-food industry. *European Review of Agricultural Economics*, *32*(3), 421–440. doi:10.1093/eurrag/jbi013

Nosecka, B., & Bugała, A (2019). *Rynek jabłek w Polsce*. Retrieved from www.agroindustry.pl/index.php/2019/04/29/rynek-jablek-w-polsce/ (accessed December 28, 2023).

Pietrzak, M., Chlebicka, A., Kraciński, P., & Malak-Rawlikowska, A. (2020). Information asymmetry as a barrier in upgrading the position of local producers in the global value chain—Evidence from the apple sector in Poland. *Sustainability*, *12*(19), 7857. doi:10.3390/su12197857

Raynaud, E., Sauvée, L., & Valceschini, E. (2005). Alignment between quality enforcement devices and governance structures in the agro-food vertical chains. *Journal of Management and Governance*, *9*(1), 47–77. doi:10.1007/s10997-005-1571-1

Shapiro, C. (1983). Premiums for high quality products as returns to reputations. *Quarterly Journal of Economics*, *98*(4), 659–679. doi:10.2307/1881782

Spence, M. (1973). Job market signaling. *The Quarterly Journal of Economics*, *87*(3), 355–374. doi:10.2307/1882010

Teuber, R. (2011). Protecting geographical indications: Lessons learned from the economic literature. Paper presented at the 2011 international congress, August 30–September 2, 2011, Zurich, Switzerland (No. 116081). European Association of Agricultural Economists. doi:10.22004/ag.econ.116081

Trienekens, J., & Wognum, N. (2013). Requirements of supply chain management in differentiating European pork chains. *Meat Science, 95*(3), 719–726. doi: 10.1016/j.meatsci.2013.03.035

Williamson, O.E. (1985). *The economic institutions of capitalism*. The Free Press.

Williamson, O.E. (2004). Transaction cost economics and agriculture: An excursion. In *Role of institutions in rural policies and agricultural markets* (pp. 19–39). Elsevier.

Zago, A. (2015). Collective Reputation in Agricultural Markets. *Économie rurale*. doi:10.4000/economierurale.4531

9 Vertical Integration, Trust, and Information Asymmetry in Quality Grain-Bakery Chains

Agata Malak-Rawlikowska,[1]
Edward Majewski,[1] *Tania Runge,*[2]
Stefano Targetti,[3] *Davide Viaggi,*[3]
Matteo Zavalloni,[4] *and Katharina Meyer*[5]

[1]*Warsaw University of Life Sciences – SGGW, Poland*
[2]*Thünen Institute, Coordination Unit Climate, Soil, Biodiversity, Germany*
[3]*University of Bologna, Italy*
[4]*University of Urbino Carlo Bo, Italy*
[5]*Research Institute of Organic Agriculture FiBL, Germany*

9.1 Introduction

Governance structures are essential to strengthen trust and reduce information asymmetry in food supply chains (Pietrzak et al., 2020). Stronger integration of chain actors in informal (implicit) or formal contractual arrangements or full vertical integration reduces costs due to improving coordination, communication, and information flow amongst supply chain partners to final consumers (Fiocco, 2016; Gulati & Singh, 1998; Güth et al., 2007; Li et al., 2020). This, in turn, leads to improved transparency, which can help to reduce uncertainty and create a more efficient and reliable food supply chain (Albanese, 2015; Karbowski & Prokop, 2019) and enhance the willingness to participate of farmers (D'Alberto et al., 2024). Additionally, vertical integration can support developing trust between food chain partners, allowing them to share information and collaborate more closely, leading to mutual benefits and the generation of a cooperation surplus (Allen & Phillips, 2000; Fee et al., 2006; Gulati & Singh, 1998; Pishchulov et al., 2023; Yang et al., 2020).

High-value-added product chains are particularly vulnerable to problems with trust and information asymmetry. Most of the value-added features of these products are based on non-experimental features and credence attributes difficult to assess even after the purchase. The attributes might be related to production methods and the delivery of agri-environmental and climate public goods, e.g., animal welfare, biodiversity, water quality, landscape, rural viability, or

DOI: 10.4324/9781032633725-11

cultural heritage. One solution that can help reduce the problem of lack of trust and enhance the value of products is to certify them, for example, with a GI (EU Geographical Indication) or another quality label (European Commission, 2021; Hofmeier et al., 2023). However, this is often less effective because the recognition of certificates among consumers is quite low (Eurobarometer No.520, European Commission, 2022; Hartmann et al., 2019), and due to their multitude on the market, the consumer does not always see the advantages of the product associated with a specific certificate (European Commission, 2010; European Commission, 2022; Malak-Rawlikowska et al., 2023).

In this chapter, we analyse the roles of different governance structures in increasing trust and reducing information asymmetry in the food chains on the example of three supply chains of quality products: Italian Barilla bakery brand Carta del Mulino with soft wheat, Polish BioBabalscy organic flour and pasta, and German Water Protection Bread Initiative (Wasserschutzbrot). All these chains offer high-value-added products whose credence attributes are difficult to assess for consumers because they are related to the provision of agri-environmental public goods. Barillas' Mulino Bianco products are produced under the "Carta del Mulino" program, which applies specific production rules for farmers in order to support biodiversity and rural viability (Eichhorn et al., 2020). The requirements include, among others, farm ISCC PLUS certification to preserve biodiversity, crop rotation, minimum area allocated to flowers, certified seeds, no use of neonicotinoids and glyphosate, segregation and traceability of the lots, etc. ISCC PLUS certification is a voluntary scheme that is applicable for the bioeconomy and circular economy for food, feed, chemicals, plastics, packaging, textiles, and renewable feedstock derived from a process using renewable energy sources. BioBabalscy organic chain is a family business, which, together with about 132 supplying farmers (in 2022), supports biodiversity and cultural heritage by preserving old varieties of wheat, which are cultivated in an organic system to produce seeds and grains for processing into various cereal products (Eichhorn et al., 2020). Water Protection Bread Initiative (Wasserschutzbrot) engages actors of the whole value chain and aims to protect ground and drinking water (Eichhorn et al., 2020). Based on voluntary commitment declarations of farmers, mills, bakeries, and water suppliers, selected wheat varieties are cultivated under specific fertilizer conditions. This allows for a significant reduction of the nitrogen surpluses in the soil and the avoidance of leaching to groundwater. Each of these three chains is characterized by a different level of integration, formal or informal contractual arrangements, which are interesting from the point of view of dealing with information asymmetry and trust issues in the chain. In our analysis, we also focus on the general role of information asymmetry and trust in the coordination of physical flows of bakery products, mechanisms of securing quality, as well as governance structures in these chains.

Data for the case studies were collected within the EU H2020 CONSOLE project (CONtract SOLutions for Effective and lasting delivery of agri-environmental climate public goods by EU agriculture and forestry Research and Innovation action: H2020 – GA 817949) in the years 2019–2021 in Poland, Italy, and Germany by personal interviews with case study representatives (mainly producers and processors) and were updated by the authors of this chapter, based on the desk-research study and available secondary sources.

9.2 Overview of the studied chains

9.2.1 Value chain structure and governance

As indicated in Chapter 3 of this book, the chain structure and its governance type can be characterized by features, such as the length of the relationship, the degree of formalization of relations, the strength of social ties, or the level of dependency in the chain. Table 9.1 shows the characteristics of the bakery supply chains and their synthetized governance structures.

BioBabalscy organic chain is a family business located in the northwest part of Poland. Aleksandra and Mieczysław Babalski are pioneers of organic farming in Poland. Babalski opted to cultivate the soil on his farm using ecological methods in the early 1980s, drawing on his expertise from extended stays and brief visits to organic farms in Switzerland, Austria, and Germany. The family started farming on 9 hectares of agricultural land. Following the conversion, the AgroBioTest Certification Body (PL EKO 07 90001) certified his farm as Poland's first certified organic farm. In 1991, a pasta production factory was constructed, and it now operates alongside the farm. Organic wholemeal pasta is one of the company's flagship goods, as it is created from traditional, ancient grain varieties. In contrast to conventional flour, the flour used to make pasta at BioBabalscy incorporates shell and peel remains, which give a nutritious fiber. The Babalscy are enthusiastic about ecology and the preservation of nature. They contribute to these by growing and protecting ancient cereal types (such as spelt, flatfish, and samarium), which have distinct nutritional and health benefits.

BioBabalscy's chain represents a very effective integration process that results in great organizational and financial synergy while maintaining the provision of agri-environmental public goods. Cooperation across the chain heavily depends on mutual confidence and pleasant connections between farmers (ca. 107 grain suppliers horizontally integrated in the EKOŁAN association + 25 supporting suppliers) and the BioBabalskcy processor – as a strong chain integrator. No formal, written contracts are used, and cooperation is based on a voluntary relational contract basis. The relational, informal type of cooperation is characterized by strong ties between farmers and processors, involving the exchange of tacit knowledge, the exchange of specific assets (seeds), and friendship ties, which play an important role. Most of the seeds used by farmers are supplied by BioBabalscy, which works closely with the Gene Bank in

Table 9.1 Characteristics of the supply chain of selected bakery products

Specification	*BioBabalscy pasta and flour (Poland)*	*Water Protection Bread (Germany)*	*Carta del Mulino Bianco by Barilla (Italy)*
Production of grains	107 farms integrated in EKOŁAN association, + 25 supporting farms (in 2022)	43 farmers (in 2024)	2600 cereal producing farms
Mills/elevators	BioBabalscy Company (elevator and mill)	9 mills	17 mills/large number of elevators
Processing into bakery products	BioBabalscy Company	43 craft bakeries (in 2024)	Barilla processor
Distribution chain	Short chains: on-farm shop, internet shop. Longer chains: sales to intermediaries (wholesalers), less often to retail.	Around 150 sales outlets of the bakeries (as of the end of 2023)	Longer chains: traders/wholesalers or directly to retail
Other chain actors	Group of grain producers EKOŁAN.	Bavarian Ministry of Environment, Lower Franconian government (Germany); FiBL (Research Institute of Organic Agriculture; project management); 20 water suppliers	Bee Mills, WWF –World Wildlife Fund, Universities of Bologna and Tuscia
Value chain governance	Farm/processing: relation-based/ equity-based alliance, Processing/distribution: spot-market in case of online shop, relational or specific contracts governance with wholesalers	Farm/mills: relation based/equity-based alliance; Processing/distribution: relation-based – local bakeries with loyal clients	Farm/elevator/mills: specification contract, captive relations; Mills/Processing: specification contract; Processing/Wholesale/Retail: spot-market, specification contract

Source: Own elaboration based on the CONSOLE project factsheets (Eichhorn et al. 2020), webpages of the companies/initiatives https://biobabalscy.pl/; https://wasserschutzbrot.de/presse/; https://www.mulinobianco.it/lacartadelmulinos); accessed on June 15, 2024.

Poland. Farmers are members of the EKOŁAN association, which is led by Mieczysław Babalski.

Over 600 tonnes of grain are processed each year by the BioBabalscy chain, with end-product sales totalling approximately 350–400 tonnes. In addition to pasta and flakes, wholemeal flour, bran, and spelt coffee are manufactured. Wholegrain pasta with the BioBabalscy brand, particularly spelt wheat, costs up to 50% more than regular pasta. Nonetheless, the number of customers who believe in the quality of BioBabalscy organic products is increasing, indicating a promising future for the brand. The majority of pasta and related products are sold to contracted wholesalers. Cooperation is based on mid- and long-term relations. The company also has an online shop and farm shop, where products are sold directly to consumers. This distribution channel is gaining popularity among consumers, especially after the Covid-19 pandemic, and is also more profitable for the producer.

Water Protection Bread Initiative (Wasserschutzbrot) was initiated in 2014 by the Lower Franconian government (Germany), with a single water provider, one farmer, one mill, and one bakery. Forty-three farmers participated in the initiative as of 2024 in Lower Franconia, Upper Franconia, Middle Franconia, and Lower Bavaria in Germany. The wheat is sent by the farmers to the participating mills, where it is processed into flour for local bakeries. The bakeries market their baked goods with a unique label. Farmers who cultivate land in water-sensitive zones or in locations near drinking water abstraction wells from public water supply are eligible to participate in the initiative. They guarantee to apply a maximum of 160 kg N/ha and avoid late fertilization of wheat, which is heavily criticized from the point of view of groundwater protection because of a high risk of nitrate leaching, and guarantee to apply a maximum of 160 kg N/ha. This enables a large, significant reduction in nitrogen surpluses in the soil and avoids leaking lower nitrate content in the leachate into groundwater (Geoteam, 2023). Farmers grow wheat from selected novel varieties that have good baking features despite having a lower protein content of 11–11.5% than instead of the usual 13% of wheat to be used for bakery purposes. A consumer-focused communication campaign is part of the project to educate people about the significance of clean groundwater and drinking water, as well as how they can help by purchasing bakery products made with this wheat at over 100 selling locations. This chain initiative is an excellent example of trust-based governance structures that rely on voluntary (relational) commitment declarations rather than formal contracts. While these declarations are not legally enforceable, those who sign them agree to abide by certain guidelines. Farmers, mills, and bakers have been involved in establishing the criteria for participation, so there is an internal motivation to follow the rules, followed by economic incentives provided by the product's higher grain prices for the farmers. This relational contract is characterized by complex ties between sellers and buyers involving exchanging knowledge and specific production techniques. Withdrawing from the initiative is related to high transaction costs related to price and reputation losses. Social ties are also important since it is a well-known local initiative with loyal consumers and government partners involved.

The Carta del Mulino label was initiated in 2019 for the Italian Barilla bakery brand Mulino Bianco to meet changing consumer preferences, which have reoriented toward environmentally friendly products, safety, and traceability. This chain integrates a solution that links the delivery of soft wheat for the production of bread and flour confectionery (e.g., biscuits) to the provision of agri-environmental public goods related to biodiversity, environmental protection, as well as rural viability. Due to the international scale of operation of the Barilla company, the program might span many locations in Europe. Most partners are in Italy, France, Germany, and Austria. The contract represents an agreement between farmers, mills, and/or agricultural elevators/storages/traders, and it includes ten production rules (defined in collaboration with WWF – World Wildlife Fund, Universities of Bologna and Tuscia) ensuring that mills, bakeries, and farmers adhere to sustainability and traceability requirements. For the "Carta del Mulino" manufacturing line, Barilla commits to obtaining 100% of the soft wheat in accordance with the 10 guidelines. The Carta del Mulino program outlines specific steps for improving biodiversity and a premium price to compensate for the opportunity costs of compliance.

The Carta del Mulino chain is vertically integrated by specific contracts, which include commitments of producers to meet 10 rules applied by the program. At the wheat production level, farmers are dependent on much larger buyers (elevators/mills), which results in high switching costs and possibly captive relations. Due to the specific knowledge required, many farmers need a significant degree of advisory in their activities and control by leading companies, resulting in a close-ties relationship. On the other hand, this improves the chain transparency and information flow. Downstream actors have extended information about the adjustments and costs necessary to be covered at the production level. Similar captive contracts may characterize the relationship between mills and Barilla processors. A very large integrator and initiator of the Carta del Mulino program contracts selected mills that meet certain criteria and follow strict program rules. The contractual relations are formal and based on long-term commitments.

9.2.2 Quality attributes and specificity of the products

Quality attributes of bakery products produced within the analysed bakery chains are not related to easy-to-assess visual features (appearance, colour, and size) or sensory features (taste and smell) but, above all, to their credence attributes related to methods of production and processing, which support the provision of agri-environmental public goods. These quality features, which are difficult for the consumer to detect, are guaranteed by a special product logo/label and brand or certificate along the value chain (Table 9.2).

BioBabalscy bakery products' attributes are assured by the organic certificate, focused on natural production methods and enhancement of farmland biodiversity. Preserving old varieties of wheat and old recipes additionally supports cultural heritage creation, another credence attributes of BioBabalscy bakery products. All these credence features are shaped at the farm and processing level and then transmitted through retail to final consumers.

Instead of building upon organic farming, the Mulino Bianco products by Barilla and the Water Protection Bread are produced under private labels (standards) focused on the provision of well-defined agri-environmental public goods within the value chain. In the Water Protection Bread Initiative, the emphasis is put on the protection of ground and drinking water, mainly by reducing fertilization at the grain-filling stage when growing high-quality wheat. For the farmers, the requirements include installing project signs along the wheat fields; cultivating wheat varieties jointly preselected with the mills and bakeries; adhering to a maximum fertilization rate of 160 kg N/ha with no late fertilization; conducting regular soil analysis on the participating fields; maintaining detailed records of all management practices; and avoiding desiccation treatments. The mills must ensure the separate collection, analysis, and storage of wheat from the water protection fields, as well as its distinct processing into flour. They are also responsible for providing quarterly reports on the wheat/flour stocks from the initiative and the amount of flour ordered by the participating bakeries. The bakeries involved must commit to replacing at least 50% of their annual wheat flour requirement with flour from the initiative. Alternatively, in the first year, bakeries can opt to sell specially labelled bread containing at least 60% of wheat flour from the initiative as an entry-level variant. Similarly to BioBabalscy chain, all these credence features are shaped mainly at the farm and processing level, and then transmitted through the retail to final consumers.

The Carta del Mulino program (Mulino Bianco products), introduced by large Italian producer Barilla, focuses on the improvement of farmland biodiversity but also water quality. The ten rules include measures for more biodiversity-friendly crop rotations, minimum share (3%) of soft wheat area allocated to flowers and pollinator habitats, specific variety selection, certified seeds, non-use of neonicotinoids and non-use of glyphosate, as well as measures guaranteeing segregation and traceability of the lots, lots' storage separated from other production, and added value distributed along the supply chain. All these credence features are shaped mainly at the farm and processing level and then transmitted through the retail to final consumers by Barilla company.

Table 9.2 Bakery products' quality attributes from the consumer perspective and location of efforts to shape them in the value chain

Quality Attributes		*Type*	*Stages (Activities) in the Value Chain*			
			Cereals Provision at the Farm	*Mills (Flour)*	*Processing (into Bakery Products)*	*Wholesaling and Retailing*
Visual	Appearance/Shape	Search	0	0	+++	++
	Colour	Search	0	0	+++	+
	Size	Search	0	0	+++	+++
Other sensory	Smell	Search/experience	+	+	+++	+++
	Taste	Experience	+++	+	+++	++
	Consistency	Experience	+	+	+++	++
Health	Health security	Credence	+++	++	+++	++
	Crop production practices/fertilization	Credence	+++	+	0	0
	Manufacturing practices/Production process	Credence	+++	++	+++	0
Symbolic	Provision of agri-environmental public goods (farmland biodiversity, rural viability, clean water)	Credence	+++	++	+++	+
	Brand/labels	Search	++	++	+++	+
Others	Durability (shelf life)	Search/experience	0	+	+++	+++
	Quality stability	Search/experience	+	+	+++	+++
	Convenience*	Search	0	0	+++	++
	Complaints, guarantees, etc.	Search/experience	0	0	++	+++

Source: Own elaboration.

* Convenience to buy, convenience to transport, convenience to eat, convenience to prepare or to process; 0 denotes marginal or none; +, ++ and +++ denote, respectively, weak, medium and strong influence and responsibility.

9.3 Roles of different governance structures in increasing trust and reducing information asymmetry

9.3.1 Vertical chain integration and trust-based relations

One way to deal with information asymmetry in the food supply chain, loss of quality, and unfair practices is close cooperation and vertical integration (European Commission, 2021; Hofmeier et al., 2023; Newman et al., 2014; Pishchulov et al., 2023). As described in Section 9.2, integration in the supply chain of the case study bakery products take different forms at subsequent stages. Although the production scale is very different, pure market exchange occurs mainly at retail sales to consumers or through intermediaries or traders for export (in the case of Mulino Bianco by Barilla). Manufacturers use various forms of partial integration in all three cases in the chain.

The trust relationship between BioBabalscy, a pasta producer, and the farmers delivering grains to the company is characterized by a unique and collaborative partnership. There is no formal, written contract, and the relationship is based on a mutual willingness to cooperate. This unique relationship is fostered by Babalski's reputation as a pioneer of organic farming in Poland and his extensive expertise in ecological production methods, which have earned him great respect and trust among farmers. Babalski's role goes beyond that of a mere buyer; he provides farmers with seeds, valuable advice, and comprehensive support, ensuring they receive fair prices for their grains. This supportive and equitable approach leads to a partnership where both the farmers and BioBabalscy have nearly equal bargaining power. Mutual respect and understanding of each other's interests help strengthen this bond. Farmers, in turn, express a high level of satisfaction with their association with BioBabalscy and follow quality requirements set by the processor. They value reliable payments, favourable prices, and the ability to sell large quantities of their produce. This positive experience is reflected in their enthusiastic feedback, with many stating a clear preference for selling their grains to Babalski due to the beneficial terms and the supportive relationship.

For the Water Protection Bread Initiative, the Bavarian Ministry of Environment provides funding for project management and communication strategy. The water management section of Lower Franconia leads the project, with FiBL (the Research Institute of Organic Agriculture) serving as the external service provider responsible for project coordination and compliance checks of participating mills and bakeries, as well as the farmers. All partners in the value chain must adhere to agreed-upon management requirements while maintaining friendly and respectful relationships with each other and the involved institutions. This initiative exemplifies trust-based relationships that rely not on written contracts but on a voluntary commitment declaration for the characteristics and requirements inherent to the initiative, complemented by normal supply contracts. Although these declarations are not legally binding, signatories pledge to follow specific rules. Criteria for participation have been established through a participatory process for farmers, mills, and bakeries. Currently, there are more farmers willing to participate than can be accommodated, with the limiting factor being the number of participating bakeries and their demand for flour from the initiative.

Also, in the case of the Barilla Initiative Carta del Mulino, the aim is to achieve a sustainable transition of the whole chain producing under the label. Involved are therefore not only farmers but also mills and elevators, all having to comply with clear obligations under written contracts. Due to quite a large group of stakeholders in the value chain, formal contracts are needed, which establish a direct relationship between farmers and mills or elevators. Through this agreement, farmers benefit from several advantages, such as optimization of agronomic inputs, restoration of soil fertility, increase in biodiversity, guaranteed product sales and a final premium price, adoption of environmentally friendly farming practices, support for farming communities, and assurance of returning good and safe products to consumers. The contract ensures that farmers receive a price premium from the mills or elevators with whom they enter into the agreement. This premium incentivizes farmers to adhere to the specified practices and standards. In turn, Barilla commits to purchasing the products from these mills or elevators, creating a stable and predictable market for the farmers' produce. This arrangement not only fosters a collaborative relationship between the farmers and the processing facilities but also aligns their practices with Barilla's sustainability and quality goals. By establishing this structured and beneficial relationship, the contract promotes sustainable agriculture and ensures that high-quality products reach consumers, supporting Barilla's commitment to environmental responsibility and community welfare. The products under Carta del Mulino certification and labelling are promoted by Barilla, and the products enjoy significant consumer trust.

9.3.2 The role of legitimacy and enforcement

Quality (including unobservable credence features) is ensured in all three analysed bakery chains through a formalized control system. In the case of BioBabalscy, regular quality controls are performed by the processor, as well as for compliance with the ecological certificate – by an authorized, external certification laboratory. In the case of Water Protection Bread, farmers are controlled for compliance with the conditions of participation either by the local water supplier or by FiBL as an external service provider. FiBL also carries out the controls of the participating mills and bakeries. In addition, the participants of the initiative committed to providing relevant information regularly. For each calendar year, the applied fertilizer amount, as well as the harvested wheat yields, the amounts of milled wheat, and the wheat flour used in bakery products are recorded. In the case of Barilla, annual audits are conducted by an independent third-party control body for all subscribers to the "Carta del Mulino" program. 30% of total farmers are tested annually.

These activities allow the creation of a system of trust in a specific label, which, in the case of BioBabalscy, is an organic certificate, and in the case of Water Protection Bread and Carta del Mulino products, a special logo, displayed on the point of sale for Water Protection Bread, and the marking of a series of products for Carta del Mulino. In many cases, certified products, especially those produced by farmers' groups, have problems with recognition, as described in Chapter 7. This is due to ineffective promotional activities of farmer groups, low cooperation, and small production scale. In such added-value chains, the integrator plays an important role. An efficient processor with a wide sales range and a significant impact on retail might be the best solution in such chains. In bakery chains analysed in this chapter, products with special labels are promoted by processors (BioBabalscy, Barilla) or bakeries and local authorities (Water Protection Bread), which allows for the transfer of information about the advantages of these products to consumers. In all cases, the demand generated by the market exceeds the supply, and the consumer who buys these products consciously agrees to pay a higher price for the quality parameters of the product. This shows the importance of close cooperation in the chain and the integrator's role in achieving appropriate transmission of information from the production level to the consumer. On the other hand, partial vertical integration (as observed in all the case study chains), via active participation of all actors, provides mutual benefits, leading to improving the total surplus of the chain. The integrating party, having an interest in the entire chain initiative, knows perfectly the rules and costs associated with meeting the participation requirements at all levels of the product chain. Thus, asymmetric information is reduced, and the temptation of chain actors to opportunistic behaviour is lowered because everyone has a sense of common interest and is playing for one goal.

9.4 Conclusions

High-value-added product chains are especially prone to trust issues and knowledge asymmetries. The majority of the value-added characteristics of such products are based on non-experimental traits and credibility factors that are difficult to judge even after purchase.

All three chains analysed in this chapter offer high-value-added products related to the provision of agri-environmental public goods. BioBabalscy bakery products are distinguished by their organic certification, emphasizing natural production methods and farmland biodiversity. By preserving old wheat varieties and traditional recipes, the processor also supports cultural heritage. These attributes are developed at the farm and processing levels and conveyed to consumers through retail channels. In contrast, Mulino Bianco by Barilla and the Water Protection

Bread initiatives focus on agri-environmental public goods within the value chain, such as protecting biodiversity and ground and drinking water. These specific credence features of bakery products are assured by a specific label, in the case of Water Protection Bread and Carta de Mulino products, are transmitted to consumers via intensive communication, promotion, or special packaging.

Vertical chain integration and trust-based relationships play a crucial role in ensuring quality and reducing information asymmetry in these bakery chains. The analysed case of BioBabalscy fosters a collaborative partnership with farmers, providing them with seeds, advice, and fair prices without formal contracts, based on mutual respect and trust. This supportive relationship ensures high-quality cereal production and satisfaction among farmers. Similarly, the second analysed case of the Water Protection Bread Initiative relies on voluntary commitment declarations rather than legal contracts, with participants adhering to specific management requirements. Due to its large, international scale of operation, the Carta del Mulino program, Barilla establishes formal contracts with farmers, mills, and elevators to ensure compliance with sustainability standards and provide farmers with a stable market and price premiums. Due to the mutual benefits of all chain actors arising from the cooperation within the partly integrated chain, asymmetric information is reduced, and the temptation of actors to engage in opportunistic behaviour is lowered because of having a sense of community.

Formalized control systems and certifications, such as organic certificates for BioBabalscy and special logos for Water Protection Bread and Carta del Mulino products, bolster trust in these bakery chains. Regular audits and compliance checks by external bodies ensure adherence to standards. Promotion of these products by processors and local authorities helps communicate their benefits to consumers, who are willing to pay higher prices for the added value. The role of integrators, such as efficient processors with broad market reach, is vital in these chains, facilitating the transmission of information and maintaining high demand for these high-quality, environmentally responsible products. While governance structures can indeed enhance trust and reduce information asymmetry, they are not a panacea. Actors involved in the food chains need to be aware of and address potential pitfalls (for example, related to administrative burden and communication breakdowns) to ensure that their governance frameworks are genuinely effective. This requires continuous evaluation, adaptation, and a commitment to fostering an environment of trust and transparency.

References

Albanese A. (2015). Vertical integration contracts in agriculture: Fair trade and efficiency of the food Chain. In L. E. San-Epifanio & M. De Renobales Scheifler (Eds.), *Envisioning a future without food waste and food poverty: Societal challenges* (pp. 89–93), Wageningen Economic Research. DOI: 10.3920/978-90-8686-820-9_9

Allen, J. W., & Phillips, G. M. (2000). Corporate equity ownership, strategic alliances, and product market relationships. *Journal of Finance*, *55*, 2791–2815.

D'Alberto, R., Targetti, S., Schaller, L., Bartolini, F., Eichhorn, T., Haltia, E., Harmanny, K., Le Gloux, F., Nikolov, D., Runge, T., & Vergamini, D. (2024). A European perspective on acceptability of innovative agri-environment-climate contract solutions. *Land Use Policy*, *141*, 107120.

Eichhorn T., Kantelhardt J., Schaller L., Amery F., Andreoli, M., Bartollini, F., Berzina, I., Botarelli L., Budniok, A., Byrne, N., de Geronimo G., de Valença, A., Dupraz, P., Fyfe, D., Hamunen, K., Hänninen, H., Hennessy, T., Iglesias, A., Issanchou, A., … Zavalloni, M. (2020). *Deliverable D2.1 catalogue of descriptive factsheets of all European case studies of CONSOLE project: CONtract SOLutions for Effective and lasting delivery of agri-environmental climate public goods by EU agriculture and forestry*. Research and Innovation Action.

European Commission. (2010). Impact assessment on geographical indications. accompanying document to the proposal for a regulation of the European parliament and of the council on agricultural product quality schemes. COM733 final 2010/0353 (COD). Commission staff working paper: 83. www.europarl.europa.eu/registre/docs_autres_institutions/commission_europeenne/sec/2010/1524/COM_SEC(2010)1524_EN.pdf

European Commission. (2021). *Commission Staff Working Document Evaluation of Geographical Indications and Traditional Specialities Guaranteed Protected in the EU SWD/2021/0427 final Brussels, 20.12.2021 commission staff working document evaluation of geographical-PART-2021-846550V1.pdf*

European Commission. (2022). *Europeans, Agriculture and the CAP. Special Eurobarometer 520/Wave EB88.4 – TNS Opinion & Social, June 2022, Europeans, Agriculture and the CAP – czerwiec 2022 – Eurobarometer survey (europa.eu)*

Fee, C. E., Hadlock, C. J., & Thomas, S. (2006). Corporate equity ownership and the governance of product market relationships. *Journal of Finance*, *61*, 1217–1251.

Fiocco, R. (2016). The strategic value of partial vertical integration. *European Economic Review*, *89*, 284–302.

GeoTeam. (2023). Kurzfassung des Abschlussberichtes zum Nmin-Monitoring Wasserschutzweizen 2020–22. https://wasserschutzbrot.de/wp-content/uploads/230804-RegUfr-NminMonitoringWSW-KurzfassungAbschlussbericht-EV_final.pdf

Gulati, R., & Singh, H. (1998). The architecture of cooperation: Managing coordination costs and appropriation concerns in strategic alliances. *Administrative Science Quarterly*, *43*, 781–814.

Güth, W., Nikiforakis, N., & Normann, H. T. (2007). Vertical cross-shareholding: Theory and experimental evidence. *International Journal of Industrial Organization*, *25*, 69–89.

Hartmann, M., Yeh, C. H., Amilien, V., Csillag, P., Filipovic, J., Giraud, G., Kuč, V., Menozzi, D., Poschwatta, O., Roos, G., Saïdi, M., Tocco, B., Veneziani, M., & Vreden, T. (2019). *Report on quantitative research findings on European consumers' perception and valuation of EU food quality schemes as well as their confidence in such measures*.

Hofmeier, M., Menapace, L., & Rahbauer, S. (2023). Adoption of Geographical Indications and origin-related food labels by SMEs – A systematic literature review. *Cleaner and Circular Bioeconomy*, *4*, 100041. https://doi.org/10.1016/j.clcb.2023.100041

Karbowski A., & Prokop J. (2019). The impact of vertical R&D cooperation on market performance of firms. *Entrepreneurial Business and Economics Review*, *7*(4), 73–89. DOI: 10.15678/EBER.2019.070405

Li, G., Liu, M., Bian, Y., & Sethi, S. P. (2020). Guarding against Disruption Risk by Contracting under Information Asymmetry. *Decision Sciences*, *51*, 1521–1559. https://doi.org/10.1111/deci.12437

Malak-Rawlikowska A., Majewski E., Kamińska I. (2023): Unlocking the potential of the European Union Quality Schemes for Polish regional and traditional food products. *Problems of Agricultural Economics. Institute of Agricultural and Food Economics National Research Institute* (Zagadnienia Ekonomiki Rolnej, Instytut Ekonomiki Rolnictwa i Gospodarki Żywnościowej – PIB), *375*(2), 95–124. DOI: 10.30858/zer/168871

Newman, C. L., Turri, A. M., Howlett, E., & Stokes, A. (2014). Twenty years of country-of-origin food labeling research: a review of the literature and implications for food marketing systems. *Journal of Macromarketing*, *34*(4), 505–519. DOI: 10.1177/0276146714529306.

Pietrzak, M., Chlebicka, A., Kraciński, P., Malak-Rawlikowska, A. (2020). Information asymmetry as a barrier in upgrading the position of local producers in the global value chain – Evidence from the apple sector in Poland. *Sustainability*, *12*(19), 7857, 1–21. DOI: 10.3390/su12197857

Pishchulov, G., Richter, K. & Golesorkhi, S. (2023). Supply chain coordination under asymmetric information and partial vertical integration. *Annals of Operations Research*, *329*, 1315–1356. https://doi.org/10.1007/s10479-022-04705-4

Yang, J., Liu, Z., & Lamb, S. W. (2020). Does uncertainty spread vertically? A theory of multilayer newsvendors under asymmetric information. *International Transactions in Operational Research*, *27*(4), 2112–2138. DOI: 10.1111/itor.12744

10 Enhancing Consumer Trust in Product Quality by Certification and Shortening the Beef Chain

Monika Gębska,[1] Adam Patkowski,[2] Roman Grzesiak,[2] and Maurizio Notarfonso[3]

[1]Warsaw University of Life Sciences, Poland
[2]AGREGO, Poland
[3]Italian National Agency for New Technologies, Energy and Sustainable Economic Development, Italy

10.1 Introduction

Poland is the sixth largest beef producer in the EU (*Database - Eurostat*, n.d.)

Eurostat data). However, this sector is currently facing enormous challenges resulting from changes in its macroenvironment. The critical challenge is the need to implement the EU "Farm to Fork" strategy, which aims to contribute to achieving climate neutrality by 2050 and changing the current food system to a more sustainable one (Muller et al., 2020). At the same time, the sector must keep up with constantly increasing EU animal welfare requirements and changes in consumer preferences.

In Poland, the beef sector is struggling with a low number of beef cattle and high fragmentation of production. There is no tradition of creating producer groups, and farmers are not experienced in producing beef from beef cattle (Bąk-Filipek, 2021). This sector's weakness is the large number of intermediaries in the live animal trade. Another challenge in Poland is expanding the difficult domestic beef market. There is no tradition of eating beef, a widely recognized brand, or a beef quality system (Bąk-Filipek, 2021). Beef meat quality is an issue because production is strongly linked to milk production. Providing consumers access to high, repeatable, predictable meat quality is difficult.

In this chapter, we review the value chain of beef cattle production in Poland and present its structure with a simplified scheme of processes. We analyse the importance of product certification to increase trust and reduce information asymmetry in the food chain, using the example of the Polish Quality Meat Program (QMP). This quality system was recognized in 2008 by the Ministry of Agriculture and Rural Development as the official national quality system for beef. Production under this quality scheme meets the requirements for a sustainable production system specified by the European Roundtable for Beef

DOI: 10.4324/9781032633725-12

Sustainability. Beef production in the QMP system is low-emission, with higher animal welfare and a higher level of prevention. This chain has a small operation scale and faces diverse challenges related to information asymmetry. In our study, we present the role of information asymmetry and trust in the farmers' cooperation, coordination of physical flows of animals and meat products, mechanisms of securing quality, governance structures, and legitimacy and enforcement. Additionally, we suggest methods to overcome the main problems.

The data for our case study were gathered during a focus group meeting as part of the EU Horizon Europa project (*Real-Time Fresh Data (DIRECT) - Data4Food2030*, 2023) in Poland in May 2023. The participants in the meeting were primarily beef producers, processors, retailers, restaurant owners, and key stakeholders in the beef production industry; in total, 13 people were present. In addition to these meetings, the authors conducted telephone interviews (CATI) in 2024 with six other significant stakeholders from the beef industry (beef farmers, Federation of Groups and Producers Wołowina Polska representatives, and certificate companies). We updated our findings based on thorough desk research and a comprehensive review of available secondary sources to ensure the data's accuracy and relevance.

10.2 Beef sector in Poland

The domestic beef market in Poland is firmly linked to milk production, and beef meat quality is an issue. Cattle are raised on over 350,000 farms, where the average number of animals is 20 (Strategia-Polska-Wołowina, 2022).

Beef production is located mainly in three voivodeships: Masovian (18.7%), Wielkopolskie (18.4%), and Podlaskie (16.4%). In the Lower Silesian, Lubuskie, Podkarpackie, and West Pomeranian Voivodeships, beef production is negligible, with none of them exceeding 2% (PZHiPBM et al., 2024; Szymańska et al., 2018). Although approximately 1.9 million cattle are slaughtered in Poland annually, the share of beef cattle in beef production is small. Of the total number of calves intended for fattening (approximately 1.35 million per year), the share of calves of beef breeds is at most 6%. In December 2022, there were 64,483 heads, 1.1% more than in 2021. Poland's most popular meat breed is Limousine, which accounts for approximately 70% of the purebred cow population. It is followed by Charolais and Hereford – approximately 12% and 6%, respectively. Other breeds are much less frequently kept in Poland and constitute only 3.8% of the pure beef cow population. Currently, the vast majority of beef, both from dairy breeds, beef breeds, and crossbreeds, is exported, and the recipients are a total of 84 markets, primarily EU countries such as Italy, Germany, France, Great Britain, and Spain (PZHiPBM et al., 2024). The high share of exports is due to higher prices in the EU and low domestic beef consumption for many years, ranging from 2.5 to 4.5 kg per capita (PZHiPBM, 2020). Meat on the domestic market comes mainly from dairy cows or crossbreeds, which affects the quality of the meat and is associated with consumers' reluctance to purchase beef. Despite the increase in meat consumption in Poland, beef is still unpopular and considered an expensive and time-consuming meat of variable quality. The opinions and choices of Polish consumers result from habits. At the same time, they indicate a lack of trust in products and producers, mainly due to the lack of access to information and the resulting problems with the transparency and traceability of the production process or the origin of meat (Aung & Chang, 2014; Żakowska-Biemans & Gutkowska, 2018). Beef on the domestic market is often sold loose, without packaging and labelling. In the case of exports, gaining consumers' trust geographically distant from the place of production is even more challenging. Consumers worldwide expect culinary beef to be characterized by high tenderness, juiciness, and palatability. These features must remain at a similar level every time, i.e., the meat will be of repeatable quality (Maltin et al., 2003). Low demand in the domestic beef market is also due to historical reasons (Bąk-Filipek, 2021). Meat plants in Poland have been avoiding the use of relatively expensive beef for the production of cold cuts since the 1990s, and the division of beef into two types in the times of the Polish People's Republic: bone-in and boneless beef resulted in low awareness of the types of beef and its culinary values. To overcome such an unfavourable situation in the beef sector, it is necessary to create appropriate standards and production models and develop modern, transparent, and easy-to-communicate quality systems and certificates. These solutions should confirm compliance with animal welfare principles, document the degree of sustainability of production, and enable effective communication with consumers. It will allow consumers to maintain a balanced and healthy diet in which animal products (including beef) play an important role. It will also have a very positive impact on maintaining food security. Certification of production should also positively impact the optimization and shortening of production chains by eliminating unnecessary intermediate links.

10.2.1 QMP program overview

In Poland, only one quality system is dedicated to cattle and beef production – QMP (Quality Meat Program). The QMP system is an open, voluntary cattle and beef production system of guaranteed high quality, recognized by the decision of the Minister of Agriculture and Rural Development as a national food quality system. The QMP system's administrator and the QMP mark's owner is the Polish Association of Beef Cattle Producers, one of the largest organizations within which representatives of the beef production chain in Poland cooperate, operating as an agricultural industry association registered in 2005. The QMP system is a national food quality system covering the entire beef production process, describing detailed standards. This quality system helps strengthen trust between individual entities participating in the supply chain and build consumer confidence in high-quality final products, which is crucial in changing market requirements. It helps objectively evaluate the product's quality attributes and enables producers to establish credible market claims (Nikolov et al., 2010).

The system certifies individual areas of the beef supply chain, starting from the production of live beef, through production and feed suppliers, transport, and ending with slaughterhouses and processors, taking into account the method of packaging and labelling.

Independent audit units regularly assess all these entities. Thanks to the certification process, all chain participants have a guarantee that production is carried out following the QMP System Standards adopted in a given area. The product is characterized by the expected quality at every stage, and the connection system is tight and resistant to undesirable situations occurring daily in the meat production sector. The comprehensive system consists of four categories of standards:

- "QMP-Bydło" (eng. "*QMP Beef Cattle"*) in the field of beef production;
- "QMP-Pasze" (eng. "*QMP Feed"*) in the field of feed manufacturing;
- "QMP-Transport" (eng. "*QMP Transport"*) in the field of animal transport;
- "QMP-Mięso" (eng. "*QMP Meat"*) in the field of meat processing.

Until the end of 2023, the standard applied only to beef produced from cattle of beef breeds, so it had limited application. Since January 1, 2024, after over three years of efforts, the Polish Association of Beef Cattle Producers obtained consent from the Ministry of Agriculture and Rural Development to extend the scope of the QPM standard to include dairy cattle. In the new edition, covering the most common Holstein Friesian (HF) breed and other dairy breeds and crossbreds with the QMP system is possible. This is a significant change because approximately 90% of calves intended for fattening come from dairy cows. Thanks to this change, almost every cattle breeder in Poland will have the opportunity to join the QMP system. Importantly, herds of various sizes can participate in the system, even the largest ones with over 150 livestock units. Many of them already meet the requirements of the QMP standard, so adding them to the system will be pretty straightforward. To clearly distinguish products from different animal breeds, two new logos, "QMP beef from meat breeds" (red) and "QMP beef from dairy breeds" (black), have been developed. Thanks to this, consumers will be able to recognize beef of guaranteed origin from beef breeds and beef from dairy breeds. Extending the standard will make it more popular, and producers will be able to obtain additional money and will confirm the high quality of cattle produced on the farm.

Certifications must be renewed annually by undergoing an independent, paid audit. Audit costs depend on the number of animals included in the certificate and range between EUR 400, including VAT (when the certificate applies to less than 20 animals), and EUR 600, including VAT (when the certificate applies to a maximum of 200 animals). The cost of the audit for larger herds is determined individually.

The QMP system was created to strengthen trust between entities, creating the supply chain "from farm to fork". The QMP mark certifies the standards of virtually the entire production process and guarantees high quality of meat and its products. Its requirements are adapted to the growing expectations of consumers. Thanks to this, Polish beef is gaining new markets around the world. This is one of the assumptions of the Beef Promotion Fund. The possibility of using additional subsidies in exchange for joining the QMP system is another step towards building a high-quality raw material base that is exported from Poland to the whole world.

Due to the need to renew certificates yearly, the number of certificates issued and the production volume under QMP vary. Similarly, meat production ranges from year to year; in 2023, it was estimated at 5,500 tonnes, while in 2022, it was estimated at 6,000 tonnes. Data obtained from an interview with the QMP owner show that the chain in 2005–2023 consisted most commonly of 530–570 beef producers, two slaughterhouses, and two processors. All meat produced under QMP is exported, so its products are unavailable in any retailer or restaurant in Poland. The situation will improve from 2024 as the standard has been extended. The latest data shows that producers are very interested in the certification system; nearly 500 certificates were issued by the end of May 2024, and more producers are submitting applications. The Polish Association of Beef Cattle Producers aims to achieve 4000 certificates a year.

In the QMP System, it is possible to certify beef production under universal – national and EU – quality systems and certificates. A new opportunity for the beef chain actors is the idea of the Polish Food Passportization. In 2021, the Polish Food Passporting pilot project used the beef production chain as an example. The pilot was completed in November 2023. The Passportization of Polish Food project envisages the construction of a digital system ensuring effective monitoring and identification of information on beef products in the supply chain, i.e. "from field to fork". If implemented, the IT system will provide a wide range of information about the food product, primarily thanks to innovative functionalities and integration with currently operating reference databases. Thus, the Polish beef sector can gain a tool containing credible, reliable, and inimitable product data.

10.2.2 Structure of the QMP Value Chain

The beef production chain in Poland is complicated, and the main reason is low integration. The Polish fragmented agrarian structure is often cited as the main reason for the lack of integration. Many small and medium-sized farms have a small average area and a low average herd size. This factor affects the production of beef cattle and dairy cattle. More than 350,000 farms are engaged

Table 10.1 Characteristics of the supply chain of QMP beef chain in 2005–2023

Specification	*Meat QMP (Poland)*
Production of suckled calves	33% own claves, born at a farm; 67% of calves purchased from other farmers or intermediaries
Production of meat (finishing farms)	530–570 farms (550 on average)
Distribution chain	Sale of livestock to slaughterhouses
Export share	Almost 100% of meat is exported. In Poland, meat is available only in 20 shops.
Stakeholders	Beef producers, industry organizations: Polish Association of Beef Cattle Producers, which registered QMP and Polish Association of Beef Cattle Breeders and Producers, Beef Sector Council
Value chain governance type	Suppliers/Calves producers/Farmer/Specification contracts (Gerefii et al., 2005) Farmer/Slaughterhouses/Processing companies: captive contracts with a high degree of formalization, high cooperation Distribution: slaughterhouse or processing company with no relation to producers

Source: Own elaboration.

in cattle breeding and fattening, but the average number of animals kept there is at most 20 per farm (PZHiPBM et al., 2024). They deliver their production through a large group of intermediaries to relatively few slaughterhouses and meat-cutting and packaging plants.

Some dairy farmers keep all calves and sell beef cattle, but most producers buy calves from dairy farms for further fattening and sell beef cattle to the slaughterhouse. This results in transporting many calves from farms far from each other. Private, independent transport companies (intermediaries) often organize the transport.

The QMP chain is similar. Table 10.1 and Figure 10.1 present the characteristics of the supply chain of the QMP beef chain and its governance structures, including the type of relationship, the degree of its formalization, the strength of social ties, or the level of dependency in the chain and its governance type. The description focuses on the QMP value chain until December 2023 without considering the standard's extension.

The primary activities of the QMP chain consist of inbound logistics, which includes all supply functions, e.g., acquisition of beef-suckler cows, bulls semen or calves, raw materials such as feed or straw coming from own farm or purchased, and inventory management. Breeding animals (suckler cows, bulls) come mainly from breeding farms responsible for national-level livestock genetic improvement (Figure 10.1, arrow 1). Important animal traits are measured

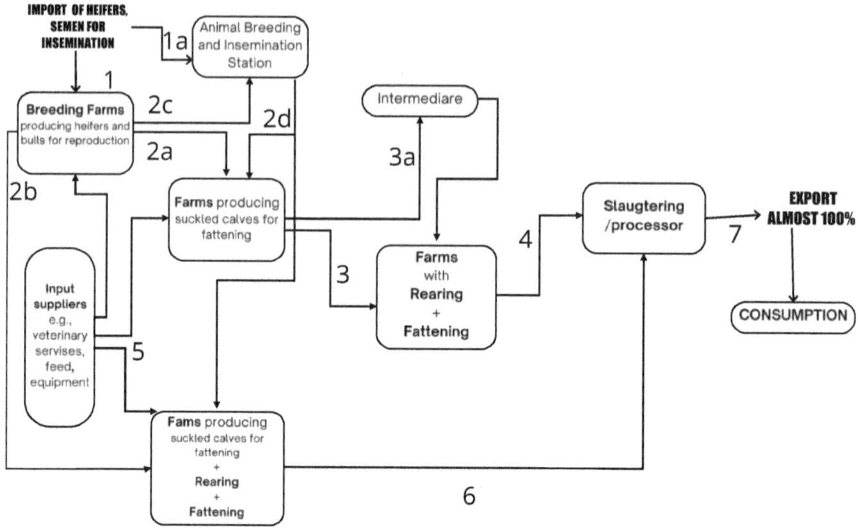

Figure 10.1 Scheme of the processes of the QMP beef value chain in Poland.

Source: Own elaboration.

at breeding farms, and the best animals are used as parent animals. The best cows and sires selected for breeding are sold to farms (Figure 10.1, arrows 2a, 2b). Some bulls go to Animal Breeding and Insemination Stations, where their semen is collected and distributed to farmers (Figure 10.1, arrow 2c, 2d). Breeding farms import some animals every five years to ensure future cattle populations' genetic diversity. About 50 pure meat breed cows and ten sires are annually imported into Poland.

In this value chain, fragmented production causes problems with the availability of calves for fattening, which complicates the supply process. About 66% of calves are purchased from other locations. Sometimes, calves are even brought from other provinces. Producers can buy calves directly from farmers producing suckled calves (Figure 10.1, arrow 3) or rely on intermediaries (Figure 10.1, arrow 3a). However, calves and their rearing must meet the requirements of the QMP system. The feed supply in the QMP chain requires pastures and other crops grown on the farm. Beef producers can purchase the missing feed from another participant in the QMP System or an equivalent feed quality assurance system, e.g., Good Manufacturing Practices Certificate (GMP+) or the QS quality system for food (QS). Poland has over 2,000 certified feed suppliers, so farmers can freely choose any supplier. However, market connections between the farmer and the supplier are covered by **specification contracts** (Gereffi et al., 2005) defining the product's characteristics and the method of obtaining it. For example, calves must be purebred from beef breed parents or a crossbred whose sire material comes from pure beef breed bulls. The purchase of all other necessary means of production, veterinary services, vaccines, cattle ear tags, and fertilizers for plant production occurs on the free market, where only the price determines the transaction. The relationships represent links governed by price, which is characteristic of a **spot market** (Gereffi et al., 2005) (Figure 10.1, arrow 5).

The second component of the QMP Value Chain's Primary Activities is farm operations, including all production and management practices. Beef production under the QMP system is usually extensive, including pasture breeding and calf grazing until finishing at 18–24 months old. Some producers do pasture breeding, and calves are first on pasture and later in feedlot finishing. Animals that are on pasture all year are subject to high environmental changes. They might need some feed supplementation to overcome winter deficiencies in the amount and quality of feed they receive. Cattle mainly receive hay and cereals or silage produced on the farm. Some farmers prefer to maintain more control over breeding, and cows calve in buildings and later go on the pasture with the offspring. There is much freedom in organizing and managing beef production. Beef cattle are kept on farms, which are mainly private, but the farmers are members of the Polish Association of Beef Cattle Producers. Producers must only follow the QMP system rules, which define appropriate breeds and ways of handling and fattening animals.

The next component of the chain is outbound logistics, which includes all activities to distribute a final product to a consumer. All farmers sell their animals directly to one of two slaughterhouses (Figure 10.1, arrows 4 and 6). This direct transport method is efficient and beneficial for the animals. It avoids additional stress caused by random intermediaries or places where animals are collected. Certified companies are responsible for cattle transport; ensuring the animals' welfare is a top priority. The QMP system also specifies how animals should be handled in slaughterhouses and during transport. The result is an average of 99.9% beef with a pH below 5.6, a clear indicator of high meat quality. The pH value measures meat quality and depends mainly on the animal's condition during slaughter. It is lower when the animal is healthy, rested, and not stressed and higher when sick, tired, and stressed. The pH value of meat up to $5.7 \div 6.0$ positively affects its durability and tenderness, which also benefits consumers.

Two private companies are currently carrying out the slaughtering stage. Sometimes, animals are transported far from the farm, which may create unnecessary stress. Extending the standard will help to produce more, allowing more slaughterhouses to be certified and reducing transport distances. Almost all meat from the QPM system is exported (Figure 10.1, arrow 7). The logo distinguishes it from other beef meat, which informs customers about specific production types and product quality.

Marketing and sales, including advertising, promotion, pricing strategies, enhancing visibility, and targeting appropriate customers, are part of a slaughterhouse's responsibility and the next actors in the country's destination.

Market links between farmers selling beef cattle and slaughterhouses are an example of a "**captive contract**" (Gereffi et al., 2005, pp. 83–84). On average, small-scale producers are dependent on larger processors. Beef producers would incur significant costs if they wanted to change slaughterhouses, primarily since only two certified ones exist. Captive value chains. In these networks, small suppliers are transactionally dependent on much larger buyers. Suppliers face significant switching costs and are, therefore, 'captive'. Such networks are frequently characterized by a high degree of monitoring and control by lead firms.

10.3 Results

10.3.1 The main challenges of the QMP beef chain related to information asymmetry and trust

One of the main characteristics of the beef QMP value chain is low production, which is based mainly on small individual beef cattle farms. However, starting in 2024, the certificate extension has excellent potential to increase livestock numbers and production.

There are many links in this chain that are not horizontally or vertically integrated. This results in frequent use of intermediaries at the farm gate, with little interaction with other links – sellers (calf breeders) or buyers (abattoirs), which creates problems of information and trust. In this case, using intermediaries results in incomplete and unreliable descriptions of calf genotype, exact age, previous feeding, health or welfare status, or prices. This shows that the information available varies from intermediary to intermediary and is imperfect for beef producers buying calves. The information problem in the QMP chain manifests itself in two ways: incompleteness and asymmetry. Incompleteness means that only some people have all the relevant information, while asymmetry indicates that the information is not evenly distributed and that some people have some confidential knowledge. Farmers with closed-cycle production, i.e., breeding, rearing, and fattening, are in a better situation. However, some also use intermediaries to transport animals to the slaughterhouse due to the long distance from the farm to one of two certified. This stage is more transparent due to the QMP standard defining rules for transporting animals for slaughter.

Another area for improvement is limited trust in the beef value chain concerning relations between producers and slaughterhouses, which comes from a subjective beef classification system. A slaughterhouse employee performs the cattle assessment before slaughter based on a visual assessment, which limits producers' trust in processors, even though the beef evaluator has authorizations granted by the Chief Inspectorate of Commercial Quality of Agricultural and Food Products. The price paid to the producer for the supplied livestock is determined depending on the rating awarded. The correctness of the classification largely depends on the experience and individual predispositions of the assessing appraiser (Houšková & Kovářová, 2012). The fact of visual assessment makes the entire process subjectivist and makes the system sensitive to abuse, e.g., lowering the class of livestock. De Oliveira et al. (2019) reported a similar example in the case of cattle purchase transactions in Brazilian slaughterhouses, where opportunistic misappropriation of value occurred due to hidden information, such as the results of animal quality measurements and the amount of remuneration for these difficult-to-measure characteristics. The lack of accessibility to information carries significant economic implications, incurring costs such as the expenses associated with searching and collecting information and potential losses due to missing information. This information gap can result in a decline in individual and collective well-being, with the possibility of adverse external effects. The cost and feasibility of acquiring information on the quality of goods are critical factors in differentiating search goods, experience goods, and credence goods (Baron, 2011). Improved animal identification systems will help maintain access to key export markets. In some situations, it may enhance the ability to quickly and successfully contain a food safety incident or a disease outbreak (Velthuis et al., 2009). Raynaud et al. (2009) stated that a reputational mechanism is crucial in mitigating rent expropriation issues in the rural context by reducing information asymmetry. They show that family tradition is an ex-ante warranty that enforces ex-post commitment agreements. Farmers with greater family tradition in cattle activity are less likely to face problems with buyers' information asymmetry advantages due to trust (Oliveira et al., 2017).

The problem of information asymmetry may manifest in the following areas: consumer trust in quality attributes and specificity of the product, market relevance, and recognition of the product.

10.3.2 Quality attributes and specificity of the product

Beef quality is a convergence between product characteristics and consumers' experiences (Liu et al., 2022). When purchasing meat, consumers assess its quality based on external and internal attributes (Banović et al., 2009; Grunert et al., 2004). As a result of this assessment, consumers formulate their expectations about the product's quality (the so-called expected quality). Food products are in this particular category of products whose quality can only be assessed after consumption (Cieszyńska et al., 2015). Hence, the "experienced quality" concept appears in the literature (Grunert, 1997). Quality attributes of QMP-certified meat are first of all related to intrinsic quality cues (appearance, colour, size, share of fat, fat marbling, and meat juice) or sensory features (taste, smell) (Grunert et al., 2004). Additionally, consumers perceive meat credence attributes such as animal breed, method of rearing, and fattening animals (Banović et al., 2009).

Consumers are interested in animal welfare aspects on farms, during transport, and during slaughtering. Finally, they expect the originality of the certified product and its security (under all supply chains) (Table 10.2). These quality features, which are difficult for the consumer to detect, are guaranteed by independent certification bodies and special product markings with the QMP logo.

The quality of meat products expected by consumers depends on visual characteristics, which depend not only on animal breeding conditions but also on transport to the slaughterhouse and pre-slaughter processing. Any exposure of beef cattle to stress affects beef quality and yield. Potentially stressful situations include hard loading and unloading, long transport in uncomfortable conditions, confinement in a slaughterhouse, lack of access to water and feed, contact with unfamiliar animals and people, unfamiliar surroundings and odours, exposure to sunlight, rain or cold, and noise. Meat is less tender in animals transported over longer distances (Hultgren et al., 2022). The risk of inappropriate behaviour is high due to the involvement of intermediaries. Although they are certified, if there is little understanding of animal welfare requirements, contracts may not be sufficient. Deeper horizontal integration of producers would be helpful, as it would be easier to organize and control larger batches of transported animals. Similarly, vertical integration in the chain will help develop a high level of formal and informal relationships between producers and slaughterhouses, the primary participants in the distribution chain (Grunert et al., 2005).

In the case of meat, appropriate storage conditions, especially temperature levels throughout the cold chain, are critical factors in maintaining product quality. One of the biggest problems with maintaining fresh meat quality is that it can only be stored for a short time (in loose or foil packaging) in wholesalers/shops. Once a consumer loses trust by purchasing a spoiled product, they will never purchase it again.

The credibility of products is unobservable through search or experience, but consumers may value credence attributes and be willing to pay a premium for their supply (Baron, 2011). Customers who buy labelled products trust manufacturers (Tonkin et al., 2015; Roe & Sheldon, 2007).

The QMP meat is sold through supply chains characterized by a lack of relational contact between the producer and the consumer. In this type of network, all supply chain participants build a relationship based on trust and a quality mark. Providing information about a product's quality characteristics to a geographically and socially distant consumer is challenging. Food labelling is a solution, a channel for communication between the food system and consumers without a face-to-face encounter (Tonkin et al., 2015). Therefore, it is essential to systematically inform the customer about the quality certificate and explain the principles of breeding, feeding, and transporting animals to

Table 10.2 Certified meat quality attributes from the consumer perspective and location of efforts to shape them in the value chain

Quality Attributes		*Type*	*Stages (Activities) in the Value Chain*			
			Breeding, Rearing and Fattening	*Transport/Trading Intermediaries*	*Slaughtering*	*Wholesaling and Retailing*
Visual	Appearance/freshness	Search	0	0	+	+++
	Colour	Search	+++	+++	+	++
	Marbling	Search	+++	+++	0	0
	Size	Search	+	+	0	+++
Other Sensory	Smell	Search/experience	+++	+	+	+++
	Taste	Experience	+++	++	++	+++
	Consistency	Experience	0	0	0	++
Health	Health security	Credence	+++	+	++	++
	Conditions for suckling cows/calves/cattle (animal welfare/pasture/other)	Credence	+++	++	+	0
	Crop production practices/ fertilization (for animal feeding)	Credence	+++	+	0	0
	Veterinary treatments	Credence	+++	+	0	0
	Manufacturing practices/ Production process	Credence	+++	+++	0	0
	QMP Label	Search	0	0	0	+++
Others	Durability (shelf life)	Search/experience	++	++	++	+++
	Quality stability	Search/experience	++	++	++	+++
	Convenience *	Search	0	0	0	+++
	Complaints, guarantees, etc.	Search/ experience	0	0	+	+++

Source: Own elaboration.

* Convenience to buy, convenience to transport, convenience to eat, convenience to prepare or to process; 0 denotes marginal or none; +, ++, and +++ denote, respectively, weak, medium, and strong influence and responsibility.

build consumer confidence in the product's reliability features. To show its legitimacy and strengthen its value, the QMP gets accreditations from the Ministry of Agriculture and Rural Development in Poland as the official national beef quality system. Leading certifications reassert their trustworthiness by emphasizing transparency, legitimacy, and accountability of their practices and governance processes (Bonroy & Constantatos, 2008; Sayogo et al., 2016). Short distribution chains (direct sales from a farm or online) are not used because there is no significant interest in premium products in Poland, such as meat with the QMP mark.

10.3.3 Market relevance

Building trust and decreasing information asymmetry in the chain is based on recognizing the QMP label.

Establishing trust and reducing information asymmetry in the QMP chain is hinged on the distinctiveness of the QMP mark and the emphasis on unique product features. Unlike Poland, other beef-exporting nations have comprehensive certification systems that encompass various aspects of the production process. The key to reaching the right consumer base lies in demonstrating that QMP beef is produced with a sole focus on high health, environmental, and welfare standards, which hold significant value in foreign markets.

A particular opportunity is the possibility of including in future information on the impact of production on the environment, such as in the Sustainable Beef and Lamb Assurance Scheme (Ireland), or on greenhouse gas emissions, such as in Life Beef Carbon (France).

The challenge is the limited scale of meat production. Even if beef producers adhere to the breeding standard, there is always room for individual interpretation of the rules, which can result in different breeding methods and cattle quality for each producer. Therefore, small batches supplied by farmers may be of different quality. When fulfilling retail orders, processors are sometimes forced to supply from many producers, so beef of different quality is often accepted to fulfil one order. Responding to the need for bigger batches, beef from dairy cattle will be included in a similar certificate, allowing them to cover a larger production volume.

Due to receiving small batches of livestock of varying quality from producers and insufficient exchange of information in the beef value chain, processors cannot constantly adjust their orders placed with producers to the retailers' expectations. Therefore, they must order large quantities of livestock, from which they select pieces to meet retailers' orders. As a result, they incur higher costs for storing and sorting purchased cattle.

The relationship between the cattle producer and the slaughterhouse is based on contracts. The bargaining power is not evenly distributed since only two slaughterhouses in Poland may be partners for QMP producers. Switching slaughterhouses is quite difficult for a farmer, which makes it rare.

As individual producers, farmers need more resources to effectively promote and protect their products against unfair practices in the supply chain. However, QMP implements projects co-financed from funds paid by PZPBM members, promotional institutions, national public funds, and European Union funds. The QMP Beef Promotion Program was implemented. The activities were implemented on the Polish market and the markets of EU countries among distributors, retail representatives, and restaurants. The main emphasis was on promoting high-quality beef produced under the QMP, which increased availability and interest in beef consumption in the country. At the same time, efforts were made in foreign markets to change the perception of Polish beef as inferior and to strengthen faith in the highest quality of Polish-certified beef. As part of the QMP Beef Promotion Program, a series of information and promotional campaigns were carried out, including information and promotional activities for consumers combined with tastings conducted in stores and restaurants and information and promotional activities for distributors in Poland and abroad – organization of information meetings.

Competing in European markets is a challenge because those markets are characterized by high beef consumption, and consumers can choose their beef quality. Good-quality beef is appreciated for its health, dietary, and taste properties, so consumers are willing to pay more (Grunert, 1997). Additionally, these countries have developed a culture of eating beef and the accompanying skills in preparing beef.

10.3.4 Governance structures

Decreasing information asymmetry in the food supply chain may result in quality improvement, eliminating unfair practices, and closer cooperation between actors. Cooperation may be strengthened into vertical integration (Newman et al., 2014). As indicated earlier, there is some integration in the QMP meat supply chain. However, it differs in parts – from the relationships typical of the spot market through contract specification to captive contracts. Additionally, at the production level, it is possible to find some good examples of cooperation between producers trying to eliminate intermediaries and take over their margin. Except that the farmers participating in the system acquire the knowledge and experience necessary to obtain a premium product. So, there is a chance to create lasting relationships between cooperating entities. This will enable greater bargaining power for livestock producers (Muller et al., 2020). Currently, bargaining power is distributed unevenly in the production and processing chain.

To increase interest in QMP certification, a new system of financial incentives (e.g., financial support for participation in quality systems) was implemented in

2024. Additionally, other incentive mechanisms for participation in certification systems will be developed (including training for producers, workshops, marketing campaigns, and additional benefits for participation in the system). In 2024, cattle breeders joining the QMP Quality System will receive additional payments under eco schemes. They will be able to count on subsidies of about 57 euros (PLN 250) for a suckler cow and about 30 euros (PLN 133) for a fattener, including for reducing the use of antibiotics. Larger farms over Livestock Unit 150 will also be supported.

10.3.5 Role of legitimacy and enforcement

An efficient control system, which includes monitoring the implementation of QMP rules and controlling production process compliance with specifications, is one of the fundamental components guaranteeing the protection of the label and reliability of unexperimental product features for the consumer. The QMP members document all activities to verify the correctness of activities resulting from the system requirements. Internal audits are carried out at least once a year, and their frequency is determined by risk analysis. There are currently five bodies that certify QMP.

EU consumers declare that labels ensure product quality and are essential to buying food products (European Commission, 2022). On the contrary, in Poland, only about 8% of Polish consumers recognize the QMP certificate, and 5% declare that their purchase decisions are based on quality marks (Stawicka, 2019). Results of many studies show that product price is more important than labelling (Gębska, 2022; Stawicka, 2019).

Due to the low scale of production and low recognition of the QMP label, the likelihood of unfair practices in the food chain is relatively low. Regulating unfair practices is difficult due to the complexity of the management structure and functioning of the food supply chain where QMP meat is available (national supply chain, EU supply chains, global chains). In every chain, there is a need for regulatory intervention in some form. Still, when the scale of unfair trade practices becomes a big problem, the challenge for decision-makers will be to determine whether national regulations are sufficient or whether an EU-wide approach will be needed.

The limitation in introducing regulations is the balance of benefits and costs of harmonizing rules on unfair commercial practices. Ensuring the effectiveness of regulations is also a considerable challenge, which includes implementing an effective enforcement mechanism and a system for monitoring unfair commercial practices.

An example of unfair practices is the use of a product logo and the sale of similar products under the QMP trademark. Such practices mislead customers. Customers pay more for a counterfeit product, thinking it is QMP certified. The product and the manufacturer lose trust because the quality is poorer, and consumers are disappointed. As a result, certified producers become less credible and trustworthy, which harms the entire chain.

10.4 Conclusions

The chapter presents and analyses the existing Poland beef meat quality labelling scheme. The scheme still has low coverage but aims to differentiate the products on the market according to the various aspects of the products and process quality. A third-party quality certification system assures consumers that the information firms supply is correct. Consumers may doubt the truth of the information provided by companies, particularly for credence goods, so certification made by independent bodies supplies consumers with an accurate evaluation of the product's quality attributes and enables producers to establish credible market claims. Although quality certification reduces the information gap between seller and consumer, the QMP case shows that the beef supply chain could be more efficient. There is still room to improve transparency and cooperation and reduce the importance of intermediaries. The QMP beef chain case study results demonstrate the product's distinctiveness and credibility. At the same time, the results indicate that the beef chain needs help with problems related to information asymmetry and low levels of recognition among consumers. Results show that vertical and horizontal integration can help build trust and positive business relations between individual stages of the chain.

Future activities in the QMP should concentrate on system and label promotion and increasing the number of participants. The program should be accessible because it includes cattle from dairy cattle and has financial incentives for producers.

References

Aung, M. M., & Chang, Y. S. (2014). Traceability in a food supply chain: Safety and quality perspectives. *Food Control*, *39*, 172–184. https://doi.org/10.1016/j.foodcont.2013.11.007

Banović, M., Grunert, K. G., Barreira, M. M., & Fontes, M. A. (2009). Beef quality perception at the point of purchase: A study from Portugal. *Food Quality and Preference*, *20*(4), 335–342. https://doi.org/10.1016/j.foodqual.2009.02.009

Baron, D. P. (2011). Credence attributes, voluntary organizations, and social pressure. *Journal of Public Economics*, *95*(11–12), 1331–1338. https://doi.org/10.1016/j.jpubeco.2011.07.005

Bąk-Filipek, E. (2021). *Uwarunkowania rozwoju rynku wołowiny w Polsce* [Conditions for the development of the beef market in Poland]. Wydawnictwo SGGW. www.ieif.sggw.pl/wp-content/uploads/2021/12/B%C4%85k-Filipek-E.pdf

Bonroy, O., & Constantatos, C. (2008). On the use of labels in credence goods markets. *Journal of Regulatory Economics*, *33*(3), 237–252. https://doi.org/10.1007/s11149-008-9058-z

Cieszyńska, K., Gutkowska, K., Wierzbicki, J., & Żakowska-Biemans, S. (2015). Oczekiwania polskich konsumentów dotyczące informacji zamieszczanych na opakowaniu mięsa wołowego [Polish consumers' expectations towards information on the packaging of beef]. *Zeszyty Naukowe Szkoły Głównej Gospodarstwa Wiejskiego W Warszawie. Ekonomika i Organizacja Gospodarki Żywnościowej*, *112*, 33–46. https://doi.org/10.22630/eiogz.2015.112.46

De Oliveira, G. M., Da Cunha, C. F., De Queiroz Caleman, S. M., & Maia, R. L. G. (2019). Information asymmetry: The case of cattle supply transaction in Brazil. *British Food Journal*, *121*(8), 1825–1837. https://doi.org/10.1108/bfj-01-2019-0041

European Commission, (2022). Europeans, Agriculture and the CAP. Special Eurobarometer 520/Wave EB88.4 – TNS Opinion & Social, June 2022, Europeans, Agriculture and the CAP – czerwiec 2022 – Eurobarometer survey (europa.eu)

Database - Eurostat (n.d.). https://ec.europa.eu/eurostat/web/agriculture/database?node_code=apro_mt_ls

Gereffi, G., Humphrey, J., & Sturgeon, T. (2005). The governance of global value chains. *Review of International Political Economy*, *12*(1), 78–104. https://doi.org/10.1080/09692290500049805

Gębska, M. (2022). Consumer trust and food purchase decisions in Poland. In *Routledge eBooks* (pp. 158–176). https://doi.org/10.4324/9781003266525-15

Grunert, K. G. (1997). What is in a steak? A cross-cultural study on the quality perception of beef. *Food Quality and Preference*, *8*(3), 157–174. https://doi.org/10.1016/s0950-3293(96)00038-9

Grunert, K. G., Bredahl, L., & Brunsø, K. (2004). Consumer perception of meat quality and implications for product development in the meat sector—a review. *Meat Science*, *66*(2), 259–272. https://doi.org/10.1016/s0309-1740(03)00130-x

Grunert, K. G., Jeppesen, L. F., Jespersen, K. R., Sonne, A., Hansen, K., Trondsen, T., & Young, J. A. (2005). Market orientation of value chains. *European Journal of Marketing*, *39*(5/6), 428–455. https://doi.org/10.1108/03090560510590656

Houšková, L., & Kovářová, K. (2012). Classification of the slaughtered cattle. *Acta Universitatis Bohemiae Meridionales/Acta Universitatis Bohemiae Meridionalis*, *9*(2), 29–34. https://doi.org/10.32725/acta.2006.015

Hultgren, J., Segerkvist, K. A., Berg, C., Karlsson, A. H., Öhgren, C., & Algers, B. (2022). Preslaughter stress and beef quality in relation to slaughter transport of cattle. *Livestock Science*, *264*, 105073. https://doi.org/10.1016/j.livsci.2022.105073

Liu, J., Ellies-Oury, M., Stoyanchev, T., & Hocquette, J. (2022). Consumer perception of beef quality and how to control, improve and predict it? Focus on eating quality. *Foods*, *11*(12), 1732. https://doi.org/10.3390/foods11121732

Maltin, C., Balcerzak, D., Tilley, R., & Delday, M. (2003). Determinants of meat quality: tenderness. Proceedings of the Nutrition Society, 62(2), 337–347. https://doi.org/10.1079/pns2003248

Muller, P., Böhm, M., Csillag, P., Donati, M., Drut, M., Ferrer-Pérez, H., Gauvrit, L., Gil, J. M., Hoang, V., Malak-Rawlikowska, A., Mattas, K., Napasintuwong, O.,

Nguyen, A., Papadopoulos, I., Ristic, B., Stojanovic, Z., Török, Á., Tsakiridou, E., Veneziani, M., & Bellassen, V. (2020). Are certified supply chains more socially sustainable? A Bargaining Power Analysis. *Journal of Agricultural & Food Industrial Organization*, *19*(2), 177–192. https://doi.org/10.1515/jafio-2019-0039

Newman, C. L., Turri, A. M., Howlett, E., & Stokes, A. (2014). Twenty Years of Country-of-Origin Food Labeling Research: A Review of the Literature and Implications for Food Marketing Systems. *Journal of Macromarketing,* 34(4), 505–519. https://doi.org/10.1177/0276146714529306

Nikolov, B., Vassileva, E., & Ivanova, D. (2010). Quality labelling and information asymmetry: Identification of quality labelling certification schemes in Bulgaria. MPRA Paper. https://ideas.repec.org/p/pra/mprapa/50070.html

Oliveira, T., Alhinho, M., Rita, P., & Dhillon, G. (2017). Modelling and testing consumer trust dimensions in e-commerce. *Computers in Human Behavior,* 71, 153–164. https://doi.org/10.1016/j.chb.2017.01.050

PZHiPBM. (2020). *Standardy Miesa Wołowego*. https://pzpbm.pl/wp-content/uploads/2020/12/standardy-miesa-wolowego.pdf

PZHiPBM, FZPDW, UPEMI, SRiWRP, & ZPM. (2024). Strategia rozwoju rynku Polska Wołowina (Polish Beef market development strategy) 2030. In https://pzpbm.pl/category/projekty/strategia/ [Pdf]. Koordynacja pracy: "Fundacja Original".

Raynaud, E., Sauvée, L., & Valceschini, E. (2009). Aligning branding strategies and governance of vertical transactions in Agri-Food chains. *Social Science Research Network.* https://papers.ssrn.com/sol3/papers.cfm?abstract_id=1481586

Real-Time Fresh Data (DIRECT) - Data4Food2030. (2023, November 8). Data4Food 2030. https://data4food2030.eu/project/direct/

Roe, B., & Sheldon, I. (2007). Credence good labelling: The efficiency and distributional implications of several policy approaches. *American Journal of Agricultural Economics*, *89*(4), 1020–1033. https://doi.org/10.1111/j.1467-8276.2007.01024.x

Sayogo, D. S., Jarman, H., Andersen, D. F., & Luciano, J. S. (2016). Labeling, certification, and consumer trust. In *Public administration and information technology* (pp. 67–88). https://doi.org/10.1007/978-3-319-27823-0_4

Stawicka, J. (2019). Znaki jakości – świadomość klientów oraz wpływ na ich decyzje zakupowe. *Zeszyty Naukowe Politechniki Częstochowskiej. Zarządzanie*, *33*(1), 232–248. https://doi.org/10.17512/znpcz.2019.1.20

Strategia-Polska-Wolowina. (2022). In Retrieved January 08, 2024, from: https://pzpbm.pl/wp-content/uploads/2020/12/Strategia-Polska-Wolowina_004-2.pdf.

Tonkin, E., Wilson, A. M., Coveney, J., Webb, T., & Meyer, S. B. (2015). Trust in and through labelling – a systematic review and critique. *British Food Journal*, *117*(1), 318–338. https://doi.org/10.1108/bfj-07-2014-0244

Szymańska, E. J., Bórawski, P., & Żuchowski, I. (2018). *Łańcuchy dostaw na wybranych rynkach rolnych w Polsce* [Chains delivery on the selected markets agricultural in Poland]. Wydawnictwo SGGW. www.uwm.edu.pl/kpros/images/monografie/lanuchydostaw.pdf

Velthuis, A. G. J., Hogeveen, H., Mourits, M. C. M., Dolman, M. A., Van Wichen, H., & Gaaff, A. (2009). Costs and reliability of livestock traceability systems for the Dutch sheep and goat sectors. *Acta Agriculturae Scandinavica. Section C, Food Economics/*

Acta Agriculturæ Scandinavica. Section C, Food Economics, *6*(1), 31–42. https://doi.org/10.1080/16507540903178464
Żakowska-Biemans, S., & Gutkowska, K. (2018). Atrybuty zaufania dotyczące jakości jako czynnik wpływający na decyzje nabywcze konsumentów żywności [Credence attributes as a factor influencing consumer food purchasing decision]. *Zeszyty Naukowe Szkoły Głównej Gospodarstwa Wiejskiego w Warszawie. Ekonomika i Organizacja Gospodarki Żywnościowej*, *121*, 115–130. https://doi.org/10.22630/eiogz.2018.121.9

11 Information Sharing and Trust in Organic Agri-Food Chains

Dušanka Gajdić
Križevci University of Applied Sciences, Croatia

11.1 Introduction

In the last decade, the production of organic food has been steadily increasing. Consequently, there are emerging questions related to the efficiency of organic agri-food supply chain (OAFSC) products. For example, what is collaboration like among stakeholders in the supply chains? To what extent do they share information, knowledge, and risks? Do they evenly distribute shared benefit? What is the level of trust among stakeholders, and does it affect the success of OAFSCs, ultimately influencing consumer trust? The lack of statistical and public data, as well as an insufficient number of empirical studies on the organic food market in EU countries, especially regarding OAFSCs in Croatia, is one of the factors complicating the search for answers to all these questions. Still, it is also one of the reasons for conducting this research.

11.1.1 Level of development of the organic food market in Croatia

Markets for organic agri-food (OAF) products vary significantly and have specific characteristics in each EU country. The European organic product market is the first largest globally, with over 54.5 billion euros of retail sales in 2021. However, it is not homogeneous due to differences in the development levels of individual countries influenced by varying income levels. Orsini et al. (2020) conducted a study in eight EU countries, categorizing organic food markets into mature and emerging markets. Developed organic markets include Germany, France, Italy, Switzerland, Sweden, United Kingdom, and Spain, while Hungary, Bulgaria, and Estonia have emerging organic markets. Croatia's organic food market is also considered one of the emerging markets based on its characteristics. Of the EU countries, Denmark has the largest total market share (13%), followed by Austria, Switzerland, and Luxembourg (approximately 11%), and Sweden (9% or more of organic products) (FiBL, 2023). These high market share figures can be attributed to the high living standards and strong ecological awareness of the population in these countries. In Croatia,

DOI: 10.4324/9781032633725-13

the market share is around 2.2% (FiBL, 2023). In 2021, the total retail value of OAF products in Croatia was approximately 99 million euros, with a per capita consumption of around 24 euros (FiBL, 2023). This places Croatia 19th in Europe in terms of organic retail sales. Consequently, the average per capita consumption of organic products in the EU is four to five times higher than in Croatia, averaging over 100 euros per person.

In Croatia, most farms engaged in organic production are family farms (hr. OPG), often covering areas smaller than 5 hectares. Although the number of organic agri-food producers (OAF producers) in Croatia has significantly increased in the last 5 years (ranking 14th in Europe in terms of the number of organic producers), Croatia lags other European countries in terms of processors, ranking 20th (FiBL, 2023). According to data from the Ministry of Agriculture of the Republic of Croatia in 2023, there were 6,132 OAF producers and only 380 processors in the country.

From the perspective of Croatian OAF producers, which is in line with research in other EU countries, some of the main obstacles to the development of OAFSCs include: underdeveloped and disorganized markets, insufficient domestic production and dependence on imported processed products, inadequate infrastructure for storage and processing, lack of collaboration and communication in the supply chain, complex legislation and certification procedures, lack of marketing knowledge, low purchase prices of OAF products, poor consumer awareness of the benefits of consuming organic products, and more (Gajdić et al., 2018; Koreleska, 2017; Kottila, 2009; Vlahović et al., 2015). According to research conducted in Croatia, retailers believe that better development of the organic market in Croatia requires the association of organic producers to increase supply and meet the quantity requirements of retailers. Additional key steps to improvement include better logistics and infrastructure, increased processing capacity, additional education for producers in marketing, negotiation, and communication skills, and other measures (Gajdić et al., 2021).

From the demand side in the supply chain, specifically from the perspective of consumers of organic products, key issues include: limited availability and choice of organic products, especially in supermarkets, high retail prices, insufficient consumer awareness of OAF products or organic labels, lack of perceived value and trust in quality, and more (Kottala & Singh, 2015; Padel & Foster, 2005; Renko & Bošnjak, 2009).

Insufficiently developed distribution channels for OAF products, especially in retail, coupled with insufficient consumer awareness, are crucial factors hindering the growth of the organic agricultural and food product market in Croatia.

11.1.2 Specificities of organic agri-food supply chain in Croatia

Previous research has shown that the use of distribution channels for OAF products depends on the different stages of development of the organic market in individual countries (e.g., emerging markets or mature markets), on the type of product (fresh or processed), and that organic producers market their products through different channels (Cavaliere et al., 2016; Gajdić et al., 2021; Hamzaoui-Essoussi et al., 2013; Orsini et al., 2020; Zander and Beske, 2014).

The main distribution channels of OAF products in developed European countries are indirect, so most organic food products can be bought in supermarket chains and specialized stores, while a smaller number of producers sell their products directly to consumers or through "alternative" chains (FiBL 2023; Orsini et al., 2020).

The distribution channels for OAF products in Croatia are mainly associated with the concepts of "local market", "alternative market", "direct sales", and "short supply chains". This is because most OAF products in Croatia are still sold through direct channels, with a smaller percentage of domestic producers distributing their products through retail (Petljak, 2013). Research by Essoussi and Zahaf (2008) has shown that small communities tend to support local producers for three reasons: (1) low availability of organic food products in supermarkets in small communities, (2) greater consumer trust in local farmers than in retailers, and (3) direct marketing and distribution of food products from local suppliers to consumers.

In Croatia, domestic OAF producers primarily market their products through direct sales. Due to competition and the significant presence of foreign organic products in supermarkets and specialized stores, only a few Croatian producers can compete with foreign producers in retail chains. This is partly due to the low capacity of farmers to operate independently in the market. Additionally, the distribution within the organic food sector is quite inefficient. The results of research (Gajdić et al., 2018) further confirm these claims. In 2018, only 13.6% of OAF producers distributed their products through indirect distribution channels (via retail and wholesale). A small number of producers sell their products through small shops and new distribution channels, such as hotels, restaurants, and cafes (Ho-Re-Ca). In terms of indirect distribution, specialized stores and small local product shops dominate the retail landscape.

Due to the specifics of organic production, small production quantities, and depending on the number of stakeholders and the type of product (fresh or processed), distribution channels may vary. Figure 11.1 provides an overview of common distribution channels for OAF products in Croatia.

Integration and collaboration are important factors that can strengthen the supply chains of organic food and the length of the supply chain and power relationships among participants are equally important as the type of supply chain.

11.1.3 Trust and information sharing between producers and retailers in OAFSC

Numerous previous studies have focused on attitudes and characteristics of consumers of OAF products and the main reasons for purchasing these products.

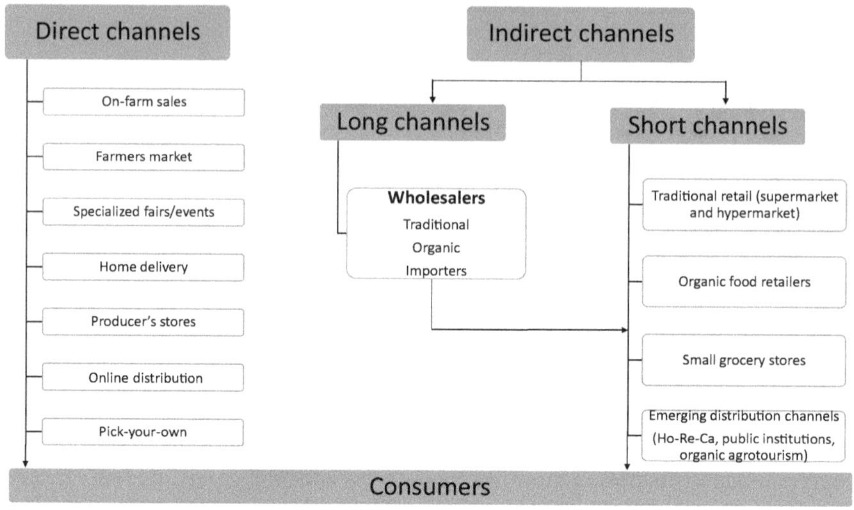

Figure 11.1 Distribution channels in Croatian organic food market.

Source: Gajdić et al. (2021).

However, there is insufficient research addressing the distribution of OAF products to the market and the challenges faced by stakeholders in OAFSCs. To further deepen the still insufficiently developed discussion from a theoretical perspective on the impact of collaboration and trust on the success of supply chains for agricultural and food products, Gajdić et al. (2023) conducted a systematic literature review and bibliometric analysis. They found that there is still a small number of empirical studies on the organic food market in EU countries. Additionally, a significantly smaller number of papers that elaborate on the research of the relationship between producers and retailers in OAFSC were found.

Trust is an important strategic prerequisite and a key factor that can enhance or limit (in the case of distrust) successful collaboration in food supply chains. For farmers, trust is a crucial foundation upon which relationships develop. As farmer satisfaction increases, so does trust, leading to long-term commitment to the relationship (Aji, 2016). Hamzaoui-Essoussi et al. (2013) state that in complex food markets "trust" is a vital element that can facilitate decision-making, linking "trust" to food safety which can be achieved through reliable and timely information. For trust to be successfully developed among business partners, certain prerequisites must be fulfilled. Findings from previous research (Batt, 2003; Puspitawati et al., 2011; Reynolds et al., 2009) indicate a series of key factors or prerequisites for trust. It is important to emphasize that the determinants of trust are significantly influenced by the specificities of the observed agri-food supply chain (AFSC), and they need to be carefully selected, as this can significantly affect the measurement of trust in the AFSC.

Given the growing importance of the organic food sector worldwide and in Croatia, as well as the need to increase the efficiency of distributing OAF products in Croatia, the main aim of this research is to examine the perceptions of producers on one side and retailers on the other side regarding the importance of mutual information sharing for the development of trust within OAFSC.

11.2 Theoretical framework and hypothesis development

Numerous authors consider mutual information sharing among stakeholders in AFSC as a crucial precursor to trust (Batt, 2003; Boniface, 2012; Fritz & Fischer, 2007; Kottila, 2009; Sun et al., 2018). Information sharing is a key feature of collaboration and trust quality since it not only reduces uncertainty among business partners but also leads to better efficiency, flexibility, and a faster response throughout the supply chain (Kache & Seuring, 2014). Responsibility for the final quality offered to end-users is widely dispersed among many actors in the chain, and the relationships between them are plagued by the issue of information asymmetry (Pietrzak et al., 2020). However, some previous research indicates a lack of trust among stakeholders in OAFSC due to problematic information flow within the supply chain, especially affecting the personal and procedural dimensions of trust (Anastasiadis & Poole, 2015).

Information asymmetry in AFSC is often associated with product quality (Jie et al., 2013; Pietrzak et al., 2020), delivery terms and conditions, and demand quantities (Batt, 2003), price transparency (Boniface et al., 2010; Puspitawati, 2011), consumer satisfaction (Fleşeriu et al., 2020; Guanqi & Husnain, 2022; Gundala & Singh, 2021; Padel & Foster, 2005; Żakowska-Biemans, 2011), trust between partners (Boniface, 2012; Kottila, 2009; Sun et al., 2018), and ultimately the overall supply chain success (Gajdić et al., 2021; Kottila, 2009; Naspetti et al., 2011; Puspitawati et al., 2011).

The results of the study by Jie et al. (2013) show that management actions to improve information quality and trust would lead to improved food quality, and these improvements, in turn, would lead to a competitive advantage and greater consumer trust.

With several factors that promote trust among partners in SC (Aji 2016; Boniface et al., 2010; Puspitawati et al., 2011; Reynolds et al., 2009; Susanty et al., 2017; Viitaharju & Lähdesmäki 2012), there are also those that can negatively impact trust development and ultimately the success of OAFSs, such as excessive use of power, dependence, and opportunism. Power is often associated with organizations that have valuable resources or control over resource distribution (Bandara et al., 2017) and is linked to the size of the organization, with the risk of opportunism increasing in certain situations in supply chains where negotiating power is not evenly distributed. Agricultural enterprises in the fresh produce supply chain usually have little negotiating power. Hence, there is a significant risk that buyers will behave opportunistically, and some examples of opportunistic behavior include when a retailer controls all information and does not share it with producers. According to Sun et al. (2018), retailers usually hold a dominant position in AFSCs, and when they emphasize information sharing, suppliers perceive it as fair.

Preliminary research conducted in Croatia through in-depth interviews in a smaller number of OAF producers and retailers (Gajdić et al., 2021) revealed that the quality of collaboration and trust between retailers and producers significantly depends on the size of the producer (*small or large*), the intensity of collaboration with retailers (*the proportion of sales through retailers compared to the total sales of the producer*), the size and type of the retailer (*small, medium, or large, specialized retailers of food products selling organic food, and general retailers of consumer goods*), as well as the type of product (*fresh or processed*).

Given the mentioned factors, the assumption is that there are differences among producers and retailers of OAF products regarding the sharing of information and mutual trust, regarding the size or type of business entities (size of producer and type of retailer). Therefore, we hypothesize as follows:

H1: There are differences in the attitudes of OAF producers regarding information sharing depending on the size of the producer.

H2: There are differences in the attitudes of retailers regarding information sharing depending on the type of retailer (specialized vs. non-specialized).

H3: There are differences in the attitudes of OAF producers about trust depending on the size of the producer.

H4: There are differences in the attitudes of retailers about trust depending on the type of retailer (specialized vs. non-specialized).

11.3 Research setting and data collection

The perceptions of OAF producers and retailers about information sharing and trust were analyzed based on a unique survey questionnaire designed to test the aim of research and proposed hypotheses. Eighty-one OAF producers and 22 retailers selling OAF products in their assortment participated in the research. The criterion for participation in the research was a minimum of 3 years of active business in the Croatian market. The research took place in the territory of the Republic of Croatia from June 2022 to January 2023 by sending links to the questionnaire to the respondents' e-mail addresses via Survey Monkey. Statistical data analysis was conducted using SPSS (Statistical Package for the Social Sciences) software.

For the development of hypotheses, a detailed literature review was conducted, and literature sources were used to design items by adopting existing measurement scales from previous studies. Additionally, new statements were created as needed, focusing on trust and mutual sharing of information among stakeholders in food chains. Table 11.1 shows used measurement scales and sources.

For many countries, especially in Central and Eastern Europe (CEE), retail data is not continuously collected (FIBiL, 2023). Also, in Croatia, there is no record of OAF producers who sell their products through retail channels, and little is known about the methods of selling products, the functioning and success of individual organic product sales channels. Therefore, the first step in the research design was creating a database of potential respondents.

For the purposes of this research, the market situation was analyzed by observing the market, employing an exploratory research technique that helps build a database. Retail stores were visited, including large retailers, specialized stores in organic or healthy food, and retailers who include OAF products in their assortment, such as specialty stores (e.g., drugstores). To obtain more accurate data and supplement the database, assistance was sought from several associations of organic food producers and supervisory bodies in Croatia. Through this process, a database of 165 Croatian producers and/or processors of organic food was created, whose products (fresh or processed) are an integral part of the retailer's assortment. Based on the market analysis, it was concluded that a surprisingly small number of OAF producers (from the total number of certified ones) collaborate with retailers. The research was conducted on a sample of 81 OAF producers, representing approximately 50% of the total number, and is considered a representative sample.

The unit of analysis, that is, the respondents of the OAF producer questionnaire, were owners of organic family agricultural holdings, companies engaged in the production of organic food. The majority of producers have continuity and long-standing operations on the Croatian market. Their agricultural farms were primarily registered as family farms. Most respondents (about 70%) had agricultural enterprises with a total area of up to 10 hectares. A total of 68.42% of respondents stated that their type of agricultural enterprise was mixed, meaning that, in addition to agriculture, at least one member of the household was employed outside the enterprise. Most of the respondents fell into the age group of 41–60 years. In the research, 59.30% of the participants were male, and 40.70% were female. The majority of respondents (53.10%) had completed higher education or obtained a college degree, 37.00% had completed secondary education, and 9.90% had either a master's or a doctoral degree.

The study involved 22 retailers offering organic and eco-friendly (OAF) products in their assortment. Considering the presence of retailers in the Croatian retail market, the sample included some of the largest retailers of mixed goods in 2021, based on the retail revenue. It also included retailers registered as specialized food stores. Previous research has shown that obtaining feedback from retailers is challenging, and the response rate for participation in

Table 11.1 Measurement scales

Construct	*Items*	*Source*
INFORMATION SHARING	INF1_Retailer and I regularly exchange information about changes that could affect our business. INF2_I find that sharing information with the retailer can improve my operational efficiency. INF3_I find that sharing information with the retailer can improve mutual financial performances. INF4_I receive timely information from the retailer about changes in demand for my product(s). INF5_I am well-informed about the retailer's business policies. INF6_Retailer regularly informs me about changes in their retail prices. INF7_Retailer promptly informs me about expected delivery schedule for my product. INF8_Retailer and I mutually share information about the quality management system and traceability procedures. INF9_Retailer regularly informs me about the needs and satisfaction of consumers of my products. INF10_Retailer and I exchange feedback on business performance.	Amentae et al. (2018); Zaheer and Trkman (2017); Bandara et al. (2017); Gellynck et al. (2011); Boniface et al. (2010); Kottila et al. (2009); Chen et.al. (2004); Batt (2003); Mentzer et.al. (2001)
TRUST	TRUST1_Retailer respects my beliefs and tradition. TRUST2_I have no doubt about the retailer's motives. TRUST3_Retailer has been fair in negotiations with me. TRUST4_I trust my retailer. TRUST5_Retailer trusts me as a supplier. TRUST6_I consider my retailer a business partner. TRUST7_The relationship between me and my retailer is characterized by strong personal connections. TRUST8_I trust the information that my retailer shares with me. TRUST9_If something goes wrong, I will remain loyal to my retailer. TRUST10_From my long-term experience, I know I can trust my retailer.	Bandara et al. (2017); Mutonyi et al. (2016); Boniface, (2012); Boniface et al. (2010); Schulze et al. (2006); Batt (2003)

surveys is often very low. Therefore, researchers conducting market-oriented studies on food supply chains often opt for case studies and individual examples (Anastasiadis & Poole, 2015; Kottila & Rönni, 2008), making it difficult to draw general conclusions. Comparing the obtained response rate with other surveys in the field of cooperation in food chains and considering that the survey was conducted on an underdeveloped OAF market, it can be concluded that the response rate is satisfactory.

The participants included employees from the procurement department, company management, company owners, company directors, business owners, and supply chain management department employees. Most of the participants had a high level of education (45.50%), followed by those with secondary education (22.70%), higher vocational education (18.20%), and master's or doctoral degrees (13.60%). Most participants were between the ages of 31 and 50. According to the current Accounting Act and the classification of companies by size, the survey included five large, four medium-sized, four small, and nine micro retailers. Among the respondents, there were a total of nine retailers that operated only in the local (Croatian) market, four retailers operated in both local and regional markets, six operated in the national market, and three retailers operated in international markets. Regarding the retail format, 50.00% of retailers operated in smaller stores, neighborhood stores, or specialized stores, 13.00% in supermarkets and hypermarkets, 9.00% in mini-markets, and one retailer was in the drugstore category.

11.4 Results and discussion

Information sharing and trust were observed as variables "information exchange" (INF) and "trust" (TRUST) between producers and retailers, with each construct being examined through a series of statements measured on a Likert scale from 1 to 5 (Table 11.1).

Information sharing was measured using several factors, including timeliness, impact on operational performance and financial results, timely delivery, changes in demand and prices, impact on quality management systems and traceability, consumer satisfaction, and the overall impact of information sharing on the business of producers and retailers. Trust was also measured through multiple indicators such as honesty, reliability, long-term experience, the establishment of partnership relations, and strong personal connections.

To establish satisfactory validity of the statements, convergent validity and construct reliability were examined, followed by discriminant validity. All external loads are statistically significant at a significant level of 1%. Convergent validity was measured through the indicator of average extracted variance (AVE). In addition, the reliability, that is, internal consistency, of each construct was examined through two indicators. The first is the Cronbach's alpha coefficient, and the second is the indicator of composite reliability. Cronbach's alpha values are significantly higher than the threshold value of 0.7, indicating the presence of internal consistency. The composite reliability indicator is also very high for all constructs and exceeds the threshold of 0.7, confirming the satisfactory reliability of the constructs in the model. In conclusion, it can be stated that all indicators effectively explain the constructs they measure – information sharing and trust.

For the purposes of this research and in accordance with the hypotheses H1 and H3, OAF producers were divided into small and large according to the size of the economy. The first group, that is, small producers, includes those with a farm size ranging from 1 to 10 hectares (small producers in total 59), while the second group comprises producers with more than 10 hectares (large producers in total 22). The aim was to investigate whether there is a statistically significant difference in the means of attitudes among producers related to information sharing and trust with retailers based on the size of the farm.

Also, for testing the H2 and H4 hypotheses, retailers were divided into specialized OAF retailers (13 in total) and non-specialized retailers (9 in total). In this case, the aim was to investigate whether differences in retailers' attitudes about information sharing and trust with producers could be justified by the type of retailer (*specialized vs. non-specialized*).

11.4.1 Testing the significance of information sharing factors among producers and retailers

Regardless of the location or type of research, most authors emphasize the quality of communication, which is achieved by the frequency of communication and the quality of information exchanged, as well as a positive experience of cooperation, as important prerequisites for trust in the OAFSC (Fritz & Fischer, 2007; Kottila, 2009; Puspitawati, 2011; Schulze et al., 2006). Quality of information encompasses several aspects, including accuracy, timeliness, appropriateness, and reliability of information, perceived honesty, and credibility of information (Batt, 2003; Zaheer & Trkman, 2017).

The results of this research indicate differences in the perceptions and importance of information sharing factors among producers and retailers. First, and in accordance with the H1 hypothesis, the aim was to investigate whether there is a statistically significant difference in the means of attitudes of OAF producers regarding the information sharing with retailers depending on the size of the farm.

Levene's test confirms that the assumption of homogeneity of variances is met for all variables that make up the information sharing construct. The statistical significance of the differences in the information sharing between producers and retailers was tested with an independent samples t-test. Although there is a difference in the perception of information sharing with retailers between small and large producers, this difference was not confirmed to be statistically significant. Based on the p-value at a significance level of 5%, farm size was identified as a statistically significant discriminator in only one variable that constitutes the information sharing construct: *INF1_Retailer, and I regularly exchange information about changes that could affect our business*. Small producers gave a higher rating to the regularity of information sharing with their suppliers compared to large producers. This is connected to the aforementioned fact that these are small producers who sell the majority of their products through direct sales channels, with a small proportion of sales to retailers in total. Timeliness of information is crucial for them due to more frequent deliveries of smaller volumes, achieving delivery flexibility to the satisfaction of both partners.

By reviewing previous studies, several key criteria measuring the quality of information sharing that can significantly impact the efficiency of the supply chain (especially in the producer-retailer relationship) have been identified, among which the timeliness of information sharing is consistently highlighted (Juan Ding et al., 2014; Rota et al., 2018). According to Susanty et al. (2017), one of the important antecedents of trust is high-quality collaborative communication, which, in addition to quality, encompasses frequency and timeliness of information exchange. Specifically, effective and timely sharing of relevant information enables supply chain members to plan and control supply chain operations and address product flow issues more quickly, facilitating more agile demand planning.

The results of the study by Gajdić et al. (2021) indicate that information sharing depends significantly on the type of retailer with whom organic food producers collaborate. With specialized retailers, information sharing was timely, more specific, and accurate compared to other retailers, described as high quality, open, and fair. Some of the smaller producers feel that they are "still learning to communicate" with retailers, and this is reflected in the quantity and type of exchanged information. Overall, the research has shown that, although OAF producers do not attach sufficient importance to the information sharing in terms of type and quantity, they still believe that the information they receive from retailers is generally accurate and timely. This is in line with preliminary research which also indicated problems in the exchange of information between OAF producers and retailers and that the exchange of information did not significantly affect producers' trust in retailers, because trust is mostly built on the previous experience of quality and honest cooperation.

Retailers' perceptions are also key to promoting the quality of relationships in food supply chains. However, previous analyses have shown that the number of papers investigating the attitudes of retailers about the quality of cooperation with their suppliers is significantly smaller. According to H2 hypothesis, the second aim was to examine whether there is a significant difference in the attitudes of retailers about information sharing regarding the type of retailer.

Based on the p-value at a significance level of 5%, type of retailer (specialized retailers of OAF products and non-specialized retailers) was identified as a statistically significant discriminator only at specialized retailers in the following variables: *INF2_I find that sharing information with my OAF producer can improve my operational efficiency; INF3_I find that sharing information with my OAF producer can improve mutual financial performances.* The results of the research show that for specialized retailers, the information sharing with OAF producers is the key to improving their operational efficiency, that is, specialized retailers believe that the information sharing can improve mutual financial performances.

Research (Naspetti et al., 2011) showed that retailers perceive regular exchange of information and high quality and open communication with their suppliers as important indicators of quality cooperation, which significantly affects trust. Research on retailers' attitudes (Jie & Gengatharen, 2019) on how trust and commitment to trading partners influence supply chain practices and the success of the Australian food supply chain also has shown that the quality of information exchange significantly affects the efficiency of the food retailer. This is in line with our research, but not fully comparable as these are very different food supply chains, regarding the members, structure, and development of the food supply chain. In conclusion, information sharing is more important for specialized retailers, because the share of OAF products in the total assortment of large non-specialized retailers is small, so it does not significantly affect their business results.

11.4.2 Testing the significance of trust factors among producers and retailers

Trust is particularly crucial in organic food systems because there are only marginal visual and sensory differences between organically and conventionally produced products, requiring consumers to trust producers' claims about the quality of these products (Thorsøe, 2015). In the long term, consumer support for organic products depends on maintaining trust within the OAFSC. Therefore, with this research, among other things, we wanted to examine the attitudes of producers and retailers of OAF products on mutual trust and determine whether there are significant differences that can affect the success and sustainability of OAFSC.

In the same way, as with the information sharing, and in accordance with the H3 and H4 hypotheses, examined the attitudes of producers and retailers about trust factors. Levene's test confirms that the assumption of homogeneity of variances is satisfied for all variables that make up the trust construct.

Here, too, the first aim was to investigate whether there is a statistically significant difference in the means of attitudes of producers regarding trust with retailers depending on the size of the farm. The statistical significance of the differences in the opinions of the producers was tested with an independent samples t-test. Based on the p-value at a significance level of 5%, farm size was identified as a statistically significant discriminator in the following variables: *TRUST4_I trust my retailer, TRUST5_Retailer trusts me as a supplier, and TRUST8_I trust the information that my retailer shares with me.*

Although previous findings indicate that in the agricultural sector trust is more important for small- and medium-sized enterprises (SMEs), which are characterized by the existence of personal relationships between business partners (Lu et al., 2012), research results indicate that larger OAF producers trust retailers more, that they also believe that retailers trust them as well and that they trust the information which retailers share with them. Formal contracts that larger producers establish with retailers, defining terms, allow for better production planning and consequently foster better development of trust in the retailer. Previous research conducted in Croatia has indicated that trust and loyalty are more pronounced in relationships between larger producers and specialized retailers of organic food. OAF producers have faith in expertise, honest advice, and information shared by retailers. For smaller producers of organic food, who often cooperate informally with smaller traders, uncertainty arises because this cooperation is not secure and the orders are not specifically and clearly defined. Given that smaller producers collaborate less with retailers, it can be concluded that they are still developing relationships and trust with their retailers. In this case, trust is based on verbal agreements, the development of close relationships, and personal trust, rather than contractual collaboration. However, this approach has certain advantages because it encourages more frequent communication between OAF producers and retailers, fostering more flexible relationships that can adapt more easily to market changes, aligning with the findings of Sahara and Gyau (2014).

Previous research has also indicated that large producers with higher collaboration intensity with retailers have significant trust in retailers due to high integrity in the supply chain and their long-term collaboration as the foundation of trust. On the other hand, collaboration and relationships with large retailers are mostly strictly business-oriented, not based on personal/friendly relationships. Findings from the study by Lobo et al. (2013) suggest that personal trust (xinyong) is a key mediator for developing close relationships (guanxi) with retailers and supplier loyalty to the buyer.

At the end, in accordance with the H4 hypothesis, an examination of the significance of the differences in retailers' attitudes about trust toward OAF producers was carried out regarding the type of retailer.

Based on the p-value at a significant level of 5%, the type of retailer was identified as a statistically significant discriminator at specialized retailers in the following variables: *TRUST7_The relationship between my OAF producer and me characterized by strong personal connections and TRUST8_I trust the information that my OAF producer shares with me.* Also, in the case of non-specialized retailers, the variable *TRUST10_From my long-term experience,*

I know I can trust my OAF producer, provided as a statistically significant discriminator.

The results of this research showed that it is important for specialized retailers to build trust with OAF producers, which is in line with the views of producers. In addition, large retailers (non-specialized) also base their trust on long-term relationships. For retailers, previous positive experiences with producers as business partners and their competences in market transactions (e.g., knowledge of the retail sector and expertise in the use of electronic ordering systems) are important, which can significantly enhance the development of trust, which is in line with research in the Finnish food chain (Viitaharju & Lähdesmäki, 2012). The research of Naspeti et al. (2011) found that trust affects performance in OAFSC, but with the assumption that the effect of trust on financial performance is not direct but mediated by stronger collaboration. Even in the developed organic apple market in Germany, where relations within the chain are characterized by a high degree of satisfaction and trust and high commitment (Zander & Baske, 2014), German retailers described the relationship with their suppliers with terms such as "reliable", "honest", "steady", and "secure", but also "market-oriented in a positive sense".

11.5 Conclusions

The short supply chain in the organic food producer-retailer relationship is present in the Croatian market. However, both previous and current research have shown that it is not sufficiently represented in Croatia. The fact is that the Croatian organic market belongs to a new market category and is still under-developed in terms of both supply and demand. The Croatian organic market is mainly characterized by direct sales, as most OAF products are still sold through direct channels. In comparison to more developed organic markets, the integration of organic products into the retail sector in Croatia is still very low, ultimately reflecting on the research results. The study reveals that for Croatian OAF producers and retailers, sharing information and developing trust are not significant by themselves. They fail to recognize the power of exchanging quality and timely information and developing mutual trust as important factors for the success of the development and sustainability of organic food supply chains. One problem is that communication and information sharing between producers and retailers mainly focus on price and delivery terms, and producers cannot express a genuine stance on these trust indicators. Consequently, it can be concluded that in Croatian organic supply chains, transactional collaboration predominates, involving simple communication and exchange of basic information between partners. Producers and retailers in the analyzed supply chain do not rely enough on shared information, but instead, trust and the development of good relationships with partners are built on previous experiences and the development of personal connections. Previous studies conducted in developed

EU countries show that sharing and the benefits of information sharing can be manifold, especially for building consumer trust in organic products. However, this study did not find a connection in that regard, and as such, it cannot discuss information asymmetry and its impact on trust as is the case with global/international food supply chains.

To provide recommendations for future research and position the research results within the framework of existing studies in the field of organic agri-food supply chains, it is necessary to reflect on the limitations of this study. First, due to the specific characteristics of OAF products and the unique features and development of the Croatian organic food market, the results of this research cannot be generalized to all other organic markets or food supply chains, also, considering cultural and economic factors that influence the findings. Another limitation, the data used in this study represents a snapshot capturing the perceptions of primary OAF producers and retailers, excluding the perspectives of other members in the food supply chain. Consumer attitudes were not considered, and the quantity and transparency of information about OAF products can influence consumer demand and the growth of this market. Croatia has significant potential for further development of OAFSC due to the availability of land suitable for increasing organic production. Areas that require additional focus include better organization of the organic product market, encouraging retailers to expand their offerings and enhance the availability of Croatian OAF products on their shelves. It is crucial to establish stronger collaboration between producers and retailers based on the quantity and quality of exchanged information and the creation of long-term trust. Additionally, networking among small OAF producers is essential for access to larger retailers.

Additionally, it is suggested to conduct further analyses, perhaps through in-depth interviews or focus groups, to explore the attitudes, reasons, motivations, and meanings for both parties. While quantitative surveys provide frequencies of the chosen responses by the participants, in the case of focus groups, we attempt to uncover why people have a positive or negative attitude toward a topic or may not be able to express it quantitatively. This approach would yield more precise data on the attitudes of producers and retailers regarding the researched topic.

References

Aji, J. M. M. (2016). Exploring farmer-supplier relationships in the East Java seed potato market. *Agriculture and Agricultural Science Procedia*, *9*, 83–94. doi:10.1016/j.aaspro.2016.02.130

Amentae, T. K., Gebresenbet, G., & Ljungberg, D. (2018). Examining the interface between supply chain governance structure choice and supply chain performances of dairy chains in Ethiopia. *International Food and Agribusiness Management Review*, *21*(8), 1061–1081. doi:10.22434/IFAMR2018.0001

Anastasiadis, F., & Poole, N. (2015). Emergent supply chains in the agrifood sector: Insights from a whole chain approach. *Supply Chain Management: An International Journal*, *20*(4), 353–368. doi:10.1108/SCM-08-2014-0259

Bandara, S., Leckie, C., Lobo, A., & Hewege, C. (2017). Power and relationship quality in supply chains: The case of the Australian organic fruit and vegetable industry. *Asia Pacific Journal of Marketing and Logistics*, *29*(3), 501–518. doi:10.1108/APJML-09-2016-0165

Batt, P. J. (2003). Building trust between growers and market agents. *Supply Chain Management: An International Journal*, *8*(1), 65–78. doi:10.1108/13598540310463378

Boniface, B. (2012). Producer relationships segmentation in Malaysia's milk supply chains. *British Food Journal*, *114*(10), 1501–1516. doi:10.1108/00070701211263046

Boniface, B., Gyau, A., Stringer, R., & Umberger, W. J. (2010). Building producer loyalty in Malaysia's fresh milk supply chain. *Australasian Agribusiness Review*, *18*, 1–29. doi:10.22004/ag.econ.114423

Cavaliere, A., Peri, M., & Banterle, A. (2016). Vertical coordination in organic food chains: A survey based analysis in France, Italy and Spain. *Sustainability*, *8*(6), 569. doi:10.3390/su8060569

Chen, I. J., Paulraj, A., & Lado, A. A. (2004). Strategic purchasing, supply management, and firm performance. *Journal of Operations Management, 22*(5), 505–523. doi:10.1016/j.jom.2004.06.002

Essoussi, L. H., & Zahaf, M. (2008). Decision making process of community organic food consumers: An exploratory study. *Journal of Consumer Marketing*, *25*(2), 95–104. doi:10.1108/07363760810858837

FiBL. The World of Organic Agriculture, Statistic & Emerging Trends. (2023). Retrieved from www.organic-world.net/yearbook/yearbook-2023.html (December 20, 2023).

Fleşeriu, C., Cosma, S. A., & Bocăneţ, V. (2020), Values and planned behavior of the Romanian organic food consumer. *Sustainability*, *12*(5), 1722. doi:10.3390/su12051722

Fritz, M. & Fischer, C. (2007). The role of trust in European food chains: Theory and empirical findings. *International Food and Agribusiness Management Review*, *10*(2), 1–24. doi:10.22004/ag.econ.8185

Gajdić, D., Kotzab, H., & Petljak, K. (2023). Collaboration, trust and performance in agri-food supply chains: A bibliometric analysis. *British Food Journal*, *125*(2), 752–778. doi:10.1108/BFJ-07-2021-0723

Gajdić, D., Mesić, Ž., & Petljak, K. (2021). Preliminary research about producers' perceptions of relationship quality with retailers in the supply chain of organic food products in Croatia. *Sustainability*, *13*(24), 1–41 doi:10.3390/su132413673

Gajdić, D., Petljak, K., & Mesić, Ž. (2018). An exploration of distribution channels: Challenges and opportunities for organic food producers in Croatia. *Економика пољопривреде*, *65*(4), 1461–1482. doi:10.5937/ekopolj1804461g

Gellynck, X., Kühne, B., & Weaver, R. D. (2011). Relationship quality and innovation capacity of chains: The case of the traditional food sector in the EU. *International Journal on Food System Dynamics, 2*(1), 1–22. doi:10.18461/ijfsd.v2i1.211

Guanqi, Z., & Husnain, M. (2022). Assessing the role of organic food supply chain traceability on food safety and consumer wellbeing: A mediated-moderation investigation. *Frontiers in Psychology*, *13*, 1073376. doi:10.3389/fpsyg.2022.1073376

Gundala, R. R., & Singh, A. (2021), What motivates consumers to buy organic foods? Results of an empirical study in the United States, *PLos One*, *16*(9), p. e0257288. doi:10.1371/journal.pone.0257288

Hamzaoui-Essoussi, L., Sirieix, L., & Zahaf, M. (2013). Trust orientations in the organic food distribution channels: A comparative study of the Canadian and French markets. *Journal of Retailing and Consumer Services*, *2*(3), 292–301. doi:10.1016/j.jretconser.2013.02.002

Jie, F., & Gengatharen, D. (2019). Australian food retail supply chain analysis. *Business Process Management Journal*, *25*(2), 271–287. doi:10.1108/BPMJ-03-2017-0065

Jie, F., Parton, K. A., & Cox, R. J. (2013). Linking supply chain practices to competitive advantage. *British Food Journal*, *115*(7), 1003–1024. doi:10.1108/BFJ-10-2010-0181

Juan Ding, M., Jie, F., Parton, A. K., & Matanda, J. M. (2014). Relationships between quality of information sharing and supply chain food quality in the Australian beef processing industry. *The International Journal of Logistics Management*, *25*(1), 85–108. doi:10.1108/IJLM-07-2012-0057

Kache, F., & Seuring, S. (2014). Linking collaboration and integration to risk and performance in supply chains via a review of literature reviews. *Supply Chain Management: An International Journal*, *19*(5/6), 664–682. doi:10.1108/SCM-12-2013-0478

Koreleska, E. (2017). Production and market of ecological product in Poland. In *International scientific conference rural development 2017* (pp. 1119–1123), doi:10.15544/RD.2017.043

Kottala, S. Y., & Singh, R. (2015). A review of sustainability, deterrents, personal values, attitudes and purchase intentions in the organic food supply chain. *Pacific Science Review B: Humanities and Social Sciences*, *1*(3), 114–123. doi:10.1016/j.psrb.2016.09.003

Kottila, M. R. (2009). Knowledge sharing in organic food supply chains. *Journal on Chain and Network Science*, *9*(2), 133–144. doi:10.3920/JCNS2009.x168

Kottila, M.-R., & Rönni, P. (2008). Collaboration and trust in two organic food chains. *British Food Journal*, *110*(4/5), 376–394., doi:10.1108/00070700810868915

Lobo, A., Leckie, C., & Li, C. (2013). The impact of guanxi, xinyong and buyer collaboration on the loyalty and financial performance of vegetable farmers in China. *Asia Pacific Journal of Marketing and Logistics*, *25*(5), 745–764. doi:10.1108/APJML-01-2013-0018

Lu, H., Feng, S., Trienekens, J.H., & Omta, S.W.F. (2012). Network strength, transaction-specific investments, inter-personal trust, and relationship satisfaction in Chinese agri-food SMEs. *China Agricultural Economic Review*, *4*(3), 363–378. doi:10.1108/17561371211263374

Mentzer, J. T., DeWitt, W., Keebler, J. S., Min, S., Nix, N. W., Smith, C. D., & Zacharia, Z. G. (2001). Defining supply chain management. *Journal of Business Logistics*, *22*(2), 1–25. doi:10.1002/j.2158-1592.2001.tb00001.x

Mesic, Ž., Molnár, A., & Cerjak, M. (2018). Assessment of traditional food supply chain performance using triadic approach: The role of relationships quality. *Supply Chain Management: An International Journal*, *23*(5), 396–411. doi:10.1108/SCM-10-2017-0336

Ministry of Agriculture of the Republic of Croatia (2023). Available online: https://poljoprivreda.gov.hr/statistika-360/360 (October 10, 2023).

Mutonyi, S., Beukel, K., Gyau, A., & Hjortsø, C. N. (2016). Price satisfaction and producer loyalty: The role of mediators in business to business relationships in Kenyan mango supply chain. *British Food Journal*, *118*(5), 1067–1084. doi:10.1108/BFJ-09-2015-0319

Naspetti, S., Lampkin, N., Nicolas, P., Stolze, M., & Zanoli, R. (2011). Organic supply chain collaboration: A case study in eight EU countries. *Journal of Food Products Marketing*, *17*(2), 141–162. doi:10.1080/10454446.2011.548733

Orsini, S., Padel, S., Gambelli, D., Lernoud, J., Sanders, J., Solfanelli, F., Stolze, M., Willer, H., & Zanoli, R. (2020). Beyond "mainstream" and "alternative" in organic food supply chains: Empirical examples of added value distribution from eight European countries. *British Food Journal*, *122*(3), 798–812. doi:10.1108/bfj-07-2019-0508

Padel, S., & Foster, C. (2005). Exploring the gap between attitudes and behaviour: Understanding why consumers buy or do not buy organic food. *British Food Journal*, *107*(8), 606–625. doi:10.1108/00070700510611002

Petljak, K., (2013). Distribution channels of organic food in the Republic of Croatia. *Business Excellence*, *7*(1), Zagreb, Croatia pp.73–97. Retrieved from https://hrcak.srce.hr/file/156309

Pietrzak, M., Chlebicka, A., Kraciński, P., & Malak-Rawlikowska, A. (2020). Information asymmetry as a barrier in upgrading the position of local producers in the global value chain—Evidence from the apple sector in Poland. *Sustainability*, *12*(19), 7857. doi:10.3390/su12197857

Puspitawati, E., Guyau, A., Stringer, R., & Umberger, W. J. (2011). Determinants of trust in the Indonesian potato industry: A comparison between groups of potato farmers. *Journal of Agribusiness*, Agricultural Economics Association of Georgia, *29*(1). doi:10.22004/ag.econ.260160

Renko, S., & Bošnjak, K. (2009). Aktualno stanje i perspektive budućeg razvoja tržišta ekološke hrane u Hrvatskoj [The actual situation and the perspectives for development of organic food market in Croatia]. *Ekonomski pregled*, *60*(7–8), 369–395. Retrieved from https://hrcak.srce.hr/40483

Reynolds, N., Fischer, C., & Hartmann, M. (2009). Determinants of sustainable business relationships in selected German agri-food chains. *British Food Journal*, *111*(8), 776–793. doi:10.1108/00070700910980919

Rota, C., Pugliese, P., Hashem, S., & Zanasi, C. (2018). Assessing the level of collaboration in the Egyptian organic and fair trade cotton chain. *Journal of Cleaner Production*, *170*, 1665–1676. doi:10.1016/j.jclepro.2016.10.011

Sahara, S., & Gyau, A. (2014). Contractual arrangements and commitment in the Indonesian supermarket channel. *British Food Journal*, *116*(5), 765–779. doi:10.1108/BFJ-03-2012-0070

Schulze, B., Wocken, C., & Spiller, A. (2006). Relationship quality in agri-food chains: Supplier management in the German pork and dairy sector. *Journal on Chain and Network Science*, *6*(1), 55–68. doi:10.3920/JCNS2006.x065

Sun, Y., Liu, Z., & Yang, H. (2018). How does suppliers' fairness affect the relationship quality of agricultural product supply chains? *Journal of Food Quality*, *5*, 1–15. doi:10.1155/2018/9313068

Susanty, A., Bakhtiar, A., Jie, F., & Muthi, M. (2017). The empirical model of trust, loyalty, and business performance of the dairy milk supply chain: A comparative study. *British Food Journal*, *119*(12), 2765–2787. doi:10.1108/BFJ-10-2016-0462

Thorsøe, M.H. (2015). Maintaining trust and credibility in a continuously evolving organic food system. *Journal of Agricultural and Environmental Ethics, 28,* 767–787. doi:10.1007/s10806-015-9559-6

Viitaharju, L., & Lähdesmäki, M. (2012). Antecedents of trust in asymmetrical business relationships: Differing perceptions between food producers and retailers. *Marketing Intelligence & Planning, 30*(5), 567–587. doi:10.1108/02634501211251061

Vlahović, B., Puškarić, A., & Šojić, S. (2015). Research into agricultural producers' motives for engaging in organic production in the Republic of Serbia. *Economic Insights – Trends and Challenges, 4*(67), 31–39. Retrieved from http://repository.iep.bg.ac.rs/233/

Zaheer, N., & Trkman, P. (2017). An information sharing theory perspective on willingness to share information in supply chains. *The International Journal of Logistics Management, 28*(2), 417–443. doi:10.1108/IJLM-09-2015-0158

Żakowska-Biemans, S. (2011). Polish consumer food choices and beliefs about organic food. *British Food Journal, 113*(1), 122–137. doi:10.1108/00070701111097385

Zander, K., & Beske, P. (2014). Happy growers! Relationship quality in the German organic apple chain. *International Food and Agribusiness Management Review, 17*(3), 1–20. doi:10.22004/ag.econ.183498

12 Information Asymmetry and Trust in the Green Energy Chain

Evidence from the Biogas Sector

Piotr Sulewski,[1] *Adam Wąs,*[1] *and Wiktor Ignaciuk*[2]

[1]*Warsaw University of Life Sciences – SGGW, Poland*
[2]*Polish Association of Agricultural Biogas Producers, Poland*

12.1 Introduction

The EU is prioritizing finding alternatives to non-renewable energy sources due to climate change and the situation with Russia and Ukraine. Agricultural biomass, particularly waste biomass converted to biogas, is a sustainable and reliable energy source. However, despite its potential, many countries, including Poland, have been slow to develop this industry. This is due to many external conditions, but we cannot ignore factors related to individual links in the green energy generation chain, especially related to biomass supply. Proper organization of substrate management is one of the most critical factors determining the functioning of agricultural biogas plants. Marks et al. (2020) and Wandera et al. (2018) emphasized the importance of cheap and effective substrates, a large spectrum of substrate usage, proper selection, and continuity of supplies. Agricultural biogas plants can either rely on their own substrates or obtain them from other entities for free or through purchase. Biogas plants that produce and sell energy must acquire some biomass from external suppliers. Optimizing substrate supply management is crucial for the economic success of a biogas plant. However, the availability and prices of substrates are highly variable, making it challenging to find the right balance. Besides substrate price and efficiency, and many other factors, such as relationships with contractors, supply interruptions, or incomplete information about substrate composition, also affect the final decisions of biogas plant managers. The accurate assessment of substrate condition, composition, and technology parameters can be complex, creating an information asymmetry between biogas producers and substrate suppliers. Using biomass contaminated with prohibited substances or technological parameters other than those declared by the supplier can cause severe disruptions in the biotechnological processes in the fermenter chamber, including process stoppage due to contamination with antibiotics. Knowledge of the quality of substrates is possessed by their suppliers but not by biogas producers. It can be assumed that

DOI: 10.4324/9781032633725-14

the existing information asymmetry makes it necessary for biogas producers to rely on trust with suppliers when performing the supply function or to incur additional transaction costs related to evaluating the raw materials purchased (similarly, the equipment used in the production process). Trust is also necessary in the relationship between biogas producers and energy consumers. These issues, even though they appear to be important in the context of the operational efficiency of biogas plants, have not yet been the subject of scientific analysis. In this context, the study's primary purpose was to assess the importance of information asymmetry and trust in biogas plant relationships with other links in the renewable energy generation chain.

12.2 Role of biogas in energy transformation challenge and the problem of trust

The transformation of the energy sector is a significant topic of discussion in many countries worldwide (Haibach & Schneider 2013; UN, 2015). This is due to the challenges of implementing climate policies (IPCC, 2022; UN, 2021) and the natural gas crisis in 2021–2022 (CNB, 2023; IEA, 2023). As a result, there is a renewed focus on finding alternative energy sources and transforming the energy sector in the EU (EC, 2022). The European Commission has proposed faster decarbonization and increased use of renewable energy across all economic sectors to combat the energy crisis in line with the Paris Agreement (UN, 2015) and the European Climate Law (Official Journal of the European Union, 2021). The goal is to reduce greenhouse gas emissions by 55% (compared to the level of 1990) by 2030 and achieve climate neutrality by 2050. These goals cannot be met without significant changes in the structure of energy sources used, given that 75–77% of GHG emissions in the EU are related to energy-sector-related processes (UNCC, 2018; European Commission, 2019). According to estimates by the European Environment Agency, only 22.5% of energy consumed in the EU in 2022 was from renewable sources. The target for 2030 is to increase this value to 42.5% (EEA, 2023). To accelerate the energy sector's transformation process, the European Commission proposed a RE-Power EU (EC, 2022) action plan to help EU countries implement the energy transition. One way to achieve this goal is by developing biogas production, including biomethane, which has many advantages (Burg, 2023; EC, 2015; Piwowar, 2020). Biogas is an alternative energy source that can help move toward a circular economy and increase energy independence. It is also stable, independent of weather conditions, reduces greenhouse gas emissions, and provides valuable agricultural fertilizer (Barrera et al., 2018). The primary advantages of biogas, apart from generating energy and increasing energy independence, include: greater stability compared to others, dependent on weather conditions, renewable energy sources, and reduction of greenhouse gas emissions not only as a result of replacing non-renewable energy with renewable energy but also as a result of changes in the method of managing organic fertilizers (in the case of agricultural biogas) (Biogas Association, 2012; Møller et al., 2022; Shih et al. 2012; Stejskal, 2008). An additional benefit is related to the digestate, a by-product of the processes taking place in the biogas plant, which is a valuable agricultural fertilizer (Czekała, 2022). In conclusion, a circular economy is an option for transforming linear and semi-linear flows of materials and energy into circular flows to increase the system's sustainability. Biogas production can be a practical example of this concept. Unfortunately, despite the advantages, biogas production is also associated with many challenges – some of which have already been the subject of scientific analysis (such as dependence on financing, technological solutions, and process conditions (Gao et al., 2019; Ignaciuk & Sulewski, 2021). So far, however, scientific analyses have ignored the problem of cooperation in the biogas supply chain, particularly the problem of asymmetry information and trust between biogas plants and substrate suppliers, on which the course and efficiency of generation processes depend.

Business entities operating in modern markets rely on information as one of their most critical resources for mutual relations and decision-making (Jakubowska, 2017). However, information asymmetry can occur when specific individuals or groups have different amounts of information, leading to negative impacts such as adverse selection and moral hazard (Prokop, 2021). Therefore, information asymmetry creates an imbalance of power in transactions, leading to inefficiency and market failure. This is particularly true for goods with trust/credibility attributes, which are difficult to assess for quality (Chlebicka, 2012). In such cases, producers/suppliers know specific features of the products that buyers cannot verify even after making a purchase (Dulleck & Kerschbamer, 2006). Consequently, buyers trust the seller when making purchasing decisions, assuming that the product has specific features they cannot verify themselves (Chlebicka, 2012). These characteristics also seem to correspond to the specifics of the relationship between biogas plant buyers of organic substrates and the various suppliers of these substrates. When ordering substrates that are some form of organic waste, biogas plant managers have limited ability to evaluate the characteristics of the product they are purchasing. Thus, when making a purchasing decision, buyers rely on trust in the seller if they do not know the parameters of the purchased product.

Trust can be defined as the belief or perception of one party (referred to as the principal) that the other party (referred to as the agent) in a particular transaction will not cheat, provided that the payoff structure can be described by the prisoner's dilemma or principal-agent game (Knack, 2001). In other words, trust means the act of a truster placing their trust in a trustee concerning a particular behavior in a specific context and at a specified time. It is worth noting that trust can change over time, as the trustee may adjust their expectations based on the actual situation (Bauer & Freitag, 2017). Regarding the research problem addressed (related to relationships in the agricultural biogas production chain), it can be noted that when deciding to purchase a particular raw material, the owner of a biogas plant trusts that he will receive material that has the assumed energy potential and does not pose a threat to the microorganisms responsible for the decomposition of organic matter. It can be assumed that the level of trust increases as the acts of cooperation are repeated. Many research studies have shown that trust is a fundamental requirement for effective collaboration (Schilke et al., 2021). When combined with commitment, it can enhance the level of integration between individuals or groups (Derek et al., 2012). Trust can significantly impact economic performance at the micro and macro levels. At the micro level, social ties and interpersonal trust can help reduce transaction costs, boost the execution of contracts, and facilitate obtaining loans. At the macro level, social cohesion, supported by trust, can contribute to strengthening democracy, improving the effectiveness of public administration, and enhancing the quality of public policies (Knack, 2001). In this context, it is reasonable to believe that the development of the agricultural biogas sector also depends on the degree of trust between partners in the business chain. The lack of such trust can be seen as a source of inefficiency preventing the realization of production potential. While the notion of trust is easy to understand, it has various dimensions that can be identified. When the level of trust is high, formal and informal contracts can be enforced without costly monitoring and investigation of performance by the parties involved (Knack, 2001). For agricultural biogas producers, this would mean, for example, not having to test the parameters of the raw material supplied to the biogas plant, which generates costs and takes time. Generally, trust can be built through the so-called first-, second-, and third-party mechanisms (Knack, 2001). First-party mechanisms are self-imposed ethical or moral codes, second-party mechanisms rely on sanctions available to the principal, and third-party mechanisms include social institutions, organizations, and government regulations. It can be assumed that each indicated mechanism in a biogas generation chain is possible and plays an important role, although these issues have not yet been empirically verified. The first-party mechanism could be expressed through the organizational culture of suppliers, the second-party mechanism through appropriate provisions in contracts (e.g., contractual penalties) between substrate suppliers, and the third-party mechanism through regulations on sanitary and other conditions that the biomass supplied to the biogas plant must meet.

It is important to note that trust is closely related to the risk concept. According to McEvily et al. (2003, p. 92), trust refers to "the willingness to accept vulnerability based on positive expectations about another's intentions or behaviors". However, such expectations are inherently risky. Similarly, Laeequddin et al. (2012, p. 557) define trust as "the willingness to assume risk". When embarking on cooperation based on trust, decision-makers managing biogas plants must also face uncertainty about the behavior and decisions of cooperators. Das and Teng (2004) argue that trust and risk are interrelated on three levels. Subjective trust and perceived risk are related, and behaviors that exhibit trust can be seen as risk taking. Personal characteristics may determine both trust and risk aversion.

Successful supply chains require cooperation to mitigate inefficiencies. Trust plays a critical role in fostering cooperation, also in biogas supply chain. Scientific studies highlight the importance of collaboration in determining enterprise competitiveness. Pomponi (2015) notes that cooperation in logistics is a key factor that drives the success of supply chains. Partners cooperating effectively can reduce inefficiencies like poor capacity utilization, empty backhaul, high transport costs, low-profit margins, and harsh environmental impacts (Daudi et al., 2016), ultimately leading to better performance. Trust is essential for building solid relationships between partners and ensuring smooth operations. It helps to overcome the challenges associated with information sharing, communication, and coordination (Naesens et al., 2009). On the other hand, a lack of cooperation can lead to waste, resulting in operational uncertainty, missed deliveries, low-quality materials, insufficient exchange of information, and weak relationships between partners. Ayers and Odegaard (2008) have linked waste to the lack of cooperation in various categories. Each of the problems mentioned above can be considered important in the case of the biogas generation chain – good cooperation, however, is particularly important here for the sake of keeping the operation running smoothly. Possible supply interruptions could result in the interruption of biotechnological processes, the resumption of which, due to the use of microorganisms, is a major challenge. Therefore, fostering a culture of collaboration and trust in biogas supply chains is essential to achieve mutual benefits. As noted by Daudi et al. (2016), developing trust in supply chains through practical behavioral factors is essential. Acting dishonestly may result in short-term gains but can have long-term negative consequences. Since trust is built over repeated interactions, individuals and companies analyze the level of uncertainty related to behavior during cooperation. Establishing trust in supply chains in the agricultural biogas sector is time-consuming, and success depends on finances, relationships, strategies, negotiations, and account management. However, suspicions, betrayal, and dishonesty can limit relationships (Renko, 2011). This can result from weak organizational and administrative structures, weak governance systems, and a unique cultural context under which collaborations exist, as noted by Derek et al. (2012).

Logistics cooperation, especially for small and medium-sized companies, can improve operational efficiency and help reduce costs (Pomponi et al., 2015). However, the condition for benefiting from logistics cooperation is the selection of appropriate business partners and trust management (Daudi et al., 2016). Numerous studies indicate that trust is critical in horizontal and vertical cooperation (between the supply chain links) (Paula et al., 2020; Pomponi, 2015). Logistics cooperation can be based on various partner relationships (Małkus 2017; Waters, 2009):

- "adversarial relationships" or "informal cooperation" (cooperation based on individual transactions, the parties to the cooperation share information of small scope, cooperate with the partner's competitors, and are often characterized by different organizational cultures);
- "contractual relationships" (based on a medium-term agreement, the scope of information exchange between partners is broader, and cooperation with the partner's competitors is somewhat limited);
- "formal alliance" (long-term agreements between cooperating parties, pretty large scope of information exchange, limited cooperation with the partner's competitors, similar organizational cultures);
- "minority investment" (relationship based on long-term connections, one party makes a minority investment in cooperation, the scope of information transferred is more significant than in the forms of cooperation indicated above, limited cooperation with the partner's competitors, similarity of organizational cultures);
- "joint venture" (cooperation based on a long-term agreement including mutual capital connections, joint sharing of risks and profits, a broad scope of information exchange, limited cooperation with the partner's competitors, common organizational culture);
- "vertical integration" involves long-term contracts, mutual information access, limited competitor cooperation, and a common culture. When one party is dependent on the other, building good relationships requires creating a climate of trust with the supplier, avoiding exploitation of their advantage.

Cooperation of biogas plants with substrate suppliers tends to take the forms of "informal cooperation" and "contractual relationships". However, if the main supplier of raw material is an entity closely integrated with the biogas plant – for example, a pig producer (piggery which is part of a larger company), the problem of information asymmetry is of lesser importance. Regarding the relationship of the biogas plant with the consumers of the renewable energy produced, it can be assumed that it is like ties based on the model of "contractual relationships" and formal rules (usually contracts with the electricity grid operator).

The biogas industry has three types of plants: agricultural, municipal, and sewage treatment plants. The plant types differ based on the input they use, such as agricultural biomass, organic waste, urban green waste, and household waste (Nikiciuk, 2019). Biogas are usually the "heat and power" plants in which anaerobic methane fermentation occurs. The substrate undergoing fermentation is various types of biomass (Marks et al., 2020), including primarily waste biomass, which brings the biogas plant operating model closer to a situation in which "one problem is the solution of the other in a sustainable way" (problematic organic waste becomes a source of the needed electricity and heat energy) (Marks et al., 2020; Savini, 2019). In the most straightforward solutions, the

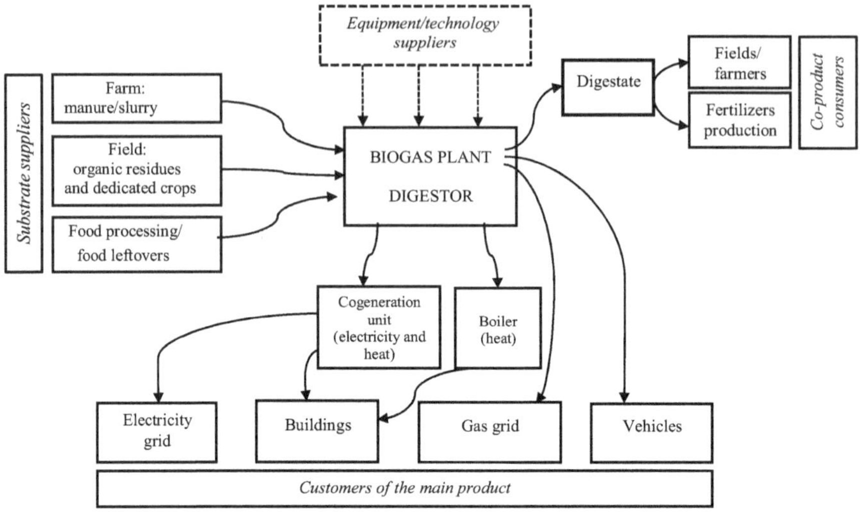

Figure 12.1 Agricultural biogas supply chain diagram.

Source: Own elaboration.

biogas generated as a result of anaerobic fermentation occurring in biogas plants (with a methane content of approximately 55–70%) can be burned in cogeneration engines (combined heat and power units), becoming a source of electricity and heat, or it can be burned in biogas boilers (Figure 12.1). There are also alternative consumption paths for the biogas produced. Biogas can be refined into biomethane and injected into the gas network in more advanced solutions. Still, the available gas infrastructure is essential (Sulewski et al., 2023). The biogas produced can also be used to power vehicles. The resulting digestate is a valuable fertilizer that can be used directly to fertilize fields or can be a component used to make organic-mineral fertilizer.

In Poland, the development of the agricultural biogas plant sector has been slow despite the country's potential for producing agricultural biogas thanks to its large agricultural sector. As of 2023, Poland had only 119 biogas plants, totaling 143 production installations. These facilities produced approximately 374 million m^3 of biogas (KOWR, 2023). Nearly 800 GWh of electricity was produced from this biogas (as all operating biogas plants in Poland convert biogas into electricity). To put this in perspective, biogas production in Germany, which has a similar area of agricultural land, is about 25 times higher than in Poland (EurObserv'ER, 2023). When we relate the electricity produced from agricultural biogas in Poland to the country's total consumption, it is clear that it meets only about 0.46% of national demand.

Central to the agricultural biogas generation chain is biomass, which is converted into useful forms of energy (electricity, heat, or biomethane) through microbial processes carried out in biogas plants. The efficiency of these processes depends on substrate parameters and technology. Therefore, ensuring a continuous supply of quality biomass is a key success factor in maintaining the operational efficiency of biogas plants. Obstacles that may occur in this regard can be considered one of the factors slowing down the development of this sector and, consequently, hindering energy transition plans. In 2020, Polish agricultural biogas plants used 4.4 million tons of organic substances, including 0.76 million tons of slurry and 0.09 million tons of manure. According to estimates from the Central Statistical Office (2019), in Poland during 2017/2018, almost 45 million tons of manure, 6.6 million m^3 of slurry, and 14.5 million m^3 of liquid manure were used for fertilization. In theory, all organic fertilizers can be processed in biogas plants. However, Poland's biogas plants' current biomass processing level is negligible. This is because some farms are too small for sensible investments, even in micro biogas plants, because of the fragmentation of Polish agriculture. Investing in farms with an animal production scale of at least 30 LU (livestock unit) is reasonable for organizational and economic reasons (Majewski et al., 2016). The optimal use of substrate potential in agricultural biogas production requires the collaboration and coordination of multiple farmers and their biogas plants. Additionally, raw materials for biogas production can be sourced from the food processing industry, either as supplementary substrates for farm-derived materials or as primary feedstocks. Estimating the quantity of food processing waste available for biogas production is challenging, as official statistics do not provide detailed coverage of all waste types. However, available data suggests that the meat processing sector can provide approximately 590,000 Mg of waste annually. In comparison, the fruit and vegetable processing sector can deliver about 377,000 Mg of waste, which can be utilized for biogas generation (Kupryś-Caruk, 2017). It is worth emphasizing, however, that the scale of unused raw materials in food processing is, in many cases, at the level of several dozen percent.

According to KOWR (National Centre for Agricultural Support) data, agricultural biogas plants have utilized a wide range of raw materials since 2011, with a list comprising 58 items, some of which are significant. However, some changes can be observed in the structure of the substrate used, which should be assessed positively, that is, the share of corn silage is decreasing, and the use of waste from the food industry is increasing. The initially popular model of feeding biogas plants with plants deliberately grown for biogas substrates (first-generation substrates – e.g., corn) is highly controversial from the point of view of the principles of sustainable development. Using energy crops for biogas production necessitates vast amounts of land, such as allocating up to 400 hectares for cultivating corn silage to supply an agricultural biogas plant with a 1 MW capacity. This practice heightens the risk of monoculture development

(Marks et al., 2020). Additionally, the use of a significant amount of energy plants for biogas production may increase price fluctuations in agricultural product markets because such activities constitute competition for the food or feed market (Majewski et al., 2016). When analyzing changes in the structure of the substrates used, we must also remember issues related to the economics of production – replacing expensive corn silage with cheaper (or even free) waste substrates helps to increase the economic efficiency of the entire project. The observed trend of decreasing the share of agricultural substrates in favor of substrates from food processing indicates an increase in the sustainability of the system, but at the same time, increases the dependence of biogas producers (farmers) on external suppliers (implying that biogas producers must rely more on trust with suppliers). The largest share among all substrates used by Polish agricultural biogas plants in 2020 had distillery vinasse. Its functional features make it particularly suitable for biogas production. Distillery vinasse, brewery spent grain, and fruit/vegetable pomace are common waste products used in biogas production. These wastes contain organic substances that bacteria can decompose to produce biogas. In dairy plants, up to 90% of the milk used in production ultimately becomes waste in the form of whey, which has good properties for biogas production (high lactose, protein, and fat content). Large amounts of waste are also generated in the processing of sugar beets. Due to the high dry matter content, production waste such as spent grain or molasses can be used as substrates to thicken the feedstock for biogas plants. Waste from the meat industry, such as post-flotation waste, is problematic but is a very efficient raw material for biogas production. Depending on the waste category, they are subject to specific pre-treatment processes, such as high-temperature hygienization. Providing particular rules for the preliminary processing of substrates, organic substrates such as expired food or shop waste can also be used in agricultural biogas plants. Due to the low purchase cost (or lack thereof), food waste is a relatively frequently used substrate in agricultural biogas plants in Poland. In 2020, almost 118,000 tons of expired food were processed into biogas. Estimates of the potential biogas yield from this type of raw materials are quite diverse because each food product has a different composition of organic substances (Majewski et al., 2016). As a result, individual substrates have various performances, which may challenge assessing their qualities and managing the production process.

Maintaining the technological regime is essential and depends on ensuring a regular supply of substrates with appropriate technological characteristics (Czekała et al., 2022; Gaworski et al., 2018). It is particularly important to consider the supply chain of larger plants when it comes to generating sustainable energy. These plants rely on raw materials from external sources, and therefore, sustainable energy generation should prioritize local suppliers. This will help to minimize the costs and pollution caused by transportation. At the same time, it should be emphasized that an adequate substrate supply is one of the key factors for the effective operation of biogas plants (Mittal et al., 2018). In the case of Poland, the largest percentage of operating biogas plants are pretty large facilities (with an installed electrical capacity above 750 kWe), which, thanks to the scale effect, allows for lower operating costs but, at the same time, requires a continuous supply of large amounts of raw material (substrate) to the plant (Kozłowski, 2021) and securing appropriate area storage (Kozłowski, 2022). It is recommended that when using biomass on a large scale, for economic and ecological reasons, unprocessed biomass should be transported over short distances – up to 50 km (Jasiulewicz, 2009).

Effective biogas plant management requires a continuous and adequate supply of high-quality substrate to avoid losses. Mechanical contamination requires additional equipment, which increases costs (Kozłowski, 2022). The quality and structure of the substrates used are essential in the case of agricultural biogas plants because the digestate produced in this case can be a valuable fertilizer for use in agriculture and horticulture. Therefore, particularly high requirements are placed on the substrates used in agricultural biogasification. According to the Renewable Energy Act (Polish Parliament, 2015), agricultural biogas plants can only use agricultural by-products, animal excrements, by-products from the processing of agricultural products, and forest biomass. Using prohibited substrates can lead to fines or plant closure. Substrate choice in agricultural biogas plants is crucial for legal and technological reasons, requiring specific substrates like methane fermentation in ruminants (Kowalczyk-Juśko & Szymańska, 2015). The quality of the input in agricultural biogas plants is as crucial for the efficiency of the biogas production process as the quality of feed in ruminant farming. The essential requirement is the non-toxicity of the feedstock, enabling the development of methane fermentation bacteria. It is equally essential to maintain the relative stability of the feedstock, as sudden changes in its composition may contribute to a decrease in the efficiency of the biogas plant (Kowalczyk-Juśko & Szymańska, 2015).

However, it is not easy to reliably assess the quality of the substrate at the time of delivery. Evaluating substrates supplied by external entities proves challenging, as they are difficult to categorize as "experience goods" or "credence goods" rather than "search goods". Especially in the case of biomass supplied to biogas plants from food processing plants, it is difficult to identify the quality of the products. In many situations, it is possible to know the actual parameters after purchase, although this may generate high costs of analyzing the composition of the supplied raw materials. The quality of the raw material can also be recognized based on the parameters of the fermentation process (but it is risky to use substrates of unknown parameters). Still, this situation brings the substrates closer to the characteristics of goods with trust/credibility attributes. It can be assumed that when making a purchase, the buyer of substrates trusts the seller that the material he supplied has specific characteristics because the buyer himself cannot thoroughly verify this and at least partially perceive biogas substrates as trustworthy goods. Thus, information asymmetry between substrate suppliers and biogas producers seems to be a significant challenge from the point of view of sector development. Despite this, the relationship between suppliers and biogas plants has not yet been the subject of scientific analysis.

12.3 Methodology of own research

The study focused on four agricultural biogas plants that had been in operation for at least eight years. This extended period allowed for a comprehensive evaluation of the analyzed phenomena over the long term. However, due to the slow development of the biogas plant sector in Poland and the limited number of installations, creating a research sample of biogas plants with sufficient operational history was challenging. Therefore, this study was partly a case study, but an average-based synthetic assessment was made in some aspects. The evaluated facilities converted biogas to electricity, with capacities ranging from 1 MWe to over 2 MWe. In the studied biogas plants, interviews were conducted with managers using an interview questionnaire.

12.4 Results

As emphasized earlier, the supplied substrates are essential for maintaining the biogas plant's operational activities. In the studied facilities, on average, the largest share in the structure of the substrates used was corn silage (average 35%, min. 20%, and max. 50%) (Table 12.1). Most of the silage for biogas production (73%) was produced in-house. Distillery stillage accounted for 25% of the substrates used. Organic fertilizers were used by only two plants (18% of substrates). The rest came from purchased substrates, mainly food processing waste (15%). These categories accounted for 93% of the total weight of the raw material. Transporting corn silage and manure/slurry over an approximately 8–9 km distance was common, while other food industry residues were transported from distances exceeding 40 km. This distance is important in terms of pollution emissions and logistics.

The relationship between technology used in biogas plants and equipment suppliers was also considered. Three out of four of the biogas plants had permanent service contracts with their technology and cogeneration unit suppliers. Some plants had contracts for remote access to external companies managing automation. Others had permanent contracts for fermentation process optimization, which included laboratory tests and microelement regulation. Entrusting crucial aspects of installation operations to external entities suggests that biogas plant managers have faith in them.

Most biogas plants have established suppliers for their substrates, but some also use unverified sources (Table 12.2 upper part). In three cases, the cooperation takes the form of signed (formal) contracts for the supply of substrates, and in two cases, the cooperation is carried out without a formal contract (including, in one case, such cooperation takes place alongside a formal contract). None of

Table 12.1 Essential characteristics of the substrates used in the tested biogas plants

Substrate	*Biogas plant*	*% of total used substrates*	*Source of origin (%)*			*Distance (km)*
			own	*purchased*	*received for free*	
Corn sillage	1	20	100	0	0	7
	2	2	100	0	0	7.5
	3	45	20	80	0	22
	4	50	70	30	0	1
	Average	35	73	28	0	9
Stillage from the distillery	1	0	-	-	-	-
	2	50	-	100	0	15
	3	20	-	20	80	70
	4	30	-	100	0	40
	Average	25	-	73	27	42
Food industry residues	1	30	-	90	10	30
	2	10	-	100	0	75
	3	0	-	-	-	-
	4	20	0	20	80	20
	Average	15	-	70	30	42
Manure	1	50	100	0	0	1
	2	0	-	-	-	-
	3	22	20	80	0	15
	4	0	-	-	-	-
	Average	18	60	40	0	8

Source: Own study.

the respondents declared frequent use of bargain purchase opportunities. Half of the respondents assessed their quality assessment capabilities quite highly during delivery. This assessment was based on compliance with the supplier's declaration. They rated their ability as 8 on a scale from 0 to 10, where 0 means "I am not able to assess the quality" and 10 means "I have no problems with assessing raw material quality". On the other hand, two people rated this possibility within the middle of the scale, with ratings of 4 and 6. At the same time, however, the respondents declared rather average knowledge of the parameters of the supplied substrates from the point of view of their suitability for biogas production. From the answers obtained, it can be concluded that the surveyed managers can only evaluate the purchased raw materials to a certain extent, so when making purchasing decisions, they rely on trust in suppliers.

The cooperation of the examined biogas plants with business partners may generate several problems. The bottom part of Table 12.2 summarizes the responses of the surveyed managers regarding the sources of problems that arise in relationships with business partners (both with suppliers of substrates and other

Table 12.2 Ways of cooperation with substrate suppliers and main problems in relations with business partners

Biogas plant	*Using only regular and well-known suppliers*	*Signed delivery contract*	*Only occasional use of unverified suppliers*	*Frequent use of bargain purchases from unverified suppliers*	*Assessment of own ability to assess the quality of the substrate (scale 0–10)*	*Knowledge of the characteristics of the raw material (scale 0–10)*
1	X	-	X	-	8	5
2	-	X	-	-	8	5
3	-	X	X	-	4	5
4	X	X	X	-	6	7

Biogas plant	*Incorrect substrate quality*	*Fluctuations in the level of supplies*	*Unclear information about the origin of the substrates*	*Mechanical contamination of the substrate*	*Composition of substrate other than the declaration*	*Volatility of substrate prices*	*Insufficient information on technology performance*	*Hidden costs related to supplies*	*Lack of access to laboratory test results*	*Financing problems*	*Bureaucracy*	*Instability of financial support*	*Residents' distrust*	*Problems with connection to the network*
1	-	x	-	-	x	x	-	x	-	-	x	-	-	-
2	x	-	-	x	x	x	x	x	x	x	x	x	x	x
3	x	x	-	-	-	x	-	-	x	-	x	x	x	-
4	x	x	x	-	x	x	-	-	-	x	x	x	x	-

Source: Own study.

business partners). All respondents mentioned "volatility of substrate prices" and "bureaucracy" (concerning procedures related to the cooperation of biogas plants with various agents) among the problems. Three out of four respondents indicated "incorrect substrate quality", "fluctuations in the level of supplies", "composition of substrate other than the declaration", "instability of financial support", and "residents' distrust" among the problems they struggle with. Less frequently mentioned problems were "hidden costs related to supplies", "lack of access to laboratory test results", "financing problems", "mechanical contamination of the substrate", and "problems with connection to the network".

The surveyed managers were also asked to assess the problems mentioned above not only from the perspective of their own experiences but also from the point of view of their importance for all agricultural biogas producers. This assessment was carried out using two criteria, that is, the frequency with which the indicated problems occur and the importance of the consequences they may generate. The presented summary shows that, on average, the most severe problems faced by biogas plants by the surveyed managers included "residents' distrust", "bureaucracy", "problems with connection to the network", "volatility of substrate prices", and "instability of financial support". Respondents noted that these problems occurred frequently and had severe consequences. It is worth noting that problems related to relationships with suppliers, such as "fluctuations in the level of supplies", "inappropriate substrate composition", "inappropriate quality", "insufficient information about the technology", or "unclear information about the origin of the raw material" were on average rated as less severe in terms of consequences, although mostly quite likely. What stands out in this list is "receiving a mechanically contaminated substrate", which was considered very likely, although the consequences were low. The answers suggest that the surveyed managers perceive relations with various elements of the environment rather than suppliers of raw materials with whom they cooperate as more problematic. Conversely, relationship issues with substrate suppliers were rated near the middle of the scale. This suggests that these relationships may not be without tensions, especially considering respondents' previous experiences discussed earlier.

The above observations are confirmed by assessing the degree of trust in various agents with which biogas plants cooperate (Figure 12.2). The surveyed managers express the greatest trust in the chain links that directly and constantly cooperate with biogas plants, that is, recipients of the generated energy (average rating 8 on a scale of 0–10) and substrate suppliers (average rating 6.75). On the other hand, the least trusted are state institutions, that is, the Inspectorate of Environmental Protection (score 1 on a scale of 0–10) and state authorities in general (score 4.5). Respondents also show a very low level of trust toward financial institutions (average rating of 3.75), relatively low trust toward the local community (average rating of 4.5), and slightly higher trust toward local authorities (average rating of 5). However, there is some variation in the formulated assessments in this respect, which results from the previous

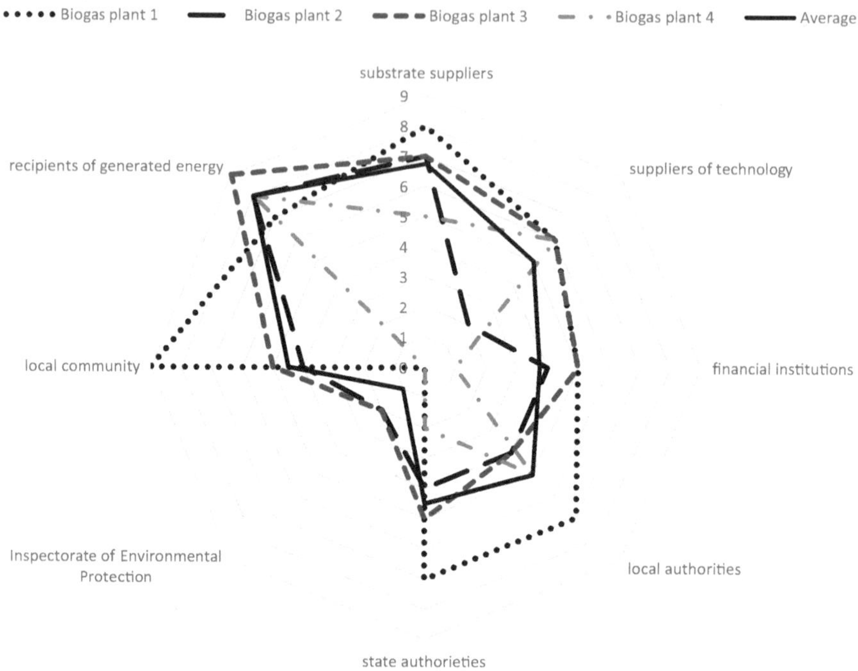

Figure 12.2 Assessment of the degree of trust of biogas plant managers toward various agents.

Source: Own elaboration.

cooperation experience with the agents mentioned above. This can be seen, for example, in the level of trust in the local community. A reasonably well-known problem is the negative attitude of residents toward constructing a biogas plant in their neighborhood. As a result, they often submit complaints to the authorities, pointing out the nuisance of biogas plants, which translates into a lack of trust toward the residents, declared by the biogas plant managers. However, the situation changes when the neighbors of the biogas plant benefit directly from, for example, obtaining cheap heat from this facility, which was the case of one of the analyzed plants (as a result, the change in the attitudes of the neighbors of the biogas plant influenced the high assessment of the level of trust toward the local community expressed by the representative of the biogas plant). Also, for example, the declared lack of trust toward environmental protection inspections is the result of previous experience – respondents perceive the activities of this institution as hindering the regular operation of biogas plants. In the context of the answers obtained, biogas plant managers show greater trust in those they can influence in some way (as part of the supply chain). Although relationships with substrate suppliers are burdened with many risk factors, biogas plants are able to exert some pressure on their business partners. Biogas plants have much less ability to exert pressure on important environmental institutions, which, however, are not part of the supply chain, which applies to state institutions or banks.

12.5 Summary

This study is one of the first attempts to assess the importance of information asymmetry and trust in the agricultural biogas industry. The case studies indicated that managers of agricultural biogas plants responsible for substrate supply face the problem of information asymmetry due to the difficulty of accurately assessing the raw material being purchased. Because of this, they have to rely to some extent on trust with suppliers. The analyzed cases show that most respondents experienced a situation where the substrate parameters deviated from expectations. At the same time, the respondents rated their ability to assess the substrate quality quite highly when receiving the substrates. However, the answers obtained were not unequivocal, which may suggest that the scale of the problem is related to the skills and experience of the particular manager and may depend on the type of substrate and supplier. It is worth noting, however, that in practically all of the analyzed biogas plants relied mainly on regular suppliers, and additionally, in some cases, they also declared having a written contract for the supply of substrates. The surveyed managers declared only occasional use of "untested suppliers". As a result, the overall level of trust in substrate suppliers in the cases analyzed was relatively high. The degree of trust in other agents that make up the micro-environment was used as a benchmark, and in such a comparison, state and financial institutions were particularly low in trust. This observation may suggest that the biogas plants' managers do not trust, in particular, those agents whose bargaining power is higher than that of them. In the "substrate supplier"–"biogas plant" relationship, there is the possibility of applying sanctions to discipline the supplier, including breaking off cooperation (although the condition is to have an alternative source of supply), while in the case of other agents, the possibility of such actions is limited. It is also worth noting the high trust biogas producers have in energy consumers. In this case, the relationship is based on a standard contract under the law and the rules of cooperation appear quite transparent, reducing information asymmetry and increasing trust.

References

Ayers, J. B., & Odegaard M. A. (2008). *Retail supply chain management*. Auerbach Publications, Taylor & Francis Group. 978-0-84939-052-4.

Barrera, S. Y., Iritani, D., Pavan A.L., & Ometto, A. (2018). Theoretical contribution of industrial ecology to circular economy. *Journal of Cleaner Production, 170*, 1514–1522.

Bauer, P. C., & Freitag, M. (2017). Measuring trust. In E. M. Uslaner (Ed.), *The Oxford handbook of social and political trust*. Online publication date: January 2017. doi:10.1093/oxfordhb/9780190274801.013.1.
Biogas Association (2012). *Farm to fuel. Developers' guide to biomethane*. Viking Strategies.
Burg, V., Rolli, C., Schnorf, V., Scharfy, D., Anspach, V., & Bowman. G. (2023). Agricultural biogas plants as a hub to foster circular economy and bioenergy: An assessment using substance and energy flow analysis. *Resources, Conservation and Recycling, 190,* 106770. ISSN 0921-3449, doi:10.1016/j.resconrec.2022.106770.
Chlebicka, A. (2012). Zarządzanie łańcuchem dostaw produktów żywnościowych a problem asymetrii informacji. *Logistyka*, *6/212*, 405–409.
CNB (Czech National Bank) (2023). The European natural gas market during the energy crisis. *Global Economic Outlook.* www.cnb.cz/export/sites/cnb/en/monetary-policy/.galleries/geo/geo_2023/gev_2023_05_en.pdf (accessed November 15, 2023).
CSO (2019). *Means of production in agriculture in the 2017/18 farming year*. GUS.
Czekała, W. (2022). Digestate as a source of nutrients: Nitrogen and its fractions. *Water, 14*, 4067.
Das, T. K., & Teng, B.S. (2004). The risk-based view of trust: A conceptual framework. *Journal of Business and Psychology*, *19*(1), 85–116.
Daudi, M., Hauge, J.B., & Thoben, K.D. (2016). A trust framework for agents' interactions in collaborative logistics. *Dynamics in Logistics*, *9*, 53–63.
Derek, F., Tukamuhabwa, B.,R., & Eyaa, S. (2012). The effect of trust and commitment on vertical collaboration and physical distribution service quality. *International Journal of Business and Behavioral Sciences*, *2*(4), 49–66.
Dulleck, U., & Kerschbamer, R. (2006). On doctors, mechanics, and computer specialists: The economics of credence goods. *Journal of Economic Literature*, *44*(1), 5–42.
EEA (2023). *Share of energy consumption from renewable sources in Europe*. www.eea.europa.eu/en/analysis/indicators/share-of-energy-consumption-from. (accessed November 17, 2023).
EurObserv'ER (2023). *Biogas Barometer.* www.eurobserv-er.org/biogas-barometer-2023/ (accessed May 15, 2023).
European Commission (2015). *Closing the loop – An EU action plan for the circular economy European Commission*. https://eur-lex.europa.eu/legal-content/EN/TXT/?uri=CELEX:52015DC0614, (accessed November 15, 2023).
European Commission (2019). Energy and the Green Deal. https://commission.europa.eu/strategy-and-policy/priorities-2019-2024/european-green-deal/energy-and-green-deal_en
European Commission (2022). Communication from the commission to The European Parliament, The European Council, The Council, The European Economic and Social Committee and The Committee of The Regions. *REPowerEU Plan*. COM(2022) 230 final.
Gao, M., Wang, D., Wang, Y., & Wang, X. (2019). Opportunities and challenges for biogas development: A review in 2013–2018. *Current Pollution Reports*, *5*, 25–35. doi:10.1007/s40726-019-00106-7
Gaworski, M., Zegardło, M., & Bloch-Michali, M. (2018). Problems of substrate supplies continuity versus biogas plan assessment. *Annals of Warsaw University of*

Life Sciences - SGGW - Agriculture (Agricultural and Forest Engineering), *71*, 109–117. doi:10.22630/AAFE.2018.71.11

Haibach, H., & Schneider, K. (2013). The politics of climate change: Review and future challenges [in] climate change: International law and global governance. In Oliver C. Ruppel, C. Roschmann, & K. Ruppel-Schlichting (Vol. II Eds.), *Policy, diplomacy and governance in a changing environment*. Nomos Verlagsgesellschaft mbH.

IEA (International Energy Agency) (2023). *Europe's energy crisis: What factors drove the record fall in natural gas demand in 2022?* www.iea.org/commentaries/europe-s-energy-crisis-what-factors-drove-the-record-fall-in-natural-gas-demand-in-2022 (accessed November 18, 2023).

Ignaciuk, W., & Sulewski, P. (2021). Conditions of development of the agricultural biogas industry in Poland in the context of historical experiences and challenges of the European Green Deal. *Problems of Agricultural Economics*, *368*(3), 55–77.

IPCC (2022). *Climate change 2022. Mitigation of climate change. Working Group III contribution to the sixth assessment report of the intergovernmental panel on climate change. Summary for Policymakers*. www.ipcc.ch/report/ar6/wg3/downloads/report/IPCC_AR6_WGIII_SPM.pdf (accessed November 15, 2023).

Jakubowska, A. (2017). Zaufanie i asymetria informacji w relacjach podmiotów na rynku finansowym – wybrane aspekty na przykładzie banków i ich interesariuszy [Trust and information asymmetry in the relationships of entities on the financial market – selected aspects on the example of banks and their stakeholders]. *Zeszyty Naukowe Politechniki Śląskiej. Organizacja i* Zarządzanie, *113*, 125–134. ISSN 1641-3466.

Jasiulewicz, M. (2009). Znaczenie rolnictwa w rozwoju energetyki rozproszonej jako formy rozwoju zrównoważonego obszarów wiejskich [The importance of agriculture in the development of distributed energy as a form of sustainable development of rural areas]. *Studia Obszarów Wiejskich*, *18*, 157–170.

Knack, S. (2001). Trust, associational life, and economic performance. *MPRA Paper 27247, University Library of Munich*.

Kowalczyk-Juśko, A., & Szymańska, M. (2015). *Poferment nawozem dla rolnictwa* [Digestate as a fertilizer for agriculture]. FDPA.

KOWR (Krajowy Ośrodek Wsparcia Rolnictwa – Krajowy Ośrodek Wsparcia Rolnictwa), (2023). Dane dotyczące działalności wytwórców biogazu rolniczego [Data on the activities of agricultural biogas producers]. www.gov.pl/web/kowr/dane-dotyczace-dzialalnosci-wytworcow-biogazu-rolniczego (accessed November 10, 2023).

Kozłowski, K. (2021). Najlepsze substraty do biogazowni [The best substrates for biogas plants]. *Rynek biogazu i biometanu*, *9*(81), 40–45.

Kozłowski, K. (2022). Przygotowanie substratów w biogazowniach [Preparation of substrates in biogas plants]. *Rynek biogazu i biometanu*, *2*(83), 59–62.

Kupryś-Caruk, M. (2017). Przemysł rolno-spożywczy źródłem substratów do produkcji biogazu [Agricultural and food industry as a source as substrates for biogas production]. *Postępy Nauki i Technologii Przemysłu Rolno-Spożywczego*, *72*(2), 69–85.

Laeequddin, M. Sahay, B.S., Sahay, V., & Waheed, K.A., (2012). Trust building in supply chain partners relationship: An integrated conceptual model. *Journal of Management Development*, *31*(6), 550–564.

Majewski, E., Sulewski, P., & Wąs, A. (2016). *Potencjał i uwarunkowania produkcji biogazu rolniczego w Polsce* [Potential and conditions of agricultural biogas production in Poland]. Wydawnictwo SGGW.

Małkus, T. (2017). Assumptions of trust in logistics cooperation. *Acta Logistica*, *4*(3), 1–4. ISSN 1339-5629.

Marks, S., Dach, J., Morales, F. J.F., Mazurkiewicz, J., Pochwatka P., & Gierz Ł. (2020). New trends in substrates and biogas systems in Poland. *Journal of Ecological Engineering*, *21*(4), 19–25.

McEvily, B., Perrone, V. & Zaheer, A. (2003). Trust as an organizing principle. *Organization Science*, *14*(1), 91–103.

Mittal, S., Ahlgren, E.O., Shukla, P.R. (2018). Barriers to biogas dissemination in India: A review. *Energy Policy*, *112*, 361–370. doi:10.1016/j.enpol.2017.10.027

Møller, H.B., Sørensen, P.,Olesen, J.E., Petersen, S.O., Nyord, T., & Sommer, S.G. (2022). Agricultural biogas production – Climate and environmental impacts. *Sustainability*, *14*, 1849. doi:10.3390/su14031849

Naesens, K., Gelders, L., & Pintelon, L. (2009). A swift response framework for measuring the strategic fit for a horizontal collaborative initiative. *International Journal of Production Economics*, *121*(2), 550–561.

Nikiciuk, M. (2019). *Potencjał ekologiczny i prowzrostowy sektora biogazowni rolniczych w województwie podlaskim* [Environmental and pro-growth potential of the agricultural biogas sector in Podlaskie Voivodeship]. https://repozytorium.uwb.edu.pl/jspui/handle/11320/7992 (accessed November 16, 2023).

Official Journal of the European Union (2021). *Regulation (EU) 2021/1119 of The European Parliament and of The Council of 30 June 2021 establishing the framework for achieving climate neutrality and amending Regulations (EC).* No 401/2009 and (EU) 2018/1999 ("European Climate Law").

Paula, I.C., Campos, E.A.R., Pagani, R.N., Guarnieri, P. & Kaviani, M.A. (2020). Are collaboration and trust sources for innovation in the reverse logistics? Insights from a systematic literature review. *Supply Chain Management*, *25*(2), 176–222. doi:10.1108/SCM-03-2018-0129

Piwowar, A. (2020). Agricultural biogas – An important element in the circular and low-carbon development in Poland. *Energies*, *13*, 1733. doi:10.3390/en13071733

Pomponi, P., Fratocchi L., & Rossi Tafuri, S. (2015). Trust development and horizontal collaboration in logistics: a theory based evolutionary framework. *Supply Chain Management: An International Journal*, *20*(1), 83–97. doi:10.1108/SCM-02-2014-0078

Prokop, J. (2021). *Co to jest asymetria informacji? Jak zapobiegać asymetrii informacji?* [What is information asymmetry? How to prevent information asymmetry?] *Gazeta SGH.* https://gazeta.sgh.waw.pl/po-prostu-ekonomia/co-jest-asymetria-informacji-jak-zapobiegac-asymetrii-informacji, (accessed November 19, 2023).

Renko, S. (2011). *Vertical collaboration in the supply chain*. www.intechopen.com/books/275 (accessed November 15, 2023).

Savini, F. (2019). The economy that runs on waste: Accumulation in the circular city. *Journal of Environmental Policy & Planning*, *21*(6), 675–691, doi10.1080/1523908X.2019.1670048

Schilke, O., Reimann, M., & Cook, K. (2021). Trust in Social Relations. *Annual Review of Sociology*, *47*, 239–259. doi:10.1146/annurev-soc-082120-082850

Shih, J.S., Burtraw, D., Palmer, K., & Siikamäki, J. (2012). Air emissions of ammonia and methane from livestock operations: Valuation and policy options. *Journal of the Air & Waste Management Association*, *58*, 1117–1129.

Stejskal, B. (2008). Practical experience from biogas station. *Infrastructure and Ecology of Rural Areas, 9*(208), 125–135. PAN.

Sulewski, P., Ignaciuk, W., Szymańska, M., & Wąs, A. (2023). Development of the biomethane market in Europe. Energies, *16*, 2001. https://doi.org/10.3390/en16042001.

UN (2015). *The Paris Agreement*. https://unfccc.int/process-and-meetings/the-paris-agreement (accessed November 15, 2023).

UNCC (United Nations Climate Change), (2018). European Union: Energy system restructuring towards a long-term low-emission pathway. Report. https://unfccc.int/documents/183908 (accessed November 15, 2023).

United Nations (2021). *Global roadmap for accelerated SDG7 action in support of the 2030 agenda for sustainable development and the Paris Agreement on climate change*. www.un.org/sites/un2.un.org/files/2021/11/hlde_outcome_-_sdg7_global_roadmap.pdf (October 15, 2022).

Wandera, S.M., Qiao, W., Algapani, D.E., Bi S., Yin, D., Qi X., Liu, Y., Dach, J., & Dong, R. (2018). Searching for possibilities to improve the performance of full scale agricultural biogas plants. *Renewable Energy*, *116*(A), 720–727. doi:10.1016/j.renene.2017.09.087

Waters, D. (2009). *Supply chain management. An introduction to logistics* (2nd ed.). Palgrave Macmillan.

13 Blockchain and Non-fungible Tokens Technology Application

Evidence from the Apiary Chain

Sławomir Jarka,[1] Grzegorz Dobiesz,[2] and Agnieszka Biernat-Jarka[1]

[1]Warsaw University of Life Sciences - SGGW, Poland
[2]IT company, Poland

13.1 Introduction

The potential of tokenization is growing, thanks to smart contracts and with the development of blockchain technology and the institutional environment, notably in the financial market infrastructure. The potential enables the tokenization of all types of assets, simultaneously reducing transaction costs. The authors state that the development of the market potential of tokens can be achieved through both adapting the existing financial market infrastructure and building new blockchain-based infrastructures. Tokenization represents a form of business digitization based on decentralized blockchain technology. It involves creating tokens and assigning them to a specific product, company or person. Discussions regarding the utilization of blockchain technology in various markets have persisted for years, with applications extending to the tokenization of unique items such as art or music (e.g., virtual sports trading cards, digital artworks). The authors of the study suggest that blockchain technology and tokenization can be effectively employed in the beehive products market, particularly in the case of high-quality honeydew honey and royal jelly.

The aim of the research is to determine the opportunities and challenges related to the use of blockchain technology in food supply chains, with particular emphasis on the market of valuable beehive products such as honey, royal jelly, bee pollen, and bee bread in areas related to ensuring the safety and quality of food products. The chapter presents the assumptions of the usefulness of the use of blockchain technology and tokenization in the honey and royal jelly market on the example of a leading producer in Poland, recognized as the winner of the "Beekeeper of the Year 2021" competition (Biernat-Jarka & Jarka, 2021).

It is postulated that the introduction of blockchain technology and tokenization in the honey and royal jelly market in Poland would elevate transparency for the stakeholders. Furthermore, it is essential to foster close collaboration among

DOI: 10.4324/9781032633725-15

bridging infrastructure providers, standardization bodies and other stakeholders. Registering and verifying events in the production and distribution processes of honey and other beehive products are intended to increase credibility, transparency, and certainty of information about the origin of the products. Consequently, the traceability of products is expected to increase as well. Nowadays, consumers expect technological solutions to allow them familiarizing themselves with the technologies used in the production chain in a friendly way. Traceability plays a "guarantor role" of food quality and safety in the production process (Hasan et al., 2023).

13.2 Literature Review: Blockchain Technology – Characteristics, Functionality, and Applications

Contemporary food supply chains include producers, suppliers, carriers, wholesalers, retailers, other intermediaries, and even customers themselves. These supply chains involve numerous diverse stakeholders, each pursuing their own independent objectives. Effectively managing these stakeholders can often pose significant challenges, particularly amid the ongoing evolution of globalization as pointed in the Chapter 1 of this book. The escalating globalization necessitates that enterprises adopt new methods and solutions to enhance the management of resources that are frequently dispersed across different regions.

These new methods can also be an important source of competitive advantage for food producers in Europe (Tiganis et al., 2023). The European agricultural model is undergoing transformation to maintain a strong competitive position in the global market. The strong competitive position can be evidenced by the growing dynamics of Polish food exports, which in 2022 reached 127%, in relation to the volume of food exports from the previous year, that is, 2021 (Yearbook Trade, 2023).

Enhancing the competitiveness of food on the global market entails improving quality control, which includes enhancing supply chain efficiency. As Paciarotti and Torregiani (2021) point out, the supply chain is a series of independent, discrete, largely autonomous events controlled by marketing, production, and distribution activities. Nowadays, the digitalization of these events is observed in enterprises, resulting from the development of technology and the accompanying infrastructure. The digitization of the economy is one of the most dynamic changes of our times, which opens up new opportunities in creating business models. At the same time, it brings uncertainty and multiple threats along, especially the social effects of the automation of production processes or broadly understood food safety (Okorie et al., 2022).

Digitization as a continuous process of convergence of the real and virtual worlds is becoming the main driver of innovation and change in most sectors of the economy (Jia et al., 2023). After three successive industrial revolutions, we are entering the era commonly referred to as the fourth industrial revolution, building on new information technologies based on large data sets, Big Data, the Internet of Things, and artificial intelligence. These new technologies open up enormous opportunities for enterprises to increase productivity, competitiveness, and create and capture added value. The implementation of the networks into the food supply chain not only creates the foundations for the efficiency development of all its participants, but also contributes to an increase in the level of safety.

The response to challenges related to the rapid development of digital technologies is the digital transformation of various areas of economic activity. Digital transformation is a special type of organizational change of an enterprise, sector, supply chain, as well as the contemporary food safety system. The availability of digital data, the automation of production processes, the interconnection of value chains, and the creation of digital customer interfaces is transforming business models and reorganizing entire industries (Mendes et al., 2022).

Blockchain technology is of particular importance in the process of supply chain control. It is considered one of the breakthrough information technologies of our time (Treiblmaier, 2018). Today, many specialists claim that we stand on the brink of transformative changes in which the main role will be played by blockchain – a technology that is expected to change the paradigms of many sectors of the economy. This technology uses chains of blocks to store and transmit information about transactions conducted on the Internet. Each block contains information about a specific number of transactions. Once a block is completed, another block of data is created, followed by subsequent blocks, thus forming a chain of blocks (Sun et al., 2022).

In the product tokenization process, the main principle is to maintain uniform, common information through the use of a collective transaction book based on blockchain technology. This technology is based on a peer-to-peer network without central computers, systems managing and verifying transactions (Almeshal et al., 2021). Any computer on the network can participate in transmitting and authenticating transactions. In the case of blockchain, these will be blocks within a transaction book. This is shown in Figure 13.1. The ledger is open to everyone, but fully protected against unauthorized access by complex cryptographic tools. The user can only view his or her transactions. Thanks to this provision, transactions are public, but available only within the access rights of a given user. Their entire history, from the very beginning of their existence, can be reviewed and verified.

Blockchain has a potential to fundamentally change the way global business transactions are conducted. Currently, some business-to-business transactions are routed through third parties to ensure their integrity and protection. However, these third parties may cause delays and increase costs. Blockchain technology enables participants in a trusted business network to transact directly while ensuring the validity and non-repudiation of transactions (Castellini et al., 2022). Once the proposed transactions are approved and an agreement has been reached on their outcomes, blockchain participants record transactions in cryptographic blocks that cannot be rejected (Seifermann et al., 2022).

Blockchain is nothing more than software for operating a distributed database, characterized by several distinguishing features (Gad et al., 2022):

- Data stored within the blockchain is distributed, and therefore each network node has an identical data structure.
- There is no central server in this solution; it lacks a superior unit. Each node in the network is equal, and each copy of the database within the network contains complete information.
- All users, particularly every node in the network, have access to all transactions recorded in the distributed ledger.
- Data within the register are inextricably linked and cryptographically secured as a result of adding new entries; therefore, they cannot be changed, and each transaction is permanently saved in all network nodes and cannot be deleted or modified.
- Every operation within a blockchain necessitates passing through an established consensus process – network participants must authorize a given transaction.

Combining these main features in one solution yields remarkable results in practice. Blockchain-based solutions are characterized primarily by Xu et al. (2020):

- High level of security – blockchain-based network cannot be shut down. There is no single place or server from which you can disconnect power and cut off the network from transactions within the database.
- Transparency – everything is public here. There is no situation in which a network participant is forced to trust the so-called black box.
- Data consistency – there is no "update" function, each subsequent confirmed block written in next chain contains a fraction of the previous one. The mechanism constructed in this way does not allow changes to the history, once data is saved, it can only be altered through a new transaction.
- Data correctness – a feature that allows transactions to be carried out without the need for an authorized party or its supervisor. It is the network participants who authorize each transaction and ensure their correctness.

Taking into account all the factors currently occurring in food markets, where producers must ensure the quality and integrity of their products in order to maintain their reputation and credibility; applying blockchain technology seems purposeful (Castellini et al., 2022). The use of this technology to create a digital representation of assets as tokens is particularly valuable for developing regulations related to limited production and regional production, as well as for combating product counterfeiting.

Tokenization refers to the process of creating a digital representation of an asset on the blockchain, which is then utilized to verify its authenticity and track its history of ownership. This technology can be applied to all types of assets – including stocks, bonds, real estate, unique production, works of art, and other unique collectibles (van Wassenaer et al., 2023). The authors of this chapter propose the use of tokenization in the beehive products market.

We differentiate between the following fungible and nonfungible tokens (Davies et al., 2024):

- Payment tokens (currency type tokens), the most popular of which is Bitcoin. They are used to make payments.
- Utility tokens work similarly to tokens and are used for practical use within your own platform. They have specific functions, such as product, payment, or loyalty functions. By investing in a utility token, an investor receives access to services or products. Utility tokens are used for Initial Coin Offering.
- Security tokens resemble or replace traditional securities from a legal standpoint. Their primary function is to provide investors with security. A Security Token Offering (STO) involves the issuance of legally protected tokens. These tokens are based on tangible assets, such as shares and bonds, which are backed by real-world assets. For example, real estate can be tokenized using security tokens.
- NFTs (non-fungible tokens) have recently gained significant popularity. Unlike fungible tokens, each NFT is unique. They are used as certificates of authenticity for items such as works of art and for tracking products in supply chains, such as in the food industry, to prevent counterfeiting.

The security during tokenization is also ensured by the so-called smart contracts, enabling parties to conduct direct transactions without the involvement of intermediaries (Szpringer & Niewińska, 2021). When selling a product, for example, there is no need to engage a notary, lawyer, or sales intermediary.

Tokens, as digital carriers of value, can have an infinite number of functions. In our chapter, we have listed only a few that we consider the most representative. Tokenization on a distributed ledger guarantees security, convenience, efficiency, and speed. Additionally, this approach is often more cost-effective than traditional methods. The digitalization of trust institutions worldwide, although gradual, is inevitable. Blockchain technology is aptly called "trust technology" for this reason.

Tokenized product registers, such as those for food, can provide the much-needed transparency and credibility in today's market. Achieving this requires close cooperation between infrastructure providers, native product registries, standardization or certification bodies, and existing stakeholders (Garcia-Teruel & Simón-Moreno, 2021).

Tokenizing real-world assets involves numerous technical and legal considerations (Garcia-Teruel & Simón-Moreno, 2021). The authors of the chapter recognize these complexities as another challenge for future research on the application of blockchain technology and tokenization in the beehive products market.

13.3 Methodology

This exploratory micro-case study aims to illustrate the use of blockchain technology and tokenization in an apiary farm and its impact on changing the position of the beekeeper and his farm in the chain of stakeholder relationships, and especially among loyal customers. This micro-case demonstrates the initial process of developing the assumptions of the blockchain concept and the subsequent tokenization of valuable beehive products such as honeydew honey and royal jelly. To investigate this transformative process, a tailored blockchain system was developed and implemented specifically to meet the requirements of an apiary farm, facilitating the tokenization of the aforementioned products. Collaboration was initiated with a leading producer of high-quality honeydew honey and royal jelly, along with various external stakeholders: knowledge institutes, suppliers of equipment, beekeeping organizations, and customers.

This form of research cooperation requires the use of an intervention research methodology. Intervention research involves a reflective process of iterative problem-solving, where researchers and members of the case organization collaborate to enhance the problem-solving cycle within the organization (ter Bogt & van Helden, 2011).

The criterion for selecting an apiary farm for research was based on the level of adoption of digital technologies and the beekeeper's willingness to implement process innovations. This decision was informed by insights gathered during interviews with the apiary owners. Further details are provided in the subsequent section of the article.

The production chain of honey and other valuable bee products involves various stakeholders: beekeepers, individual consumers, corporate customers, banking sector entities, and government regulatory agencies (Figure 13.1). Today, the increasing demand for honey across all levels of the food chain – from consumers to wholesalers and distributors – is driven by population growth, rising incomes, and societal enrichment. Consequently, there is a growing emphasis from discerning customers on the origin of honey and the verification of its authenticity. The introduction of blockchain technology and tokenization in the surveyed apiary farm aligns seamlessly with these market expectations.

13.4 The Origins of Królewskie Miody Apiary Farm

In order to familiarize the readers with the concept of implementing tokenization based on blockchain technology at the Królewskie Miody (Kings' Honey) apiary farm, a synthetic description of the activity is presented below (Blajer, 2023).

The Królewskie Miody apiary farm operates in the Podkarpackie Voivodeship, in the south-eastern part of Poland. The adventure with bees by Piotr Blajer, the owner of the Kings' Honey apiary farm, began in 1986. At that time, his father received 3 bee families from his friend (Mr. Jan) – a very large beekeeper at that time, as he had 150 bee families. His first visual contact with the bees took place from the "top of the apple tree" under which the three bee families he received were standing. He watched the first inspection of these families and the basic instructions that Mr. Jan gave his father. This first exemplary contact has stuck in his mind to this day and left him in an "awe". He then asked himself a question: How can such small insects have such work process organization and what motivates them to achieve such a level of the development? He started his adventure with running an apiary with his father from 3 hives in 1986, to reach 1,100 hives in 2023. The beginnings were not easy, "*however, we never lost the entire apiary during this period despite various types of weather, utility or financial difficulties*", as indicated by the owner of the apiary. Over the following 15 years, the apiary farm developed gradually, reaching 80 bee families in 2001. At that time, production was carried out in various types of hives, that is, Styrofoam and wooden hives. This lack of standardization of apiary equipment "*knocked me out of my work rhythm*", as Piotr Blajer admits. After graduating from the Faculty of Forestry, he and his wife (also a university graduate) made a joint decision to continue their professional career in beekeeping. At that time, after 2001, there was a very dynamic development of the apiary, which around 2005 numbered 250 hives, then 500 hives. The quantitative development in the apiary was accompanied by qualitative development, that is, first, Styrofoam hives were introduced for honey production and the genetic potential of the apiary was improved. These activities resulted in the yield of the very valuable honeydew honey increasing from the initial 20 kg to 60 kg from one hive.

The next stage of the apiary's development took place in 2017, when electronic monitoring of honey production using digital technology was introduced. This was the beginning of the implementation of digital solutions, thanks to which the beekeeper had real-time up-to-date data from various locations of the apiary, including following: temperature in the hive, humidity, weight gain/loss spread across the time/hours, and rainfall. This significant technological innovation radically improved the organization of work in the apiary. As the beekeeper points out, "*empty inspection trips between apiaries were eliminated, so each trip had a specific purpose*", for example, adding a body to the hive if the weight exceeded, for example, 20 kg. The end of honey harvesting if the honeydew honey scale after heavy rain showed negative values for 3 days in a row, etc. In 2017, the apiary already had 800 hives, with a simultaneous increase in work efficiency.

With the development of the apiary, the offer of varietal honeys also increased, including the most valuable – honeydew honey. A side effect of the increase in the range of honey produced were problems related to packaging for retail sales. In 2018, the beekeeping workshop expanded. A completely new facility was built with a cold storage facility that serves as a heating facility during honey centrifugation. At that time, the apiary farm took steps to build trust among customers, which became the base for long-term profits. Although the Internet had already been used to contact customers, it was only the information and marketing campaigns conducted on Facebook and Instagram that made the group of loyal customers grow, which in turn guaranteed the stability of sales levels. These activities prompted the beekeeper to further expand the apiary to the previously mentioned 1,100 hives.

13.5 Introduction of Blockchain Technology and Tokenization

The origins of the Kings' Honey apiary farm and the subsequent stages of its development provide the basis for introducing further innovations in apiary production, this time using modern digital technologies such as tokenization. This applies primarily to honeydew honey and royal jelly, products that are the showcase of the apiary's offer.

The decision to introduce blockchain technology and tokenization was motivated by internal factors on the apiary farm, namely the focus on further development of the farm. However, the final decision was made by external factors, and above all by the expectations of demanding customers of honeydew honey and royal jelly, who expect authentic products of known origin. Undoubtedly, blockchain technology and the tokenization process contribute to meeting these expectations. Preparatory work is currently underway to implement this technology on an apiary farm, which corresponds to Stage 1 (Table 13.1).

Table 13.1 Stages of the tokenization process of honeydew honey and royal jelly

Stage	*Activities undertaken*
Stage 1	Project approval and budget allocation.
Stage 2	Preparation of project documentation
Stage 3	Configuration of technical infrastructure.
Stage 4	Installation and configuration of the tokenization system.
Stage 5	System tests, checking usage scenarios.
Stage 6	Production launch of the token distribution platform.

Source: Own work.

In this innovative setup, the Kings' Honey offers a purchase of a unique product such as royal jelly and honeydew honey in cooperation with the Academy of Beekeeping and Environmental Sustainability Foundation, through the issuance of tokens issued especially for this purpose by the Association (Figure 13.1). The role of the Association is to carry out certification of the apiary farm and confirm the highest quality standards for the processing of honeydew honey and royal jelly. Furthermore, it aims to provide a sales platform using tokenization to contract the products and build relationships (matching) with end customers.

In the tokenization system implemented at Kings' Honey apiary farm, each token represents 50 g of royal jelly and 1 kg of honeydew honey. Unlike traditional cash prepayments, this token-based system enables purchasers to acquire a stake in future production. Through this method, buyers commit to purchasing a specified quantity of the product in advance, while also agreeing to pay for and receive their allocated quantity within a predetermined timeframe. The details of this tokenization approach are illustrated in the second figure.

During the arrangements with the product tokenization expert, it was assumed that the ERC-20[1] standard would be used in the Ethereum[2] network. Before creating a token, it is crucial to define its intended function. The manufacturer determines the role of the token beforehand. Tokens are generated using a specialized programming environment, typically a platform designed for creating custom tokens. By replacing traditional trust institutions, such as registries, with blockchain technology, there are notable improvements in process efficiency and speed. Furthermore, this approach tends to be more cost-effective and less susceptible to human errors.

All of this is facilitated through the use of an NFT, which represents digital ownership rights to production. According to the manufacturer, this approach simplifies production planning and provides sales guarantees. For the recipient – namely, the buyer of such a token – it ensures access to a sought-after and valuable product, facilitating free trade in these products thereafter. This method enhances transparency, trust, and efficiency within the supply chain of valuable beehive products like honeydew honey and royal jelly.

End-users and consumers of honeydew honey and royal jelly will significantly benefit from this innovative process. Blockchain technology authenticates the origin of the product, greatly reducing the potential for counterfeiting and falsification during production. Moreover, the use of NFTs creates a "product passport", enabling traceability of the product's journey from the manufacturer to the final seller through unique entries. This transparency and traceability enhance consumer confidence in the authenticity and quality of these valuable beehive products.

The following stages can be distinguished in the tokenization process of honeydew honey and royal jelly at the Kings' Honey apiary farm (Table 13.1).

Based on the previous professional experience of the project team, the project implementation time was set at six months, that is, the implementation of

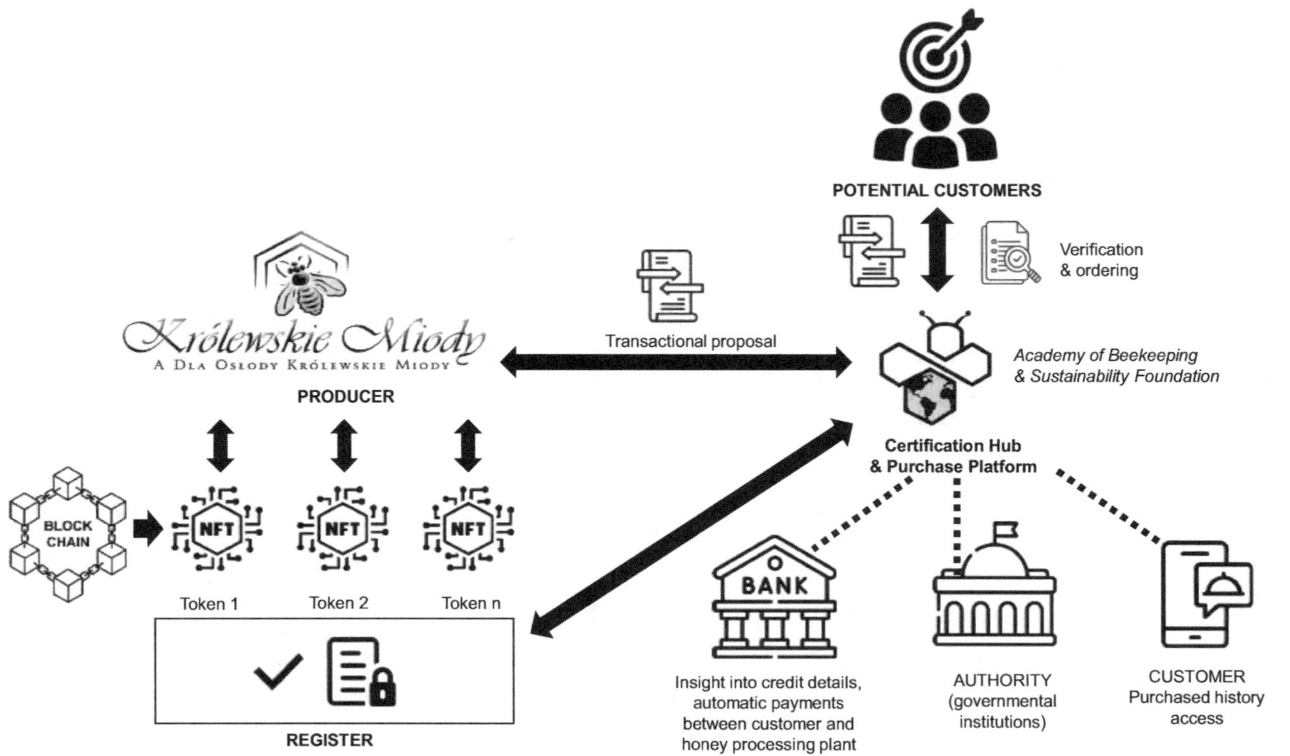

Figure 13.1 The concept of implementing tokenization of honeydew honey and royal jelly on an apiary farm Kings' Honey (Królewskie Miody).

Source: Own study.

the aforementioned stages. Taking into account that the project is financed by the Kings' Honey apiary's own funds, proper management of project costs is extremely important. Any discrepancies between the schedule and the actual progress of the project should trigger a procedure for additional monitoring of project costs, aimed at checking for any deviations between the assumed budget and the actual costs incurred.

The use of such a solution on an apiary farm shortens the supply chain as much as possible, and the interaction between the parties allows the manufacturer to determine the demand for a given product at a specific time and the recipient to contract the product for a given time when he will need it. This order and transaction model allows for better planning of production in line with demand without creating losses associated with production to stock. This chain model can be used in all types in which the resulting product is expensive to produce and at the same time delicate to store.

Previous research and design implementations have shown that blockchain technology has already had a significant impact on the reliability of the production. There is also a certain weakness as tokenized beehive products may be of different quality. Potentially, a batch of a given product may differ in quality.

One of the key benefits of tokenizing beehive products is the transparency of the entire system. Everyone can independently verify the quality, origin, and quantity of their batch. Tokenization allows us to hard-code certain terms or actions into transactions. This opens up many new possibilities. For example, royalties in each part of the token can be programed when a batch of products (honeydew honey and royal jelly) were traded.

Blockchain technology enables the harnessing of human creativity and serves as a fertile ground for numerous innovative applications (Xu et al., 2020). In the Web3 space, new functionalities can be proposed or validated by any stakeholder from anywhere in the world.

13.6 Conclusions

The initial implementation of blockchain and NFT technologies at Kings' Honey apiary farm demonstrates substantial potential to enhance transparency within the honeydew honey and royal jelly market chain. This technology offers a secure and tamper-resistant information pathway, ensuring the authenticity of these distinctive and valuable beehive products and their quality certifications. Additionally, it provides all involved entities with an immutable record of all transactions conducted. These advantages are compelling more enterprises in the agri-food sector and advanced technology firms to collaborate on innovative projects leveraging blockchain technology.

In addition to the numerous opportunities presented by blockchain and tokenization in apiary farms, there are also challenges and barriers that could hinder broader adoption of this technology in the food chain (Ge et al., 2017).

One significant barrier to implementing blockchain technology in managing the beehive product chain could be the lack of sufficient financial resources needed to make the necessary investments. In Poland, commercial apiary farms represent a small fraction of the overall farm population, accounting for less than 5%. However, some beekeepers can leverage existing hardware infrastructure with Internet access, which can potentially reduce the required investment costs. A significant challenge in enhancing the effectiveness of systems for identifying and verifying valuable beehive products lies in the limited opportunities for collaboration among different producers. Future research should investigate the impacts of implementing blockchain technology and tokenization in apiary farms of varying scales, such as those catering to selective customer segments known for their high product quality standards. Piotr Blajer, owner of Kings' Honey apiary farm, highlighted these points during an interview.

Notes

1 ERC-20 is a standard for fungible tokens, having a property that makes each token exactly the same (in type and value) as another token. For example, the ERC-20 token works similarly to ETH, it means that one token is and will always be equal to all other tokens.

2 Ethereum is a decentralized blockchain with smart contract functionality. It is open-source software.

References

Almeshal, T. A., & Alhogail, A. A. (2021). Blockchain for businesses: A scoping review of suitability evaluations frameworks. *IEEE Access*, *9*, 155425–155442.

Biernat-Jarka, A., & Jarka S. (2021). Zarządzanie innowacjami w organizacjach z uwzględnieniem gospodarstw pasiecznych (Innovation management in organizations, including apiary farms). In A. Biernat-Jarka, S. Jarka, & J. Pawłowska-Tyszko (Eds.), *Nowe technologie w gospodarce pasiecznej – wyzwania i ograniczenia* [New technologies in beekeeping – challenges and limitations] (pp. 84–95). IERiGŻ- PIB.

Blajer, P. (2023). Kings' Honey Apiary Farm. Typescript copied. Chorzów.

Castellini, G., Lucini, L., Rocchetti, G., Lorenzo, J. M., & Graffigna, G. (2022). Determinants of consumer acceptance of new technologies used to trace and certify sustainable food products: a mini-review on blockchain technology. *Current Opinion in Environmental Science & Health*, *30*, 100403.

Davies, J., Sharifi, H., Lyons, A., Forster, R., & Elsayed, O. K. S. M. (2024). Non-fungible tokens: The missing ingredient for sustainable supply chains in the metaverse age? *Transportation Research Part E: Logistics and Transportation Review*, *182*, 103412.

Gad, A. G., Mosa, D. T., Abualigah, L., & Abohany, A. A. (2022). Emerging trends in blockchain technology and applications: A review and outlook. *Journal of King Saud University-Computer and Information Sciences*, *34*(9), 6719–6742.

Garcia-Teruel, R. M., & Simón-Moreno, H. (2021). The digital tokenization of property rights. A comparative perspective. *Computer Law & Security Review*, *41*, 105543.

Ge, L., Brewster, C., Spek, J., Smeenk, A., Top, J., van Diepen, F., Klaase, B., Graumans, C., & de Ruyter de Wildt, M. (2017). Blockchain for agriculture and food: Findings from the pilot study. Wageningen Economic Research report; No. 2017-112. Wageningen Economic Research.

Hasan, A. T., Sabah, S., Daria, A., & Haque, R. U. (2023). A peer-to-peer blockchain-based architecture for trusted and reliable agricultural product traceability. *Decision Analytics Journal*, *9*, 100363.

Jia, Y., Su, J., Cui, L., Wu, L., & Tan, K. H. (2023). Platform business model innovation in the digitalization era: A "driver-process-result" perspective. *Journal of Business Research*, *160*, 113818.

Mendes, J. A. J., Carvalho, N. G. P., Mourarias, M. N., Careta, C. B., Zuin, V. G., & Gerolamo, M. C. (2022). Dimensions of digital transformation in the context of modern agriculture. *Sustainable Production and Consumption*, *34*, 613–637.

Okorie, O., Russell, J., Jin, Y., Turner, C., Wang, Y., & Charnley, F. (2022). Removing barriers to blockchain use in circular food supply chains: Practitioner views on achieving operational effectiveness. *Cleaner Logistics and Supply Chain*, *5*, 100087.

Paciarotti, C., & Torregiani, F. (2021). The logistics of the short food supply chain: A literature review. *Sustainable Production and Consumption*, *26*, 428–442.

Seifermann, S., Murti, I. H., & Oberle, J. (2022). Tracking and tracing in manufacturing supply chains using blockchain technology. *Procedia CIRP*, *115*, 172–177.

Sun, Y., Jiang, S., Jia, W., & Wang, Y. (2022). Blockchain as a cutting-edge technology impacting business: A systematic literature review perspective. *Telecommunications Policy*, *46*(10), 102443.

Szpringer, W., & Niewińska, K. (2021). Tokenizacja – próba oceny potencjału rynkowego [Tokenization – an attempt to assess market potential]. *Marketing i Rynek*, *10*, 17–25.

ter Bogt, H., & van Helden, G. (2011). The role of consultant-researchers in the design and implementation process of a programme budget in a local government organization. *Management Accounting Research*, 22(1), 56–64.

Tiganis, A., Grigoroudis, E., & Chrysochou, P. (2023). Customer satisfaction in short food supply chains: A multiple criteria decision analysis approach. *Food Quality and Preference*, *104*, 104750.

Treiblmaier, H. (2018). The impact of the blockchain on the supply chain: a theory-based research framework and a call for action. *Supply Chain Management: An International Journal*, *23*(6), 545–559.

van Wassenaer, L., Verdouw, C., Kassahun, A., van Hilten, M., van der Meij, K., & Tekinerdogan, B. (2023). Tokenizing circularity in agri-food systems: A conceptual framework and exploratory study. *Journal of Cleaner Production*, *413*, 137527.

Xu, J., Guo, S., Xie, D., & Yan, Y. (2020). Blockchain: A new safeguard for agri-foods. *Artificial Intelligence in Agriculture*, *4*, 153–161.

Yearbook Trade of Foreign Statistics of Poland 2023, www.stat.gov.pl (31.03.2024)

Key Insights and Conclusions

Michał Pietrzak[1], *Joanna Domagała*[2], *and Aleksandra Chlebicka*[1]

[1]*Warsaw University of Life Sciences – SGGW, Poland*
[2]*University of Georgia, USA*

The theoretical insights from Part I of the book collectively underscore the complex nature of information asymmetry and trust in agri-food supply chains. Addressing these issues requires a comprehensive approach that integrates functionally and geographically separate stages of agri-food chains, enhances information sharing and inter-organizational learning among chain partners, fosters effective governance for trust-building cooperation, and, last but not least, utilizes advanced information technologies:

- **The concept of supply chains** has evolved to extend beyond the boundaries of a single company, encompassing a series of linked entities that are interconnected vertically through the flow of products, information, and financial resources, effectively managing the journey from raw material sources to the final point of demand (from farm to fork);
- In non-integrated chains, these multiple entities often operate independently, which can lead to inefficiencies and misalignments, many of which could be overcome through **information sharing**;
- Information is not merely data but is deeply intertwined with knowledge and context. Effective **knowledge management** in supply chains requires understanding the complexities of information interpretation, the role of tacit knowledge, and the importance of **learning processes** among supply chain partners; the prerequisite for such learning is trust;
- **Trust** emerges as a critical factor in overcoming information asymmetry and enhancing cooperation within supply chains. It could be enhanced by including credible strategic moves, repeated interactions, and reputational mechanisms. Therefore, it can be cultivated through socialization, learning, and the establishment of self-enforcing agreements that align long-term interests;
- The issues of information asymmetry and trust are revealed by flaws in proper coordination of **physical flows** and the lack of mechanisms for **securing quality**. Both could be smoothed out by establishing adequate **governance**

structures. These often take the form of hybrid organizations bundling formal and informal coordination mechanisms and fostering a cooperative environment that balances power dynamics and builds sustainable relationships;
- **Information technology** plays a pivotal role in addressing information asymmetry by enhancing transparency, and data integrity. This can be achieved by key contemporary technologies, such as traceability systems, the Internet of Things, and blockchain technology.

The empirical illustrations from Part II of the book reinforce the theoretical conclusions regarding the role of chain integration, quality assurance, and adequate modes of governance in mitigating information asymmetry and lack of trust in agri-food chains. **The diverse case studies** demonstrate the varying degrees of success and challenges faced by different products and regions, highlighting the importance of strong governance, effective communication, and robust collaboration among stakeholders.

Central to the discussion in this part of the book is the challenge of information asymmetry, where consumers lack sufficient information to assess product quality accurately. This issue is particularly pronounced for products with experience attributes and even more with credence attributes (which cannot be easily evaluated even after purchase). Various mechanisms, such as certifications like **Protected Designation of Origin (PDO)** and **Protected Geographical Indication (PGI)**, aim to bridge this gap by signaling quality and origin to consumers. However, these mechanisms are not foolproof and often require robust governance and enforcement to be effective. The cases of Parmigiano Reggiano, Comté, and Koryciński Swojski cheeses highlight the mixed success of Protected Geographical Indications. While **Parmigiano Reggiano** and **Comté** benefit from strong chain integration and effective counterfeiting measures, **Koryciński Swojski** faces challenges due to weaker governance and cooperation. The successful PGIs chains exhibit strong vertical integration and trust-based relationships, which help mitigate information asymmetry and ensure consistent quality. The comparative analysis of **Pink Lady (club variety)** and **Jabłka Grójeckie (PGI)** apples reveals different strategies for addressing information asymmetry. Pink Lady's success is driven by strong branding and legal protections accompanied by quasi-vertical integration within the whole chain. On the other hand, Jabłka Grójeckie struggles with market recognition and strategic differentiation of the product. These both cases underscore the importance of branding and proactive integration of the whole chain in overcoming information asymmetry and achieving market success.

The **BioBabalscy** pasta chain, **Barilla's Mulino Bianco**, and the **Water Protection Bread** initiative illustrate the benefits of formalized **control systems** and **certifications**, which enhance trust and ensure adherence to quality standards, leading to higher consumer confidence and a willingness to pay premium prices. Also, the **QMP** (the Polish beef meat quality labeling scheme, which aims to differentiate products based on quality aspects) certification assures consumers of the accuracy of information provided by companies. Although certification reduces the information gap, the QMP case reveals inefficiencies in the beef supply chain and highlights the need for higher transparency and better cooperation.

Another empirical illustration addresses issues related to organic products, where information plays a crucial role in providing traceability. The **Croatian organic food market** is characterized by direct sales and low retail integration. The **predominant transactional collaboration** and focus on price and delivery terms reflect the early stage of market development, contrasting with more developed markets where trust and information sharing are prioritized.

The **biogas sector** case study reveals the importance of trust in copying with information asymmetry related to substrate quality. As regards geographically limited supplies, the **regular suppliers** and **occasional written contracts** help maintain trust and ensure quality. However, challenges arise when green energy producers scale their operations and must source inputs outside the regional market.

The final case study demonstrates the potential role of blockchain and non-fungible token (NFT) technologies in the **premium beehive products** chain for enhancing transparency and traceability. **NFT technology** can provide a reliable and manipulation-resistant information path of the origin and quality of these products. The challenge lies in the costs of adopting these technologies.

The aforementioned cases show, that relationships between producers, processors, and consumers in agri-food chains are **prone to information asymmetry**. They also illustrate that **trust** emerges as a **critical element** in reducing the uncertainties associated with quality in agri-food chains. Various forms of **quasi-vertical integration** and **close cooperation** within supply chains enhance quality assurance by fostering mutual trust, better communication of product attributes to consumers, and aligning incentives. **Intermediaries**, such as producer organizations (i.a. cooperatives) and processors, could play a crucial role in transmitting quality information and building consumer trust. They can help in aggregating and standardizing the **quality signals**. Moreover, the third-parties can act as **validators of quality**. Despite these efforts, challenges remain in ensuring the **credibility and relevance of quality certifications**. The absence of robust governance can lead to distrust and diminish the market relevance of quality-assured products.

The book also underscores that different sectors face **unique challenges** regarding information asymmetry, necessitating **tailored solutions** that consider sector-specific dynamics and stakeholder relationships. These insights could be valuable for policymakers, industry stakeholders, and researchers aiming to enhance quality management and consumer trust in the agri-food sector.

Index

Note: Figures are indicated by *italics*. Tables are indicated by **bold**. Endnotes are indicated by the page number followed by 'n' and the endnote number e.g., 20n1 refers to endnote 1 on page 20.

MIX
Papier | Fördert gute Waldnutzung
FSC® C083411

Kolibri 360 GmbH
Ferdinand-Jühlke-Straße 7
99095 Erfurt, Deutschland
produktsicherheit@kolibri360.de